Roadside
Silhouettes

1 MOURNING DOVE
2 HOUSE SPARROW
3 GRACKLE
4 STARLING
5 COWBIRD
6 RED-WING
7 KINGFISHER
8 BLUE JAY
9 MOCKINGBIRD
10 SONG SPARROW
11 SHRIKE
12 FLICKER
13 BLUEBIRD
14 NIGHTHAWK
15 ROBIN
16 KILLDEER
17 PHEASANT
18 PURPLE MARTIN
19 BARN SWALLOW
20 CLIFF SWALLOW
21 SPARROW HAWK
22 CARDINAL
23 MEADOWLARK
24 KINGBIRD
25 HORNED LARK
26 PHOEBE
27 BOB-WHITE
28 CROW

A Field Guide to the Birds

A Field Guide to the Birds

Giving Field Marks of all Species
Found East of the Rockies

Text and Illustrations by
ROGER TORY PETERSON

Second Revised and Enlarged Edition

Sponsored by
National Audubon Society

HOUGHTON MIFFLIN COMPANY BOSTON
The Riverside Press Cambridge

The Riverside Press
CAMBRIDGE · MASSACHUSETTS
PRINTED IN THE U.S.A.

To
CLARENCE E. ALLEN
and
WILLIAM VOGT

Learning Bird Songs

IN learning bird voices (and some birders do 90 per cent of their field work by ear), there is no substitute for the actual sounds. Authors often attempt to fit songs into syllables, words, and phrases. Musical notations, comparative descriptions, and even ingenious systems of symbols have been employed. But since the advent of sound recording, these older techniques have been eclipsed.

Use the *Field Guide to Bird Songs* in conjunction with this book. This new album (published September 1959) contains the most comprehensive collection of sound recordings yet attempted. It includes the calls and songs of more than 300 land and water birds — a large percentage of all the species found in Eastern and Central North America. Two 12-inch LP records prepared under the direction of Dr. Peter Paul Kellogg and Dr. Arthur A. Allen of the Laboratory of Ornithology, Cornell University, have been arranged to accompany, page by page, this *Field Guide to the Birds*, Second Revised Edition.

The song descriptions in this book are merely reminders, for handy use in the field. To prepare yourself for your field trips play the records. Read each description in the *Field Guide* for an analysis. Play the records repeatedly and compare similar songs. Repetition is the key to learning bird voices. Remember, however, that there are "song dialects": birds in your locality may not always sing precisely as the ones on the record do. However, the quality will be the same and the general effect will be recognizable.

CONSERVATION NOTE

BIRDS and all wildlife are necessary to healthy land and contribute to our happiness and standard of living.

Help support the cause of wildlife conservation by taking an active part in the work of the National Wildlife Federation (232 Carroll St., N.W., Washington 12, D.C.) and the National Audubon Society (1130 Fifth Avenue, New York City) and your local Audubon Society. These and other conservation organizations deserve your support.

To
CLARENCE E. ALLEN
and
WILLIAM VOGT

Learning Bird Songs

IN learning bird voices (and some birders do 90 per cent of their field work by ear), there is no substitute for the actual sounds. Authors often attempt to fit songs into syllables, words, and phrases. Musical notations, comparative descriptions, and even ingenious systems of symbols have been employed. But since the advent of sound recording, these older techniques have been eclipsed.

Use the *Field Guide to Bird Songs* in conjunction with this book. This new album (published September 1959) contains the most comprehensive collection of sound recordings yet attempted. It includes the calls and songs of more than 300 land and water birds — a large percentage of all the species found in Eastern and Central North America. Two 12-inch LP records prepared under the direction of Dr. Peter Paul Kellogg and Dr. Arthur A. Allen of the Laboratory of Ornithology, Cornell University, have been arranged to accompany, page by page, this *Field Guide to the Birds*, Second Revised Edition.

The song descriptions in this book are merely reminders, for handy use in the field. To prepare yourself for your field trips play the records. Read each description in the *Field Guide* for an analysis. Play the records repeatedly and compare similar songs. Repetition is the key to learning bird voices. Remember, however, that there are "song dialects": birds in your locality may not always sing precisely as the ones on the record do. However, the quality will be the same and the general effect will be recognizable.

CONSERVATION NOTE

BIRDS and all wildlife are necessary to healthy land and contribute to our happiness and standard of living.

Help support the cause of wildlife conservation by taking an active part in the work of the National Wildlife Federation (232 Carroll St., N.W., Washington 12, D.C.) and the National Audubon Society (1130 Fifth Avenue, New York City) and your local Audubon Society. These and other conservation organizations deserve your support.

Preface

THOSE of us who have read Ernest Thompson Seton's semi-autobiographical story, *Two Little Savages*, remember how the young hero, Yan, discovered some mounted ducks in a dusty showcase and how he painstakingly made sketches of their patterns.

This lad had a book which showed him how to tell ducks when they were in the hand, but since he only saw the live ducks at a distance, he was usually at a loss for their names. He noticed that all the ducks in the showcase were different — all had blotches or streaks that were their labels or identification tags. He decided that if he could put their labels or 'uniforms' down on paper, he would know these same ducks as soon as he saw them at a distance on the water.

Many of us, later on, when the sport of bird-study first revealed its pleasurable possibilities, tried to locate a book — a guide — that would treat *all* birds in the manner that Yan and the ducks had suggested. We found many bird books, but although descriptions were complete and illustrations authoritative, the one thing we wished for — a 'boiling-down,' or simplification, of things so that any bird could be readily and surely told *from all the others* at a glance or at a distance — that, except fragmentarily, we were unable to find.

We would study a colored plate of Warblers, thorough in its treatment of dull-colored juveniles and autumn plumages, but confusing in the similarity of them all. We would select some point on each bird as being perhaps the diagnostic feature, though we could not be certain. Fancied differences were noted, while the really distinctive characteristics were overlooked. This shadow of uncertainty that darkened many of our earlier finds of 'rare' birds marred our enjoyment of the study.

Hence this handbook — designed to complement the standard ornithological works, a guide to the field marks of Eastern birds, wherein live birds may be run down by impressions, patterns, and distinctive marks, rather than by the anatomical differences and measurements that the collector would find useful.

Without the prompting or the constant help of William Vogt, former editor of *Bird-Lore*, and now conservation chairman of the Pan-American Union, this guide would probably never have been undertaken or completed. He was the spark plug.

Those who were fortunate enough to go on trips with the late Mr. Charles A. Urner, of Elizabeth, New Jersey, agree that he was truly phenomenal in his ability afield. He graciously criticized a large part of the original edition, especially those sections dealing with the water-birds.

Doctor John B. May, of Cohasset, Massachusetts, examined the manuscript and helped especially with the Hawks and Owls, the two groups in which lie his especial interest.

Mr. Francis H. Allen, of Boston, who for many years has been one of the most active and observant of field enthusiasts in New England, contributed many valuable notes and has been responsible for a complete perusal and polishing-off of the original text as well as the present revision.

As it is quite generally and rightfully agreed that Mr. Ludlow Griscom, of Cambridge, is a court of last resort in matters of field identification, I have always turned to him for a final appraisal of difficult species and knotty problems. He has unselfishly given me the benefit of his long and varied field experience The responsibility for any errors of omission or commission is, however, the author's.

To the following I am also indebted for notes and other aid in the original edition: Miss Phyllis M. Bergen, T. Donald Carter, S. Gilbert Emilio, William G. Fargo, John F. Kuerzi, Joseph Hickey, Francis Lee Jaques, John T. Nicholas, Mark C. Rich, Charles H. Rogers, and Alexander Sprunt, Jr.

In preparing the original edition I used the collections at the Museum of Comparative Zoölogy at Cambridge, Massachusetts, the Museum of the Boston Society of Natural History, the American Museum of Natural History in New York City, and the Natural History Museum of Buffalo, New York.

The first completely revised edition of the *Field Guide* appeared in 1939. Additional notes on identification were added as well as cross-references between text and plates, size of birds in inches, sections on song and range, etc. New illustrations were added, and the area covered by the Guide was extended from the ninetieth to the hundredth meridian, which runs through the Great Plains, a much more practical line of division between the east and the west.

For assistance in the second edition I was indebted to Robert P. Allen, Etting Arnold, Paul Brooks, Samuel A. Eliot, Jr., David L. Garrison, Samuel Harriot, Mildred Peterson, Frank Pitelka, R. H. Pough, Gardiner Rea, John Smith, Wendell Taber, Allan Thomas, Lovell Thompson, Alexander Wetmore, and J. T. Zimmer.

With the advent of this second revised edition (1947) I believe the book is coming of age — for the changes are quite extensive, retaining the virtues of the older book and ironing out the rough spots. All the illustrations are new, there is much more color; black and white pattern is used only when it is more of an aid to identification than color would be. The cross-reference between plates and text will make the book easier to use as will the abbreviated line of field marks for each species on the key pages opposite the illustrations. Plates of the bills of Terns, Ducks overhead as the sportsman sees them, and the confusing fall Warblers are among the innovations. The greatest change in the text is the addition of sections on *Similar species*, for that, after all, is what everyone asks himself when he tentatively identifies a bird: 'What else could it be?' *Accidentals* (birds recorded less than twenty times in Eastern North America) and *Subspecies* are put into appendixes in the back of the book, where they will not confuse the beginner. This also makes future revision simpler as new subspecies will be described by the hard-working museum taxonomists and new accidentals will be recorded by field men. Little else will change greatly. Periodically, then, the book can be brought up to date by revising only these sections.

References were made to almost every piece of ornithological literature that might be of help. In addition to dozens of regional lists and the files of the *Auk, Condor, Wilson Bulletin*, and *Audubon Magazine*, I made most frequent reference to the following works: *Fourth A.O.U. Check-List of North American Birds* (and the nineteenth, twentieth, and twenty-first supplements), Alexander's *Birds of the Ocean*, Bailey's *Handbook of Birds of the Western United States*, Bent's *Life Histories of North American Birds*, Bond's *Birds of the West Indies*, Brooks's *Birds of West Virginia*, Chapman's *Handbook of Birds of Eastern North America*, Chapman's *The Warblers of North America*, Coward's *Birds of the British Isles and Their Eggs*, Cruickshank's *Birds around New York City*, Eaton's *Birds of New York*, Forbush's *Birds of Massachusetts and other New England States*, Griscom's *Birds of the New York City Region*, Greene, Griffin, Odum, Stoddard, and Tompkins's *Birds of Georgia*, Haecker, Moser, and Swenk's *Check-List of the Birds of Nebraska*, Hoffmann's *Guide to the Birds*, Hoffmann's *Birds of the Pacific States*, Howell's *Florida Bird Life*, Kortright's *The Ducks, Geese, and Swans of North America*, May's *The Hawks of North America*, Murphy's *Oceanic Birds of South America*, Oberholser's *Bird Life of Louisiana*, Pearson and Brimley's *Birds of North Carolina*, Peterson's *A Field Guide to Western Birds*, Phillips's *Natural History of the Ducks*, Roberts's *Birds of Minnesota*, Saunders's *A Guide to Bird Songs*, Stone's *Bird Studies at Old Cape May*, Taverner's *Birds of Canada*, Todd's *Birds of Western Pennsylvania*, Wayne's *Birds of South Carolina*, and Witherby, Jourdain, Ticehurst, and Tucker's *The Handbook of British Birds*.

The myriad details of helping me put the manuscript into finished form was the long, devoted task of my wife, Barbara, and Miss Sigrid Lee.

Guy Emerson has been my most constant spur, critic, and advisor. He has followed the new book every step of the way. But there have been others: Ludlow Griscom with his continued help on the many tough problems; Francis Allen, again the editor and also contributor of numerous notes; Doctor John Aldrich of the Fish and Wildlife Service, who carefully checked the subspecies, James Boswell Young who helped me with the confusing fall Warblers, and Doctor Alexander Wetmore, secretary of the Smithsonian In-

stitution, who kept me informed of the latest changes in nomen-
clature contemplated by the A.O.U. check-list committee, of which
he is chairman.

About a dozen species with which my own experience is limited
were written at my request by men who know these birds well.
These signed entries were contributed by Maurice Broun, Ludlow
Griscom, Doctor Robert Cushman Murphy, Alexander Sprunt,
Jr., Doctor George Miksch Sutton, and Doctor Josselyn Van Tyne.

Doctor Alexander Wetmore, Doctor Herbert Friedmann, and
Doctor John Aldrich extended the facilities of the National
Museum and the United States Fish and Wildlife Service to me,
and I constantly used their combined collections, which are second
to none in North American material.

Anywhere from one or two suggestions to a hundred or more
were offered by the following: Donald C. Alexander, Charles C.
Ayres, Jr., John H. Baker, Herbert H. Beck, Irsten Barnes, Mrs.
Ely B. Beard, E. J. Besson, Charles H. Blake, John Bull, E. J.
Buchwald, Mrs. E. J. Buchwald, T. D. Burleigh, Paul Brooks,
Maurice Brooks, Roland Clement, Kenneth Close, Ellen Cone, Wil-
liam J. Calvert, Edward Chalif, Herbert S. Cutler, Allan Cruickshank,
Allan Duvall, Samuel A. Eliot, Jr., John Elliott, Eugene Eisenmann,
Earle Greene, Fred Griffin, Mrs. Jack Hagar, Charles L. Handley,
Mrs. Paul Hannemann, Sydney Heckler, Philip B. Heywood, Richard
Herbert, Margaret Brooks Hickey, Joseph J. Hickey, Elsie Hervey
Hopkins, Richard G. Johnson, Edith Keeler, Haven Kolb, Muriel
Kendrick, S. Charles Kendeigh, Robert Knickmeyer, M. A. Linton,
George Lowery, Harold Mayfield, C. Russell Mason, Donald
McHenry, Don Maxwell, Locke MacKenzie, C. H. Manley, J. T.
Nichols, H. C. Oberholser, R. A. O'Reilly, Jr., Allan Phillips,
Hustace Poor, Charles C. Poole, Fred M. Packard, Richard H. Pough,
R. Dudley Ross, Austin Riggs II, Oscar Root, Chandler Robbins,
George Sigel, Robert Smolker, Robert Stewart, Mrs. Albert Smith,
Walter Spofford, Wayne Short, Martha Stiles, George M. Stirrett,
Wendell Taber, Richard Tousey, F. G. Trulan, Edwin Way Teale,
Lovell Thompson, Roger Williams, Allyn Wood, Francis M. Weston,
Doctor Alexander Wetmore, Ethel Wolfe, Doctor Miles Pirnie, and
Morton H. Baker.

I suppose I received from these correspondents between 1000
and 1500 filing cards with suggestions for this new revision. In
addition, scores of other users of the guide have given me their
verbal comments. So I can truly say that this book is written not
only *for* the bird students of America, but *by* them.

The author is working on a book that he hopes will be a useful
companion to this guide, a sort of Baedeker that will tell you *where*
to look for birds. Bird enthusiasts travel about a lot, and this
guide will point to some of the key spots in different states. I
would welcome ideas about this.

Contents

Illustrations

AREA
COVERED BY THIS GUIDE
(unshaded part of map)

Roughly, eastern and central North America from the Atlantic to the 100th meridian in the Great Plains

Species found in southern Texas, especially the Lower Rio Grande Valley, and nowhere else in the United States are described in A FIELD GUIDE TO WESTERN BIRDS . . . Observers in southern and central Texas and the western parts of Oklahoma, Kansas, Nebraska, and the Dakotas will require both this book and its western companion volume to cover their regions adequately.

How to Use This Book

VETERANS who have watched birds for years will know how to use this book. Beginners, however, should spend a few moments becoming familiar, in a general way, with the illustrations: the briefest examination will be sufficient to get an idea of the shapes of birds and the groups to which they belong. Ducks, it will be seen, do not resemble Loons; Gulls are readily distinguishable from the Terns. The needle-like bills of the Warblers immediately distinguish them from the seed-cracking bills of the Sparrows. Birds that could be confused are grouped together where easy comparison is possible. Thus, when a bird has been seen, the observer can turn to the pictuie most resembling it and feel confident that he has reduced the possibilities to the few species in its own group.

In most instances the pictures tell the story without help from the text. The short arrows point to the most outstanding field marks and these are briefly explained on the key page opposite. In every case it is well to check identifications by referring to the text. The plates give visual field marks; the text gives aids such as range, habitat, manner of flight, etc., that could not be pictured, and, in addition, mentions the birds that might be confused with a given species.

Far from helping only the beginner who can scarcely tell a Gull from a Duck, it is hoped that the advanced student will find this guide useful in recognizing the rarities that sometimes appear in his territory. The *accidentals*, birds that have been recorded less than twenty times in Eastern North America, are briefly treated in a section in the back of the book.

Some of the assertions of the ease with which certain birds may be distinguished will possibly be questioned because older works stated that they are 'very difficuit' or 'impossible' to identify except in the hand. Doubting Thomases need but take a trip with one of our present-day field experts — someone like Ludlow Griscom — to realize the possibility of identifying almost any bird, with amazing certainty, at the snap of a finger. It is but a matter of seeing a bird often enough and knowing exactly what to look for.

Most of the 'rare finds' are made by people who are alive to the possibilities and know just what to look for on a bird. It is the discovery of rarities that puts real zest into birding, a zest that many of us would like to interpret as 'scientific zeal' rather than the quickening of our sporting blood.

Field birding, as most of us engage in it, is a game — a most absorbing game. As we become more proficient, we attempt to list as many birds as we can in a day. The May 'big day,' 'century run,' 'lethal trip,' 'grim grind,' or whatever you choose to call it, where the day's goal is a hundred species or more, is the apogee of this sort of thing. Some ornithologists minimize the scientific value of this type of bird work. Truly, it has but little. Recognition is not the end and aim of ornithology, but is certainly a most fascinating diversion, and a tool which the person who desires to contribute to our knowledge of ornithology might profitably learn to master.

A total of 440 species are included in the main body of this book, plus 7 hybrids and varietal forms. In the appendixes there are 74 accidentals and 181 additional subspecies. This makes a total of 702 forms treated in this guide.

Make this Guide a personal thing. It is gratifying to see a copy marked on nearly every page, for I know that it has been well used. Although the cover is waterproofed, I have seen many copies with home-made oilcloth jackets; I have seen copies torn apart, reorganized and rebound to suit the owner's taste; others have been tabbed with index tabs, or fitted with flaps or envelopes to hold daily check-lists. I have even seen special pockets made in clothing and on car doors to accommodate the *Guide*. The new cross-reference between plates and text will eliminate the necessity of inking in numbers, and I have included a life list, so that the owner will not need to mark up the index for this purpose.

The illustrations. The plates and cuts throughout the text are intended as diagrams, arranged so that quick, easy comparison can be made of the species that most resemble one another. As they are not intended to be pictures or portraits, modelling of form and feathering is often subordinated to simple contour and pattern. Some birds are better adapted than others to this simplified handling, hence the variation in treatment. Even color is sometimes unnecessary, if not, indeed, confusing. In many of the waterfowl, which we seldom see at close range, this is especially true, therefore many of the diagrams are carried out in black and white. With most small birds, however, color is quite essential to identification.

Area. The area covered by this book is roughly North America east of the hundredth meridian. Rather than draw a hard and fast political boundary, an ecological one has been deemed more practical. The logical division of the bulk of North American species comes in the belt between the hundredth meridian (central North and South Dakota, central Nebraska, western Kansas and western Oklahoma) and the foothills of the Rockies. This is by no means a sharp division and people living in that area will need both Eastern and Western *Field Guides* to cover their region adequately. In a general way, the Eastern species follow the river valleys westward while the Western forms edge eastward along the more arid uplands. Subspecies of essentially Eastern species which occur in southern Texas are included in this book. Species which occur in the southern tip of Texas, notably around Brownsville, and no-where else in the United States, are included in the Western *Guide*. Those few European forms which occur in Greenland but never on the American continent proper are excluded.

Range. A thorough acquaintance with any existing State or local list should be made. The writer has given only an abbreviated account of the ranges of each species; an account of the exact range and seasonal distribution would have doubled the size of this handbook. Only the range in Eastern North America is given. Many species have a much wider distribution. The Mallard, as an example, is found over a large part of the globe. If the bird leaves the United States entirely in winter, that is mentioned, for the probable presence or absence of a species is a useful tool in identification.

Subspecies. It is a challenge to be able to identify some of the more well-marked subspecies, but in this book subspecies are merely listed with their breeding ranges, unless field distinctions are fairly obvious. Advanced students, using skins in their museum, might work out ways of telling others, but a too thorough treatment in these pages might only make the beginner overconfident, and would lead to many errors. A discussion of the subspecies problem will be found in the back of this book. Be sure to read it.

Voice. We make our first identification of a species, as a rule, by sight. Then we become familiar with its song or notes. A 'sizzling trill' or a 'bubbling warble' conveys but a wretched idea of the voice of any particular bird. Though inadequate descriptions, they do help to fix a note or song in our minds. Word syllabifications in most books vary greatly, each author giving his own interpretation. There are a few species whose voices we often hear long before we become acquainted with the bird in life. Who has known the Whip-poor-will before hearing its cry at night, or the Oven-bird before its *teacher-teacher-teacher* was familiar? Then there are those few, such as the small Flycatchers, that are far more easily recognized by voice than by appearance.

Many birds have a variety of notes and often more than one song. Many Warblers, for example, have two songs. These pages will attempt to treat the voices of birds only briefly. In several cases I have resorted to a system of symbols similar to that developed by Aretas Saunders. The serious student should secure a copy of his classic book *A Guide to Bird Songs* (D. Appleton-Century Company). The other way to learn songs at home is by actual sound recordings. *American Bird Songs* (Albert R. Brand Bird Song Foundation), is published by the Comstock Publishing Co., of Ithaca, New York. Seventy-two songs are recorded on six double-disc records.

Identification by Elimination. Identification by elimination is important in field work. For example, five brown Thrushes are found in the East. In the lowlands of the Southern States only one stays to nest, the Wood Thrush. The student in Georgia, knowing this, does not bother about the other four in the summertime, once having ascertained the bird to be a Thrush. In like manner, on Long Island all five occur in migration, but in winter any Thrush could be called, with almost complete certainty, the Hermit Thrush. Here the value of a local list is evident.

Suppose that a Thrush is in the field of our glass with its back turned. It has no hint of rusty color anywhere. We know then, that it is not a Veery, a Wood Thrush, or a Hermit Thrush. The bird faces about; it has grayish cheeks and a dim eye-ring. By experience or consultation of the text we know that the Olive-backed Thrush has a conspicuous eye-ring and buffy cheeks. Our bird then, must be the Gray-cheek. It is almost as helpful to know what a bird could not be as what it might be.

Then, of course, there is *elimination by habitat*. One expects the Veery in the wet woods at the foot of a New England mountain and the Gray-cheek (Bicknell's Thrush) near timber-line.

I have briefly indicated habitat preferences in this guide, but in migration birds might turn up anywhere, so it is not unlikely to see a Blackburnian Warbler, a bird of the northern evergreens, busily searching for insects in a palmetto while on its brief passage through Florida.

Caution in Sight Records. One should always use caution in making identifications, especially where rarities are concerned. Not long ago, some ornithologists would not accept sight records unless they were made along the barrel of a shotgun. Today it is difficult for the average person to secure collecting privileges; moreover, a large proportion of the rarities show up in parks, sanctuaries, or on municipal property where collecting is out of the question. There is no reason why we should not trust our eyes — at least after we have a good basic knowledge of the commoner species. Caution should be the keynote. A quick field observer who does not temper his snap judgment with a bit of caution is like a fast car without brakes.

My Life List

......COMMON LOON
......PACIFIC LOON
......RED–THROATED LOON
......HOLBOELL'S GREBE
......HORNED GREBE
......EARED GREBE
......WESTERN GREBE
......PIED–BILLED GREBE
......SOOTY SHEARWATER
......AUDUBON'S SHEARWATER
......GREATER SHEARWATER
......CORY'S SHEARWATER
......FULMAR
......LEACH'S PETREL
......WILSON'S PETREL
......WHITE PELICAN
......BROWN PELICAN
......BLUE–FACED BOOBY
......WHITE–BELLIED BOOBY
......GANNET
......EUROPEAN CORMORANT
......D.–C. CORMORANT
......MEXICAN CORMORANT
......WATER–TURKEY
......MAN–O'–WAR–BIRD
......GREAT WHITE HERON
......WÜRDEMANN'S H. (HYBRID)
......GREAT BLUE HERON
......AMERICAN EGRET
......SNOWY EGRET
......REDDISH EGRET
......LOUISIANA HERON
......LITTLE BLUE HERON
......GREEN HERON
......B.–C. NIGHT HERON
......Y.–C. NIGHT HERON
......AMERICAN BITTERN
......LEAST BITTERN
......WOOD IBIS
......EASTERN GLOSSY IBIS
......W.–F. GLOSSY IBIS
......WHITE IBIS
......ROSEATE SPOONBILL
......MUTE SWAN
......WHISTLING SWAN
......CANADA GOOSE
......BRANT
......WHITE–FRONTED GOOSE
......SNOW GOOSE
......BLUE GOOSE
......FULVOUS TREE–DUCK
......MALLARD
......BLACK DUCK
......MOTTLED DUCK
......GADWALL

......EUROPEAN WIDGEON
......BALDPATE
......PINTAIL
......EUROPEAN TEAL
......GREEN–WINGED TEAL
......BLUE–WINGED TEAL
......SHOVELLER
......WOOD DUCK
......REDHEAD
......RING–NECKED DUCK
......CANVAS–BACK
......GREATER SCAUP DUCK
......LESSER SCAUP DUCK
......AMERICAN GOLDEN–EYE
......BARROW'S GOLDEN–EYE
......BUFFLE–HEAD
......OLD–SQUAW
......HARLEQUIN DUCK
......COMMON EIDER
......KING EIDER
......WHITE–WINGED SCOTER
......SURF SCOTER
......AMERICAN SCOTER
......RUDDY DUCK
......HOODED MERGANSER
......AMERICAN MERGANSER
......R.–B. MERGANSER
......TURKEY VULTURE
......BLACK VULTURE
......SWALLOW–TAILED KITE
......MISSISSIPPI KITE
......EVERGLADE KITE
......GOSHAWK
......SHARP–SHINNED HAWK
......COOPER'S HAWK
......RED–TAILED HAWK
......HARLAN'S HAWK
......RED–SHOULDERED HAWK
......BROAD–WINGED HAWK
......SWAINSON'S HAWK
......SHORT–TAILED HAWK
......AM. ROUGH–LEGGED HAWK
......GOLDEN EAGLE
......BALD EAGLE
......MARSH HAWK
......OSPREY
......AUDUBON'S CARACARA
......GYRFALCON
......DUCK HAWK
......PIGEON HAWK
......SPARROW HAWK
......SPRUCE GROUSE
......RUFFED GROUSE
......WILLOW PTARMIGAN
......ROCK PTARMIGAN

......PRAIRIE CHICKEN
......L. PRAIRIE CHICKEN
......SHARP–TAILED GROUSE
......BOB–WHITE
......HUNGARIAN PARTRIDGE
......RING–NECKED PHEASANT
......WILD TURKEY
......WHOOPING CRANE
......SANDHILL CRANE
......LIMPKIN
......KING RAIL
......CLAPPER RAIL
......VIRGINIA RAIL
......SORA
......YELLOW RAIL
......BLACK RAIL
......PURPLE GALLINULE
......FLORIDA GALLINULE
......COOT
......OYSTER–CATCHER
......PIPING PLOVER
......SNOWY PLOVER
......SEMIPALMATED PLOVER
......WILSON'S PLOVER
......KILLDEER
......GOLDEN PLOVER
......BLACK–BELLIED PLOVER
......RUDDY TURNSTONE
......WOODCOCK
......WILSON'S SNIPE
......LONG–BILLED CURLEW
......HUDSONIAN CURLEW
......UPLAND PLOVER
......SPOTTED SANDPIPER
......SOLITARY SANDPIPER
......WILLET
......GREATER YELLOW–LEGS
......LESSER YELLOW–LEGS
......KNOT
......PURPLE SANDPIPER
......PECTORAL SANDPIPER
......W.–RUMPED SANDPIPER
......BAIRD'S SANDPIPER
......LEAST SANDPIPER
......CURLEW SANDPIPER
......RED–BACKED SANDPIPER
......DOWITCHER
......STILT SANDPIPER
......SEMI. SANDPIPER
......WESTERN SANDPIPER
......BUFF–BR. SANDPIPER
......MARBLED GODWIT
......HUDSONIAN GODWIT
......RUFF
......SANDERLING
......AVOCET
......BLACK–NECKED STILT
......RED PHALAROPE
......WILSON'S PHALAROPE
......NORTHERN PHALAROPE
......POMARINE JAEGER

......PARASITIC JAEGER
......LONG–TAILED JAEGER
......NORTHERN SKUA
......GLAUCOUS GULL
......ICELAND GULL
......GR. BLACK–BACKED GULL
......HERRING GULL
......CALIFORNIA GULL
......RING–BILLED GULL
......BLACK–HEADED GULL
......LAUGHING GULL
......FRANKLIN'S GULL
......BONAPARTE'S GULL
......LITTLE GULL
......IVORY GULL
......KITTIWAKE
......SABINE'S GULL
......GULL–BILLED TERN
......FORSTER'S TERN
......COMMON TERN
......ARCTIC TERN
......ROSEATE TERN
......SOOTY TERN
......LEAST TERN
......ROYAL TERN
......CABOT'S TERN
......CASPIAN TERN
......BLACK TERN
......NODDY
......BLACK SKIMMER
......RAZOR–BILLED AUK
......COMMON MURRE
......BRÜNNICH'S MURRE
......DOVEKIE
......BLACK GUILLEMOT
......PUFFIN
......WHITE–CROWNED PIGEON
......ROCK DOVE
......MOURNING DOVE
......GROUND DOVE
......MANGROVE CUCKOO
......YELLOW–BILLED CUCKOO
......BLACK–BILLED CUCKOO
......ROAD–RUNNER
......SMOOTH–BILLED ANI
......BARN OWL
......SCREECH OWL
......HORNED OWL
......SNOWY OWL
......HAWK OWL
......BURROWING OWL
......BARRED OWL
......GREAT GRAY OWL
......LONG–EARED OWL
......SHORT–EARED OWL
......RICHARDSON'S OWL
......SAW–WHET OWL
......CHUCK–WILL'S–WIDOW
......WHIP–POOR–WILL
......POOR–WILL
......NIGHTHAWK

......CHIMNEY SWIFT
......R.-THR. HUMMINGBIRD
......BELTED KINGFISHER
......FLICKER
......RED-SHAFTED FLICKER
......PILEATED WOODPECKER
......RED-BELLIED WOODP.
......RED-HEADED WOODP.
......YELLOW-B. SAPSUCKER
......HAIRY WOODPECKER
......DOWNY WOODPECKER
......RED-COCKADED WOODP.
......ARCTIC THREE-T. WOODP.
......AM. THREE-T.-WOODP.
......EASTERN KINGBIRD
......GRAY KINGBIRD
......WESTERN KINGBIRD
......SCISSOR-T. FLYC.
......CRESTED FLYCATCHER
......PHŒBE
......YELLOW-B. FLYCATCHER
......ACADIAN FLYCATCHER
......ALDER FLYCATCHER
......LEAST FLYCATCHER
......WOOD PEWEE
......OLIVE-SIDED FLYC.
......VERMILION FLYCATCHER
......HORNED LARK
......TREE SWALLOW
......BANK SWALLOW
......ROUGH-WINGED SWALLOW
......BARN SWALLOW
......CLIFF SWALLOW
......PURPLE MARTIN
......CANADA JAY
......BLUE JAY
......FLORIDA JAY
......AMERICAN MAGPIE
......RAVEN
......CROW
......FISH CROW
......BLACK-C. CHICKADEE
......CAROLINA CHICKADEE
......BROWN-C. CHICKADEE
......TUFTED TITMOUSE
......WHITE-BR. NUTHATCH
......RED-BR. NUTHATCH
......BROWN-H. NUTHATCH
......BROWN CREEPER
......HOUSE WREN
......WINTER WREN
......BEWICK'S WREN
......CAROLINA WREN
......LONG-B. MARSH WREN
......SHORT-B. MARSH WREN
......MOCKINGBIRD
......CATBIRD
......BROWN THRASHER
......ROBIN
......WOOD THRUSH
......HERMIT THRUSH

......OLIVE-BACKED THRUSH
......GRAY-CHEEKED THRUSH
......VEERY
......EASTERN BLUEBIRD
......BLUE-G. GNATCATCHER
......GOLDEN-CR. KINGLET
......RUBY-CR. KINGLET
......AMERICAN PIPIT
......SPRAGUE'S PIPIT
......BOHEMIAN WAXWING
......CEDAR WAXWING
......NORTHERN SHRIKE
......LOGGERHEAD SHRIKE
......STARLING
......BLACK-CAPPED VIREO
......WHITE-EYED VIREO
......BELL'S VIREO
......YELLOW-THR. VIREO
......BLUE-HEADED VIREO
......B.-WHISKERED VIREO
......RED-EYED VIREO
......PHILADELPHIA VIREO
......WARBLING VIREO
......B. AND WHITE WARBLER
......PROTHONOTARY WARBLER
......SWAINSON'S WARBLER
......WORM-EATING WARBLER
......GOLDEN-W. WARBLER
......BLUE-W. WARBLER
......BREWSTER'S W. (HYB.)
......LAWRENCE'S W. (HYB.)
......BACHMAN'S WARBLER
......TENNESSEE WARBLER
......ORANGE-CR. WARBLER
......NASHVILLE WARBLER
......PARULA WARBLER
......YELLOW WARBLER
......MAGNOLIA WARBLER
......CAPE MAY WARBLER
......B.-THR. BLUE WARBLER
......MYRTLE WARBLER
......B.-THR. GREEN WARBLER
......CERULEAN WARBLER
......BLACKBURNIAN WARBLER
......Y.-THR. WARBLER
......CHESTNUT-S. WARBLER
......BAY-BREASTED WARBLER
......BLACK-POLL WARBLER
......PINE WARBLER
......KIRTLAND'S WARBLER
......PRAIRIE WARBLER
......PALM WARBLER
......OVEN-BIRD
......N. WATER-THRUSH
......LA. WATER-THRUSH
......KENTUCKY WARBLER
......CONNECTICUT WARBLER
......MOURNING WARBLER
......YELLOW-THROAT
......YELLOW-BREASTED CHAT
......HOODED WARBLER

......WILSON'S WARBLER
......CANADA WARBLER
......AMERICAN REDSTART
......HOUSE SPARROW
......EUR. TREE SPARROW
......BOBOLINK
......MEADOWLARK
......WESTERN MEADOWLARK
......YELLOW-H. BLACKBIRD
......RED-WING
......ORCHARD ORIOLE
......BALTIMORE ORIOLE
......RUSTY BLACKBIRD
......BREWER'S BLACKBIRD
......BOAT-TAILED GRACKLE
......PURPLE GRACKLE
......BRONZED GRACKLE
......COWBIRD
......SCARLET TANAGER
......SUMMER TANAGER
......CARDINAL
......ROSE-BR. GROSBEAK
......BLUE GROSBEAK
......INDIGO BUNTING
......PAINTED BUNTING
......DICKCISSEL
......EVENING GROSBEAK
......PURPLE FINCH
......PINE GROSBEAK
......BRITISH GOLDFINCH
......HOARY REDPOLL
......REDPOLL
......PINE SISKIN
......GOLDFINCH

......RED CROSSBILL
......WHITE-W. CROSSBILL
......TOWHEE
......LARK BUNTING
......IPSWICH SPARROW
......SAVANNAH SPARROW
......GRASSHOPPER SPARROW
......BAIRD'S SPARROW
......LECONTE'S SPARROW
......HENSLOW'S SPARROW
......SHARP-TAILED SPARROW
......SEASIDE SPARROW
......DUSKY S. SPARROW
......CAPE SABLE SPARROW
......VESPER SPARROW
......LARK SPARROW
......PINE-WOODS SPARROW
......SLATE-COLORED JUNCO
......OREGON JUNCO
......TREE SPARROW
......CHIPPING SPARROW
......CLAY-COLORED SPARROW
......FIELD SPARROW
......HARRIS'S SPARROW
......WHITE-CR. SPARROW
......WHITE-THR. SPARROW
......FOX SPARROW
......LINCOLN'S SPARROW
......SWAMP SPARROW
......SONG SPARROW
......McCOWN'S LONGSPUR
......LAPLAND LONGSPUR
......SMITH'S LONGSPUR
......CHESTNUT-C. LONGSPUR
......SNOW BUNTING

Accidentals, Strays, and Others

....
....
....
....
....
....
....
....
....
....

A Field Guide to the Birds

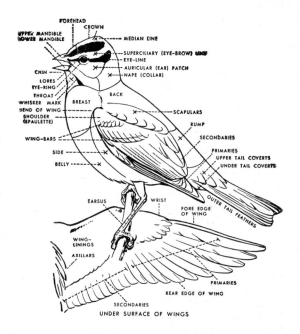

TOPOGRAPHY OF A BIRD
Showing terms used in this volume

Loons: Gaviidæ

LARGE submarine-like swimming birds, much larger than most Ducks and with shorter necks than Geese. The sharp-pointed bill is a characteristic feature. They are thicker-necked than Grebes, and like them are expert divers. In flight the outline is hunch-backed and gangly, with a slight downward sweep to the neck and the big feet projecting beyond the tail.

COMMON LOON. *Gavia immer.* Subsp.   p. 6.
   Field marks: — Size of a small Goose (28–36). A Loon on the water is a long-bodied, low-lying bird, a sort of avian submarine. Sometimes it swims with only the head and neck above water. In flight Loons appear like big Mergansers but with big feet trailing out behind, and a downward droop of the neck, giving a curved look. Their wing-beats are slower than those of any Duck. *Breeding plumage:* — Head and neck glossy black with white collar; *back checkered with black and white;* under parts white. *Winter plumage:* — Mostly grayish; top of head, back of neck, and back dark gray; cheek, throat, and under parts white. Immature birds are often blotched with black and white. Beginners sometimes think these queer-looking birds a rarer species.
   Similar species: — Cormorants resemble Loons but are blacker, especially in winter, and in flight the longer neck and tail are evident. Cormorants swim with the bill pointed slightly upward at an angle. Mergansers slightly resemble Loons. See Red-throated Loon.
   Voice: — On breeding grounds, weird yodeling calls and quaver-ing laughter; at night or before a storm, a ringing *ha-oo-oo*.
   Range: — Breeds on lakes from n. edge of United States n. to Labrador and Newfoundland. Migrates through interior and along coast to Gulf of Mexico. Winters mainly on salt water.

PACIFIC LOON. *Gavia arctica pacifica.*   p. 6.
   Field marks: — 23–24. Similar in size to Red-throated Loon; bill quite as slender as that of the Red-throat, but *straight,* the lower mandible never curving up; depth at base *only half* that of Common Loon. *Breeding plumage:* — Resembling Common Loon, but whole top of head and hind neck *pale smoke-gray*: the squarish white spots on the back arranged in *four distinct patches,* two on each side. *Winter adult:* — Like Common Loon, but head and hind neck often *grayer* and *lighter* than blackish back; the bill character should be noted. *Young:* — Distinguishable only when small size and bill shape can be positively made out.
   Similar species: — Pacific Loons in winter plumage are often assumed to be Red-throated Loons because of small size and slender bill. They are blackish above, never brownish gray.

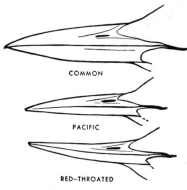

COMMON

PACIFIC

RED-THROATED

BILLS OF LOONS

Moreover the feathers have *large pale edgings*, giving a scaly effect, instead of a profusion of small white specks.
Range: — In recent years found to be regular on New England coast (October to May), rarely Long Island.

LUDLOW GRISCOM

RED-THROATED LOON. *Gavia stellata.*   p. 6.
  Field marks: — Smaller than Common Loon; nearer size of Merganser (24–27). *Breeding plumage:* — Gray head and rufous-red throat-patch unmistakable, but seldom seen in this plumage in U. S. waters. *Winter plumage:* — Mainly grayish above and white beneath (see below).
  Similar species: — In winter, similar to Common Loon but smaller and back *spotted* with white, giving the bird a paler appearance. In many individuals, the gray on the head and hind neck is pale, merging into the white and offering none of the dark contrast of the Common Loon. The bill is the best field mark. It seems to be slightly *upturned*: this is apparent at a considerable distance. The bill of the Common Loon is stouter and straighter. Another good mark is the snaky profile of the present species.
  Range: — Breeds in Arctic; winters chiefly along coast, from New England to Gulf of Mexico. Scarce migrant inland.

Grebes: Colymbidæ

THE GREBES are duck-like swimming water-birds; poor fliers but expert divers. They may be distinguished from the Ducks by the pointed bill, narrow head and neck, and tailless appearance. The Grebes normally hold their necks quite erect; Loons and Ducks do so mostly when alarmed.

HOLBOELL'S GREBE. *Colymbus grisegena holböllii.* p. 6.
Field marks: — Much larger than other Eastern Grebes, large as a fair-sized Duck (18–20). *Breeding plumage:* — Body gray; neck rufous-red; *cheeks whitish*: crown black; bill *yellowish*. *Winter plumage:* — The most familiar plumage. Grayish in color; top of head darker; *conspicuous white crescent-shaped mark* on side of gray head (often absent in first-year birds). In flight shows two white patches on each wing.
Similar species: — There are three species of diving birds found during the colder months with which it is often confused. The Holboell's Grebe may be separated from the Horned Grebe by its larger size, much heavier head and neck, large dull *yellow* bill, and more uniform gray coloration. (The Horned Grebe has contrasting white cheeks, white neck, and a dark bill.) It can be distinguished from the Red-throated Loon by its grayer face and neck and dull yellow bill. The Loon, on the water, at a distance, appears as a long-bodied bird with a proportionately shorter neck, whereas the Grebe is a shorter-bodied bird that seems to be all head and neck. In flight, at a distance, this Grebe resembles the female Red-breasted Merganser, but it beats its wings more slowly, has two white patches on each wing instead of one, and holds its neck bent slightly downward — this last a very good field character. The Merganser flies with its neck and body held perfectly horizontal.
Range: — Breeds on prairie lakes from w. Minnesota and North Dakota, north. Winters chiefly along coast, s. to North Carolina; less common inland.

HORNED GREBE. *Colymbus auritus.* p. 6.
Field marks: — 13–15. A small duck-like bird with a small pointed bill; typical of lakes, bays, and large bodies of water. *Breeding plumage:* — Head black, with *conspicuous buff-colored ear-tufts*: neck and flanks rufous-red. *Winter plumage:* — Contrastingly patterned with dark and white. Top of head, line down back of neck, and back dark gray; under parts, neck, and cheeks clear white and sharply defined.
Similar species: — On Plains see Eared Grebe.
Range: — Breeds from Arctic south to lakes of Maine, Minnesota, and n. Nebraska; winters from New England and Great Lakes south to Gulf of Mexico.

EARED GREBE. *Colymbus nigricollis californicus.* p. 6.
Field marks: — 12–14. A small, long-necked diving bird, dark above, light below; in the breeding season with a *crested* black head and two golden ear tufts.

Similar species: — The Horned Grebe in breeding plumage also has buffy ear tufts. The Eared Grebe can always be told by its helmet-like *crown* and *black* neck (Horned Grebe, chestnut). *Winter plumage:* — Very similar to Horned Grebe. Dark gray of head and neck *broader and less clearly defined*, giving a 'dirtier' look. There is almost invariably a suffused whitish patch in the gray on each side of the head just back of the ear (see diagram). Neck is more slender; bill is *slimmer and appears slightly upturned.*

Range: — Western; breeds on prairie lakes east to North Dakota, Nebraska, w. Minnesota, and nw. Iowa. Casual or accidental east of Great Plains.

WESTERN GREBE. *Aechmophorus occidentalis.*   p. 6.
Field marks: — A very large Grebe (22–29), with an extremely long slender neck. In any plumage it is an all *black-and-white* bird. (See diagram.) The bill is light yellow.
Similar species: — The winter Holboell's Grebe, has *two* white patches on each wing (Western, one), and is a dingy gray-looking instead of a clean-cut black-and-white bird. Loons are shorter-necked, have no wing-patches.
Range: — West; breeds in Dakotas, Nebraska, and w. Minnesota. Casual east of Great Plains (accidental on Atlantic coast).

PIED–BILLED GREBE. *Podilymbus podiceps podiceps.*   p. 6.
Field marks: — 12–15. A 'chicken-billed' diver. The common Grebe of the ponds, creeks, and marshes; the breeding Grebe of the eastern United States. *Breeding plumage:* — Gray-brown, darkest on top of head and back; black throat-patch and *black ring around bill. Winter plumage:* — Browner, without throat-patch and bill-mark. Young birds in summer have the head striped with white.
Similar species: — The thick, *rounded* bill of the Pied-bill will distinguish it in profile, in any plumage, from the Horned Grebe with its slender, pointed bill. The Pied-bill has no well-marked white patches in the wing as have the others of the group.
Voice: — A cuckoo-like *cow-cow-cow-cow-cow-cow-cowk-cowk* or *kum-kum-kum,* etc.
Range: — Breeds from Gulf States to Nova Scotia, Quebec, and Saskatchewan. Winters north to Middle States and rarely to New York and Ohio.

Shearwaters and Fulmars: Procellariidæ

LOOK FOR Shearwaters way out at sea. They are gull-like birds, uniform sooty, or dark above and white below. Their flight, several flaps and a sail, banking on stiff wings in the wave-troughs, is distinctive. A Shearwater's wings are proportionately narrower than a Gull's, and the tail not so fanlike. Fulmars are more robust than Shearwaters.

SOOTY SHEARWATER. *Puffinus griseus.* p. 7.
Field marks: — Size of a Laughing Gull (16–18). A gull-like sea-bird that looks all black at a distance and scales over the waves on narrow stiff wings. It is uniformly dark dusky brown except the under surface of the wings, which is pale or whitish.
Similar species: — Dark Jaegers always show white at the base of the primaries and fly with swift hawk-like wing-beats. Young Laughing Gull has white rump.
Range: — Oceanic; breeds in southern hemisphere; summer and autumn migrant off Atlantic and Gulf Coasts, north to Labrador.

AUDUBON'S SHEARWATER. *Puffinus lherminieri.* p. 7.
Similar species: — A very small black-capped Shearwater (12), not much more than half size of Greater Shearwater, more slender and with much more rapid wing-motion. Resembles Greater Shearwater in pattern (black above and white below, with black cap), but does not show any white ring at base of tail.
Range: — Breeds in Bahamas. Occurs off Atlantic coast of Southern States, particularly off Cape Hatteras, North Carolina.

GREATER SHEARWATER. *Puffinus gravis.* p. 7.
Field marks: — 18–20. Gull-like birds, dark above and white below, scaling on narrow stiff wings over the surface of the ocean, are very likely this species or the next. The Greater Shearwater is slightly smaller than the Herring Gull with a *black cap, sharply defined* against white of throat; *white ring at base of tail*; bill black.
Similar species: — The Cory's Shearwater does not have the black cap (sides of head gray) and the white patch at the base of the tail is less distinct or lacking.
Range: — Open ocean n. to Greenland; May to September.

CORY'S SHEARWATER. *Puffinus diomedea.* Subsp. p. 7
Similar species: — Similar to Greater Shearwater, but larger (21) and paler. The *gray* color of the head *blends* into the white of the throat, whereas the Greater Shearwater has a black-capped

LOONS AND GREBES

HORNED GREBE   p. 3.
  Summer: Buffy 'ears': rufous neck.
  Winter: Black and white pattern, thin dark bill.

EARED or BLACK-NECKED GREBE   p. 3.
  Summer: Buffy 'ears'; black neck.
  Winter: Like Horned Grebe; grayer neck, upturned bill.

PIED-BILLED GREBE   p. 4.
  Any plumage: Rounded bill, white under tail coverts.

WESTERN GREBE   p. 4.
  Black body, long white neck.

HOLBOELL'S or RED-NECKED GREBE   p. 3.
  Summer: Reddish neck, white chin and cheek.
  Winter: Grayish neck, yellow bill.

RED-THROATED LOON   p. 2.
  Summer: Gray head; rusty throat.
  Winter: Pale color; upturned bill.

PACIFIC or ARCTIC LOON   p. 1.
  Summer: Gray crown; spots in patches.
  Winter: Dark as Common Loon; bill as slender as Red-
    throats, but not upturned.

COMMON LOON   p. 1.
  Summer: Black head, checkered back.
  Winter: Dark back; straight, stout bill.

 Loons in flight are hunch-
backed and gangly, with a
slight downward sweep to the
neck and the feet projecting
behind.

HORNED GREBE
Summer Winter

EARED GREBE
Summer Winter

PIED-BILLED GREBE
Summer Immature

WESTERN GREBE

HOLBOELL'S GREBE
Summer Winter

Summer **RED-THROATED LOON** Winter

Summer **PACIFIC LOON** Winter

Summer **COMMON LOON** Winter

CORY'S
SHEARWATER

GREATER   SHEARWATER

Dark
Phase

Light
Phase

FULMAR

SOOTY
SHEAR-
WATER

AUDUBON'S
SHEARWATER

LEACH'S
PETREL

WILSON'S
PETREL

SKUA

Light Phase

Dark
Phase

PARASITIC JAEGER

LONG-TAILED JAEGER   POMARINE JAEGER

Plate 2   7

OCEANIC BIRDS

CORY'S SHEARWATER   **p. 5.**
    Blended face pattern, yellow bill.

GREATER SHEARWATER   **p. 5.**
    Black cap, white patch at base of tail.

SOOTY SHEARWATER   **p. 5.**
    Dark body.

AUDUBON'S SHEARWATER   **p. 5.**
    Small; black cap, no patch at base of tail.

FULMAR   **p. 8.**
    Bull-headed; stubby bill; northern (see text).
    Light phase: Light patch at base of primaries.

SKUA (NORTHERN)   **p. 109.**
    White wing-patches, broad blunt tail.

LEACH'S PETREL   **p. 8.**
    White rump, forked tail.

WILSON'S PETREL   **p. 9.**
    White rump, square tail.

LONG-TAILED JAEGER *   **p. 108.**
    Very long central tail feathers.

PARASITIC JAEGER *   **p. 108.**
    Pointed central tail feathers.

POMARINE JAEGER *   **p. 108.**
    Blunt central tail feathers.

  * Jaegers are hawk-like and show a white flash in the wing. There are light, intermediate, and dark phases. Immatures have stubby central tail feathers and are very difficult to identify.

look. The thick bill of the Cory's Shearwater is *yellow*; the Greater Shearwater's thinner bill is black. The Cory's Shearwater lacks the light patch on the rump or has an indistinct one. (The two species are not often seen together except off New England.)

Range: — Open ocean from North Carolina to Newfoundland; July to November.

FULMAR. *Fulmarus glacialis glacialis.*   p. 7.
Field marks: — An oceanic glider, a little larger than a Kittiwake (18–20). *Light phase:* — Head and under parts white; back, wings *and tail* gray; wings darker toward tips; bill yellow; very stubby and thick at the base. *Dark phase:* — Smoky gray; wing-tips darker; bill yellow. In flight, the bird glides and banks on stiff wings in the style of a Shearwater. It follows boats, and often comes near enough for the peculiar bill shape to be made out.
Similar species: — In the light phase, it resembles a Gull but the neck and bill are thicker and the manner of flight different (above). The Fulmar has dusky primaries, lacks the sharply defined black markings toward the tips shown by most Gulls. In dark plumage it suggests a Shearwater but is too pale and too stubby-billed to be mistaken for the dark Sooty Shearwater with its dark slender bill.
Range: — Northern oceans; in United States only on fishing banks far off New England coast during colder months.

Storm Petrels: Hydrobatidæ

LITTLE BLACK birds with white rump-patches flitting over the surface of the water far out at sea ar certainly Petrels. A number of species of Petrels have been recorded in eastern North America, but most of them have appeared accidentally, on but one or more occasions, and would be very unlikely to fall under ordinary field observation. Thus only our two common kinds will be considered here. For the others see Accidentals — Oceanic Birds.

LEACH'S PETREL. *Oceanodroma leucorhoa leucorhoa.*   p. 7.
Field marks: — 8. Wing-spread greater than that of Purple Martin. The breeding Petrel of the North Atlantic (but seldom seen abroad by day); dark sooty, with a pale band of light brown across the wing. The rump-patch is white, and the *tail forked*, the black feet barely showing beyond it. In flight it bounds about erratically like a Nighthawk and often glides like a Shearwater. It does not follow boats.
Similar species: — The best-known Petrel, the Wilson's, is blacker, has a *square* tail, and much longer legs (the yellow

webbed feet projecting *half an inch* beyond the tail). The Leach's Petrel's bounding, butterfly-like flight marks it at a long distance — its best field character (Wilson's skims like a Swallow).

Voice: — At night on breeding grounds, a rhythmic series of eight or nine notes, *wick'-ah wick'-ah wĭ-hĭ-hĭ-hĭ-hĭ* (F. H. Allen).

Range: — Atlantic Ocean; breeds on sea islands from Greenland to Maine and Massachusetts (Penikese Id.) Comes and goes at night. Migrates off coast.

WILSON'S PETREL. *Oceanites oceanicus oceanicus.* p. 7.
Field marks: — Smaller than the Purple Martin (7). Black, with conspicuous white rump-patch; tail even at end. The yellow-webbed feet extend beyond tail's tip. Skims like a Swallow, pausing to flutter and patter over surface of water.

Similar species: — As the Wilson's Petrel is far commoner off our shores than the Leach's, most sight records of Petrels are automatically referred to this species. It habitually follows in the wake of boats; Leach's rarely does. (See Leach's Petrel.)

Range: — A summer traveler on the open ocean; north to Labrador. Breeds in the Antarctic.

Tropic-birds: Phæthontidæ

YELLOW-BILLED TROPIC-BIRD. *Phaëthon lepturus catesbyi.*
p. 9.
Field marks: — Tropic-birds spend most of their life at sea, far from sight of land, flying pigeon-like on strong, quick wings over

YELLOW-BILLED TROPIC-BIRD

CORMORANTS, WATER-TURKEY, GANNET AND BOOBIES

Cormorants sit upright on rocks or posts, often hold a 'spread-eagle' pose. They swim with bill pointed upward more than Loons.

DOUBLE-CRESTED CORMORANT   p. 15.
    Adult: Black body, yellow-orange throat pouch.
    Immature: Pale breast blending into dark belly.

EUROPEAN CORMORANT   p. 14.
    Adult: Large; throat pouch pale yellow.
            In breeding plumage, white flank patches.
    Immature: Belly whitish to under tail coverts.

WATER-TURKEY or ANHINGA   p. 15.
    Serpentine neck, long fan-shaped tail.

GANNET   p. 14.
    Adult: White; pointed tail, large black wing-tips.
    Immature: Brown; pointed tail.
    Changing immature: White patched with dark.

BLUE-FACED BOOBY   p. 13.
    Black on rear edge of wing; black tail.

WHITE-BELLIED BOOBY   p. 13.
    Blackish breast against clear white belly.

DOUBLE-
CRESTED
CORMORANT

Adult

Immature

Breeding
Adult

Immature

EUROPEAN
CORMORANT

WATER-TURKEY

Changing

Immature

GANNET

Adult

BLUE-
FACED
BOOBY

WHITE-
BELLIED
BOOBY

Summer   BLACK GUILLEMOT   Winter

Immature

Summer   PUFFIN   Winter

Summer   DOVEKIE   Winter

Immature

Summer   RAZOR–BILLED AUK   Winter

Summer   BRUNNICH'S MURRE   Winter

"Ringed" Murre

Summer   COMMON MURRE   Winter

Plate 4

11

ALCIDAE (Auks, etc.)

ALCIDS are duck-like sea birds with stubby necks. They have a buzzy flight and a straddle-legged look when about to land.

BLACK GUILLEMOT　　　　　　　　　　　　　　　p. 126.
Summer: Black body, pointed bill, large white patches.
Winter: Whitish body, large white wing-patches.

PUFFIN (ATLANTIC)　　　　　　　　　　　　　　p. 126.
Summer: Triangular red bill.
Winter: Triangular bill, dusky cheeks.
Immature: Smaller bill, dusky cheeks.

DOVEKIE　　　　　　　　　　　　　　　　　　　p. 125.
Starling size, stubby bill.

RAZOR–BILLED AUK　　　　　　　　　　　　　　p. 124.
Adults: Heavy head, flat bill with white mark.
Immature: Smallish bill, with curved ridge.

BRÜNNICH'S MURRE　　　　　　　　　　　　　　p. 125.
Summer: Light mark on gape.
Winter: Dark cap to below eye.

COMMON MURRE　　　　　　　　　　　　　　　　p. 125.
Summer: Long thin bill, no gape mark.
'RINGED MURRE': White eye-ring.
Winter: Black line on white cheek.

the open ocean. They are somewhat smaller than the Herring Gull, white with black shoulder-patches and two extremely long *central tail-feathers* (19 inches) — so long and streaming that they distinguish *Phaëthon* from all other sea-birds. These streamers are much longer than the needle-pointed fork of the Terns.

Similar species: — Old-Squaws have been called Tropic-birds! **Range:** — Breeds in Bermuda (called 'Long-tail'). Occasional off Florida Keys. Casual along coast to New England after hurricanes.

Pelicans: Pelecanidæ

HUGE, BULKY water-birds with long flat bills and tremendous throat-pouches. Pelicans fly in orderly lines, alternating several flaps with a short sail, each bird in the flock playing follow-my-leader, flapping and sailing in rhythm, apparently taking the cue from the bird in front. In flight they draw their heads back on their shoulders.

WHITE PELICAN. *Pelecanus erythrorhynchos.*   p. 12.
Field marks: — Huge (55–70). Wing-spread 9 ft. White with black primaries and a great yellow throat-pouch. Flies with head hunched back on shoulders, and long flat bill resting on curved neck. Often flies at a great height.

BROWN PELICAN

WHITE PELICAN

PELICANS IN FLIGHT

Similar species: — Swans have no black in wings. The Wood Ibis and very rare Whooping Crane have black primaries but fly with necks extended and long legs trailing. Snow Goose is much smaller; flies with neck extended, and has a small bill. Along Florida coast Gannets are often called White Pelicans by beginners.

Range: — Migrates from Northwest diagonally across prairie states to Gulf Coast and Florida. Accidental in Northeast.

(EASTERN) BROWN PELICAN. *Pelecanus occidentalis caro-linensis.* p. 12.
Field marks: — Huge (45–54). Wing-spread 6½ ft. A ponderous dark water-bird with white about the head and neck (in adults). Immatures have dark heads. Flies with its head hunched back on its shoulders and its long flat bill resting comfortably on its breast. Its bulk and its flight — a few flaps and a sail — indicate a Pelican; its dusky color and habit of plunging headlong into the water proclaim it this species. Lines of Pelicans often scale very close to the water, almost touching it with their wing-tips.

Range: — Atlantic and Gulf Coasts from North Carolina to Texas; winters in Florida and along Gulf Coast.

Gannets and Boobies: Sulidæ

VERY LARGE gull-like sea-birds with much longer necks and larger bills than Gulls. As the Gannet is the only one of the group normally found on the Atlantic Coast of the United States, it should be the basis of comparison for the more or less accidental members of the family.

BLUE–FACED BOOBY. *Sula dactylatra dactylatra.* p. 10.
Field marks: — 27. A white Booby, or Gannet-like bird, with a *black tail.*
Similar species: — Gannet is larger, has *white* tail and black toward ends of wings only (Blue-faced Booby has black on *entire rear edge of wing*). The immature Blue-faced Booby is dusky-brown with a white belly. It resembles the White-bellied Booby but is not so clean-patterned and has a whitish patch on the upper back and a whitish rump.

Range: — Occasional off s. Florida (Dry Tortugas). Sits on buoys.

WHITE–BELLIED BOOBY. *Sula leucogaster.* p. 10.
Field marks: — 28–30. A blackish Booby with a *clear white belly,* in clean-cut contrast to a dark breast.

Similar species: — A young Gannet would not show the well-defined contrast of white belly and dark breast. The immature Booby resembles a young Gannet more closely, but is much blacker, with yellow feet. See immature Blue-faced Booby.

Range:— Occasional off Florida, particularly Dry Tortugas. Sits on buoys.

GANNET. *Moris bassana.* p. 10.
Field marks: — 35–40. Goose-sized white birds with extensive *black wing-tips* wheeling in wide circles over the ocean waves are quite certainly Gannets. They are twice the size of Herring Gulls, with much longer necks and larger bills, which are carried pointed toward the water, and pointed, not fan-shaped tails. This gives them a 'pointed at both ends' look. When fishing over the sea, they drop Kingfisher-like into the waves. Young birds are dusky all over, but actions and pointed 'cigar shape' identify them. Changing young have a piebald or 'coach-dog' look; mottled, with dark heads, or boldly splotched with brown and white.

Similar species: — Gulls sometimes drop into the water for food, but the plunge is not spectacular. They do not show so much black in the wing-tips.

Range: — Breeds on islands in Gulf of St. Lawrence; winters at sea from s. New England to Florida.

Cormorants: Phalacrocoracidæ

LARGE, DARK water-birds, much larger than any of the Ducks. To be confused only with Loons, or Geese, but the tail is longer and wing-action more rapid. In flight the neck is held slightly above the horizontal (Loon's neck droops slightly). Cormorants can be told by their very blackness, especially the adults, which are black beneath as well as above. Loons are clear white below. Flocks of Cormorants usually fly in line or wedge formation very much like Geese. A large dark bird perched in an *upright position* on some rock or buoy over the water can hardly be anything else. They often strike a 'spread-eagle' pose. Swimming they lie low like Loons, but with necks more erect and snakelike, and bills pointed upwards *at an angle.*

EUROPEAN CORMORANT. *Phalacrocorax carbo carbo.* p. 10.
Field marks: — 34–40. Most Cormorants seen in midwinter in New England can be automatically assigned to this species. The adult at close range shows a light yellow chin-pouch bordered by a *white throat-patch.* In spring it has a white 'pocket' on the flanks (acquired in February).

Similar species: — This species is a much larger bird than the commoner Double-crest, but unless comparison is available, size cannot be relied upon. The bill of the Double-crest is not so heavy and the throat-pouch is more *orange* (birds with bleached yellowish pouches sometimes complicate matters). Typical immature birds are whiter below than immature Double-crests, the white extending clear to the under tail-coverts. The browner white of the other bird blends into black on the lower belly. Worn and faded Double-crests, however, will have very white or mottled breasts and abdomens, but are seen chiefly in late spring or late summer and early fall. 'The molts are irregular and protracted, worn or delayed individuals are frequent and the greatest caution is urged with immatures when either species is rare or unseasonable' (Ludlow Griscom).

Range: Breeds from Arctic south to Gulf of St. Lawrence; winters along coast to Long Island (and, occasionally, Virginia).

DOUBLE-CRESTED CORMORANT. *Phalacrocorax auritus,*
Subsp. p. 10.

Field marks: — 30–35. The common Cormorant of the Atlantic Coast, and the only one likely to be found on inland lakes and rivers. Southern race is known as Florida Cormorant. (See remarks under Cormorants and European Cormorant.)

Range: — Breeds locally from James Bay and Gulf of St. Lawrence s. to Florida and Gulf of Mexico. Winters mostly along southern coasts; a few n. to Long Island.

MEXICAN CORMORANT. *Phalacrocorax olivaceus mexicanus.*

Field marks: — 25. Similar to Double-crest, but looks slimmer, very much smaller, and dingier both in plumage and in color of pouch. In the breeding season the pouch is edged by a *narrow border of white*.

Range: — Coast of Texas and sw. Louisiana. Both Cormorants occur in Texas but the great majority along the coast are Mexicans during the summer and Double-crests in winter.

Darters: Anhingidæ

WATER-TURKEY. *Anhinga anhinga leucogaster.* p. 10.

Field marks: — 34. Cypress swamps and ricefields in the South are the home of the Water-Turkey, or, as it is variously called, Snake-bird or Anhinga. It is blackish with large silvery patches on the fore part of the wings, a long tail, and a long, serpentine neck. Females have pale buffy breasts, males black. Immature birds are brownish instead of blackish. In flight it progresses with alternate flapping and sailing, the slender neck extended in

WATER–TURKEY

front, the long tail spread fan-wise. It often soars high over-head, hawk-like.

Similar species: — It perches like a Cormorant, in upright pos-ture, on some tree or snag, but the neck is much snakier. The pale-breasted females in particular suggest immature Cormor-ants. Cormorants do not have the light wing-patches. In flight the Anhinga's tail is much longer than that of a Cormorant, and much like that of a Turkey, hence 'Water-Turkey.'

Range: — Lowland swamps north locally to North Carolina, ne. Tennessee, s. Illinois, and Arkansas; winters in Florida and Gulf States.

Man-o'-War-birds: Fregatidæ

MAN–O'–WAR BIRD. *Fregata magnificens rothschildi.*   p. 17.

Field marks: — 40. Wing-spread 7½ ft. In warmer seas we often see long-winged black birds, with long scissor-like tails (usually folded in a long point), soaring with an ease that Gulls and Swallows can hardly match. These are the Man-o'-Wars, or Frigate-Birds. Their extremely long wings seem to have a hump in the middle when the birds are soaring. *Male:* — Black,

MAN-O'-WAR-BIRD

with orange throat-pouch. *Female:* — White breast. *Immature:* — Whole head and under parts white.
Similar species: — The beginner in southern Florida might mistake the white-headed immature for a Swallow-tailed Kite (but Man-o'-War has *black* linings under the wing and is *much* larger).
Range: — Coastal; chiefly s. Florida and Louisiana.

Herons and Bitterns: Ardeidæ

STORK-LIKE wading birds with long necks, long legs, and pointed bills. In sustained flight their heads are tucked back to their shoulders in an S, and their long legs trail behind; their wing beats are slow and 'bowed.' Cranes and Ibises, also long-legged waders, fly with necks outstretched.

GREAT WHITE HERON. *Ardea occidentalis occidentalis.* p. 86.
   Field marks: — Largest American heron, inhabiting the most restricted range of any. Pure white with yellow beak and *greenish-yellow legs*, the latter an infallible character separating it from the smaller American Egret, which has black legs. Never abundant, persecution and natural disasters reduced it to about

GEESE AND SWANS

BRANT p. 32.
Black chest and 'stocking'; neck spot.

CANADA GOOSE p. 31.
Black 'stocking,' white cheek patch.

HUTCHINS'S CANADA GOOSE p. 259.
There are several races of the Canada Goose, varying in size and color, but identification in the field is seldom safe. The Hutchins's or Richardson's Goose (visitor to Plains and Texas) is the small extreme.

BARNACLE GOOSE p. 32.
A European stray.
White face, black eye-mark.

BLUE GOOSE p. 33.
Adult: White head, dark body.
Immature: Dusky with dark bill, pale wings.

BLUE–SNOW HYBRID
Hybrids, looking like Blue Geese with white bellies, etc., are frequent.

WHITE–FRONTED GOOSE p. 32.
Adult: White at base of bill.
Immature: Dusky with pale bill.

SNOW GOOSE p. 33.
Adult: White with black wing-tips.
Immature: Similar but duskier.

WHISTLING SWAN p. 31.
Black bill, long straight neck.

MUTE SWAN p. 30.
Knobbed orange bill, more curved neck.

HUTCHINS'S GOOSE

CANADA GOOSE

BRANT

BARNACLE GOOSE

Immature

BLUE GOOSE

Adult

Adult

Immature

WHITE-FRONTED GOOSE

BLUE-SNOW HYBRID

Immature

SNOW GOOSE

Adult

WHISTLING SWAN

MUTE SWAN

CANADA GOOSE

BRANT

Lower

Upper

WHITE-FRONTED GOOSE

Adult

Immature

BLUE GOOSE

Immature

SNOW GOOSE

Upper

BLUE GOOSE

Adult

Upper

WHISTLING SWAN

Plate 6   19

GEESE AND SWANS

Many Geese and Swans fly in line or wedge formation.

CANADA GOOSE   p. 31.
    Black 'stocking,' light chest, white throat patch.

BRANT   p. 32.
    Small; black 'stocking,' black chest, black head.

WHITE–FRONTED GOOSE   p. 32.
    Adult: Gray neck, black splotches on belly.
    Immature: Dusky; light bill, light feet.

SNOW GOOSE   p. 33.
    White body, black wing-tips.

BLUE GOOSE   p. 33.
    Adult: Dark body, white head.
    Immature: Dusky; pale wing-linings, dark bill, dark feet.

WHISTLING SWAN   p. 31.
    Very long neck; wings with no black.

150 birds in 1935. Rigid protection has increased it to more normal status. Nests in scattered groups of from two or three pairs to a dozen or more, in dense mangrove growth.

Range: — Extreme south Florida and the Keys. Almost unknown north of Miami except for a few isolated wanderers (South Carolina, North Carolina, Mississippi, and Pennsylvania).

ALEXANDER SPRUNT, JR.

WURDEMANN'S HERON. *Ardea wurdemanni.*
   Field marks: — A hybrid between the Ward's Great Blue Heron and the Great White Heron; like a Great Blue with a pure white head, *lacking the black plume.* Look for it in the Florida Keys.

GREAT BLUE HERON. *Ardea herodias.* Subsp.   p. 86.
   Field marks: — 42–52. This great bird, often called 'crane' by country people, stands about four feet tall, and is, next to the Sandhill Crane, the largest wading bird found in the Northern States. Its long legs, long neck, and sharp-pointed bill, and, in flight, its folded neck and trailing legs mark the bird as a Heron. The great size (spread of an Eagle) and the blue-gray coloration, whiter about the head and neck (in adults), identify it as this species.
   Voice: — Low, hoarse croaks; *frahnk, frahnk, frawnk.*
   Range: — Breeds from Florida Keys and Gulf Coast north to Nova Scotia, Quebec, and Manitoba. Winters in s. United States north rarely to Great Lakes and s. New England.

AMERICAN EGRET. *Casmerodius albus egretta.*   p. 86.
   Field marks: — 37–40. A large Heron of snowy-white plumage, with black legs and feet and a *yellow bill.*
   Similar species: — The Snowy Egret and the immature Little Blue Heron are also white, but are much smaller and have *black or blackish* bills instead of yellow.
   Voice: — A low, hoarse croak.
   Range: — Breeds in s. United States n. in wooded swamps to Tennessee and New Jersey; wanders in summer to Ontario and Maine; winters from South Carolina to Texas.

SNOWY EGRET. *Leucophoyx thula thula.*   p. 86.
   Field marks: — The Heron with the 'golden slippers.' A medium-sized white Heron (20–27) with a black bill, black legs, and *yellow feet.* When feeding, it shuffles about with its feet so as to stir up the food, a habit not noticeable in the other white herons. Young Snowies have a yellow stripe up the back of the leg and look yellow-legged when walking away from the observer.
   Similar species: — The American Egret is much larger and has *black feet and a yellow bill.* The Little Blue Heron in the white

plumage is about the same size as the Snowy, but has *dark feet*. Its bill is bluish at the base.

Range: — Breeds in s. United States; north rarely to New Jersey; occasionally wanders in summer to Great Lakes and s. New England.

REDDISH EGRET. *Dichromanassa rufescens rufescens.* p. 86.
Field marks: — 29. A medium-sized Heron, neutral gray, with a rusty-brown head and neck, and a *flesh-colored, black-lipped bill*. There is also a scarcer white phase (1 to 400 in Texas, 50–50 in West Indies). When feeding, the quickest way to pick this species out is by its clowning actions. It lurches about and often acts quite drunk. It is loose-feathered and when fluffed, its neck is very shaggy.
Similar species: — Dark phase resembles adult Little Blue Heron, which is darker, with a bill that is *pale bluish* at the base. White phase appears like American Egret but shorter and stouter, legs blue. The only *necessary* recognition mark for either plumage is the *flesh-colored* black-tipped bill.
Range: — Gulf coast of Texas; rare in s. Florida (becoming increasingly resident in the Keys).

LOUISIANA HERON. *Hydranassa tricolor ruficollis.* p. 86.
Field marks: — A slender, graceful, medium-sized Heron (26) dark in color, with a clear white belly and a white rump. The contrasting white belly is the key-mark in any plumage.
Similar species: — Some young Little Blues changing from the white to the blue plumage might be dark winged and white-bellied like a Louisiana, but they would also show scattering white feathers on the back and neck.
Range: — Breeds near coast from Texas to North Carolina; a few wander north in summer to New Jersey, casually to Massachusetts.

LITTLE BLUE HERON. *Florida cœrulea cœrulea.* p. 86.
Field marks: — A medium-sized (20–29), slender Heron, slaty-blue (blackish at a distance); legs dark. The immature bird is snowy white with a tinge of blue in the primaries; legs dull *greenish*; bill *bluish* tipped with black. White birds changing to adulthood are boldly patched with blue, unlike plumage of any other Heron.
Similar species: — The adult, like the Green Heron, appears blackish at a distance, but the latter bird is smaller, with much shorter *yellowish* or *orange* legs. Some Snowy Egrets, especially young birds, are frequently suspected of being young Little Blues because of a stripe of yellow or greenish up the posterior side of the legs visible as the bird walks away. The thicker bill, with the bluish base, and the lack of the shuffling foot motions, so characteristic of the Snowy, will identify this species.

DUCKS IN FLIGHT

(Through the binoculars)

NOTE: Males are analyzed below. Females are somewhat similar.

GADWALL p. 37.
  White speculum.

BLACK DUCK p. 37.
  Dark body, paler head (see Plate 9).

MALLARD p. 36.
  Dark head, two white borders on speculum, neck ring.

PINTAIL p. 40.
  Needle tail, one white border on speculum, neck stripe.

BALDPATE p. 42.
  Large white shoulder-patches.

SHOVELLER p. 43.
  Spoon bill, large bluish shoulder-patches.

WOOD DUCK p. 43.
  Stocky; long dark tail, white border on dark wing.

BLUE-WINGED TEAL p. 41.
  Small; large bluish shoulder-patches.

GREEN-WINGED TEAL p. 41.
  Small, dark-winged; green speculum.

HOODED MERGANSER p. 51.
  Merganser shape; small wing-patch.

AMERICAN MERGANSER p. 52.
  Merganser shape, white chest, large wing-patches.

RED-BREASTED MERGANSER p. 52.
  Merganser shape, dark chest, large wing-patches.

Mergansers fly with bill, head, neck, and body held in a horizontal line.

BLACK DUCK

Sexes
Similar

MALLARD

GADWALL

♂

PINTAIL

BALDPATE

SHOVELLER

BLUE-WINGED
TEAL

GREEN-
WINGED
TEAL

WOOD
DUCK

AMERICAN MERGANSER

HOODED MERGANSER

RED-BREASTED
MERGANSER

GREATER SCAUP

REDHEAD

RING-NECKED DUCK

CANVAS-BACK

BUFFLE-HEAD

AMERICAN GOLDEN-EYE

RUDDY DUCK ♂

OLD-SQUAW

HARLEQUIN DUCK

KING EIDER ♂

COMMON EIDER

WHITE- WINGED SCOTER

SURF SCOTER

AMERICAN SCOTER

Plate 8   23

DUCKS IN FLIGHT
(Through the binoculars)

NOTE: Males are analyzed below.   Some females are similar.

REDHEAD   p. 44.
  Gray back, broad gray wing-stripe.

GREATER SCAUP   p. 45.
  Broad white wing-stripe (see Lesser Scaup).

RING–NECKED DUCK   p. 44.
  Black back, broad gray wing-stripe.

CANVAS–BACK   p. 45.
  White back, long profile.

AMERICAN GOLDEN–EYE   p. 46.
  Large white wing-squares, short neck, black head.

BUFFLE–HEAD   p. 47.
  Small; large wing-patches, white head-patch.

RUDDY DUCK   p. 51.
  Small; dark with white cheeks.

OLD–SQUAW   p. 48.
  Dark wings, white on body.

HARLEQUIN DUCK   p. 48.
  Stocky, dark; small bill, white marks.

KING EIDER   p. 49.
  Whitish fore parts, black rear parts.

COMMON or AMERICAN EIDER   p. 48.
  White back, white fore wings, black belly.

WHITE–WINGED SCOTER   p. 49.
  Black body, white wing-patches.

SURF SCOTER   p. 50.
  Black body, white head-patches.

AMERICAN SCOTER   p. 50.
  All black plumage.

Range: — Breeds in s. United States north to New Jersey (casually Massachusetts); wanders to New England and s. Canada: (chiefly white birds in late summer); winters in s. United States.

(EASTERN) GREEN HERON. *Butorides virescens virescens.*

p. 87.

Field marks: — The Green Heron looks quite black and crowlike at a distance, but flies with slower, more arched, wing-beats. It is a small dark Heron (16–22) with comparatively short *greenish-yellow or orange* legs. Elevates a shaggy crest when alarmed. At close range neck is rich chestnut. Normally the most generally distributed small Heron in the North.

Similar species: — It often shows more blue than green, so don't think you have a Little Blue Heron.

Voice: — A series of *kucks* or a loud *skyow* or *skewk.*

Range: — Breeds from Gulf of Mexico, n. to Minnesota, s. Quebec, and Nova Scotia; winters from Florida south.

BLACK–CROWNED NIGHT HERON. *Nycticorax nycticorax hoactli.*

p. 87.

Field marks: — 23–28. A chunky, rather short-legged Heron. *Adult:* — The only Heron that is black-backed and pale gray or white below; wings gray. *Immature:* — Brown, spotted and streaked with white.

Similar species: — The immature resembles the American Bittern, but is a grayer brown, rather than a rich, warm brown. In flight, it flaps its wings more slowly, in a wider arc, and lacks the broad black wing-tips of the Bittern.

Voice: — Call, a flat *guok!* or *guark!* is unmistakable; most often heard in the evening.

Range: — Breeds from Florida and Gulf of Mexico n. to s. Manitoba and e. Quebec; winters n. to s. New England (a few), s. New York, and Ohio (occasionally).

YELLOW–CROWNED NIGHT HERON. *Nyctanassa violacea.*

p. 87.

Field marks: — 22–28. *Adult:* — A chunky gray Heron with a *black head* ornamented with white cheek-patch and whitish crown. Immature: — See below.

Similar species: — The adult lacks the contrast of black above and white below of the Black-crowned Night Heron. The immatures are very similar. The Black-crown is browner with larger spotting on the back. The Yellow-crown is more slate-colored, and is more finely speckled. Its bill is slightly stouter, the legs longer and yellower. In flight, the entire foot and a short space of bare leg extend clear of the end of the tail — a very good field character.

Voice: — *Quak,* higher pitched than note of Black-crown.

Range: — Chiefly swamps of Southern States breeding north sparingly to Missouri, Tennessee, Maryland, New Jersey, and, rarely, Long Island and Massachusetts. Winters from Florida south.

AMERICAN BITTERN. *Botaurus lentiginosus.* p. 87

Field marks: — 23–34. In crossing a marsh we flush this large stocky brown bird. It is rarely ever seen perching in trees like other Herons. In flight the black wing-tips, contrasting with the streaked buffy brown of the rest of the bird, is a good point Standing, it points its bill skyward.

Similar species: — The brown young Night Heron resembles it but is grayer without the black wing-tips. When silhouetted in flight, the faster wing-beats and the less curved wings are the Bittern's marks, and its bill is held more horizontal. The Least Bittern resembles it but little; the latter is a tiny bird contrastingly patterned with buff and black.

Voice: — The pumping, the 'song' of the Bittern, which we hear in the swamps in spring is a slow, deep *oong-ka-choonk — oong-ka-choonk — oong-ka-choonk*, etc. Distorted by distance, the *ka* is often the only audible syllable and sounds like a mallet driving a stake into the mud. Flushing note, a rapid throaty *kok-kok-kok.*

Range: — Breeds in marshes from Gulf of Mexico, n. to Newfoundland and n. Manitoba; winters n. to s. Illinois and Virginia, rarely farther.

(EASTERN) LEAST BITTERN. *Ixobrychus exilis exilis.* p. 87

Field marks: — The midget of the Heron family (11–14), nearer the bulk of a Rail or a Meadowlark. When discovered, it usually flushes close by from its hiding-place in the marsh, flies weakly for a short distance, and drops in again. The *large buff wing-patches*, black back, and small size identify it.

Similar species: — Rails lack the buff wing-patches and are without much pattern. Beginners sometimes call Green Herons Least Bitterns. (Green Heron's wings are dark, almost black.) See American Bittern.

Voice: — The call, a low rapid *coo-coo-coo* coming from the marsh is often the best indication of the bird's presence (cuckoo-like, but not in long series).

Range: — Breeds from Gulf of Mexico north to s. Maine, Ontario, and Minnesota; winters from s. Georgia and s. Texas south.

CORY'S LEAST BITTERN. *Ixobrychus neoxenus.*

Field marks: — A very rare local color-phase of the Least Bittern. Identical in pattern with Least Bittern, but buff color of that bird replaced by deep chestnut. Formerly more frequent.

DUCKS OVERHEAD
(As the sportsman often sees them)

NOTE: Only males are analyzed below.

BLACK DUCK (BLACK MALLARD*)   p. 37.
    Dusky body, white wing-linings.

GADWALL   p. 37.
    White belly, white rear wing-patches.

MALLARD   p. 36.
    Dark chest, light belly, neck-ring.

PINTAIL (SPRIG*)   p. 40.
    White breast, thin neck, needle tail.

BALDPATE (WIDGEON*)   p. 42.
    White belly, dark pointed tail.

SHOVELLER (SPOONBILL*)   p. 43.
    Dark belly, white chest; big bill.

WOOD DUCK   p. 43.
    White belly, dusky wings, long square tail.

BLUE-WINGED TEAL   p. 41.
    Small Teal size; dark belly.

GREEN-WINGED TEAL   p. 41.
    Small Teal size; light belly, dark head.

HOODED MERGANSER *   p. 51.
    Merganser shape; dusky wing-linings.

AMERICAN MERGANSER *   p. 52.
    Black head, white body, white wing-linings.

RED-BREASTED MERGANSER *   p. 52.
    Merganser shape; dark breast-band.

* The sportsman usually calls Mergansers 'Sheldrakes.' The names
in parentheses are also common gunners' names.

BLACK DUCK
(Sexes similar)

MALLARD

GADWALL
Male

PINTAIL

BALDPATE

SHOVELLER

WOOD DUCK

BLUE-WINGED TEAL

GREEN-WINGED TEAL

HOODED MERGANSER

AMERICAN MERGANSER

RED-BREASTED MERGANSER

GREATER
SCAUP DUCK

RING–NECKED
DUCK

REDHEAD

CANVAS–BACK

AMERICAN
GOLDEN–EYE

BUFFLE–HEAD

OLD–
SQUAW

RUDDY
DUCK   Male

HARLEQUIN
DUCK

SURF SCOTER

WHITE–WINGED
SCOTER

AMERICAN
SCOTER

Plate 10   27

DUCKS OVERHEAD

(As the sportsman often sees them)

NOTE: Only males are analyzed below.
The first four all have black chests and white wing-
linings, and look very much alike.

GREATER SCAUP DUCK (BLUEBILL *)   p. 45.
Black chest, white stripe showing through wing.

REDHEAD   p. 44.
Black chest, round rufous head.

CANVAS-BACK   p. 45
Black chest, long profile.

RING-NECKED DUCK   p. 44.
Not safe to tell from Scaup overhead (except possibly
for lack of white rear wing-stripe).

AMERICAN GOLDEN-EYE (WHISTLER *)   p. 46.
Blackish linings, white patches.

BUFFLE-HEAD (BUTTERBALL *)   p. 47.
Like small Golden-eye; note head pattern.

OLD-SQUAW   p. 48.
Solid dark wings, white belly.

RUDDY DUCK   p. 51.
Stubby; white face, dark chest.

HARLEQUIN DUCK   p. 48.
Solid dark color, white spots, small bill.

WHITE-WINGED SCOTER *   p. 49.
Black body, white wing-patches.

SURF SCOTER *   p. 50.
Black body, white on head.

AMERICAN SCOTER *   p. 50.
Black body, silvery flight feathers.

* The three Scoters are often called 'Coots' by sportsmen. The names
in parentheses are also common gunners' names.

Storks and Wood Ibises: Ciconiidæ

WOOD IBIS. *Mycteria americana.*   pp. 29, 87.
   Field marks: — 35–47. A very large white Stork with a dark, naked wattled head and *extensive black wing-areas*; bill long, thick at the base and decurved. Immature birds are dingier in color with much lighter head and neck, but they still look like Wood Ibises.
   Similar species: — Distinguished in flight from the White Herons by the outstretched neck and the black in the wings and by the alternate flapping and sailing; from the White Ibis by its entirely dark head, stouter bill, and much larger size (near that of the Great Blue Heron). The White Ibis has a very small area of black in the wing-tips. In flight at a distance the Wood Ibis much resembles the White Pelican except for its very different proportions (long neck and legs).
   Range: — Southern United States, chiefly near coast from South Carolina to Texas.

Ibises and Spoonbills: Threskiornithidæ

IBISES are long-legged wading birds with long, slender, *decurved* bills, similar to those of the Curlews. Unlike the Herons they fly with necks *outstretched*. The name alone describes the Spoonbills. No other heron-like birds have bills at all resembling theirs.

EASTERN GLOSSY IBIS. *Plegadis falcinellus falcinellus.*
                                                                   p. 87.
   Field marks: — 22–25. A medium-sized marsh wader with a long, decurved bill; largely bronzy-chestnut, but at a distance appearing quite black, like a large black Curlew. It flies with neck outstretched, with much quicker wing-beats than a Heron, alternately flapping and sailing.
   Similar species: — The immature Glossy is less metallic, but an all-dark bird. (Immature White Ibis has white rump and belly.) Winter Glossies have some white speckling about the head (see Limpkin). In Texas see White-faced Glossy Ibis.
   Range: — Breeds in peninsular Florida; wanders rarely to Northern States.

WHITE–FACED GLOSSY IBIS. *Plegadis mexicana.*
   Similar species: — Similar to the preceding species, but with a white patch about the base of the bill. Many Glossy Ibises show

WHITE IBIS AND WOOD IBIS

Note the great amount of black in the Wood Ibis.

a narrow strip of whitish or bluish skin between the bill and the eye and are thus mistaken for the White-face, but in this species the white goes *in back of the eye and under the chin*. It is said that the White-faced Glossy loses the white face in winter.

Range: — Southern Texas and s. Louisiana; occasional in Florida.

WHITE IBIS. *Guara alba.*   p. 87.
   Field marks: — 22–27. Few sights in the bird world are as impressive as long streamers of the so-called 'White Curlews' drifting about over some Southern marsh. Seen close at hand, they are medium-sized white birds with black wing-tips, red legs, *red faces*, and long, decurved bills. They fly with necks outstretched, alternately flapping and sailing. The dark young birds are quite evidently Ibises by their shape. They have white bellies and show conspicuous *white rumps* as they fly away.
   Similar species: — No white Heron has black-tipped wing-feathers. The Wood Ibis is very much larger and the black areas are much more extensive. The young Glossy Ibis can be told from the similarly sized young White Ibis by its uniformly dark coloration.
   Range: — Low country from South Carolina to Texas.

ROSEATE SPOONBILL. *Ajaia ajaja.*   p. 86.
   Field marks: — 32. A *pink* wading bird with a flat spatulate bill. When feeding, the bill is swung rapidly from side to side.

In flight the neck is extended like an Ibis, and the bird often sails
between wing-strokes. Adults are bright pink with a vivid red
'drip' along the shoulders. Immature birds are white, acquiring a glow of pink as they become older.

Similar species: — Two other pink or red waders have occurred
in the South — the Scarlet Ibis and the Flamingo — but they
are so vastly different in shape that they could hardly be confused. The Ibis is accidental; the Flamingo rare, far less likely
to be seen than the Spoonbill.

Range: — Breeds locally on Texas Coast; less commonly in s.
Florida (mangrove coasts); very locally in Louisiana.

Flamingos: Phœnicopteridæ

FLAMINGO. *Phœnicopterus ruber.*   p. 86.
  Field marks: — 45. An extremely slender *rose-pink* wading
  bird, with a broken 'Roman nose'; as tall as a Great Blue
  Heron, but much more slender. In flight it shows large black
  wing-areas, and its extremely long neck is extended droopily in
  front and its long legs trail similarly behind, giving the impres-
  sion that the bird might as easily fly backward as forward! Do
  not trust a 'wild' Flamingo unless it is *bright* pink. Pale washed-
  out birds are likely escaped captives.
  Similar species: — See Roseate Spoonbill.
  Range: — Occasional on Florida coast. The birds at Hialeah
  Race Track and at the Bok Sanctuary are captive.

Swans: Cygninæ

HUGE WHITE swimming birds, larger and with much longer necks
than Geese. Like some of the Geese, they migrate in stringy lines
or V-shaped flocks. Their extremely long, slender necks and the
lack of black wing-tips distinguish them from all other large white
swimming birds (Snow Goose, White Pelican, etc.). Young birds
are tinged with brown.

MUTE SWAN. *Cygnus olor.*   p. 18.
  Field marks: — 58. In most parts of the East any wild Swan
  can be called, without hesitation, a Whistling Swan, except
  where the Mute Swan, the park variety, has established itself in
  a wild state. It is a more graceful-looking bird than the somewhat smaller Whistler, nearly always swimming with an S curve
  in its neck, its wings raised in an arch over its back, and its
  knobbed orange bill pointing downward toward the water.

Similar species: — The Whistling Swan's bill is *black* with no knob. At attention it is quite straight-necked, its head and bill jutting out at a right angle. It tends to sit lower in the water with less stern visible, and works with its head and neck beneath the surface of the water a good deal more than does the Mute. Young Whistlers in the brown-tinged plumage have dull pinkish bills. The brownish young Mute Swan has a darker bill that is blackish at the base.

Range: — Long Island, New Jersey coast, and Hudson Valley (The Whistling Swan is rare in this area).

WHISTLING SWAN. *Cygnus columbianus.*   pp. 18, 19.

Field marks: — 48–55. The common wild Swan of the East. Usually heard long before the wavering wedge-shaped flock can be detected high in the blue. Their pure white wings and long necks stretched full length mark them as Swans. On the water one can sometimes approach close enough to see the small yellow spot at the base of the black bill. Young birds are not white, but quite dingy-appearing with dull pinkish bills.

Similar species: — Snow Geese have black in the wings and much shorter necks. (See Mute Swan.)

Voice: — Loud high-pitched cooing notes, less harsh than honking of Canada Goose; 'A musical, loud *woo-ho, woo-woo, woo-ho*' (J. Moffitt).

Range: — Winters chiefly on large bays from Chesapeake to North Carolina (occasionally on Great Lakes and Gulf Coast); migrates through Great Lakes region to the Arctic.

Geese: Anserinæ

LARGE waterfowl; larger, heavier-bodied, and with longer necks than Ducks. In flight they are noisy and some species assemble in line or V-formation. As is not the case with most of the Ducks, the *sexes are alike* at all seasons. They are more terrestrial than Ducks and feed mainly on land (except Brant); are to be looked for in grassy marshes, grain or stubble fields. Cormorants fly in line or V-formation; they suggest Geese, but are *black* and *silent*.

CANADA GOOSE. *Branta canadensis.* Subsp.   pp. 18, 19.

Field marks: — 25–43. The most widespread of its tribe in North America, and the only Goose seen in many localities. Gray-brown, with a black head and neck or 'stocking' that contrasts sharply with the light-colored breast. The most characteristic mark is the *white cheek patch* that runs from under the chin on to the side of the head. People in some sections are very

familiar with the long strings of Geese migrating high overhead
in V-formation. Their musical honking, or barking, often her-
alds the approach of a flock long before it can be seen.
Voice: — A deep double-syllabled 'honking' note, *ka-ronk* or
ha-lunk (second syllable higher).
Range: — Breeds from Arctic Coast south to South Dakota and
Gulf of St. Lawrence; also a few in New England (wild birds?);
winters from Great Lakes and Nova Scotia south to Gulf of Mexico.

BRANT.   *Branta bernicla.*   Subsp.   pp. 18, 19.
Field marks: — A small black-necked Goose hardly larger than
a Mallard (23–30). It is almost strictly coastal, bunching erratically in large, irregular flocks rather than in the organized V-
formation of most other Geese. (See below.)
Similar species: — The Brant resembles the Canada Goose
somewhat, but is much smaller. The fore parts of a Brant are
black, *to the water-line*; a Goose's breast flashes whitish above the
water. At a distance a Goose shows dingy sides and *two* pale
areas, fore and aft; a Brant is much more white on the sides and
its white rear is very conspicuous. The Brant has a small white
patch *on the neck* instead of a large white patch on the face. Its
wing-beats are less slow and labored.
Voice: — A throaty *cr-r-r-ruk* or *krrr-onk, krrr-onk.*
Range: — Breeds in Arctic; winters in large bays along coast
from Massachusetts to North Carolina. Casual inland.

BARNACLE GOOSE.   *Branta leucopsis.*   p. 18.
Field marks: — 26. A European salt-water species that has
occurred almost a score of times on this side of the Atlantic. It
is so boldly patterned and so well worth looking for that I have
included it here rather than on the accidental list. Black, white
and gray, with a *white face and forehead*, and a black mark joining
the eye to the bill.
Similar species: — Told from Brant by white of head, from Canada Goose by white forehead and black chest.

WHITE–FRONTED GOOSE.   *Anser albifrons.*   pp. 18, 19.
Field marks: Smaller than common Canada Goose; near size of
Snow Goose or Brant (27–30). A gray-brown Goose showing at
close range a pink bill, a clear white patch *on the front of the face*,
and black barring on the belly (variable in amount). The feet
are yellow or orange. *Immature:* — Dusky with *yellow or orange*
feet but otherwise without the distinctive marks of the adult.
No other Goose has yellow or orange feet.
Similar species: — At a distance this species shows no contrast
of black 'stocking' and light belly as in the Canada Goose or
Brant. When flying overhead with either of them, the more uni-

form color below is at once apparent. The immature Blue Goose is also uniformly dusky but has dusky feet.

Voice: — 'Flight note, *kah—lah—a—luck*, high-pitched "tootling," usually uttered from one to three times' (J. Moffitt).

Range: — Breeds in Arctic; migrates chiefly west of Mississippi River to Gulf Coast; casual on Atlantic Coast.

SNOW GOOSE. *Chen hyperborea.* Subsp.   pp. 18, 19.

Field marks: — 23–38. A *white* Goose, smaller than the Canada, with *black wing-tips.* Young birds are duskier, but still pale enough to be recognizable as Snow Geese.

Similar species: — Swans have *no black* in the wings, are much larger and have much longer necks. On the water when wing-tips are often hard to see, Swans can be told by their different shape (see diagram).

Voice: — Monosyllabic flight notes: 'loud, nasal, resonant *whouk* or *houck*, uttered singly, twice, or rarely three times' (J. Moffitt).

Range: — Breeds in Arctic, migrates mainly through Mississippi Valley and plains (Lesser Snow Goose); winters along Gulf Coast of Louisiana and Texas (Lesser Snow Goose) and in large coastal bays from Delaware to North Carolina (Greater Snow Goose).

BLUE GOOSE. *Chen cærulescens.*   pp. 18, 19.

Field marks: — 25–30. A dark Goose, smaller than the Canada, with a *white* head and neck. Some individuals have white breasts, possibly hybrids with Snow Goose blood. A dark Goose in a flock of Snows is most likely a Blue. Intermediates are frequent.

Similar species: — The young bird is dusky in color, very similar to the immature White-front, but has dark feet instead of yellow, and paler, bluish wings.

Voice: — Exactly like Snow Goose.

Range: — Migrates from Arctic through Mississippi Valley to Gulf Coast of Louisiana. Rare on Eastern seaboard.

Tree-Ducks: Dendrocygninæ

FULVOUS TREE-DUCK: *Dendrocygna bicolor helva.*   p. 38.

Field marks: — 20–21. This long-legged, goose-like Duck of the Gulf Coast does not ordinarily frequent trees. Its tawny body and broad creamy stripe on the sides identify it. In flight the long legs extending beyond the tail, slightly drooped neck, and slow wing-beats (for a Duck) are distinctive. On the wing the bird looks dark, with blackish wing-linings and a white ring at the base of the tail. On land it has a tall gangly look (long neck, long legs). The sexes are alike.

Voice: — A squealing double-noted whistle. (Called Squealer.)

Range: — Marshes and rice fields of s. Texas and Louisiana.

BAY DUCKS

Diving Ducks (Bay Ducks and Sea Ducks) run and patter along the water when taking flight. Surface-feeding Ducks (Marsh Ducks, Plate 14), spring directly up.

CANVAS-BACK   p. 45.
     Male: White body, rusty head, sloping profile.
     Female: Grayish; dark chest, sloping profile.

REDHEAD   p. 44.
     Male: Gray; black chest, round rufous head.
     Female: Indistinct face-patch near bill (see text).

RING-NECKED DUCK   p. 44.
     Male: Black back, white mark before wing.
     Female: Eye-ring and ring on bill (see text).

LESSER SCAUP DUCK   p. 45.
     Male: Black chest, black head (purple gloss), blue bill.
     Female: Sharp white patch at base of bill.

GREATER SCAUP DUCK   p. 45.
     Male: Like preceding; head rounder (green gloss).
     Female: Like preceding (see text).

BARROW'S GOLDEN-EYE   p. 47.
     Male: White crescent on face; blacker above.
     Female: Like female American Golden-eye (see text).

AMERICAN GOLDEN-EYE   p. 46.
     Male: Round white spot before eye.
     Female: Gray body, brown head, light collar.

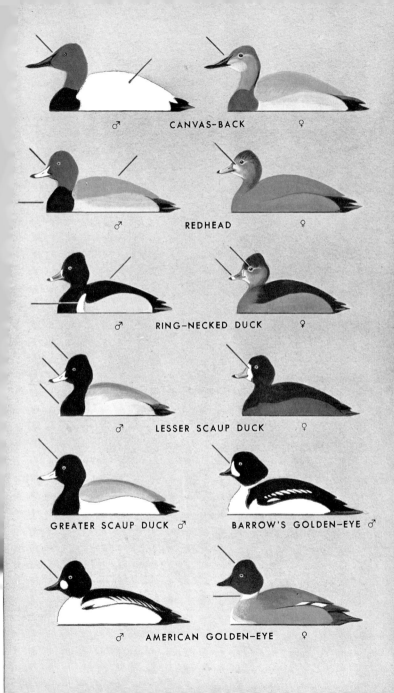

CANVAS-BACK ♂ ♀

REDHEAD ♂ ♀

RING-NECKED DUCK ♂ ♀

LESSER SCAUP DUCK ♂ ♀

GREATER SCAUP DUCK ♂　　BARROW'S GOLDEN-EYE ♂

AMERICAN GOLDEN-EYE ♂ ♀

♂ Summer OLD-SQUAW ♀ Winter
♂ Winter

♂ HARLEQUIN DUCK ♀

♂ SURF SCOTER ♀

♂ WHITE-WINGED SCOTER ♀

♂ AMERICAN SCOTER ♀

KING EIDER ♂

♀ COMMON EIDER ♂

Plate 12   35

SEA DUCKS

OLD-SQUAW   p. 48.
    Male in summer: Needle tail, white face patch.
    Male in winter: Needle tail, pied pattern.
    Female: Dark wings; much white around head.

HARLEQUIN DUCK   p. 48.
    Male: Dark; rusty flanks, harlequin pattern.
    Female: Face spots, small bill.

SURF SCOTER   p. 50.
    Male: Black body, white head patches.
    Female: Light face spots, no white in wing.

WHITE-WINGED SCOTER   p. 49.
    Male: Black body, white wing patch.
    Female: Light face spots, white wing patch.

AMERICAN SCOTER   p. 50.
    Male: Black body, orange on bill.
    Female: Light cheek, dark crown.

KING EIDER   p. 49.
    Male: White foreparts, black rear parts.
    Female: See below.

COMMON or AMERICAN EIDER   p. 48.
    Male: White above, black below.
    Female: Brown; heavily barred.

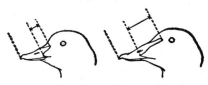

KING EIDER ♀   COMMON EIDER ♀

Female Eiders can be told at close range by their bills; stubbier in the King with less feathering on the side of the bill; more sloping in the Common Eider with a long lobe extending onto the forehead.

Surface-Feeding Ducks: Anatinæ

DUCKS of this group, although not always confined to small bodies of water, are most characteristic of creeks, ponds, and marshes. They obtain their food by dabbling and tipping up rather than by diving. When frightened, they spring directly into the air instead of pattering before getting under way. They swim as a rule with the tail held quite clear of the water. Most birds of this group have a metallic *speculum*, or '*mirror*,' a rectangular patch situated at the hind edge of the wing.

In summer the males of most Ducks desert their mates and moult their bright plumage. They acquire a plumage known as the 'eclipse plumage.' I have not covered this phase in the following pages, first, because most Ducks are not much in evidence during this trying period, and secondly, because they look so much like the females of their species as to be readily identifiable. In another month or so, they commence a second moult in which they regain their bright winter pattern. See Kortright's *The Ducks, Geese, and Swans of North America* for pictures and descriptions of eclipse plumages.

Many of our Ducks hybridize occasionally. Over the years I have seen in the field birds that I felt sure were the following hybrids: Mallard-Black, Mallard-Gadwall, Mallard-Pintail, Gadwall-Pintail, and Green-winged-European Teal.

MALLARD. *Anas platyrhynchos platyrhynchos.*   pp. 22, 26, 39.
Field marks: — Like the puddle Mallard of the parks and barnyards, but smaller (20–28). Has a liking for wooded swamps as well as marshes. *Male:* — Grayish with *green head, narrow white ring around neck*, ruddy breast, and white tail. *Female:* — A mottled brown Duck with whitish tail and conspicuous white borders *on each side* of metallic violet-blue wing-patch.
Similar species: — A few other Ducks have heads glossed with greenish and are therefore mistaken for Mallards, but the white neck-ring and dark ruddy breast are diagnostic (the very different Red-breasted Merganser has a similar combination, however — green-black head, white collar, ruddy breast). In flight Mallards and Blacks have a characteristic wing-stroke; it is slower than in most Ducks, and the downward sweep does not carry the wings much below the level of the body. Stray female Mallards when mixed in with flocks of Blacks, appear much lighter in color, with *whitish tails*. This and the *white borders* on each side of the wing-patch, or speculum, are definitive field marks. Female Pintails are similar mottled-brown Ducks but are more streamlined and have a white border on only one side of the speculum. The bill of the Pintail is gray; that of the Mallard usually orange. In flight overhead the Mallard's wing-linings are whiter.

Voice: — Female quacks like a barnyard Duck (as do females of Black Duck and Gadwall). Male, a reedy *yeeb—yeeb.*
Range: — Breeds in w. North America e. to Great Lakes area; a few farther e. and s. Winters from Great Lakes and s. New England s. to Gulf of Mexico.

BLACK DUCK. *Anas rubripes.*   pp. 22, 26, 39
Field marks: — 21–25. The Black Duck in flight, with its uniform *dark coloration* and *flashing white wing-linings* is unmistakable. The sexes are similar, dark sooty-brown with a lighter yellowish-brown head and a metallic violet patch in the wing. The feet are anywhere from brown to red and the bill dull greenish or yellowish. For some years two races of the Black Duck were recognized by both taxonomists and field students; the common Black Duck (*A. r. tristis*) and the Red-legged Black Duck (*A. r. rubripes*). This division has lately been repudiated. It is believed by many that the differences in size, leg coloration, etc., are due mainly to season and the ages of the birds. The arguments for and against are very well stated in Kortright's fine book *The Ducks, Geese, and Swans of North America.* The case, however, is still not closed, in the opinion of some.
Similar species: — Black Ducks which resort to the ocean are sometimes confused with the Scoters. See female Mallard.
Voice:—Female quacks similarly to a barnyard Duck (so do females of Mallard and Gadwall). Male has a low croak.
Range: — E. North America, breeding from Labrador s. to North Carolina (a few), Pennsylvania, Ohio, and n. Illinois, and w. to Wisconsin and Minnesota. Winters from Great Lakes and New England s. to Gulf of Mexico and Florida.

MOTTLED or DUSKY DUCK. *Anas fulvigula.* Subsp.   p. 39
Field marks: — 20. Like a pale brownish edition of the Black Duck. The light buffy of the unstreaked throat and the yellow bill are good marks.
Similar species: — Mottled Duck has the coloration of the female Mallard but lacks the dark blotches on its *yellow bill.* The general pattern (dark tail and single white line on speculum) suggests the Black Duck, from which it is readily told by its tawny color and tan instead of gray-brown head.
Range: — Florida (local race is better known as Florida Duck) and coastal belt of Louisiana and Texas.

GADWALL. *Anas strepera.*   pp. 22, 26, 39
Field marks: — 19–21. *Male:* — A slender *gray* Duck with a *black rump.* It has a *white patch* on the *hind* edge of the wing, a white belly, and yellow feet. *Female:* — Brown, mottled, but with *white speculum* and yellow feet.
Similar species: —Male resembles Black Duck but is smaller,

MERGANSERS AND OTHER DUCKS

WOOD DUCK p. 43.
>*Male:* Distinctive face pattern.
>*Male in eclipse:* Duller, face pattern similar.
>*Female:* White spot around eye.

BUFFLE-HEAD p. 47.
>*Male:* Large white head-patch, white sides.
>*Female:* Small; dark head, white cheek-spot.

HOODED MERGANSER p. 51.
>*Male:* White crest, dark sides.
>*Female:* Dark head, buffy crest.

RED-BREASTED MERGANSER p. 52.
>*Male:* White collar, crest.
>*Female:* Crested rufous head, *blended* throat and neck.

AMERICAN MERGANSER or GOOSANDER p. 52.
>*Male:* Long white body, dark head.
>*Female:* Crested rufous head, *sharply marked* throat and neck.

FULVOUS TREE-DUCK p. 33.
>Tawny color, white side-stripe; sexes similar.

RUDDY DUCK p. 51.
>*Male in spring:* Rufous, white cheeks.
>*Male in winter:* Gray, white cheeks.
>*Female:* White cheek crossed by dark line.
>*Note:* Ruddy Ducks often cock their tails.

| Marsh and Pond Ducks (Dabblers) | Bay and Sea Ducks (Divers) | Mergansers (Divers) | Ruddy Duck (Diver) | Tree-ducks (Dabblers) |

POSTURES OF DUCKS ON LAND

Male in eclipse

WOOD DUCK

♂   ♀

BUFFLEHEAD

♂   ♀

HOODED MERGANSER

♂   ♀

RED-BREASTED MERGANSER

♂   ♀

COMMON MERGANSER

♂   ♀

FULVOUS TREE DUCK

♀

♂ Winter

♂ Spring

RUDDY DUCK

MOTTLED DUCK

BLACK DUCK
Sexes similar

GADWALL ♂

MALLARD ♂ ♀

PINTAIL ♂ ♀

EUROPEAN WIDGEON ♂

AMERICAN WIDGEON ♀ ♂

SHOVELER ♀ ♂

BLUE-WINGED TEAL ♀ ♂

GREEN-WINGED TEAL ♀ ♂

COMMON TEAL ♂

CINNAMON TEAL ♂

Plate 14   39

MARSH AND POND DUCKS
(Surface-feeding Ducks)

BLACK DUCK   p. 37.
Dusky body, pale head; sexes similar.

MOTTLED or DUSKY DUCK   p. 37.
Browner, buffy throat, yellow bill.

GADWALL   p. 37.
Male: Gray body, black rear.
Female: White patch (in flight); yellowish bill.

MALLARD   p. 36.
Male: Green head, white neck-ring.
Female: Orange on bill, whitish tail.

PINTAIL   p. 40
Male: Needle tail, neck-stripe.
Female: Gray bill, slim pointed tail.

EUROPEAN WIDGEON   p. 42.
Male: Rufous head, buffy crown.
Female: See text.

BALDPATE or AMERICAN WIDGEON   p. 42.
Male: White crown.
Female: Gray head, brown body.

SHOVELLER   p. 43.
Male: Shovel bill, dark chestnut sides.
Female: Shovel bill.

BLUE–WINGED TEAL   p. 41.
Male: White face crescent, blue wing-patch.
Female: Small size, blue wing-patch.

GREEN–WINGED TEAL   p. 41
Male: Vertical white mark on body.
Female: Small size, dark wing.

EUROPEAN TEAL   p. 40
Male: Horizontal white stripe.
Female: Like female Green-wing.

CINNAMON TEAL   p. 41
Male: Deep rufous; blue wing-patch.
Female: Like female Blue-wing.

grayer, more slender, and has white belly. The white speculum
is diagnostic. On the water the gray feathers of the flanks
usually conceal this patch; then the best mark is the black
around the tail, which contrasts sharply with the pale gray of
the wing coverts. *Female:* — Resembles female Pintail, but has
white speculum and yellow feet. These cannot be seen when
the bird is swimming, but at close range, there is a telltale touch
of yellow in the Gadwall's bill. Ordinarily, she is best told by
the company she keeps. The female Baldpate is more ruddy-
colored with a gray head. The location of the white wing-patch
is the best mark; that of the Baldpate is on the *fore edge* of the
wing. Some young Baldpates in the fall show so little white in
the wing that they might be easily confused with the Gadwall,
but they ride more lightly on the water with the rear end lifted
high in typical Baldpate fashion.

Voice: — 'Female quacks. Male, a loud *kack—kack*, and a shrill
whistled call' (Kortright).

Range: — Breeds from sw. Canada s. to Kansas, n. Iowa, and
s. Wisconsin (and locally e. to w. Pennsylvania and coastal
Delaware and North Carolina); migrates to Gulf of Mexico; rare
in e. New York and New England.

PINTAIL. *Anas acuta tzitzihoa.*   pp. 22, 26, 39.
Field marks: — 26–30. Male Pintails are slender white-breasted
Ducks with long, slim necks and long, *needle-pointed* tails, quite
different in cut and appearance from the other surface-feeding
Ducks of the ponds and marshes. A conspicuous white point
runs from the neck onto the side of the brown head. *Female:* —
A mottled brown Duck with a slender neck and a somewhat
pointed tail. In flight the light border on the rear of the wings
is a good character.

Similar species: — The only other Duck with a long pointed
tail is the Old-squaw, not a marsh Duck. The female resembles
the female Mallard but is more slender, has a more pointed tail,
gray bill (Mallard, olive or orange and black) and lacks the
white-bordered blue speculum. It can easily be confused with
female of Baldpate and Gadwall (see those species).

Voice: — Male utters Teal-like wheezy mewing notes; also a
double-toned whistle. Female occasionally utters a low quack.

Range: — Breeds in w. North America from Hudson Bay s. to
Nebraska and Iowa and casually e. to w. Pennsylvania. Winters
from Missouri, s. Ohio, and Long Island to Gulf Coast.

EUROPEAN TEAL. *Anas crecca.*   p. 39.
Similar species: — Male, very similar to male Green-winged
Teal, but lacks vertical white mark in front of wing. Has,
instead, a *horizontal* white stripe on the scapulars, *above* the

wing. Easily identified, even at a distance. Female indistinguishable.

Range: — Rare visitor in Northern States on ponds along coast.

GREEN–WINGED TEAL. *Anas carolinensis.* pp. 22, 26, 39.
Field marks: — 13–15½. When Ducks fly up from the marsh, Teal are conspicuous by their half-size proportions. If they show no large light-colored patches on the wings, they are this species. *Male:* — A small gray Duck with brown head and conspicuous *white mark* in front of wing. In sunlight, shows an iridescent green speculum in wing and green patch on side of head. Has a cream-colored patch toward the tail. *Female:* — A little speckled Duck with an iridescent green speculum.
Similar species: — Blue-winged Teal (both sexes) have light blue wing-patches. In flight, from below, male Blue-wings show dark bellies; Green-wings, white bellies. Female Green-wings, though smaller, shorter-necked, and shorter-billed are difficult to distinguish unless absence of blue wing-patch is seen.
Voice: — Male utters a single-noted whistle, sometimes repeated two or three times; female, a crisp quack.
Range: — Breeds from James Bay s. to n. Nebraska, s. Minnesota, n. Michigan, and s. Ontario; winters from n. Nebraska, s. Illinois, and Long Island to Gulf of Mexico.

BLUE–WINGED TEAL. *Anas discors.* pp. 22, 26, 39.
Field marks: — 15–16. Little half-sized marsh Ducks with large light-colored patches on the front of the wing can quite safely be called this species. *Male:* — Small, dull-colored, with large *white crescent in front of eye,* and large *chalky-blue patch on fore edge of wing.* The blue, at a distance in some lights, looks whitish. *Female:* — Mottled, with large blue patch on fore part of wing.
Similar species: — The somewhat larger Shoveller has pale blue wing-patches too, but can immediately be recognized by its tremendous bill. Female Scaup has white patch in front of eye. (See Green-winged Teal.)
Voice: — On wing, males utter chirping and peeping notes; females a light quack.
Range: — Breeds from Saskatchewan, and s. Ontario, s. to Kansas, Missouri, Illinois, Ohio and New Jersey; winters from South Carolina and Gulf Coast s.

CINNAMON TEAL. *Anas cyanoptera cyanoptera.* p. 39.
Field marks: — 15½–17. *Male:* — A small, dark *cinnamon-red* Duck with large chalky-blue patches on front edges of wings. *Female:* — A small mottled brown Duck with blue wing-patches like male.
Similar species: — On wing resembles Blue-winged Teal (female

cannot be separated in field from female Blue-wing). Only other small rufous Duck is male Ruddy Duck.

Range: — W. United States; occasional e. to Prairie States. Accidental e. of Mississippi River.

EUROPEAN WIDGEON. *Mareca penelope.* p. 39.
Field marks: — 18–20. The male is a *gray* Widgeon with a *reddish-brown head* and buffy crown.

Similar species: — Suggests, upon first acquaintance, Redhead Duck (but lacks black chest). The male Baldpate, or 'American Widgeon,' is a *brown* Widgeon with a gray head and *white* crown. When too distant to show color, the head of the European Widgeon appears much darker than the rest of the bird, quite unlike the Baldpate. *Female:* — Very similar to female Baldpate, but in good light head is distinctly tinged with *reddish*, whereas that of Baldpate is gray. The surest point, but one that can be noted only when the bird is in the hand, or very rarely when the bird flaps its wings, is the axillars — dusky in this species, white in the Baldpate.

Range: — Uncommon to rare visitor in e. North America; chiefly near coast in fall and winter, inland in spring.

BALDPATE. *Mareca americana.* 22, 26, 39.
Field marks: — 18–22. The shining white crown of the male, which gives it its name, is the character by which most beginners learn this bird. The Baldpate in flight can be recognized at a good distance by the large white patch covering the *front* of the wing; in other Ducks possessing white patches they are placed on the hind edge. (The similarly placed blue wing-patches of the Blue-winged Teal and Shoveller often appear whitish at a distance, however.) *Male:* — Brownish with gray head and white crown; patch on side of head glossy green, visible only in good light; patch on fore part of wing white; bill blue with a black tip. *Female:* — Ruddy brown with gray head and neck; belly and fore part of wing whitish. Immature birds that have not acquired the white wing-patch are nondescript, brownish Ducks with a paler gray head and neck, and a white belly which contrasts sharply with the brown breast.

Similar species: — See European Widgeon. The female is most easily confused with female Gadwall and female Pintail. Her gray head contrasting with the brown color of her breast is the best mark. In flight she shows pale wing-patches similar to the white ones of the male.

Voice: — A whistled *whee whee whew* (male).

Range: — Breeds in W. North America e. to Nebraska and Minnesota, and casually to w. Pennsylvania. Winters from Long Island s. to Gulf of Mexico. Prefers ponds and bays.

SHOVELLER. *Spatula clypeata.* pp. 22, 26, 39.
Field marks: — 17–20. Bill large and spatulate. *Male:* —
Largely black and white; belly and *sides rufous-red*; head blackish glossed with green; breast white; pale blue patch on fore
edge of wing. Broadside in the water, or flying overhead, the
pattern of the drake is unique, five alternating areas of light
and dark, thus: dark, white, dark, white, dark. *Female:* —
Mottled brownish, with large blue wing-patch as in male. The
Shoveller is a small Duck, somewhat larger than a Teal; best
identified in all plumages by its spatulate bill, which in flight
makes the wings appear set far back. On the water the bird sits
squatty and low, with the bill pointed downward, presenting a
distinctive appearance.
Similar species: — Wing pattern suggests Blue-winged Teal.
Voice: — Female, a Mallard-like quack, male a lower quack.
Range: — Breeds from Saskatchewan s. to Nebraska and w.
Iowa; locally e. to w. Pennsylvania and Delaware; winters on
ponds and marshes from Long Island to Gulf of Mexico; rare in
northeast.

WOOD DUCK. *Aix sponsa.* pp. 22, 26, 38.
Field marks: — 17–20. Appropriately named, the Wood Duck
is a bird of the forested bottomlands and woodland streams.
The male is the most highly colored North American Duck. On
the wing, the white belly of the Wood Duck contrasts very
strikingly with the dark breast and wings. This, the long square
dark tail, the short neck, and the angle at which the bill is
pointed downward, are all good aids in identification. *Male in
winter and spring plumage:* — Highly iridescent, descriptive
words fail; the pattern diagram explains it much better. *Male
in eclipse plumage* (summer): — Similar to female, but with the
white face-markings and red and white bill of the spring male.
Female: — Dark brown with lighter flanks, white belly, dark
crested head, and *white patch surrounding eye*.
Similar species: — Female and young Baldpates in air suggest
female Wood Duck but have pointed tails.
Voice: — A distressed *whoo—eek*, shrill and raucous (female); and
a finch-like *jeeee* with rising inflection (male).
Range: — Breeds in wooded swamps and river timber from Gulf
of Mexico to s. Ontario and s. Manitoba; winters n. to s. Illinois
and Virginia; rarely farther.

Diving Ducks: Aythyinæ

'SEA DUCKS' or 'Bay Ducks' they are called for convenience, but
many are found commonly on the lakes and rivers of the interior;

primarily, they are birds of the more open bodies of water, although they breed in marshes. They all dive for food, whereas the surface-feeding Ducks rarely dive. In taking wing, they do not spring directly upward from the water, but find it necessary to patter along the surface while getting under way.

REDHEAD. *Aythya americana.*   pp. 23, 27, 34.
Field marks: — 18–23. *Male:* — Mostly gray, with a black chest and a *round red-brown head*; bill blue with a black tip. *Female:* — A brownish Duck with a broad *gray* wing-stripe and a *suffused light patch* about base of bill.
Similar species: — The male resembles the Canvas-back, but is much grayer; the Canvas-back is very white. The Redhead has a high, abrupt forehead and a blue bill, in contrast to the Canvas-back's long sloping forehead and blackish bill. The comparative profiles of the two birds can be made out at fairly long range. Redheads are shorter and chunkier, much more like the Greater Scaup in general contour. On the wing the gray wing-stripe distinguishes the more uniformly colored Redhead from the contrastingly patterned Scaup. The female differs from the female Scaup in having a gray wing-stripe and an indistinct buffy area about the base of the bill, instead of a white wing-stripe and a well-defined white patch at the base of the bill. The only other female Ducks with broad gray wing-stripes are the Canvas-back and the Ring-neck. The Canvas-back is larger and paler, with the long profile; the Ring-neck is smaller, darker, and has a conspicuous ring on the bill and a white eye-ring.
Range: — Breeds in interior from Saskatchewan and Manitoba s. to cent. Nebraska, s. Wisconsin, and se. Michigan, rarely farther e.; winters on lakes and bays from w. New York s. to Gulf of Mexico.

RING–NECKED DUCK. *Aythya collaris.*   pp. 23, 27, 34.
Field marks: — 16–18. *Male:* — A black-backed Scaup. Head, chest, and back black; sides light gray with *conspicuous white mark in front of wing*; bill crossed by two white rings. In flight, the only black-backed Duck having a broad *gray* wing-stripe. The name Ring-billed Duck would be much more appropriate, as an examination at very close range is necessary to be aware of the dull chestnut ring that encircles the neck. The rather peaked triangular head-shape is distinctive in both sexes. *Female:* — Brown, darkest on crown of head and back; wing-stripe *gray*; indistinct whitish area about base of bill; white eye-ring, and *ring on bill*; belly, white.
Similar species: — Female Scaup has a definite white face 'mask,' a *white* wing-stripe and lacks the white eye-ring, and ring on the bill; the female Redhead is larger, paler, with less

contrast, and lacks the conspicuous rings about the eye and on the bill. Female Ring-necks are a little difficult to tell from the Scaup with which they so often associate, but the males can be picked out at a great distance, as no other species of this distinctive black-chested genus has a black back.

Range: — Breeds in interior from Saskatchewan and w. Ontario s. to n. Nebraska and n. Iowa, locally e. to w. Pennsylvania and Maine. Migrates throughout United States to Gulf of Mexico. Winters n. to Great Lakes and Massachusetts. Has a preference for wooded lakes.

CANVAS-BACK. *Aythya valisineria.* pp. 23, 27, 34

Field marks: — 20–24. *Male:* — A very white-looking Duck with a rusty-red head and neck, black breast, and a long blackish bill. *Female:* — Grayish, with a suggestion of the red of the male bird on the head and neck. The *long, sloping profile* will separate either sex from any of the other species which they superficially resemble. In flight, Canvas-backs string out in lines or in V-formation. The long head, neck, and bill give the bird a front-heavy appearance, as if the wings were set far back.

Similar species: — See Redhead. Female Mergansers are red-headed but have crests and whitish chests.

Range: — Breeds in w. North America e. to Dakotas, Nebraska, and Minnesota (occasionally to s. Wisconsin). Winters from cent. New York (Finger Lakes) s. chiefly on salt or brackish bays to Gulf of Mexico.

GREATER SCAUP DUCK. *Aythya marila nearctica.*

pp. 23, 27, 34

Field marks: — 17–20½. *Male:* — The two Scaups on the water appear to be 'black at both ends and white in the middle.' The flanks and back are finely barred with gray, but at any distance those parts appear quite white. The bill is blue; hence the gunner's nickname, 'Blue-bill.' *Female:* — Brown, with broad white wing-stripe and a well-defined white 'mask' at the base of the bill. The two Scaups are our only Ducks possessing a broad white wing-stripe.

Similar species: — At a great distance on the water, drake Golden-eye and Scaup look somewhat alike, but where the Golden-eye has only a black head the Scaup is black to the water-line. See Lesser Scaup. Mallard has superficial resemblance but seldom dives.

Range: — Breeds chiefly in Arctic; winters on bays along coast from New England to North Carolina, also along Gulf Coast. Less common inland (Great Lakes, etc.).

LESSER SCAUP DUCK. *Aythya affinis.* p. 34

Similar species: — *Male:* — Similar to Greater Scaup, but

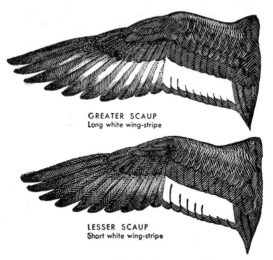

GREATER SCAUP
Long white wing-stripe

LESSER SCAUP
Short white wing-stripe

WINGS OF SCAUP DUCKS

slightly smaller (15–18), and grayer on flanks; head more angular-looking (suggesting Ring-necked Duck), glossed in some lights with *dull purple* (Greater has rounder head, glossed with green). These differences are tricky and can be made sure of only when the bird is near-by in good light. The length of the wing-stripe is the easiest way to separate typical individuals of both sexes in the field. The white in the Lesser extends about half way along the hind edge of the wing, while in the Greater Scaup this stripe extends considerably farther toward the wing-tip (see diagram). This character does not always hold as the birds sometimes seem to intergrade, but most individuals can be told in this way. The Greater is the winter Scaup of the Great Lakes and the coast of northern United States, while the Lesser is the Scaup so abundant on every lake and river inland during migration and along southern coasts in winter.

Range: — Breeds from Hudson Bay to se. Ontario; migrates s. to Gulf of Mexico. The commonest Scaup in inland localities.

AMERICAN GOLDEN-EYE. *Glaucionetta clangula americana.*
pp. 23, 27, 34.

Field marks: — 17–23. *Male:* — A white-looking Duck with a black back and a puffy green-glossed head (black at a distance). A large round white spot between the eye and the bill is the best identification mark. In flight the bird is short-necked and the wings show large white patches. *Female:* — Gray with a white collar and a dark-brown head; wings with large square white patches. The whistling or 'singing' of the Golden-eye's wings, which has earned for the bird the name 'Whistler,' is often useful in identification.

Similar species: — The male at a distance bears a slight resemblance to a Scaup but lacks the black chest. Only the head is black; in this it bears a closer resemblance to a male Merganser, but is stocky and short-necked, with a large round or triangular head, quite unlike the long-geared Merganser. Look for the face spot.

Voice: — Courting males have a double note, suggesting Night-hawk.

Range: — Breeds from Hudson Bay and n. Labrador s. to North Dakota, n. Minnesota, n. Michigan, n. New York, and cent. Maine; winters to South Carolina and middle Gulf Coast.

BARROW'S GOLDEN-EYE. *Glaucionetta islandica.*   p. 34.
Field marks: — 20–23. Similar to American Golden-eye. Rare.
Male: — The *crescent*-shaped white patch in front of eye is the thing to look for. (American Golden-eye has a *round* white spot). The Barrow's shows a greater amount of black on the sides of the body (see diagram) but American Golden-eye in summer eclipse plumage can be similar (though it is then never jet black on head or wings). The head of Barrow's is glossed with *purple* instead of green and is of a very different shape — a more abrupt forehead and a low rounded crown. Try to see *all* these characters before you put this rare bird on your list. *Female:* — Very difficult to tell in field from female Golden-eye, but bill shorter and deeper, forehead more abrupt. As the breeding season approaches the bill of the female Barrow's becomes *all* yellow (female American, yellow tip). In the winter it is not safe to tell females except by the males they are with.
Range: — Labrador, s. in winter along coast to Massachusetts.

BUFFLE-HEAD. *Glaucionetta albeola.*   pp. 23, 27, 38.
Field marks: — 13–15. One of the smallest Ducks. *Male:* — Mostly white, with black back and large, puffy head marked with *great white patch* that extends from eye around back of head; large white wing-patches in flight. (On the wing suggests small Golden-eye.) *Female:* — Dark little Duck with large head, white cheek-spot, and white wing-patch.
Similar species: — The Buffle-head is sometimes mistaken for the less common Hooded Merganser, which is very dark instead of very white. The white crest of the latter is bordered with black. The dark female Buffle-head can be mistaken for a male Hooded Merganser with its crest laid back. Look for the Merganser's spike-like bill.

Range: — Breeds chiefly in w. Canada; winters from Great
Lakes and New England s. to Gulf of Mexico.

OLD–SQUAW. *Clangula hyemalis.*   pp. 23, 27, 35.
Field marks: — ♂ 21, ♀ 17.   Old-squaws are the only Sea
Ducks combining *white on the body and unpatterned dark wings.*
They bunch in irregular flocks rather than in long, stringy lines
like the Scoters, their dark, pointed wings dipping low with each
beat. *Male in winter:* — Boldly patterned with dark brown and
white. Head, neck, belly, and scapulars white; breast, back,
and wings dusky brown; dark patch on side of head; short bill
banded with black and pink; long, needle-pointed tail-feathers.
Male in summer: — Mostly dark with white flanks and belly,
and white patch surrounding eye. *Female in winter:* — Lacks
long, pointed tail-feathers of male. Dark above and white
below; head white with black crown and cheek-spot. *Female in
summer:* — Similar but darker.
Similar species: — The long pointed tail-feathers of the male
suggest no other Duck except Pintail, which is a Duck of
marshes and rivers, not the ocean.
Voice: — Talkative; musical cries, *onk—a—lik, ow—owdle—ow,*
etc.
Range: — Arctic coasts; winters s. to Great Lakes, and along
coast to North Carolina.

(EASTERN) HARLEQUIN DUCK.   *Histrionicus histrionicus
histrionicus.*   pp. 23, 27, 35.
Field marks: — 15–17½. Dark and bizarre. *Adult male:* — A
rather small dark blue-gray Duck (blackish at a distance) with
reddish-brown sides and odd white patches and spots. A glance
at the diagram explains the bird's strange appearance. In flight
it has the shape, short neck, and manner of a Golden-eye, but
stands out as a uniformly dark bird. Often cocks its tail like
the Ruddy Duck. *Female:* — Dusky brown with two or three
round white spots on side of head; no wing-patch.
Similar species: — Female may be distinguished from female
Buffle-head (which has *one* elongated white face spot) by absence
of white on wing; from female Scoter by its smaller size and
stubbier bill. In a general way it is a small Duck with the
pattern of a female Surf Scoter, and the shape and slight bill
of a Buffle-head.
Range: — Arctic coasts, s. in winter to Maine and Massachusetts, rarely farther; found about wave-washed rocks and ledges.

COMMON EIDER. *Somateria mollissima.* Subsp.   pp. 23, 35.
Field marks: — 22–26. The Eiders are among the most oceanic
of all the Ducks, living their lives about shoals off the northern
coasts. They are bulky and thick-necked, and their flight is

sluggish and low over the water. The head is rather low-hung, and the birds often progress with alternate flapping and sailing. No other Duck flies like them. *Male:* — Only Duck with *black belly* and *white back*. Breast and fore part of wing white; head white with black crown. *Female:* — A large brown Duck with a long flat profile; body heavily *barred* (many other female Ducks are mottled and streaked on the breast, but only female Eiders are *barred*). Immature males are at first grayish brown, later dusky with a white collar; still later may have chocolate heads or breasts, the white areas coming in irregularly.

Similar species: — Male King Eider has *black* back. Female Eiders resemble female Scoters because of their chunky proportions, but are of a richer, warmer brown color. None of the female Scoters have the heavy black barrings. Females of the Common and the King Eiders are very difficult to tell apart, but it can be done. The bill of the Common Eider is longer and gives the bird a more sloping canvas-back-like profile. See diagram of bills, page 35.

Range: — Breeds from Arctic s. to Maine Coast; winters to Massachusetts and Long Island (a few).

KING EIDER. *Somateria spectabilis.* pp. 23, 35.
Field marks: — 21–24. *Male:* — A large, heavy Duck. At a distance the fore parts appear white, the rear parts black. No other Duck gives this effect. On the water it suggests slightly a Black-backed Gull. Back and belly black; wings with large white patches; fore parts whitish; top of head pearl-gray; cheeks tinged with greenish; bill and large knob or shield on forehead orange. *Female:* — A chunky Duck, warm brown, heavily barred with black. *Immature male:* — Among the few birds of this species that visit us there seems to be a large percentage of young males. These appear dusky with light breasts and dark brown heads. The amount of white varies in birds changing to adult plumage.

Similar species: — Male Common Eider has a *white* back. Some female King Eiders have unstreaked throats, giving the head a contrasted effect the female Common Eider does not have. All other color differences which have been claimed prove unreliable or imaginary. (See diagram of bills.) Immature male might possibly be confused with female Golden-eye, which also has a chocolate-brown head, but Golden-eye is grayer with square white wing-patches.

Range: — Arctic, s. in winter sparingly to Long Island and Great Lakes.

WHITE-WINGED SCOTER. *Melanitta fusca deglandi.*
pp. 23, 27, 35.
Field marks: — 20–23. The Scoters are the large, chunky,

blackish Ducks commonly seen coastwise, flying in stringy formation low over the waves. They are sometimes called 'Coot' by gunners. The White-wing, easily identified by its wing-patches, is the commonest and largest of the three species. The wing-patch is often covered by the flank feathers in swimming birds. Wait for them to flap their wings. *Male:* — Black with white wing-patches and a small patch just below the eye. *Female:* — Dusky brown with white wing-patch and two light patches on side of head (sometimes obscure, but more pronounced in young birds).

Similar species: — See Surf and American Scoters.

Range: — Breeds across Canada from Alaska to Gulf of St. Lawrence, s. to s. Manitoba and central North Dakota (local); winters to South Carolina, Great Lakes, and Gulf Coast (a few). A few non-breeding birds along coast in summer.

SURF SCOTER. *Melanitta perspicillata.* pp. 23, 27, 35.
Field marks: — 18–22. The 'Skunk-head Coot.' *Male:* — Black, with one or two white patches on crown of head — hence the nickname. *Female:* — Dusky brown with two light patches on side of face (sometimes obscured). These face-patches are more conspicuous on young birds.

Similar species: — The female White-wing is similarly marked around the head, but has white wing-patches (which often do not show until the bird flaps). Female American Scoter lacks wing-patch but has different head pattern (light cheek, dark cap).

Range: — Breeds in nw. Canada; winters from Maine to Florida, chiefly off-shore along coast.

AMERICAN SCOTER. *Oidemia nigra americana.* pp. 23, 27, 35.
Field marks: — 17–21. *Male:* — The only American Duck with *entirely* black plumage. This, and the bright yellow-orange base of the bill are diagnostic. In flight from below the American Scoter shows a 'two-toned' wing effect (because of black linings and silvery primaries). This is more pronounced than in the other Scoters. *Female:* — Dusky brown, with light cheeks contrasting with a dark cap.

Similar species: — Females of the other two Scoters have two light patches on each side of the head. The female American Scoter can be confused with the winter Ruddy Duck (which is smaller, paler, and has a white chest).

Range: — Breeds in Arctic; winters along coast from Maine to South Carolina and Florida (rarely). Rare inland.

Ruddy and Masked Ducks: Erismaturinæ

RUDDY DUCK. *Erismatura jamaicensis rubida.* pp. 23, 27, 38.
Field marks: — 14–17. In the air, in any plumage, the Ruddy is a small, chunky Duck, *unpatterned except for conspicuous white cheeks.* The short wing-stroke gives the bird a very 'buzzy' flight. On the water it often spreads its tail and cocks it vertically, like a Wren. *Male in breeding plumage:* — Rusty-red with *white cheeks,* black cap, and large blue bill. *Male in winter:* — Gray with white cheeks, blackish cap, and dull blue bill. *Female:* — Similar to winter male, but with light cheeks crossed by dark line.
Similar species: — It is possible to misidentify a female American Scoter as a Ruddy Duck — both are unpatterned except for light cheeks. The Ruddy Duck is very much smaller with a light chest and a definitely shovel-shaped bluish bill. The Ruddy prefers fresh water, the Scoter salt.
Range: — Breeds from Manitoba s. to Nebraska, n. Illinois, se. Michigan, and rarely farther e. Winters chiefly along coast from Long Island (a few) to Florida and Gulf Coast.

Mergansers: Merginæ

OUR THREE Mergansers, or fish-eating Ducks, lack the broad and flattened bills so characteristic of most Ducks; the mandibles are slender, with toothed edges, well adapted for seizing slippery fish. Most species have crests and are long-geared, slender-bodied birds. In flight, the bill, head, neck, and body are held perfectly horizontal; at a distance, this gives them an unmistakable long-drawn appearance, quite unlike other Ducks.

HOODED MERGANSER. *Lophodytes cucullatus.* pp. 22, 26, 38.
Field marks: — 16–19. *Male:* — Black and white; head with fan-shaped white crest which it frequently spreads. Breast white with two black bars in front of wing; wing with white patch; flanks brownish. *Female:* — Recognized as a Merganser by the narrow, spike-like bill, and in flight by the long-drawn appearance, with bill, head, neck, and body in a horizontal line. Known as this species by its small size, dark coloration, *dark head and neck,* and buffy crest. Flocks bunch more than the other two Mergansers, which fly in lines.
Similar species: — The male can be confused with the male Buffle-head. The Buffle-head is smaller and chubbier, with

white flanks; those of the Merganser are dark. The white crest of the Merganser is outlined with a dark border. (See female Buffle-head.) The female Hooded Merganser is a dark bird. The other female Mergansers are larger, grayer, with rufous-red heads. The female Wood Duck is also dark with a crest, but the square white wing-patch, spike-like bill, and flight identify the Merganser. Both frequent woodland pools.

Range: — Breeds from New Brunswick, s. Ontario, and Manitoba s. very locally or rarely to Southern States. Winters from Gulf of Mexico n. to s. New England and Great Lakes.

AMERICAN MERGANSER. *Mergus merganser americanus.*

pp. 22, 26, 38.

Field marks: — 22–27. In line formation, low over the water, the rakish, long-bodied American Mergansers follow the winding course of the creeks and rivers. *Male:* — Long white body with a black back and a green-black head; bill and feet orange; breast tinged with a delicate peach-colored bloom. In flight, the whiteness of the bird and the Merganser shape, with bill, head, neck, and body all held horizontal, identify it. *Female:* — Gray with a *crested* rufous-red head, red bill and feet, and a large square white patch on the wing.

Similar species: — The male Merganser and Golden-eye resemble each other at a distance, but the Golden-eye, aside from having the white eye-spot, is chubbier, shorter-necked, and puffier-headed. The rusty-headed females suggest Canvas-backs or Redheads to the beginner, but these birds have black chests and no crests. Males are sometimes mistaken for Mallards (because of green head). See Red-breasted Merganser (females are very similar).

Range: — Breeds from Newfoundland and Hudson Bay to n. edge of United States; winters from s. edge of Canada to Gulf States (rarely). Commonest cold-weather Duck on northern rivers.

RED-BREASTED MERGANSER. *Mergus serrator.*

pp. 22, 26, 38.

Field marks: — 20–25. *Male:* — Black head glossed with green and *conspicuously crested*; area on breast at water line rusty separated from head by *wide white collar*; bill and feet red. *Female:* — Gray, with crested dull-rufous head and large square white patch on wing; bill and feet reddish.

Similar species: — The male American Merganser is whiter than the Red-breast, without the collar and breast-band effect or the crest. The females are very similar but in the Red-breast the rufous of the head is paler and it *blends* into the white of the throat and neck. In the American the white chin and white chest are sharply defined. The Red-breasted Merganser is more characteristic of the ocean than is the American, which is chiefly a fresh-water species. Both birds may, at times, be found on the same bodies of water.

Range: — Breeds from Arctic s. to n. parts of United States; winters from Great Lakes and New England coast s. to Florida and Gulf (abundantly).

Vultures: Cathartidæ

VULTURES are great blackish Eagle-like birds, usually seen soaring in wide circles high in the heavens. Their naked heads are so small for the size of the bird that at a great distance they sometimes appear to be almost headless. Hawks and Eagles have larger, well-proportioned heads.

TURKEY VULTURE. *Cathartes aura.* Subsp.   p. 58.
  Field marks: — 30. Wing-spread 6 ft. This species, the better-known of the two eastern Vultures, is nearly Eagle-size with great 'two-toned' blackish wings (the flight feathers are notice-ably lighter). It is usually seen soaring, with its wings held above the horizontal (forming a dihedral). The big bird rocks and tilts unsteadily as it floats along. At close range the red head of the adult can be seen. Young birds, however, have black heads.
  Similar species: — The diminutive head and slimmer tail at once distinguish the Turkey Vulture from the Eagles. It soars with wings above the horizontal, Eagles with flat outstretched wings, Ospreys with a kink or crook in the wings. See Black Vulture.
  Range: — Breeds from Gulf of Mexico n. to w. Connecticut, w. New York, and n. Minnesota. Winters from s. New Jersey and Ohio Valley s.

BLACK VULTURE. *Coragyps atratus.*   p. 58.
  Field marks: — 24. Wing-spread under 5 ft. This big black bird is quickly identified by the short square tail which barely projects from the hind edge of the wings and by a whitish patch on the under surface of each wing toward the tip. It flies with several rapid flaps and a short sail — a mark as far as you can see the bird.
  Similar species: — The tail of the Turkey Vulture is longer and slimmer. The Black Vulture has much less 'sail area'; not only is the tail stubby but the wings are shorter and wider. It can be spotted immediately by its quick, labored flapping. The Turkey flaps slowly and deliberately, soars more. Young Tur-

BUTEOS OR BUZZARD HAWKS

 BUTEOS have heavy bodies, short wide tails.

SWAINSON'S HAWK   p. 64.
  Prairies; dark chest band (adult).

RED–TAILED HAWK   p. 61.
  Adult: Rufous tail.
  Immature (and adult): Light chest, streaked belly.

RED–SHOULDERED HAWK   p. 63.
  Adult: Rufous shoulders; narrow white tail-bands.
  Immature: Streaked on both breast and belly.

ROUGH–LEGGED HAWK   p. 64.
  Light phase: Dark belly; white tail with black band.
  Dark phase: Dusky body; see text.

BROAD–WINGED HAWK   p. 63.
  Adult: Wide white tail-bands.
  Immature: Like immature Red-shoulder but tail shorter.

HARLAN'S HAWK   p. 62.
  Dark body; whitish, mottled tail; prairies.

KRIDER'S RED–TAILED HAWK   p. 260.
  Pale body; white or pale rufous tail; prairies.

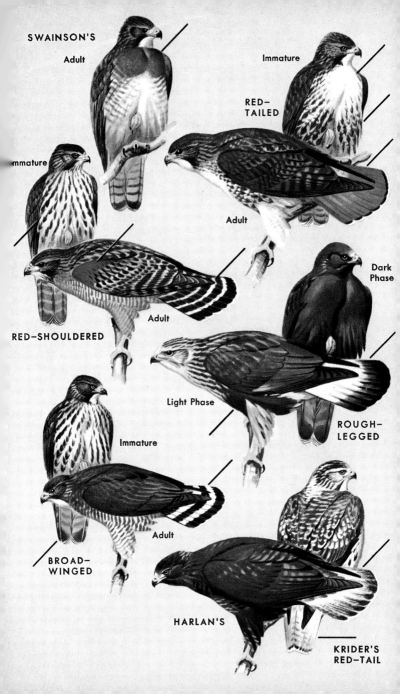

SWAINSON'S

Adult

Immature

RED-
TAILED

Immature

Adult

Adult

RED-SHOULDERED

Dark
Phase

Light Phase

ROUGH-
LEGGED

Immature

BROAD-
WINGED

Adult

HARLAN'S

KRIDER'S
RED-TAIL

COOPER'S HAWK

Adult

Immature

GOSHAWK

Adult

Immature

SHARP-SHINNED HAWK

Adult

Immature

SPARROW HAWK (KESTREL)

♂ ♀

PIGEON HAWK (MERLIN)

♂ ♀

Adult

Immature

PEREGRINE FALCON

MARSH HAWK (HARRIER)

♂ ♀

Plate 16   55

HAWKS

ACCIPITERS (True Hawks)
Small head, short wings, long tail.
Adults, barred breasts; immatures, streaked.

COOPER'S HAWK   p. 61
Crow-sized, rounded tail.

GOSHAWK   p. 60
Adult: Pearly breast, light gray back.
Immature: Large; pronounced eye-stripe.

SHARP–SHINNED HAWK   p. 60
Small; notched or square tail.

FALCONS
Large head, broad shoulders.
Long pointed wings, long tail.

SPARROW HAWK or * KESTREL   p. 74
Both sexes: Rufous back, rufous tail.

PIGEON HAWK or * MERLIN   p. 73
Male: Small; slaty back, banded gray tail.
Female: Dusky back, banded tail.

DUCK HAWK or * PEREGRINE FALCON   p. 73
Adult: Slate back, light breast, black mustaches.
Immature: Brown, streaked; typical mustaches.

HARRIERS
Small head, long body.
Longish wings, long tail.

MARSH HAWK or * HARRIER   p. 68
Male: Pale gray back, white rump.
Female: Brown, with white rump.

* Author's preference.

key Vultures have black heads and are sometimes mistaken for Black Vultures.

Range: — Resident in s. United States n. to Maryland, West Virginia, s. Ohio, s. Indiana, and Missouri.

The Names of Hawks

IN OLD ENGLAND (and today) the only birds called 'Hawks' were the bird-killing diurnal birds of prey, the *Accipiters*, birds like our Sharp-shin, Cooper's Hawk, and Goshawk. The colonists who settled here were not naturalists, so they applied the name Hawk to almost all the day-flying raptores. This has been a great handicap to the conservationist, who can prove by food-habit studies that most of these birds are beneficial, or are, at least, an important cog in the balance of nature. In spite of his charts and tables he has a difficult time securing protection for these birds because of the stigma attached to the name Hawk.

I should like to advocate a return to the old English names in some cases:

> Harrier — instead of Marsh Hawk
> Peregrine — instead of Duck Hawk
> Merlin — instead of Pigeon Hawk
> Kestrel — instead of Sparrow Hawk

Through the efforts of Doctor Walter Spofford in Tennessee, the field students in that state now use these names without being self-conscious about it.

The Old-World name for the Buteos is 'Buzzards.' Unfortunately, the name Buzzard in North America has been corrupted in popular usage to mean our Vultures. The connotation being what it is, it is perhaps impracticable to try to change the names of the Buteos to Red-tailed Buzzard, Broad-winged Buzzard, etc.

Kites: Elaninæ

HAWKS of southern distribution; most nearly resembling the Falcons in shape of wing — except the Everglade Kite.

WHITE-TAILED KITE. *Elanus leucurus majusculus.* p. 66.
   Field marks: — 15½. This rare whitish species is Falcon-shaped, with long, pointed wings and a long tail. Like other Kites it soars and glides like a Gull, and often hovers like a Sparrow Hawk. *Adult:* — Pale gray with white head, *tail*, and under parts, and a *large black patch* toward fore edge of wing.

No other Falcon-like bird (except White Gyrfalcon) has a white tail. *Immature:* — Similar, with rusty breast-band and pearly gray tail.
Range: — Now accidental in East; formerly Florida and probably South Carolina and Oklahoma. Still found in s. Texas.

SWALLOW-TAILED KITE. *Elanoides forficatus forficatus.*

p. 66.

Field marks: — 24. Shaped like a Barn Swallow, this medium-sized, Hawk flies with swallow-like grace. The black upper parts, the white head and under parts, and the long, *forked* tail, make it a striking, well-marked bird.
Similar species: — See immature Man-o'-War Bird.
Range: — Chiefly river swamps of Florida, South Carolina, and Louisiana.

MISSISSIPPI KITE. *Ictinia misisippiensis.* p. 66.
Field marks: — 14. Falcon-shaped; graceful and gray. Dark above, light below; head *very pale pearly gray*; tail *black*. No other Falcon-like Hawk has black unbarred tail. In flight it shows from above a broad pale patch or stripe on the rear edge of wings, a good confirmatory mark. Immature birds have heavy brown streakings on the under parts but have the Falcon-like shape and distinctive black tail (somewhat barred below).
Range: — From Gulf States n. to Kansas, s. Missouri, and sw. Tennessee; also e. to ne. Florida and South Carolina (a few). Migrates from n. part of range.

EVERGLADE KITE. *Rostrhamus sociabilis plumbeus.* p. 58.
Field marks: — Very unlike other Kites in having wider wings and tail; very similar to Marsh Hawk at any distance, but *without wavering, tilting flight* of that bird. Flies at low elevations on an 'even keel' with head at right angles to body, like a Tern, as it searches the *fresh-water* marshes for its sole food of snails. Latter are taken to a favorite feeding post, and extracted with the peculiar, very hooked beak. Adult male completely black except for white patch at base of square tail; legs red. Female heavily streaked with dark lines on buffy body; white line over eye and white tail-patch. Shows surprising tameness.
Similar species: — Only other dark hawk in Florida with white at base of tail is Caracara, which has white breast and white wing-patches. Marsh Hawk similar but flight erratic; body and wings more slender. Female and immature Kites have blackish tails and white eye-stripes.
Range: — Fresh-water marshes of Florida. Now rare and confined to few localities, notably Lake Okeechobee.

ALEXANDER SPRUNT, JR.

VULTURES, CARACARA, EVERGLADE KITE AND BUTEOS

TURKEY VULTURE   p. 53.
  Two-toned wings, small head, longish tail.

BLACK VULTURE   p. 53.
  Stubby tail, white wing-patches.

CARACARA (AUDUBON'S)   p. 69.
  White chest, pale patches toward wing-tips.

EVERGLADE KITE   p. 57.
  Adult male: Black body, white base of tail.
  Immature: Brown, streaked; white base of tail.

ROUGH–LEGGED HAWK   p. 64.
  Dark phase: Dark body, whitish flight feathers; tail light
      from below.

HARLAN'S HAWK   p. 62.
  Shape of Red-tailed Hawk; dark body; tail whitish above,
  mottled.
  Indistinguishable from melanistic Red-tail below.

SHORT–TAILED HAWK   p. 64.
  Dark phase: Black body, pale banded tail.
                Only small black Buteo in Florida.

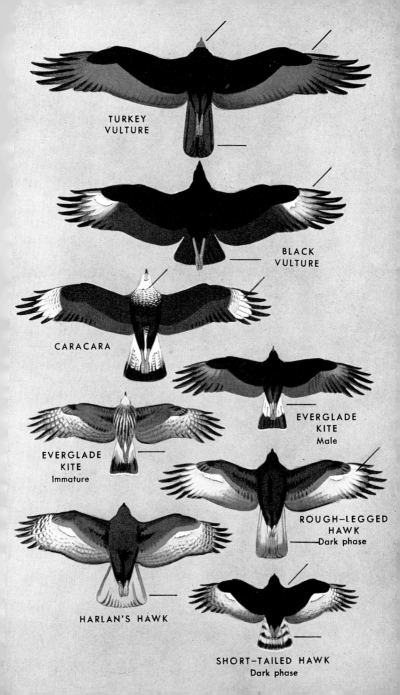

TURKEY
VULTURE

BLACK
VULTURE

CARACARA

EVERGLADE
KITE
Male

EVERGLADE
KITE
Immature

ROUGH-LEGGED
HAWK
Dark phase

HARLAN'S HAWK

SHORT-TAILED HAWK
Dark phase

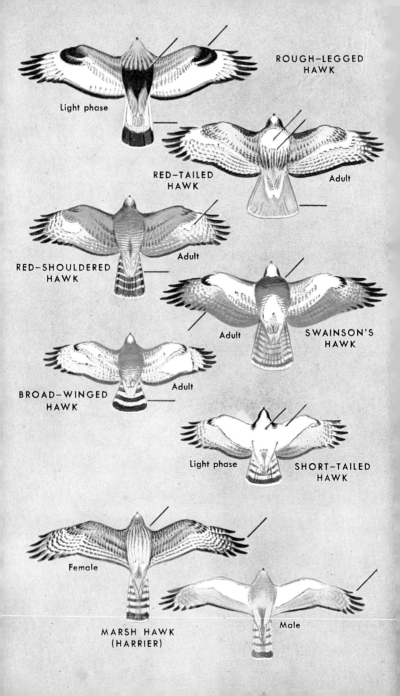

ROUGH-LEGGED HAWK

Light phase

RED-TAILED HAWK

Adult

RED-SHOULDERED HAWK

Adult

SWAINSON'S HAWK

Adult

BROAD-WINGED HAWK

Adult

SHORT-TAILED HAWK

Light phase

MARSH HAWK (HARRIER)

Female

Male

Plate 18   59

BUTEOS AND HARRIERS

The birds shown opposite are adults.

Buteos or Buzzard Hawks are chunky, with broad wings and broad rounded tails. They soar and wheel high in the open sky.

ROUGH–LEGGED HAWK (Light phase)   p. 64.
    Dark belly, black wrist marks.
    Whitish tail with broad band.

RED–TAILED HAWK   p. 61.
    Light chest, streaked belly.
    Tail with little or no banding.

RED–SHOULDERED HAWK   p. 63.
    Banded tail (white bands narrow).
    Translucent wing 'windows' (not infallible).

SWAINSON'S HAWK   p. 64.
    Dark chest, light belly, dark flight feathers.

BROAD–WINGED HAWK   p. 63.
    Banded tail (white bands wide).

SHORT–TAILED HAWK (Light phase)   p. 64
    Clear white belly and wing-linings.
    Only Florida Buteo so colored.

Harriers are slim, with long rounded wings and long tails. They fly low with a vulture-like dihedral.

MARSH HAWK or * HARRIER   p. 68.
    Male: Whitish with black wing tips.
    Female: Harrier shape; brown, streaked.

Both Rough-legged Hawk (left) and Marsh Hawk (right) show some white at the base of the tail from above.

* Author's preference.

Accipiters, or Short-Winged Hawks: Accipitrinæ

LONG-TAILED Hawks with short, rounded wings; woodland birds that do not soar in circles high in the air so much as the Buteos. The typical flight is several short quick beats and a sail.

(EASTERN) GOSHAWK. *Accipiter gentilis atricapillus.* pp. 55, 66.
Field marks: — 20–26; spread 40–47. *Adult:* — A large, robust hawk, with long tail and broad, rounded wings. Crown and stripe behind the eye black, *stripe over the eye white.* The breast is pale gray, and the back blue-gray, paler than the back of a Cooper's or a Sharp-shin. *Immature:* — Very much like the immature Cooper's, but larger, and usually distinguished by the light stripe over the eye. Identification by size is not always reliable, as young Cooper's may be almost as large as a Goshawk.
Similar species: — Adults are easily told from the Cooper's, which it resembles in shape, by its much larger size — considerably larger than a Crow: Cooper's is smaller than a Crow. The gray-backed adult Cooper's is reddish below; the Goshawk is whitish or *pale gray.* The flight of the three bird hawks, or 'blue darters,' is much alike, characterized by alternate flapping and sailing; they seldom soar like the Buteos.
Range: — Breeds in wooded regions of Canada s. to n. Michigan, n. New York, and n. New England and sparingly in mountains to Pennsylvania. Winters irregularly to Missouri, Kentucky, and Virginia.

MAURICE BROUN

SHARP-SHINNED HAWK. *Accipiter striatus velox.* pp. 55, 66.
Field marks: — 10–14. A small woodland Hawk with a *long* tail and *short*, rounded wings. Flies with several quick beats and a sail. Adults have blue-gray backs, rusty-barred breasts. Immatures are brown, heavily streaked.
Similar species: — The two other small Hawks, the Sparrow and Pigeon Hawks, are Falcons and have long pointed instead of short rounded wings. Large female Sharp-shins are often near the size of small male Cooper's. The two are almost identical in pattern, but generally the Cooper's has a *rounded* tail and the Sharp-shin a *square-tipped* tail (slightly notched when folded). It can be very tricky separating small male Cooper's Hawks from large female Sharp-shins. They are not much different in size and the Sharp-shin's square-tipped tail can even look slightly rounded when spread fanwise. The tail shape works best when the tail is folded.
Voice: — Like Cooper's Hawk but shriller.

Range: — Breeds from n. Florida and Gulf Coast n. to tree iimit in Canada; winters n. to Northern States.

COOPER'S HAWK. *Accipiter cooperii.*   pp. 55, 66.
Field marks: — 14–20. A short-winged, long-tailed Hawk; not quite so large as a Crow. Keeps to the woods and does not soar high in the open as often as many other Hawks. Adults have blue-gray backs, rusty breasts. Immatures are brown, streaked. Tail *rounded*.
Similar species: — There are two other Accipiters (long tail, short wings). The smaller Sharp-shin has a *notched* or *square tail*; the Goshawk is much larger. (See Sharp-shinned Hawk and Goshawk.) Immature Cooper's Hawks are usually more sharply and narrowly streaked below than immature Sharp-shins.
Voice: — About nest a rapid *kek, kek, kek*, etc.; suggests Flicker or Pileated Woodpecker.
Range: — Breeds throughout most of United States, n. to Gulf of St. Lawrence, s. Ontario, and cent. Alberta; winters n. to Northern States.

Buteos, or Buzzard Hawks: Buteoninæ (in part)

LARGE HAWKS with broad wings and broad, rounded tails, which habitually soar in wide circles, high in the air. There is considerable variation in individuals within most of the species. Those figured in the pattern-diagrams are in the most characteristic plumages. Young birds are similar to the adults, but in most species are *streaked lengthwise* below.

Black or melanistic phases often occur in birds of this group, especially in the Rough-legged Hawk. In the Prairie States these melanos are most frequent (Red-tail, Rough-leg, Swainson's, etc.) and one must indeed be an expert to tell some of them apart.

RED-TAILED HAWK. *Buteo jamaicensis.* Subsp. pp. 54, 59.
Field marks: — 19–25. When this large broad-winged, round-tailed Hawk veers in its soaring, the rufous-red of the upper side of the tail can be seen. From beneath, adults have whitish tails which in strong light overhead might transmit some of the red color. Young birds have dark gray tails which might or might not show banding. The under parts of the Red-tail are more or less 'zoned' (light breast, broad band of streakings across belly). There is much variation particularly in the Prairie States where more than one race occurs. There, individuals range from the white Krider's Hawks to rufous Western Red-

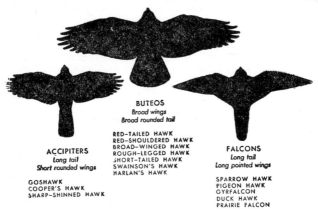

BUTEOS
Broad wings
Broad rounded tail

RED–TAILED HAWK
RED–SHOULDERED HAWK
BROAD–WINGED HAWK
ROUGH–LEGGED HAWK
SHORT–TAILED HAWK
SWAINSON'S HAWK
HARLAN'S HAWK

ACCIPITERS
Long tail
Short rounded wings

GOSHAWK
COOPER'S HAWK
SHARP–SHINNED HAWK

FALCONS
Long tail
Long pointed wings

SPARROW HAWK
PIGEON HAWK
GYRFALCON
DUCK HAWK
PRAIRIE FALCON

SILHOUETTES OF THREE COMMON TYPES OF HAWKS

tails and even dusky melanos. The Harlan's Hawk (*Buteo harlani*) was until recently considered a dark race of the Red-tail. See section on Subspecies in Appendix.

Similar species: — With practice one can identify the Buteos by shape alone. The Red-tail is chunkier, with wider wings and a shorter tail than the Red-shoulder. The Red-shoulder has a banded tail and is more uniformly patterned below (rufous in adult; dark streaks on both breast and belly in immature); whereas the Red-tail is 'zoned' (light breast, streaked belly). *Black adults usually show red tails*, a point of distinction from other black Buteos. Immatures are often light at base of tail, leading to confusion with Rough-leg.

Voice: — A rasping squeal, *keeer—r-r* (slurring downward).

Range: — Breeds in dry woodlands from Newfoundland, n. Ontario, and Saskatchewan s. to Gulf of Mexico and Florida. Winters n. to Iowa, Ohio, and s. Maine.

HARLAN'S HAWK. *Buteo harlani*.   pp. 54, 58.

Field marks: — Until recently this black prairie Buteo was called a subspecies of the Red-tailed Hawk. It will be known from melanistic (black) Red-tails, which are also frequent on the Plains, by the lack of rufous in the tail. Instead, the tail is very white with a *finely mottled black terminal band*. The whiter tail and the Red-tail proportions distinguish it from the black Rough-leg.

Range: — Breeds in w. Canada; migrates through the Mississippi Valley to the Gulf States.

RED-SHOULDERED HAWK. *Buteo lineatus.* Subsp.

pp. 54, 59.

Field marks: — 18–24. Recognized as a Buteo by the ample tail and broad wings; as this species by the heavy dark bands across both sides of the tail. Adults have rufous shoulders (not visible nine times out of ten) and pale Robin-red under parts. A good mark, not often shared by the other Buteos, is a diffuse light-colored patch or 'window' toward the tip of the wing, at the base of the primaries. Immature birds are streaked below, as are most other young Hawks. They can be identified by the tail-banding, proportions, and, in flight overhead by the 'wing windows,' a helpful (but not infallible) mark.

Similar species: — The adult Cooper's Hawk also has rusty under parts but a very different shape (proportionately shorter wings and a longer tail). The Broad-winged Hawk has a banded tail, too, but in the adult the white bands are *as wide as the black.* Young Broad-wings with their more narrowly barred tails are frequently called Red-shoulders by hawk-watchers. See Broad-winged Hawk and Red-tailed Hawk.

Voice: — A piercing whistle, *kee—yer*, with dropping inflection (more two-syllabled than Red-tail's slurred squeal). Blue Jays often imitate this cry.

Range: — Breeds in moist woodlands and river timber from Nova Scotia, s. Quebec, and Ontario s. to Florida and Gulf of Mexico and w. to Great Plains. Winters n. to n. United States (a few).

BROAD-WINGED HAWK. *Buteo platypterus platypterus.*

pp. 54, 59.

Field marks: — A small chunky Buteo, the size of a Crow (14–18½). The manner of banding on the tail of the adult is the best mark — *the white bands are about as wide as the black.* Often migrates in large soaring flocks.

Similar species: — Young birds are more difficult, as the dark tail-bands are more numerous, crowding out the white. The banded tail then resembles that of a Red-shoulder, but the bird is of different proportions, with a stubbier tail and shorter wings, more like a little Red-tail. Its under-wing pattern is usually whiter without the translucent windows of the Red-shoulder, but it is safer to go by shape.

Voice: — A high-pitched shrill whistle, suggestive of Wood Pewee; a plaintive *p—wee-e-e-e-e.*

Range: — Breeds in dry forests and wooded hills from cent. Texas and Gulf Coast n. to New Brunswick, Quebec, and Saskatchewan. Winters chiefly from Florida s. into Tropics.

SWAINSON'S HAWK. *Buteo swainsoni.* pp. 54, 59.
Field marks: — 19½–22. A Buteo of the Plains; proportioned
like a Red-tail but wings slightly more pointed. The wings
when soaring are somewhat above the horizontal (slightly Vulture-like or Marsh-Hawk-like). In typical adults the *wide brown
breast-band* is the best mark. Overhead the *unmarked light buffy
wing-linings* contrast with the *darker-toned flight feathers* (see
diagram). From above the tail is gray, often shading to white
at base. (Do not confuse with Rough-leg.)
Similar species: — Typical adult usually told by dark breast
band (Red-tail is lightest on chest). There are confusing lighter
individuals where the breast-band nearly disappears and blackish birds which are hard to tell from other melanistic Buteos,
except by elimination, but the under-wing pattern, with its
dusky flight feathers, is often a good mark. Black Swainson's
Hawks lack the rusty tail of the black Red-tail and the snowy
white primaries and secondaries on the under-wing surface which
are so distinctive in black Rough-legs. In the Swainson's these
flight feathers are often paler than the wing-linings but are
clouded, not white.
Voice: — 'Shrill plaintive whistle, *kree-e-e-e.*' (A. C. Bent.)
Range: — W. North America, breeding e. to Plains in Minnesota, Nebraska, Kansas, etc. Casual farther e. in migration.
Migrates in large circling flocks; winters in Argentina.

SHORT-TAILED HAWK. *Buteo brachyurus.* pp. 58, 59.
Field marks: — 17. A small Buteo, the size of a Crow. Two
color-phases occur — the 'Black Hawk' with black belly and
black under wing-coverts, and the white phase, where the same
areas are white. No other small Florida Buteo would be clear
white or jet-black below. At close range black birds show a
conspicuous white patch on the forehead near the bill. Immature
birds are enough like the adults to be recognized.
Range: — S. Florida (rare and local) and the Keys.

AMERICAN ROUGH-LEGGED HAWK. *Buteo lagopus s.jo-
hannis.* pp. 54, 58, 59.
Field marks: — 20–23½. Look for the Rough-leg in open
country. It is a Buteo by shape, but larger, with longer wings
and tail than most of the others. The tail is *white with a broad
black band at the end.* The light phase, from below, has a *black
belly* and a conspicuous *black patch at the wrist of the wing.*
Light-bellied birds sometimes are seen. Black Rough-legs are
frequent. These lack the large amount of white on the upper
side of the tail, but from below usually show much white in the
flight feathers (see diagram). This is the only eastern Buteo
that *habitually* hovers with beating wings, Kingfisher-like, or
like an Osprey, in one spot.

Similar species: — As it usually flies low in open country, it might easily be taken for a Marsh Hawk, especially because of the white base of the tail, but the Marsh Hawk is a slender bird with a slim tail and long slim wings. The black phase can be told from the black Red-tail by the characteristic flight pattern and the lack of rusty on the tail. On Great Plains see Ferruginous Rough-legged Hawk and Swainson's Hawk.

Range: — Arctic; winters from s. edge of Canada s. to North Carolina, n. Louisiana, and n. Texas.

FERRUGINOUS ROUGH-LEG. *Buteo regalis.*

Field marks: — 23–24. A large Buteo of the Plains, dark rufous above and whitish below with a *whitish tail.* A very good mark in typical adults overhead is a dark V formed by the dark feathers on the legs. Shows two light patches on upper surface of wings. Immature birds are dark above and white below without the rufous and without the dark V formed by the legs.

Similar species: — The Krider's Red-tail (see Subspecies) can be confused with light birds of this species but lacks the rufous back. American Rough-leg is darker with a broad black tail-band. In the scarce dark phase the Ferruginous Rough-leg resembles the black American Rough-leg closely. The long tail is paler, often whitish, without any suggestion of a broad black band at the tip.

Range: — W. North America e. to Minnesota, Nebraska, and Texas.

Eagles: Buteoninæ (in part)

EAGLES are at once recognizable from the 'Buzzard Hawks,' or Buteos, which they somewhat resemble, by their immense size and proportionately longer wings. The powerful bill of an Eagle is nearly as long as the head, a point of distinct difference from the lesser Hawks.

GOLDEN EAGLE. *Aquila chrysaëtos canadensis.*   p. 67.

Field marks: — 30–40. Wing-spread 6½–7½ ft. Rare in the East. *Adult:* — Evenly black below, or with white at the base of the tail. When the bird wheels, showing the upper surface, the white tail, with its contrasting dark terminal band identifies it. The amount of white varies. The light 'gold' on the hind neck is of occasional importance as a field mark. *Immature:* — From above and below, typical individuals show *a white flash in he wing* at the base of the primaries, and a white tail with a *broad dark terminal band.* All manner of variation exists between this 'ring-tailed' plumage of the immature and the plumage of the adult, described above.

ACCIPITERS, FALCONS, AND KITES

Accipiters have short rounded wings, long tails. They fly with several rapid beats and a short sail.

COOPER'S HAWK   p. 61.
  Near size of Crow; rounded tail.

GOSHAWK   p. 60.
  Adult: Very large, pale gray breast.
  Immature: See text.

SHARP-SHINNED HAWK   p. 60.
  Small; tail square or notched.

Falcons have long pointed wings, long tails. Their wing strokes are strong and rapid.

GYRFALCON   p. 72.
  Black phase: Blacker below than Duck Hawk.
  Gray phase: More uniformly colored than Duck Hawk.
  White phase: White as a Snowy Owl.

SPARROW HAWK or * KESTREL   p. 74.
  Banded rufous tail.

PIGEON HAWK or * MERLIN   p. 73.
  Banded gray tail.

DUCK HAWK or * PEREGRINE FALCON   p. 73.
  Falcon shape; size near that of Crow; face pattern.

Kites (except Everglade Kite) are Falcon-shaped but are buoyant gliders, not power fliers. They are Southern.

SWALLOW-TAILED KITE   p. 57.
  White below, long forked tail.

WHITE-TAILED KITE   p. 56.
  Falcon-shaped with whitish tail.

MISSISSIPPI KITE   p. 57.
  Falcon-shaped with black tail.
  * Author's preference.

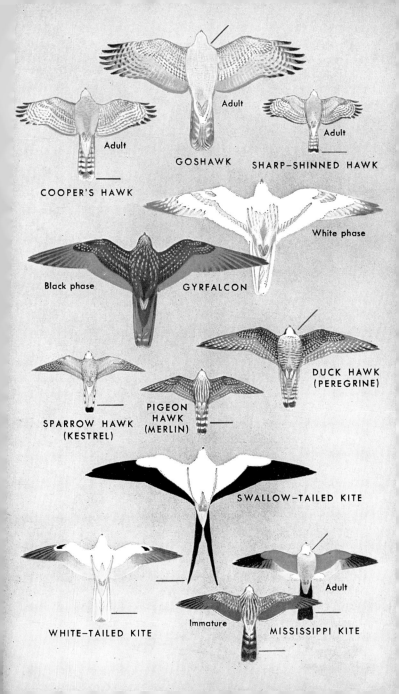

Adult

GOSHAWK

Adult

COOPER'S HAWK

Adult

SHARP-SHINNED HAWK

White phase

Black phase

GYRFALCON

SPARROW HAWK
(KESTREL)

PIGEON
HAWK
(MERLIN)

DUCK HAWK
(PEREGRINE)

SWALLOW–TAILED KITE

WHITE–TAILED KITE

Immature

Adult

MISSISSIPPI KITE

BALD EAGLE   Adult

BALD EAGLE   Immature

GOLDEN EAGLE   Adult

GOLDEN EAGLE   Immature

OSPREY

Plate 20   67

EAGLES AND OSPREY

BALD EAGLE   p. 68.
    Adult: White head and white tail.
    Immature: Some white in wing linings.

GOLDEN EAGLE   p. 65.
    Adult: Almost uniformly dark; wing linings dark.
    Immature: 'Ringed' tail; white patches at base of primaries.

OSPREY   p. 69.
    Clear white belly; black wrist marks.

Where the Bald Eagle, Turkey Vulture and Osprey all are found, they can be separated at a great distance by their manner of soaring; the Bald Eagle with flat wings; the Turkey Vulture with a dihedral; the Osprey with a kink or crook in its wings.

Similar species: — If you lack experience, be very careful. The adult resembles the immature Bald Eagle, but is darker. Young Bald Eagles usually have much white in the wing-linings and sometimes on the body. They often have a tail mottled with white at the base, but not a sharply banded tail. The legs of the Golden Eagle are feathered to the toes, the Bald Eagle has bare tarsi; a taxonomic character that sometimes can be used in the field. The present species flaps less and soars more than the Bald. Even the general contour is different; the head and massive bill of the Bald Eagle project more. The wings of the Golden Eagle are shorter and wider, the tail more ample. In brief, the Golden is more buteo-like, reminding one of a black Rough-legged Hawk. However, the black Rough-leg usually has very little white at the base of the tail, above (see flight patterns).

Range: — Mountainous regions of Canada, s. locally in Appalachians to Southern States, also w. edge of Great Plains.

BALD EAGLE. *Haliœetus leucocephalus.* Subsp.   p. 67.
Field marks: — 30–31. Wing-spread 6–7½ ft. Our national bird with its *white head* and *white tail* is 'all field mark.' The immature bird has a dusky head and tail. It usually shows some whitish in the wing linings and breast.
Similar species: — Melanistic Buteos (black Rough-legs, etc.) are much smaller (see flight diagrams). Immature Bald Eagles are sometimes confused with the Golden Eagle. Although in many individuals there may be some white on the under surface of the wings, it is usually in the linings rather than at the base of the primaries. See Golden Eagle.
Voice: — A harsh, creaking cackle, *kweek-kik-ik-ik-ik-ik* or a lower *kak-kak-kak.*
Range: — Chiefly near ocean, rivers, and lakes from Gulf of Mexico n. to Arctic; winters n. as far as ice-free water permits.

Harriers: Circinæ

MARSH HAWK, or HARRIER. *Circus cyaneus hudsonius.*
                                                      pp. 55, 59.
Field marks: — 18–24. The *white* rump-patch is the badge of the species. *Adult males* are pale gray; *females*, streaked brown. In ordinary flight, the bird glides buoyantly low over the meadows and marshes with the wings held perceptibly above the horizontal, suggesting the Turkey Vulture's dihedral. The white rump is always conspicuous. Overhead, the wing-tips of the whitish male have a 'dipped in ink' pattern.
Similar species: — The Rough-leg, a winter Hawk, has white at

the base of the tail, but is much more heavily proportioned. When the Marsh Hawk is flying high, the long square-tipped tail might suggest a Falcon, but the wings are not pointed. The Accipiters (which sometimes appear white-rumped from the side) have much shorter wings.

Voice: — A weak nasal whistle *pee, pee, pee.* Also a lower pitched *chu-chu-chu.*

Range: — Breeds in meadows and bushy marshes from Gulf of Mexico n. to Gulf of St. Lawrence. Winters n. to s. New England and Great Lakes (a few).

Ospreys: Pandionidæ

OSPREY. *Pandion haliætus carolinensis.* p. 67.
　　Field marks: — 21–24. Wing-spread 4½–6 ft. A large water-loving, eagle-like Hawk — blackish above and *clear white* below only *large* bird of prey so patterned. Head largely white, suggestive of Bald Eagle, but has *broad black patch through cheeks.* Flies with decided kink or crook in wings. The habit of hovering on beating wings, and plunging feet first for fish, is characteristic.
　　Voice: — A series of short, sharp, cheeping whistles, *cheep, cheep,* or *chewk chewk,* etc.; sounds annoyed.
　　Range: — Breeds near water from Gulf of Mexico n. to Hudson Bay and s. Labrador; winters from Gulf States s.

Caracaras: Polyborinæ

AUDUBON'S CARACARA. *Polyborus cheriway auduboni.*
　　　　　　　　　　　　　　　　　　　　　　　　p. 58, 72.
　　Field marks: — 22. The 'Mexican Buzzard' is often seen on fence posts or on the ground feeding with Vultures, where its *black crest* is its outstanding feature. It is a large, long-legged, long-necked dark Hawk, about size of Osprey. In flight, the under body presents three alternating areas of light and dark — whitish throat and breast, black belly, and white, dark-tipped tail. The *pale-colored patches* at the wing-tips are conspicuous from above or below. These are determinative, especially when seen in conjunction with the white breast area. At close range it shows a red face.
　　Range: — Prairie regions of cent. Florida and s. Texas.

CHICKEN-LIKE BIRDS

NOTE: The birds on the page opposite are males unless otherwise noted.

RING—NECKED PHEASANT   p. 77.
   Male: Highly colored; neck-ring, long tail.
   Female: Brown; long pointed tail.

SHARP—TAILED GROUSE   p. 76.
   White tail, short point.

PRAIRIE CHICKEN   p. 76.
   Barred; short dark tail.

RUFFED GROUSE   p. 74.
   Fan tail with black band.
   (Tail can be rusty or gray.)

SPRUCE GROUSE   p. 74.
   Dusky; black tail, rusty tip.

HUNGARIAN PARTRIDGE   p. 77.
   Rusty tail.

BOB—WHITE   p. 77
   Small size; head-stripes, short dark tail.

WILLOW PTARMIGAN   p. 75.
   Summer: Dark body, white wings.
   Winter: White body, black tail.

| Ruffed | Female | Sharp-tailed | Prairie |
| Grouse | Pheasant | Grouse | Chicken |

RING-NECKED PHEASANT

♂

♀

SHARP-TAILED GROUSE

RUFFED GROUSE

PRAIRIE CHICKEN

SPRUCE GROUSE

HUNGARIAN PARTRIDGE

BOB-WHITE

Summer

Winter

WILLOW PTARMIGAN

CLAPPER RAIL

KING RAIL

VIRGINIA RAIL
Adult
Juvenile

Adult
SORA
Immature

YELLOW RAIL

BLACK RAIL

COMMON GALLINULE
Downy Young

COOT
Downy Young

KING RAIL
Downy Young

PURPLE GALLINULE

COMMON GALLINULE

AMERICAN COOT

Plate 22   71

RAILS, GALLINULES, AND COOT

CLAPPER RAIL   p. 80.
    Salt marshes; large, gray.

KING RAIL   p. 80
    Fresh marshes; large, rusty brown.
    Downy young: Glossy black; white on bill.

VIRGINIA RAIL   p. 81.
    Small; gray cheeks, long bill.
    Juvenile: Blackish.

SORA RAIL   p. 81.
    Adult: Gray; short yellow bill.
    Immature: Buffy brown; short bill.

YELLOW RAIL   p. 81.
    Buffy; striped back, white wing-patch.

BLACK RAIL   p. 82.
    Small; slaty with black bill.
    All young Rails are black, so do not call them Black Rails.

PURPLE GALLINULE   p. 82.
    Blue frontal shield, purple neck.

FLORIDA GALLINULE   p. 82.
    Adult: Red bill, white flank stripe.
    Downy young: Glossy black; red bill.

COOT   p. 83.

    Adult: White bill.
    Downy young: Orange-red head.

Coots and Gallinules skitter
over the water when taking
flight.

AUDUBON'S CARACARA

Falcons: Falconinæ

THE MOST streamlined of the Hawks. Know them by this combination: long, *pointed* wings and longish tails. The wing-strokes
are rapid; the slim wings are built for speed, not sustained soaring
in the manner of the Buteos. When they do soar, however, they
lose something of the pointed effect and naturally are puzzling to
the inexperienced.

GYRFALCON. *Falco rusticolus obsoletus.*   p. 66.
   Field marks: — 20–24½. A rare Arctic visitor; a very large
Falcon, much larger than the Duck Hawk, slightly longer-tailed
and more uniformly colored. It had been assumed that three or
four races occur in North America, with a distinction made between black, gray, and white types. Recent studies have led to
the conclusion that there is only one Gyrfalcon in North America
(Friedmann), and that the various 'races' are color phases, possible in the same brood.
   Similar species: — White birds are distinguished from the
Snowy Owl by the smaller head, pointed wings, and quicker,
falcon flight. Black birds are much larger and blacker-breasted
than the Duck Hawk. There are many intermediates. These
gray birds are paler-headed and more uniformly colored, than the
Duck Hawk, without such marked contrast between dark upper
parts and light under parts. The contrasting dark hood and
clean cut 'mustaches' of the Duck Hawk offer a fairly good distinction. The wing-beats of the 'Gyr' are deceptively slower,

almost gull-like. Only those who know the Duck Hawk from A
to Z should attempt to recognize this rare bird.
Range: — Arctic, rarely reaching n. United States in migration
and winter.

PRAIRIE FALCON. *Falco mexicanus.*
Field marks: — 17. Don't expect to see this Falcon east of the
Plains. Very much like Peregrine Falcon in size and cut of jib,
but of a paler, sandy color. 'Like a faded Peregrine' (Taverner).
In flight overhead the Prairie Falcon shows *blackish patches*
(formed by the dark flanks and axillars) where the wings join the
body. (See Illus. in *A Field Guide to Western Birds.*)
Similar species: — Peregrine has contrasting face pattern (wide
black 'mustaches') and contrasting dark back (slaty black in
adult, dark brown in immature). Female Sparrow Hawks are
smaller and darker.
Range: — W. North America, e. to Great Plains.

DUCK HAWK, or PEREGRINE FALCON. *Falco peregrinus anatum.* pp. 55, 66.
Field marks: — 15–20. Recognized as a Falcon by its long,
pointed wings and long, narrow tail, and its quick, 'rowing'
wing-beats that are not unlike the flight of a Pigeon. Its size,
near that of a Crow, identifies it as this species. On perching
birds the heavy dark 'mustaches' are distinctive. Adults are
slaty-backed, barred on the belly. Young birds are browner,
heavily streaked below.
Similar species: — Sparrow Hawk (Kestrel) and Pigeon Hawk
(Merlin) are smaller, hardly larger than Robin. In Great Plains
see Prairie Falcon.
Voice: — Noisy around eyrie; a repeated *we'chew*; a rapid rasping *cack cack cack*, etc., and a wailing note.
Range: — Breeds mainly on cliffs from Arctic s. locally to n.
Georgia and n. Louisiana. Winters from n. United States s. to
Gulf of Mexico.

(EASTERN) PIGEON HAWK, or MERLIN. *Falco columbarius columbarius.* pp. 55, 66.
Field marks: — 10–13½. A small Falcon, not much longer than
a Jay. Male, bluish-gray above, with broad black bands on the
tail. Female and young, dusky brown.
Similar species: — Suggests a miniature Duck Hawk. The
pointed wings and Falcon-like wing-action separate it from the
little Sharp-shinned Hawk, which has short rounded wings. The
lack of rufous-red on the tail or back distinguishes it from the
other small Falcon, the Sparrow Hawk. In flight it sails less between strokes than the Sparrow Hawk. During migration to be
looked for in open country, on coastal marshes, etc.

Range: — Breeds in conifers from n. edge of United States to limit of trees; winters from Gulf States s.

SPARROW HAWK, or KESTREL. *Falco sparverius.* Subsp.

pp. 55, 66.

Field marks: — 9–12. A small swallow-like Falcon, not much larger than a Robin. No other *small* Hawk has a rufous-red tail. Males have blue-gray wings. Both sexes have a handsome black-and-white face pattern. It is the only common *small* Hawk that habitually hovers on rapidly beating wings, kingfisher-like, in one spot. The Sparrow Hawk sits fairly erect with an occasional but characteristic jerk of the tail. Look for it on telegraph poles.
Similar species: — Flying, note the narrow, pointed wings (Sharp-shin has short, rounded wings). Its rufous back and tail distinguish it from either Sharp-shinned or Pigeon Hawk.
Voice: — Rapid, high *klee klee klee* or *killy killy killy.*
Range: — Breeds in tree cavities from Florida and Gulf of Mexico n. to Newfoundland, s. Quebec, and Saskatchewan; winters n. to s. Ontario.

Grouse: Tetraonidæ

GROUND-DWELLING, chicken-like birds that scratch for a living; larger than Quail, and without the long tails of Pheasants.

SPRUCE GROUSE. *Canachites canadensis.* Subsp. p. 70.
Field marks: — 15–17. In the deep wet coniferous forests of the north we look for this tame slate-colored Grouse. The male is splotched with black and white beneath. At close range, such as a Spruce Grouse allows, the male shows a comb of bare red skin above the eye and a chestnut band on the end of the tail. The female is browner, thickly barred, and lacks the black under parts.
Similar species: — Female is much darker than Ruffed Grouse and lacks the broad black band at the end of the tail. She is *barred* with black above, not spotted.
Range: — Spruce forests of Canada from Labrador to Alberta and s. locally to n. New England, n. New York, n. Michigan (in jack pines), and n. Minnesota.

RUFFED GROUSE. *Bonasa umbellus.* Subsp. p. 70.
Field marks: — 16–19. A large, *red-brown* or *gray-brown* chicken-like bird of the brushy woodlands, usually not seen until it springs into the air with a startling whir. It has a fan-shaped tail with a broad black band near its tip. Two color phases occur: 'red' birds with rufous on the tail and 'gray' birds with gray tails.

Although red birds are in the preponderance in the southern part of the range and gray birds northward, it is not considered a sub-specific distinction in individuals.

Similar species: — Female Pheasants are similar, but have pointed, instead of fan-shaped tails, and prefer more open country. They flush with less of a whir, generally croaking as they go.

Voice: — The drumming of the male might be overlooked as a distant motor starting up, or an outboard on some far-distant lake. The 'booming' starts off slowly, gaining speed until it ends in a whir: *bup ... bup ... bup ... bup .. bup . bup . up . r-rrrrr.* At a distance the muffled thumping is so hollow that sometimes it hardly registers as an exterior sound, but seems rather to be a disturbing series of vibrations within the ear itself.

Range: — Resident from s. Labrador and s. James Bay, Canada s. to New Jersey (and in Appalachians to Georgia and Alabama. Also s. in the Mississippi Valley to Michigan, Wisconsin, and ne. Iowa, and very locally to Ohio, Indiana, and Missouri).

WILLOW PTARMIGAN. *Lagopus lagopus.* Subsp. p. 70.
Field marks: — 15–17. Ptarmigan are small Arctic or Alpine Grouse that change their brown summer plumage for white feathers when winter sets in. They frequent bleak Arctic tundra and rocky slopes above timberline where few other birds would long survive. The two species found in eastern Canada are very much alike; in the breeding plumage, rusty-brown with white wings, and in the winter, white with black tails.

Similar species: — There is no easy way to distinguish the two Ptarmigans in the field when they are in the brown plumage but the Willow is usually more uniformly rufous on the head and breast. In winter the Rock Ptarmigan has a *black mark* extending from the bill through the eye. Its smaller, more slender bill is apparent when the bird is in the hand. As their names suggest, there is a difference in habitat: the Willow resorts to the willows and sheltered valleys in winter and the open tundra and slopes in summer; the Rock Ptarmigan is restricted to the highest, most barren hills.

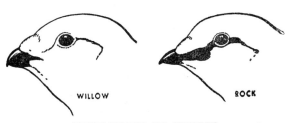

WILLOW   ROCK

PTARMIGANS IN WINTER

Range: — Arctic America, s. to s. Quebec, cent. Ontario, and s. Saskatchewan.

ROCK PTARMIGAN. *Lagopus mutus.* Subsp. p. 75.
See Willow Ptarmigan.
Range: — Arctic, s. to n. Quebec, Labrador, and Newfoundland.

PRAIRIE CHICKEN. *Tympanuchus cupido.* Subsp. p. 70.
Field marks: — 18. A large, brown hen-like bird of the prairies and brushy grasslands; known by its *short rounded dark tail* (black in males, barred in females) and, when close, by the *heavy barring* on the under parts.
Similar species: — Female Pheasant has a long pointed tail, Sharp-tailed Grouse a pointed whitish tail. Ruffed Grouse lives in woods, has a large fan-shaped tail.
Voice: — Courting males in spring make a hollow three-syllabled 'booming' *oo-loo-woo,* suggesting the sound made by blowing across the opening of a Coca-Cola bottle.
Range: — Prairies from s. Saskatchewan and s. Manitoba s. to Illinois, Missouri, and Arkansas, and e. to Michigan (local) and Indiana. Also coast of Texas and sw. Louisina.

LESSER PRAIRIE CHICKEN. *Tympanuchus pallidicinctus.*
Field marks: — Like a small, pale Prairie Chicken.
Range: — A very limited area in sw. Kansas, e. Colorado, w. Oklahoma (Beaver, Texas, and Cimarron Counties), n. Texas, and ne. New Mexico.

SHARP-TAILED GROUSE. *Pediœcetes phasianellus.* Subsp.
p. 70.
Field marks: — 17½. In the prairie brushland we see a pale Grouse with a *short pointed tail.* In flight the tail appears *white.*
Similar species: — Female Pheasants have *long* pointed tails; Prairie Chickens, *short, rounded, dark* tails; Ruffed Grouse, *fan-shaped* tails.
Voice: — Courting note a single *coo,* lower and shorter than notes of Mourning Dove. Also a cackling *cac-cac-cac,* etc.
Range: — Prairie brushland and open forests; from n. Quebec and n. Manitoba s. to w. Wisconsin, Minnesota, and cent. Nebraska.

Quails, Partridges, and Pheasants: Phasianidæ

QUAIL and Old World Partridges are small, scratching, chicken-like birds, smaller than Grouse or Pheasants. Pheasants are chicken-sized with long sweeping tails.

BOB–WHITE. *Colinus virginianus.* Subsp. p. 70.
Field marks: — 8½–10½. A small, ruddy, chicken-like bird, near the size of a Meadowlark. On the ground or perched the male shows a conspicuous white throat and stripe over the eye, the female buffy.
Similar species: — Distinguished from Ruffed Grouse by smaller size and short tail; from Woodcock, by smaller head, stubby bill, and more blustering flight; and from Meadowlark in flight, by lack of white outer tail-feathers.
Voice: — A clearly enunciated whistle *Bob-White!*, or *Poor Bob-Whoit!* (last note loud and ringing). 'Covey call,' a shrill *ka-loi-kee?* answered by *whoil-kee* (T. S. Roberts).
Range: — Chiefly farming country from Gulf of Mexico n. to South Dakota, s. Minnesota, s. Ontario, and sw. Maine.

HUNGARIAN, or EUROPEAN, PARTRIDGE. *Perdix perdix perdix.* p. 70.
Field marks: — 12–14. In flight this rotund grayish Partridge shows a *short rufous tail*. It is smaller than any of the Grouse and larger than a Bob-white, has a dark splotch on the belly and broad chestnut-colored bars on the flanks. It is found locally in open farming country.
Voice: — A loud hoarse *kar-wit, kar-wit* (B. W. Tucker).
Range: — Introduced locally in a number of Eastern States; most successful in Upper Mississippi Valley.

RING–NECKED PHEASANT. *Phasianus colchicus torquatus.* p. 70.
Field marks: — ♂ 33–36, ♀ 20½. A large chicken-like or gamecock-like bird with a *long, sweeping pointed tail*. The male is highly-colored with a *white neck-ring*; the female is mottled brown with a moderately long pointed tail.
Similar species: — Brown female can be confused with Ruffed and Sharp-tailed Grouse, but *long pointed tail* is characteristic.
Voice: — Courting males utter a loud double squawk followed by a whir of wings (not audible at a distance).
Range: — Established in farming country mainly n. of Mason and Dixon Line (Delaware, n. Maryland, s. Ohio, s. Indiana, Missouri, and n. Oklahoma) and n. only as far as deep snows will allow (s. Maine, n. New York, s. Ontario, s. Michigan, Minnesota, and s. Saskatchewan).

Turkeys: Meleagrididæ

TURKEY. *Meleagris gallopavo.* Subsp. **p. 78.**
Field marks: — ♂ 48, ♀ 36. A streamlined version of the

TURKEY

familiar Turkey of the barnyard. The domestic Turkey has
white tips to the tail-feathers; the Wild Turkey, *chestnut*. This
would be all well enough if the wild form did not sometimes
breed with stray barnyard birds. As a result, it is often difficult
to determine their true identity.

Voice: — Similar to 'gobbling' of domestic Turkey.

Range: — Southern woodlands n. to Pennsylvania, e. Kentucky,
and se. Missouri.

Cranes: Gruidæ

LONG-LEGGED, long-necked birds, superficially a little like large
Herons, but more robust, with long feathers on the back, which
curl down over the ends of the wings giving a tufted appearance.
They also have shorter bills, and bare red skin about the face.
Their blaring trumpet-like calls dispel any doubt as to their identity.

WHOOPING CRANE. *Grus americana.*   p. 79.

   Field marks: — Larger than Sandhill Crane or Great Blue Heron
(50). A large *white* Crane with a red face; neck outstretched in
flight, primary wing-feathers black.

   Similar species: — Large size, black-and-white wing-pattern
create similarity at great distance with Wood Ibis, White Pelican
and Snow Goose.

   Range: — Very rare. Prairies of nw. Canada, migrating s. *via*
Nebraska to Texas coast and Mexico.

WHOOPING CRANE

Compare its flight pattern with Wood Ibis and White Pelican.

SANDHILL CRANE. *Grus canadensis.* Subsp. p. 86.
Field marks: — 40–48. A long-legged, long-necked gray bird with a bald *red* forehead. Some birds are tinged with brick-red, probably because of iron in the water. On the ground, the tufted appearance of the feathers over the tail is a good mark. In flight, the neck is fully *extended*. The wing-motion is distinctive, a smart jerk or flap of the wings above the body level. (Herons have deep, bowed down stroke.)
Similar species: — Great Blue Heron is often called Crane but is less robust of body. In sustained flight it carries its neck in a loop with the head drawn back to the shoulders, while the Crane flies with neck extended and legs trailing, like a 'flying cross.'
Voice: — A deep rolling *k-r-r-r-oo* repeated several times.
Range: — Breeds from prairies of Canada s. to Michigan, Wisconsin, and South Dakota; also in Florida and s. Georgia. Migrates w. of Mississippi River to Gulf Coast.

Limpkins: Aramidæ

LIMPKIN. *Aramus guarauna pictus.* p. 87.
Field marks: — 28. In Florida we find this large brown swamp wader. It is about the size of a Bittern, but with much longer,

dark legs, a longer neck, and a long, slightly drooping bill which gives it a slightly ibis-like aspect. No Ibis is brown with *white spots and streakings*. The flight is Crane-like (wings making a smart jerk or flap above the level of the body).

Similar species: — See American Bittern, immature Night Herons, immature White Ibis, and immature Glossy Ibis.

Voice: — A piercing, repeated wail *kree-ow*, *kra-ow*, etc., etc., especially at night or on cloudy days.

Range: — Swamps, marshes; Florida, s. Georgia (Okefinokee).

Rails, Gallinules, and Coots: Rallidæ

RAILS are plump, somewhat chicken-like marsh-birds of secretive habits, shy rather than wary, and much more often heard than seen. When flushed, they rise from the reeds close at hand, fly feebly with legs dangling for a short distance, and drop back again into the marsh.

Gallinules and Coots resemble Ducks except for their smaller heads and rather chicken-like bills.

KING RAIL. *Rallus elegans elegans.*   p. 71.
  Field marks: — 15–19. A large reddish Rail with a long, slender bill; twice size of Virginia Rail, or about that of a chicken.
  Similar species: — The Virginia Rail is half the size and has slaty-gray cheeks. King and Clapper Rails are of similar proportions, but one is more brown, the other more gray; the King inhabits fresh-water marshes; the Clapper, salt marshes. Birds in typical habitats give no trouble but in borderline areas (brackish-salt marshes) it is difficult to distinguish them — particularly in the South where some races of the Clapper are almost as rusty as the King.
  Voice: — A low, grunting *bup-bup*, *bup-bup-bup*, etc. or *chuck-chuck-chuck* not descending the scale as does the Virginia Rail's call, and deeper.
  Range: — Breeds from Gulf of Mexico n. to Massachusetts, s. Ontario, and s. Minnesota, w. to Kansas; winters n. to New Jersey.

CLAPPER RAIL. *Rallus longirostris.* Subsp.   p. 71.
  Field marks: — 14–16. The large gray or gray and tan Rail of the coastal marshes, the 'Salt-water Marsh Hen' of the gunners. Its hen-like appearance, grayish coloration, strong legs, long bill, and white patch under the short tail identify it. It sometimes swims; then it is a baffling-looking bird.

Similar species: — Most like the King Rail which prefers fresh marshes (but is sometimes found in brackish near Clapper). The King Rail is larger, has blacker stripes on the back and flanks, and is *rusty-brown* on the wings. Its breast is cinnamon, but the Clapper often shows similar warm buff on these parts. In fact the two approach each other so closely in some ways and in some places that did they not often breed in adjacent marshes, they might be suspected of being races of the same species.

Voice: — A clattering *kek-kek-kek-kek*, etc., or *cha-cha-cha-cha-cha*, etc.

Range: — Salt marshes along Atlantic and Gulf Coast n. to Connecticut; winters from Long Island (occasionally) south.

VIRGINIA RAIL. *Rallus limicola limicola.* p. 71.

Field marks: — 9–10½. A small reddish Rail, with *gray cheeks* and a long, slightly decurved bill; the only small Rail, near size of a Bob-white, with a *slender* bill. Full-grown young in late summer are sooty black.

Similar species: — Sora has short *yellow* bill. (See King Rail.)

Voice: — *Wak-wak-wak*, etc., and *kid-ick-kidick* besides various 'kicking' and grunting sounds.

Range: — Breeds mainly in fresh marshes from Nova Scotia, s. Quebec, and Saskatchewan s. to Nebraska, Missouri, Kentucky, and e. North Carolina; winters from Gulf of Mexico n. to North Carolina (rarely s. New England).

SORA. *Porzana carolina.* p. 71.

Field marks: — 8–9¾. The adult Sora is a small plump gray-brown Rail with a black patch on the face and throat, and a short, *yellow* bill. The immature bird lacks the black throat-patch, and is buffy-brown.

Similar species: — The short yellow bill will distinguish the Sora from the only other similarly sized fresh-water Rail, the Virginia Rail, which has a long, slender bill. The immature can be confused with the smaller and rarer Yellow Rail.

Voice: — 'Song,' a descending whinny. In spring, a plaintive whistled *ker-wee* (with rising inflection). In the fall, a sharp *keek* when a stone is tossed into the marsh.

Range: — Breeds in fresh marshes from Nova Scotia, lower St. Lawrence River, and Saskatchewan s. to Maryland, s. Ohio, n. Missouri, and Kansas. Winters in southern United States, rarely in North.

YELLOW RAIL. *Coturnicops noveboracensis noveboracensis.*

p. 71.

Field marks: — 6–7½. Rare. A small yellowish Rail, resembling a week-old chicken; shows a *white* wing-patch in flight —

the only Rail so marked. Yellow Rails are so mouse-like that it requires the services of a bird dog to find them unless one is familiar with their notes. They prefer grassy marshes.

Similar species: Immature Sora might be taken for Yellow Rail but is larger, not so yellow, and lacks the white wing-patch. Notice back pattern in color plate.

Voice: — Ticking notes, often in long series; *tic-tic, tic-tic-tic; tic-tic, tic-tic-tic,* etc. (groups of two and three). 'Some observers describe another call: *kĭ kĭ kĭ kĭ kĭ kreeah,* last note with a rolling quality' (Francis H. Allen).

Range: — Summers locally in n. parts of United States and n. to Nova Scotia, cent. Quebec, and n. Manitoba; winters from Gulf of Mexico n. to North Carolina.

BLACK RAIL. *Laterallus jamaicensis pygmæus.* p. 71.
Field marks: — 5–6. A tiny slaty or blackish Rail with a black bill; about the size of a young Song Sparrow with a bobbed tail. Back speckled with white. Inhabits wet meadows and salt marshes with stretches of fine wire grass. Very difficult to glimpse or flush.

Similar species: — All young Rails in downy plumage are glossy black (often called Black Rails by the inexperienced).

Voice: — Male utters *kik* notes lighter and more metallic than those of other Rails. Female has a Cuckoo-like *croo-croo-croo-o* (do not confuse with Least Bittern).

Range: — Breeds from Florida along coast to Massachusetts; local inland to Iowa and Kansas; winters s. of United States.

PURPLE GALLINULE. *Porphyrula martinica.* p. 71.
Field marks: — 12–14. This southern Gallinule is one of the most beautiful of all water-birds. The head and under parts are deep purple, the back bronzy-green, the bill red tipped with yellow, frontal shield on the forehead light *blue,* legs *yellow.*

Similar species: — Besides the deep purple under parts, the *blue* frontal shield will distinguish it from the Florida Gallinule, and, in flight the dangling bright *yellow* legs.

Voice: — A hen-like cackling *kek, kek, kek,* given when flying; also guttural notes.

Range: — Lowland swamps from Florida and Texas n. to South Carolina and Tennessee. Occasionally wanders north. Winters from Florida (rarely) and s. Texas south.

FLORIDA GALLINULE. *Gallinula chloropus cachinnans.* p. 71.
Field marks: — 12–14½. Gallinules are duck-like marsh-lovers with stout, rather chicken-like bills, equally at home swimming in the open water or wading among the reeds. A slate-gray duck-like bird with a red bill is certainly this species. It has a band of white feathers on the flanks, another sure mark. Pumps head and neck when swimming.

Similar species: — Coot is stockier, shorter-necked, and has a *white bill.* (See Purple Gallinule.)

Voice: — A croaking *curruk* repeated, and *kik-kik-kik*; hen-like notes, some complaining, others loud and harsh.

Range: — Breeds from Gulf of Mexico n. to Vermont, New York, s. Ontario, Minnesota, and Nebraska; winters n. to South Carolina, rarely farther.

COOT. *Fulica americana.* p. 71.

Field marks: — 13–16. The only slate-gray duck-like bird with a *whitish bill.* Its head and neck are blacker than the body and it has a white patch under the tail. Like the Gallinule, when swimming, it pumps its neck and head back and forth. In deep water it dives expertly. When it takes wing, it patters its feet for a considerable distance. In flight a white border shows on the hind edge of the wing.

Similar species: — A Coot in the company of Gallinules is larger with a somewhat bigger head. Gallinules have *red* bills. Coots are more duck-like, flock more and resort more to lakes, bays, and open water.

Voice: — A guttural *kuk-kuk-kuk-kuk* and various other cackling and croaking notes.

Range: — Breeds in marshes from New Brunswick, s. Quebec, and Saskatchewan s. to Arkansas and New Jersey, a few to Florida; winters from Gulf of Mexico n. to Great Lakes (a few) and Long Island (a few).

Oyster-Catchers: Hæmatopodidæ

AMERICAN OYSTER-CATCHER. *Hæmatopus palliatus palliatus.* pp. 90, 103.

Field marks: — 17–21. A very large, dark and white shorebird, with white wing-patches and a *large red bill.*

Similar species: — See Black Skimmer.

Voice: — A piercing whistled note, *wheep!*, rapidly repeated as the birds fly about.

Range: — Breeds and winters locally along coast from Virginia to Texas.

Plovers and Turnstones: Charadriidæ

WADING BIRDS, more compactly built, thicker-necked and more boldly patterned than Sandpipers. They also have shorter, stouter bills and larger eyes. The notes of the various Plovers are so distinctly different that they can be used to advantage in identifying them.

PIPING PLOVER. *Charadrius melodus.* Subsp.   pp. 91, 102.
  Field marks: — 6–7½. As pale as a beach flea is this small whitish Plover. It has a more or less complete or incomplete black ring about the neck. In flight it is as pale as a winter Sanderling without so bold a wing pattern.
  Similar species: — The back of the Semipalmated Plover is the dark color of wet sand or mud; that of the Piping is pale like the sun-bleached, dry sand of the beaches it inhabits.
  Voice: — Plaintive whistle; *peep-lo* (first note higher).
  Range: — Breeds along coast from Gulf of St. Lawrence s. to North Carolina and locally inland from s. Ontario and s. Saskatchewan s. to Erie, Pennsylvania, n. Ohio, ne. Illinois, and Nebraska. Winters on coast from South Carolina to Texas.

(CUBAN) SNOWY PLOVER. *Charadrius alexandrinus tenuirostris.*
                                                        p. 102.
  Similar species: — 6. Slightly smaller and even whiter than the Piping Plover, with a *slim, black bill* and *dusky legs* (Piping Plover, yellow legs). The 'ring' is reduced to a black mark on each side of the breast. In winter when the two are together, the stubby bills of most Piping Plovers are also *all black*; use then the leg color, the whiter look of the Snowy, and the dark mark back of the eye.
  Voice: — 'A low-pitched, musical whistle, *kik kik kroor ri*' (J. T. Nichols); '*pe-wee-ah* or *o-wee-ah*' (F. M. Weston).
  Range: — Gulf Coast from Florida to Texas.

SEMIPALMATED PLOVER. *Charadrius hiaticula semipalmatus.*
                                                        pp. 91, 102.
  Field marks: — 6½–8. A small shore-bird with a *black collar* across its chest; *dark* brown above; half the size of the Killdeer.
  Similar species: — Killdeer is twice as large, its tail is twice as long and it has *two* black rings across its chest (Semipalmated, one). The Piping Plover is more like it in size and pattern but is much paler and whiter.
  Voice: — A plaintive *chi-we* or *tooi*, second note higher.
  Range: — Breeds from Arctic s. to Nova Scotia; migrates along coast and inland to s. Atlantic and Gulf coasts.

WILSON'S PLOVER. *Charadrius wilsonia wilsonia.*   p. 102.
  Field marks: — 7–8. A 'ringed' Plover, larger than either the Semipalmated or Piping Plover, easily distinguished by its proportionately *long, heavy, black bill*.
  Similar species: — The stubby little bills of the Piping and Semipalmated Plovers are black only at the tip except in fall

SEMIPALMATED   WILSON'S

COMPARATIVE BILL-LENGTHS OF TWO
RINGED PLOVERS

immatures. These black-billed fall birds can be told not only
by their size and bill proportion but by *yellowish legs*. Wilson's
legs are flesh-gray. Along Gulf Coast see Snowy Plover.
Voice: — An emphatic whistled *whitl* or *wheep!*
Range: — Breeds on coastal islands from Virginia to Texas;
winters from Florida to Texas.

KILLDEER. *Charadrius vociferus vociferus.* pp. 91, 102.
  Field marks: — 9–11. The Killdeer is the common noisy breed-
  ing Plover of the plowed fields and pasture-lands. It is larger
  than the other 'ringed' Plovers, has *two* breast-bands, instead of
  one, and, in flight, shows a golden-red rump and a longish tail.
  Voice: — Noisy; a loud insistent *kill-dee* or *kill-deeah*, repeated.
  Also a plaintive *dee-ee* with rising inflection.
  Range: — Breeds from Florida and Gulf of Mexico n. to s.
  Quebec and n. Ontario; winters n. to s. Illinois and Long Island
  Sound.

GOLDEN PLOVER. *Pluvialis dominica dominica.* pp. 91, 102.
  Field marks: — 10–11. A trifle larger than a Killdeer. Breeding adults are dark shore-birds, spangled with golden spots above,
  and solid black on the belly. A broad white stripe extends over
  the eye down the side of the neck. Young birds and winter
  adults are brown, darker above than below. They are recognized as Plovers, as distinct from Sandpipers, by their stocky
  proportions and short, stout bill; and in flight from the other
  Plovers by their lack of conspicuous pattern. See below.
  Similar species: — The Black-bellied Plover is pale gray above,
  not golden-brown and has *white rump and tail*. (Golden has a
  brown tail.) In mixed flocks the Black-belly shows white in the
  wings and tail and a black axillar patch (beneath wings where
  they join the body); Golden Plovers are smaller, darker, and without pattern.
  Voice: — The harsh, whistled *queedle* or *quee* is quite unlike the
  plaintive *wheer-ee* of the Black-belly.

LONG-LEGGED WADERS

LOUISIANA HERON   **p. 21.**
    White belly.

LITTLE BLUE HERON   **p. 21.**
    Adult: Dark body, dark bill and legs.
    Immature: White body; dark bill and feet.

REDDISH EGRET   **p. 21.**
    Gulf Coast
    Dark phase: Dark; flesh-colored bill.
    White phase: White; flesh-colored bill.

SNOWY EGRET   **p. 20.**
    Yellow feet.

AMERICAN EGRET   **p. 20.**
    Yellow bill, dark legs.

GREAT WHITE HERON   **p. 17.**
    Large, with yellowish legs; Florida Keys.

GREAT BLUE HERON   **p. 20.**
    Large, gray.

SANDHILL CRANE   **p. 79.**
    Red forehead; tufted rear.

FLAMINGO   **p. 30.**
    Pink; very long neck.

ROSEATE SPOONBILL   **p. 20.**
    Pink wings, spoon bill.
    Immature birds whitish.

Herons fly with their necks folded back to their shoulders; cranes with their necks extended.

LOUISIANA HERON

LITTLE BLUE HERON
Adult

REDDISH EGRET
Dark Phase

SNOWY EGRET

LITTLE BLUE HERON
Immature

REDDISH EGRET
White Phase

AMERICAN EGRET

GREAT WHITE HERON

GREAT BLUE HERON

SANDHILL CRANE

FLAMINGO

ROSEATE SPOONBILL

GREEN HERON

Adult — YELLOW-NIGHT CROWNED HERON

Adult — BLACK-CROWNED NIGHT HERON

Immature — BLACK-CROWNED NIGHT HERON

Adult — GREEN HERON

LEAST BITTERN

AMERICAN BITTERN

Immature — YELLOW-CROWNED NIGHT HERON

Immature — BLACK-CROWNED NIGHT HERON

WHITE IBIS

Immature

GLOSSY IBIS

LIMPKIN

Adult — WHITE IBIS

WOOD IBIS

Plate 24   87

LONG-LEGGED WADERS

YELLOW–CROWNED NIGHT HERON p. 24.
    Adult: Gray body, black head, light crown.
    Immature: Like Black-crown but slatier, more finely
            speckled, legs longer.

BLACK–CROWNED NIGHT HERON p. 24.
    Adult: White breast, black back, black crown.
    Immature: Brown, large spots on back.

GREEN HERON p. 24.
    Small dark Heron, short legs.

LEAST BITTERN p. 25.
    Tiny; back and crown black, wings buff.

AMERICAN BITTERN p. 25.
    Tawny; black neck-mark; bill pointed up.

WHITE IBIS p. 29.
    Adult: Red face, decurved bill.
    Immature: Decurved bill, white belly, white rump.

GLOSSY IBIS p. 28.
    Dark body, decurved bill.

LIMPKIN p. 79.
    Spotted; decurved bill.

WOOD IBIS p. 28.
    Naked gray head, large black wing areas.

Herons and Bitterns fly with necks folded; Ibises and Limpkins with necks extended.

Range: — Breeds in Arctic; migrates chiefly through Mississippi Valley in spring; far off Atlantic Coast in fall, except when driven to land by strong east or northeast winds. Favors burned fields, golf courses, dry flats.

BLACK-BELLIED PLOVER. *Squatarola squatarola.* pp. 91, 102.
Field marks: — 10½–13½. In breeding dress this Plover, with its black breast and almost whitish back, resembles no other shore-bird except the rare Golden Plover, which is much browner-backed. Winter birds and immatures are gray-looking and are recognized as Plovers by their stocky proportions and short, stout bills. In any plumage the *black axillar feathers under the wing,* and the white rump and tail, are determinative.
Similar species: — See Golden Plover.
Voice: — A plaintive slurred whistle, *whee-er-eee* (middle note lower).
Range: — Arctic; migrates through eastern North America; winters along coasts n. to North Carolina, occasionally farther.

RUDDY TURNSTONE. *Arenaria interpres morinella.*
pp. 91, 102.
Field marks: — 8–9½. A squat, robust, orange-legged shore-bird, larger than a Spotted Sandpiper. In breeding plumage with its russet-red back and fantastic black face and breast markings, it is handsome enough, but when the bird flies the real revelation occurs. This harlequin pattern is best explained by the diagram. Young birds and winter adults are more sober in color, but retain enough breast pattern to be recognizable. The striking wing-pattern is quite constant.
Voice: — A *low* chuckling *ket-a-kek* or *kut-a-kut*; also a single sharp *kewk*.
Range: — Breeds in Arctic; migrates through e. North America (principally along coast and Great Lakes); winters along coast n. to North Carolina. Aside from pebbly beaches and flats, best looked for on seaweed-covered rocks and jetties.

Woodcock, Snipe, Sandpipers, Etc.: Scolopacidæ

SMALL or medium-sized waders with more slender bills than Plovers. Most species are of plain or sober coloration.

WOODCOCK. *Philohela minor.* pp. 98, 118.
Field marks: — 10–12. A large, chunky, almost neckless, warm-brown bird with a 'dead-leaf pattern'; a little larger than a

Bob-white, with an *extremely long bill*. It is usually flushed from a woodland swamp or leafy thicket, and makes away on a straight course, often producing a whistling sound with its *short, rounded* wings.

Similar species: — Wilson's Snipe is slimmer, has *pointed* wings, prefers open boggy spots or wet meadows and makes off in a *zigzag* fashion when flushed.

Voice: — At dusk or on moonlit nights in spring, mating male emits a low nasal *beezp* or *peent*; suggests call of Nighthawk. Aerial 'song' starts as a chippering trill (made by wings) as bird ascends, and bursts like warbling of bubble pipe at climax.

Range: — Breeds from n. Florida and s. Louisiana to Nova Scotia, s. Ontario, ne. Minnesota, and s. Manitoba; winters n. to New Jersey and Ohio Valley.

WILSON'S SNIPE. *Capella gallinago delicata.* pp. 98, 118.
Field marks: — 10½–11½. Brown, larger than a Spotted Sandpiper, with a striped back and an *extremely long, slender bill*. When flushed, it makes off in a *zigzag*, showing a *short orange tail* and uttering a rasping note. Its preferred habitat is open boggy margins of little streams and marshes.
Similar species: — See Woodcock and Dowitcher.
Voice: — Nasal, rasping note when flushed.
Range: — Breeds from Newfoundland and n. Manitoba s. to nw. Pennsylvania, n. Illinois, and South Dakota; winters from Gulf of Mexico n. sparingly to Northern States.

LONG–BILLED CURLEW. *Numenius americanus.* p. 103.
Field marks: — 20–26, bill 5–7. The rare 'Sickle-bill' is much larger than the Hudsonian Curlew, more buffy, and lacks the contrasting head-striping (i.e., dark line through eye, stripes on crown, etc.). In flight, overhead, the *bright cinnamon winglinings* make the surest mark. In many individuals the bill is seven inches long or twice as long as that of the average Hudsonian, but in a few birds bill-lengths approach each other. Then use the other marks.
Similar species: — See Hudsonian Curlew, Marbled Godwit.
Voice: — A harsh *cur-leel* with rising inflection. Also a rapid, whistled *kli-lĭ-lĭ-lĭ.*
Range: — Very rare visitor on Atlantic coast, increasing in South Carolina. Common along Texas coast. Migrant on Plains.

HUDSONIAN CURLEW. *Numenius phæopus hudsonicus.*
pp. 90, 103.
Field marks: — 15–18, bill 2¾–4. Curlews are very large brown shore-birds with long *down-curved* bills. The bills of Godwits turn up. In flight they appear as large as some Ducks, and

LARGE SHORE-BIRDS

AVOCET   p. 105.
   Black and white back pattern, thin upturned bill.

BLACK–NECKED STILT   p. 105.
   White below; black unpatterned wings.

OYSTER–CATCHER (AMERICAN)   p. 83.
   White wing patches, black head, red bill.

HUDSONIAN GODWIT   p. 104.
   Upturned bill, ringed tail.

MARBLED GODWIT   p. 104.
   Long upturned bill, tawny brown color.

HUDSONIAN CURLEW   p. 89.
   Decurved bill, brown color, striped crown.

AVOCET

Spring

(Left) BLACK-NECKED
STILT

OYSTER-CATCHER

Fall

(Left) HUDSONIAN
GODWIT

MARBLED GODWIT

HUDSONIAN CURLEW

SEMIPALMATED PLOVER

PIPING
PLOVER

KILLDEER

Below

BLACK–BELLIED
PLOVER
(Spring)

Below

GOLDEN
PLOVER
(Spring)

Below

Above

BLACK–
BELLIED
PLOVER
(Fall)

Above

Below

GOLDEN PLOVER
(Fall)

RUDDY TURNSTONE
(Spring)

Plate 26 91

PLOVERS AND TURNSTONE

PIPING PLOVER p. 84.
    Pale sand-color, black tail spot.

SEMIPALMATED or RINGED PLOVER p. 84.
    Mud-brown; dark tail with white borders.

KILLDEER p. 85.
    Tawny-red rump, longish tail.

BLACK–BELLIED PLOVER p. 88.
    Spring: Black breast, white under tail-coverts.
    Fall: Black axillars, white in wing and tail.

GOLDEN PLOVER p. 85.
    Spring: Black breast, black under tail-coverts.
    Fall: Lack of pattern above and below.

RUDDY TURNSTONE p. 88.
    Harlequin pattern.

often fly in line or wedge formation, with sickle bills extended and legs trailing.

Similar species: — See Long-billed Curlew (rare in East).

Voice: — Four, five, or six short rapid whistles, *kŭ-kŭ-kŭ-kŭ* (F. H. Allen) or *whĭ-whĭ-whĭ-whĭ*.

Range: — Breeds in Arctic; migrates chiefly along coast, rarer inland (mostly spring). Winters in South America.

ESKIMO CURLEW. *Numenius borealis.*

Field marks: — 12–14. Bill 1¾–2½, *slightly curved* only. Body only half the bulk of a small Hudsonian. Blacker above and on top of head, the feathers with warm buffy-brown tips. Under parts warm buffy, *appearing lighter* than upper parts. (The Hudsonian Curlew appears a uniform dirty grayish brown, with a more conspicuously striped head.) In flight under surface of wings *conspicuously cinnamon buff.* Legs *dark greenish,* instead of bluish gray.

Similar species: — It is most unfortunate that the older books confused the two species, gave erroneous bill-lengths and leg-color, and circulated the idea that the Eskimo Curlew was prac-tically indistinguishable from a small young Hudsonian Curlew with a very short bill. It was inevitable, therefore, that most reports in recent decades of Eskimo Curlew have been based on young Hudsonians which looked so small and so short billed that they 'had to be' the smaller species.

Voice: — The usual flight call different from that of any other shore-bird, a sharp squeak with a squealing quality strongly suggesting the single note of a Common Tern, but weaker. Other notes do not resemble those of the Hudsonian (described as soft twittering or whistling in quality).

Range: — Formerly outer coast of New England and Long Island in fall, coastal prairies of Texas and Great Plains in spring. Practically extinct, but there are several recent sight records.

LUDLOW GRISCOM

UPLAND PLOVER. *Bartramia longicauda.* pp. 99, 103.

Field marks: — 11–12½. A large streaked buffy-brown shore-bird, 'pigeon-headed,' larger than a Killdeer but with no really distinctive markings; inhabits extensive fields, prairies, burnt meadows, etc. It habitually perches on fence-posts and even poles. The general brown coloration, the rather short bill (shorter than head), the comparatively small-headed, thin-necked, long-tailed appearance, and the habit of holding the wings elevated upon alighting are all helpful points. It flies 'on the tips of its wings' like a Spotted Sandpiper.

Similar species: — Can hardly be confused with any other sand-piper-like bird in the grass country. Curlews and Godwits are very much larger; Pectoral Sandpiper much smaller.

Voice: — *Kip-ip-ip-ip.* Also a rolling note in flight. 'Song,' two weird long-drawn wind-like whistles: *whooooleeeeee, wheeee-loooooooooooo* (first part starts with a rattle, ascends; second part descends).

Range: — Breeds from s. Maine, s. Quebec, Wisconsin, and Manitoba s. to n. Virginia, s. Illinois, s. Missouri, and Oklahoma. Migrates through e. United States (stopping on golf-courses, airports, etc.); winters in s. South America.

SPOTTED SANDPIPER. *Actitis macularia.*   pp. 98, 119.

Field marks: — 7–8. The common breeding Sandpiper; found at some time or other on nearly every lake and stream the breadth of the country. It teeters up and down between steps as if it were too delicately balanced on its slim legs. In breeding plumage the breast is covered with *large round spots* like those of a Wood Thrush; many Sandpipers are streaked, but this is the only one that is definitely spotted. Juvenile birds and fall and winter adults lack this spotting. They are olive-brown above and whitish below, with a white line over the eye. A white mark on the shoulder is a good aid. The constant teetering is as good a characteristic as any. The wing-stroke is short, below the horizontal, the wings maintaining a stiff, bowed appearance, entirely unlike the deeper wing-strokes of other small shore-birds. This is the most useful distinction of all when Sandpipers rise from the margin.

Voice: — A well enunciated *peet-weet!* first note higher. (See Solitary Sandpiper.)

Range: — Breeds from tree-limit in Canada s. to n. South Carolina, Alabama, and s. Louisiana; winters from South Carolina and Louisiana south.

(EASTERN) SOLITARY SANDPIPER. *Tringa solitaria solitaria.*   pp. 98, 118.

Field marks: — 7½–9. A dark Sandpiper, blackish above and whitish below, with a white eye-ring. The Solitary may best be described as a *dark-winged Sandpiper with flashy white sides to the tail, which are very conspicuous in flight.*

Similar species: — Resembles a little Yellow-legs, and nods like one, but has a dark rump instead of white, and dark legs instead of yellow. The Spotted Sandpiper *teeters* more than it nods and has a white stripe in the wing, which the dark-winged Solitary lacks. The Spotted has a narrow wing-arc; the Solitary, a darting, almost Swallow-like wing-stroke. Both frequent similar places (margins of pools, lakes, streams), but Solitary strictly avoids salt margins.

Voice: — *Peet!* or *peet-weet-weet!* (higher than Spotted).

Range: — Summers in Canadian wilderness, s. to n. edge of United States. Migrates through e. United States; winters in tropics.

WILLET. *Catoptrophorus semipalmatus.* Subsp.　　pp. 99, 118.
Field marks: — 14–17.　*Flashy black and white wing-pattern*
makes this large gray and white shore-bird absolutely unmistakable (see diagram).　At rest, when the banded wings cannot
be seen, the bird is of a rather uniform gray appearance and
quite nondescript.　The legs are bluish.
Similar species: — Smaller than the brown Godwits and Curlews, and a little larger than the Yellow-legs, which shows much
more contrast between the tones of the upper and under parts,
has a slimmer bill and, of course, has yellow legs.
Voice: — A musical oft-repeated *pill-will-willet* (in breeding
season); a loud *kay-tee* (second note lower).　Also a rapidly
repeated *kip-kip-kip*, etc.
Range: — Breeds in Nova Scotia and along coast from Delaware Bay to Texas; also in prairies from s. Manitoba and Saskatchewan s. to Iowa and Nebraska.　Occurs in Northeast during migration; winters along coast from North Carolina to Texas.

GREATER YELLOW-LEGS. *Totanus melanoleucus.*　　p. 118.
Field marks: — 13-15.　The *bright yellow legs* are the mark of
this rather large Sandpiper.　Flying, it appears as a *dark*-winged
shore-bird with a *whitish rump and tail*.　It has no wing-stripe.
Similar species: — See Lesser Yellow-legs.
Voice: — The three-or four-syllabled whistle, *whew-whew-whew*,
or *Dear! Dear! Dear!* is distinctive.　Also in spring, a fast-
repeated *whee-oodle, whee-oodle*, etc.
Range: — Mudflats and margins.　Breeds from Labrador and
Hudson Bay s. to Gulf of St. Lawrence and s. Manitoba; migrates throughout United States; winters along Atlantic and
Gulf coasts n. to Carolinas (occasionally farther).

LESSER YELLOW-LEGS. *Totanus flavipes.*　　pp. 98, 118.
Similar species: — Like Greater Yellow-legs but considerably
smaller (9½–11).　The smaller, slimmer bill of the Lesser is
perfectly straight; that of the Greater often appears *slightly
upturned*.　Most easily identified by calls (below).　(See fall
Stilt Sandpiper and fall Wilson's Phalarope.)
Voice: — The call most often given by the Greater is a clear
three-syllabled *whew-whew-whew*.　The corresponding call of the
Lesser is a flatter, less penetrating cry of one or two notes, *cu*
or *cu-cu*.
Range: — Breeds in Canada from n. Quebec to Manitoba and
Alaska.　Migrates throughout e. North America; winters in
South America.

KNOT. *Calidris canutus rufus.*　　pp. 98, 118, 119.
Field marks: — 10-11.　Chunky with a rather short bill; much
larger than a Spotted Sandpiper.　*Spring:* Breast pale Robin-
red, back mottled gray and black.　*Fall:* More nondescript,

breast whitish. A dumpy light-grayish shore-bird with a short bill and a whitish rump. Often feeds in closely packed flocks.
Similar species: — The spring Dowitcher, also red-breasted, has a long snipe-like bill (Knot's bill is short, about as long as head). In fall, the washed-out gray color, size and shape are the best clues. Sanderlings are smaller and whiter, Red-backs smaller and darker. (Both have dark rumps.) In flight, the Knot's whitish rump does not show so conspicuously as that of the Yellow-legs, nor does it extend so far up the back as in the Dowitcher.
Voice: — A low *knut* and a low two-syllabled whistle.
Range: — Breeds in Arctic; migrates along coast; rare inland. Winters in South America; occasionally on coast of United States.

PURPLE SANDPIPER. *Erolia maritima.*   pp. 99, 119.
  Field marks: — 8–9½. Dark Sandpipers flying about rocky, wave-washed islets or breakwaters off the northern coast in winter can safely be assigned to this species — hardier than the rest of the kin. The rock-feeding habits, stocky build, and rather Junco-like coloration, with slate-gray back and breast and white belly, are good field marks. It can easily be approached close enough to see the short yellow legs and the yellow base of the bill. In breeding plumage (rarely seen here) the bird is browner with a few rusty marks on the back and a heavily-streaked breast.
  Similar species: — See winter Red-backed Sandpiper.
  Voice: — A low *weet-wit* or *twit.*
  Range: — Arctic, s. in winter to New England and on rock jetties along coast to New Jersey (occasionally South Carolina). Said to be occasional on Great Lakes breakwaters.

PECTORAL SANDPIPER. *Erolia melanotos.*   pp. 99, 119.
  Field marks: — 8–9½. A streaked Sandpiper, larger than Spotted; prefers grassy mudflats and short-grass marshes. The rusty-brown back is streaked with black and lined snipe-like with white. The outstanding thing is the brownish breast streaking, which *ends abruptly* against the white belly like a bib.
  Similar species: — The Least Sandpiper is colored similarly, but is half the size. The top of the head is darker and the neck longer than in any of the other small shore-birds with which it might be confused. There is much difference in size between the sexes, and small individuals are likely to be confused with White-rumped and Baird's Sandpipers.
  Voice: — A reedy *krik, krik* or *trrip-trrip,* heavier than note of Semipalmated Sandpiper.
  Range: — Arctic; migrates throughout e. North America (rare on Atlantic Coast in spring). Winters in South America.

WHITE-RUMPED SANDPIPER.   *Erolia fuscicollis*. pp. 99, 119.
  Field marks: — 7–8.   The only *small* streaked Sandpiper with
a *white rump*, conspicuous in flight.   It is larger than the Semipalmated Sandpiper, smaller than the Pectoral.   In spring it is
quite rusty; in the fall, grayer than the other 'Peep.'
  Similar species: — The other small streaked Sandpipers ('Peep')
have only the *sides* of the rump white.   The similarly sized
Baird's Sandpiper does not have the conspicuous back-stripings
of this bird.   The fall Red-back is somewhat similar but larger,
with a much longer, more decurved bill.   *If in doubt, flush the
bird and look for the white rump.*
  Voice: — A thin mouse-like *jeet*, of similar quality to the *jee-jeet*
note of the Pipit.   Like the scraping of two flint pebbles.
  Range: — Arctic; migrates through Mississippi Valley and along
Atlantic coast.   Winters in s. South America.

BAIRD'S SANDPIPER.   *Erolia bairdii*.   pp. 99, 119.
  Field marks: — 7–7½.   A 'Peep' Sandpiper, larger than a Semipalmated or Western and paler, with *a buffy head and breast*, a
rather short bill, and blackish legs.
  Similar species: — The three smaller 'Peep' (Least, Semipalmated, and Western), the similarly sized White-rump, and the
larger Pectoral are more or less *striped* on the back; the Baird's
has a more *scaly* appearance, and the predominating color is
buff-brown.   The Buff-breasted Sandpiper is buffy from throat
to under tail-coverts, not on breast alone, and has *yellowish*, not
blackish, legs.   Do not confuse with spring and summer Sanderlings, which often show much orange-buff or rusty around the
head and breast (Baird's lacks the wing-stripe).
  Voice: — Note, *kreep*.
  Range: — Breeds in Arctic; migrates chiefly through Mississippi
Valley and Plains; rarest of 'Peep' Sandpipers on coast.   Prefers
sandy shores to mudflats.   Winters in s. South America.

LEAST SANDPIPER.   *Erolia minutilla*.   pp. 99, 119.
  Field marks: — 5–6½.   Collectively we call the small sparrow-
sized Sandpipers 'Peep' (Least, Semipalmated, Western, Baird's,
and White-rump).   All have a characteristic streaked, brown
pattern.   The Least is the smallest.   It may be known from the
slightly larger Semipalmated Sandpiper by the *yellowish* or
greenish, instead of blackish or greenish-black, legs, browner
coloration, *thinner* bill, and more streaked breast.   Least Sandpipers prefer the grassy and muddy parts of the marsh flats and
so are called 'mud peep,' Semipalmated Sandpipers are called
'sand peep.'   This is an aid, not a rule, as they sometimes mix.
  Similar species: — See above.
  Voice: — A sharp thin *kree-eet* more drawn out than that of
Semipalmated (more of an *ee* sound).

Range: — Breeds from Labrador to Nova Scotia; migrates through e. North America; winters along coast n. to North Carolina.

CURLEW SANDPIPER. *Erolia ferruginea.*   pp. 99, 118, 119.
Field marks: — 7–9. One of the rarest of shore-birds; characterized by the slim, *down-curved*, slightly curlew-like bill and a *whitish rump.*
Similar species: — In breeding plumage, reddish-breasted, a little like a spring Dowitcher, but the Dowitcher's bill is longer and straighter and its white rump more extensive. In winter plumage it is easily passed by as a winter Red-back, but is longer-legged, less streaked on the breast, and the bill is *curved slightly throughout its length,* not drooped only at the tip. All these things are differences of degree only. There is one definite point: the *whitish rump*; that of the Red-back is whitish along the sides only. The White-rumped Sandpiper is shorter-legged, shorter-billed, and like the Red-back shows more gray on the breast.
Voice: — *Chirrip* (less grating than Red-back) (Ticehurst).
Range: — Siberian; rare visitor to e. North America.

RED–BACKED SANDPIPER. *Erolia alpina pacifica.* Subsp.
pp. 99, 102, 119.
Field marks: — 8–9. Slightly larger than a Spotted Sandpiper. *Spring plumage:* — Rusty-red above, with a *black patch across the belly.* The only *Sandpiper* with a black belly. *Winter plumage:* — Plain unpatterned mouse-gray above, with a gray suffusion across the breast (not clean white like a Sanderling); the best mark is the rather long stout bill, which has a marked *downward droop* at the tip.
Similar species: — No other *Sandpiper* has a black belly (but Black-bellied and Golden Plovers and Turnstone have black on under parts). In fall or winter, lighter than a Purple Sandpiper, dingier than a Sanderling. Use the gray color and bill shape.
Voice: — A nasal, rasping *cheezp.*
Range: — Arctic; migrates through Great Lakes and along coast to Gulf of Mexico; winters sparingly n. to Long Island.

DOWITCHER. *Limnodromus griseus.* Subsp.   pp. 98, 118.
Field marks: — 11–12½. *The only snipe found on open shores.* (However, some people use the name 'Snipe' as a nickname for all shore-birds.) In any plumage recognized by the very long straight *snipe-like bill* and *white* lower back, rump, and tail. The white rump extends *up the back* in a long point (much farther than in other shore-birds with white rumps). In spring plumage the breast is washed with cinnamon-red; in fall, with light gray. The Dowitcher feeds like a sewing-machine, rapidly jabbing its long bill perpendicularly into the mud.

SNIPE, SANDPIPERS, AND PHALAROPES

WILSON'S SNIPE   p. 89.
   Long bill, pointed wings, orange tail, zig-zag flight.

WOODCOCK   p. 88.
   Long bill, rounded wings, dead-leaf color.

DOWITCHER   p. 97.
   Snipe bill, white tail and lower back.

SOLITARY SANDPIPER   p. 93.
   Dark wings, conspicuous white sides to the tail.

LESSER YELLOWLEGS   p. 94.
   Dark wings, whitish rump and tail.

STILT SANDPIPER   p. 100.
   Like preceding but legs greenish (see text).

SPOTTED SANDPIPER   p. 93.
   Identify by very short wing-stroke (giving a stiff bowed appearance).

WILSON'S PHALAROPE   p. 106.
   Fall: Suggests Yellowlegs; breast whiter, bill needle-like.

KNOT   p. 94.
   Fall: Stocky; grayish with light rump.
       Compare with Yellowlegs and Dowitcher.

SANDERLING   p. 105.
   Has most flashing stripe of any small shore-bird.
   Follows retreating waves like a clockwork toy.

NORTHERN PHALAROPE   p. 107.
   Fall: Sanderling-like, wing-stripe shorter, bill more needle-like.

RED PHALAROPE   p. 106.
   Fall: Sanderling-like, wing-stripe less contrasting; bill thicker than Northern Phalarope, legs yellowish.

Phalaropes swim on water; spin and dab.

WOODCOCK

WILSON'S
SNIPE

DOWITCHER

Fall

LESSER
YELLOW
LEGS

Fall

STILT
SANDPIPER

SOLITARY
SANDPIPER

Fall

WILSON'S
PHALAROPE

Fall

KNOT

SPOTTED
SANDPIPER

Fall

SANDERLING

Fall

NORTHERN
PHALAROPE

Fall

RED PHALAROPE

LEAST
SANDPIPER

SEMIPALMATED
SANDPIPER

BAIRD'S
SANDPIPER

WHITE-
RUMPED
SANDPIPER

PECTORAL
SANDPIPER

Below

BUFF-
BREASTED
SANDPIPER

Fall

CURLEW
SANDPIPER

PURPLE
SANDPIPER

Fall

RED-BACKED
SANDPIPER

UPLAND
PLOVER

WILLET

Plate 28   99

SANDPIPERS

LEAST SANDPIPER*   p. 96.
 Very small, brown; faint wing-stripe.

**SEMIPALMATED SANDPIPER ***   p. 101.
 Larger, grayer; identify by notes (see text).

**BAIRD'S SANDPIPER ***   p. 96.
 Still larger, browner, dark rump (see text).

**WHITE–RUMPED SANDPIPER ***   p. 96.
 White rump (only 'Peep' so marked).

PECTORAL SANDPIPER   p. 95.
 Like double-sized Least Sandpiper.
 Wing-stripe faint or lacking.

BUFF–BREASTED SANDPIPER   p. 101.
 Even buff below, contrasting with white wing-linings.

CURLEW SANDPIPER   p. 97.
 Fall: Suggests Red-backed Sandpiper, but rump *white*.

PURPLE SANDPIPER   p. 95.
 Slaty color; wave-washed rocks.

RED–BACKED SANDPIPER or DUNLIN   p. 97.
 Fall: Plain gray; larger than 'Peep,' darker than Sander-
     ling.

UPLAND PLOVER   p. 92.
 Brown; small head, long tail.
 Often flies like Spotted Sandpiper.

WILLET   p. 94.
 Large size, flashing wing-pattern.

  * The five small streaked Sandpipers are collectively nick-named
'Peep' (this includes the Western Sandpiper).

Similar species: — Wilson's Snipe, the only bird with similar proportions, is rarely found on open beaches and mud flats. It has a *dark* rump and tail.

Voice: — A rapid trebled *tu-tu-tu*, metallic and slightly yellow-legs-like. Some birds utter a single thin *keek*, occasionally trebled (see Subspecies).

Range: — Mud flats and margins. Breeds from Hudson Bay to Alaska; migrates along coast and less commonly inland; winters from Florida and Louisiana to South America.

STILT SANDPIPER. *Micropalama himantopus.*   pp. 98, 118.

   Field marks: — 7½–9. Long-legged; in spring, easily recognized; heavily marked with *transverse bars* beneath, and has a *rusty cheek patch*. In fall, gray above and white below; dark-winged and white-rumped. Not so easy to identify (see below).

   Similar species: — Suggests Dowitcher, particularly in fall. Is often found in its company and feeds like it (with a rapid perpendicular chopping motion of the head and bill) and, like it, often wades up to its belly and submerges its head. Its whiter under parts, shorter bill and longer legs distinguish it. Most writers liken it to a Yellow-legs, because of its flight pattern (dark wings and white rump), but it is smaller, with a conspicuous white stripe over the eye and *greenish*, not yellow, legs. The bill, which is proportionately longer and heavier, tapering markedly and with a slight droop at the tip gives the bird its dowitcher-like look (Long Island baymen thought it to be a cross between the Yellow-legs and Dowitcher).

   Voice: — A single note, like Lesser Yellow-legs, but lower and hoarser.

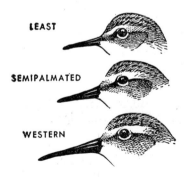

LEAST

SEMIPALMATED

WESTERN

TYPICAL BILLS OF 'PEEP'

Range: — Arctic; migrates chiefly w. of Mississippi; less common on Atlantic Coast (chiefly in fall). Winters in South America.

SEMIPALMATED SANDPIPER. *Ereunetes pusillus.* pp. 99, 119.
Field marks: — 5½–6½. The commonest of the 'Peep' in the East. Compared to the Least, the shorter, *stouter* bill is the most constant distinction. The bird is noticeably larger, grayer above, and usually has *blackish* legs.
Similar species: — Least Sandpiper is smaller, browner, thinner-billed and has *yellowish* legs. (See Western Sandpiper.)
Voice: — Commonest note a single *cherk* or *cheh*.
Range: — Arctic; migrates through e. North America; winters along coast n. to South Carolina.

WESTERN SANDPIPER. *Ereunetes mauri.* p. 119.
Similar species: — 6–7. This one is a sticker, hard to identify; when with Semipalmated Sandpipers, it appears a little larger and more coarsely marked. In typical birds the bill is *very noticeably longer, and thicker at the base,* and often droops slightly at the tip. It is usually carried pointing downward more. In breeding plumage it is rustier on the back and crown than the Semipalmated. A trace of rusty is often evident on the scapulars in the fall. This gives a two-toned effect — *rusty against gray.* Many individuals are noticeably pale-headed. The legs are black; hence there is no confusion with the smaller Least Sandpiper. The Western frequently forages in deeper water than is usual with the other 'Peeps.' In fall migration, it reaches its peak after the first of September, later than the others.
Voice: — A thin *jeep* or *jee-rp*, thinner than note of Semipalmated — more like squeak of White-rump.
Range: — Alaska; migrates along Atlantic Coast from New England s.; scarcer inland (Great Lakes, etc.). Commonest on coasts of Southern States, where it winters.

BUFF–BREASTED SANDPIPER. *Tryngites subruficollis.*
pp. 99, 119.
Field marks: — 7½–8½. A small, buffy shore-bird (slightly chunkier than Spotted) with short bill, round head, and yellowish legs; looks long-necked like a miniature Upland Plover, and like that bird frequents prairies and dry fields in preference to shores. No other small Sandpiper is so evenly buff-colored or yellowish. The under surface of the wing is *white* with a marbled tip. It is very tame.
Similar species: — The Baird's Sandpiper is buffy only across the breast; the throat and belly are white. The Baird's legs are *black* (Buff-breasted, yellowish).

SHORE-BIRDS

SNOWY PLOVER   p. 84.
    Dark legs, dark ear-patch, *slender* black bill; Gulf Coast.

PIPING PLOVER   p. 84.
    'Ringed'; color of *dry* sand (pale).

SEMIPALMATED or RINGED PLOVER   p. 84.
    'Ringed'; color of *wet* sand (dark).

WILSON'S PLOVER   p. 84.
    Large black bill.

KILLDEER   p. 85.
    Two breast rings.

BLACK–BELLIED PLOVER   p. 88.
    Spring: Black below, pale above.
    Fall: Plover shape; pale above, gray.

GOLDEN PLOVER   p. 85.
    Spring: Black below, dark above.
    Fall: Plover shape; dark above, brown.

RED–BACKED SANDPIPER or DUNLIN   p. 97.
    Spring: Rusty back, black belly.

RUDDY TURNSTONE   p. 88.
    Spring: Rusty back; face-pattern.
    Fall: Dark breast, orange legs.

WILSON'S PHALAROPE   p. 106.
    Female in spring: Dark neck stripe.
    Male in spring: Paler.

NORTHERN PHALAROPE   p. 107.
    Female in spring: Rusty neck, white throat.
    Male in spring: Duller.

RED PHALAROPE   p. 106.
    Female in spring: Rusty below, white cheeks.
    Male in spring: Duller.

SEMIPALMATED PLOVER

PIPING PLOVER

SNOWY PLOVER

WILSON'S PLOVER

KILLDEER

Fall

Fall

BLACK-BELLIED PLOVER

AMERICAN GOLDEN PLOVER

Spring

Spring

Spring

DUNLIN

Spring

Fall

RUDDY TURNSTONE

♂

♀

♂

♀

NORTHERN PHALAROPE
Spring

♂

♀

WILSON'S PHALAROPE
Spring

RED PHALAROPE
Spring

AMERICAN
OYSTERCATCHER

Spring

AMERICAN
AVOCET

BLACK–
NECKED
STILT

Spring

HUDSONIAN
GODWIT

Fall

MARBLED   GODWIT

LONG–BILLED
CURLEW

WHIMBREL

UPLAND
PLOVER

Plate 30   103

SHORE-BIRDS

AVOCET p. 105.
    Upturned bill, black and white back.
    Rusty neck (spring).

OYSTER–CATCHER (AMERICAN) p. 83.
    Large size, dark head, red bill.

BLACK–NECKED STILT p. 105.
    Black above, white below, red legs.

HUDSONIAN GODWIT p. 104.
    Spring: Upturned bill, rusty breast.
    Fall: Upturned bill, grayish breast.

MARBLED GODWIT p. 104.
    Upturned bill, brown.

UPLAND PLOVER p. 92.
    Small head, short bill, thin neck, long tail.

LONG–BILLED CURLEW p. 89.
    Very long bill; buffy, no head stripes.

HUDSONIAN CURLEW p. 89.
    Decurved bill, striped head.

Voice: — A low trilled *pr-r-r-reet* (Alexander Wetmore).
Range: — Arctic; migrates through prairies w. of Mississippi; rare on Atlantic Coast. Winters in Argentina and Uruguay.

MARBLED GODWIT. *Limosa fedoa.* pp. 90, 103.
Field marks: — 16–20. The Godwits are large shore-birds with very long, straight or perceptibly *upturned bills*. The uniform rich *buff-brown* coloration identifies this species.
Similar species: — The bills of Curlews turn *down*. See Long-billed Curlew and Hudsonian Godwit.
Voice: — A harsh *kret* or *kerret* (or '*godwit*').
Range: — Rare in most of East. Breeds from s. Canadian prairies to w. Minnesota and the Dakotas. In migration along coast from New England to Texas. Casual in Mississippi Valley; winters locally along coast from South Carolina s.

HUDSONIAN GODWIT. *Limosa hæmastica.* pp. 90, 103.
Field marks: — 14–16½. The large size (larger than the Greater Yellow-legs) and the long, straight or slightly *upturned* bill distinguish this bird as a Godwit; the tail, *ringed broadly with black and white*, proclaims it this species. In the spring it is dark reddish-breasted and looks almost black at a distance. In the fall, it is gray-backed and whitish-breasted. Flying overhead, the bird shows a *blackish under-wing surface*, very distinctive.
Similar species: — The Marbled Godwit is at all times mottled buffy-brown, without tail-pattern. The Hudsonian is more likely to suggest a very long-billed Willet.
Voice: — 'A low *qua qua*' (Wetmore); also sandpiper-like chattering; usually silent.
Range: — Rare, chiefly Atlantic Coast in fall, Mississippi Valley in spring. Breeds near Arctic; winters in s. South America.

RUFF; REEVE. *Philomachus pugnax.* p. 118.
Field marks: — 10–12½. Usually associates with Yellow-legs. Body size in *between the two species*, but *shorter legs* make it stand no higher than Lesser; bill *shorter* and *stouter* than Lesser, *yellow at base*; legs *dull ochre yellow or olive green*; in flight tail with striking pattern of broad *black central stripe* with *oval white patch on each side*. Males much larger than females. *Adult male, breeding:* — With striking ruffs and ear-tufts, which may be black, white, brown, buff, or barred, in all possible combinations. Very rare in New World. *Adults in remains or beginnings of breeding plumage:* — Brown above with much black spotting and mottling; throat and breast *equally dark*, in *sharp contrast* with whitish chin and white belly. Rare. *Adults, winter:* — *Brownish gray* above with paler edgings; whitish below, with *ashy brown* wash on *breast and sides*. Occasional. *Immature:* — Still browner with buffy edgings; whole chest and sides warm buff. Occasional.

Similar species: — Always browner than Yellow-legs *without white speckling*; Ruff never has black markings on flanks.
Range: — A straggler from the Old World. Over thirty records; recorded almost annually on coast in recent years.

LUDLOW GRISCOM

SANDERLING. *Crocethia alba.* pp. 98, 119.
Field marks: — 7–8½. A small, plump Sandpiper of the sand flats and outer beaches, where it chases the retreating waves 'like a clockwork toy.' It has a *flashing white stripe in the wing.* Other small shore-birds have wing-stripes, but in none does the stripe contrast so boldly or extend so far along the wing. It is a little larger than a Spotted Sandpiper; usually buffy to bright rusty about the head and breast in the spring; *the whitest of the Sandpipers in the fall* (nicknamed 'whitey'). Bill and legs stout and black.
Voice: — A short *kip* or *quit*, distinctive.
Range: — Arctic; migrates through e. North America; winters along coast n. to New Jersey and Long Island (occasionally).

Avocets and Stilts: Recurvirostridæ

AVOCET. *Recurvirostra americana.* pp. 90, 103.
Field marks: — 16–20. A very large shore-bird with a slender *upturned* somewhat godwit-like bill. This and the striking white and black pattern make it unique. In the breeding season the head and neck are pinkish-tan.
Voice: — A sharp *wheek*, or *kleek*, excitedly repeated.
Range: — Breeds in w. United States e. to North Dakota and n. Iowa (rare). Very rare e. of Mississippi.

BLACK–NECKED STILT. *Himantopus mexicanus.* pp. 90, 103.
Field marks: — 13½–15½. A large, slim wader; black above and white below, with *extremely long red legs.* In flight it is white beneath, with black, *unpatterned* wings.
Voice: — A sharp yipping.
Range: — Breeds in Florida, coastal South Carolina (a few) and on coast of Louisiana and Texas. It winters from Louisiana and Texas s.; a rare migrant in the w. plains.

Phalaropes: Phalaropodidæ

SMALL sandpiper-like birds with longer necks than most small
waders; equally at home wading or swimming. Two species, the
Northern and the Red Phalarope, are most commonly seen out at
sea, where, especially in the fall, they much resemble Sanderlings
except for their swimming habits. When feeding, they often spin
around like tops, rapidly dabbing their thin bills into the roiled
water. The females wear the bright colors, the males the dull —
a reversal of nature's usual order.

RED PHALAROPE. *Phalaropus fulicarius.*   pp. 98, 102, 119.
  Field marks: — 7½–9. The most maritime species of the family
  in migration, rarely occurring inland. The sea-going habits
  (swimming buoyantly like a tiny Gull) distinguish it as a Phalarope; in breeding plumage, the *reddish under parts* (blackish at
  a distance in poor light) and the white face designate it this
  species. The male is duller than the female but has her pattern.
  In fall and winter this species is blue-gray above and white
  below (see following).
  Similar species: — In fall it resembles a Sanderling but has a
  characteristic dark '*Phalarope-mark*' through the eye. In this
  plumage it is very similar to the Northern Phalarope, but is a
  little larger and paler *without back striping.* In flight the white
  wing-stripe of the Red does not contrast so much with the dark
  gray of the wing. The stripe can, in the Northern, be compared
  to that of a Sanderling, and, in the Red, to that of a Piping
  Plover. At close range, the thicker, shorter bill of the Red,
  yellowish toward the base, will identify it positively. The Northern has a more *needle-like* black bill.
  Voice: — Similar to Northern Phalarope.
  Range: — Breeds in Arctic; migrates along Atlantic Coast, well
  offshore; winters in South Atlantic.

WILSON'S PHALAROPE. *Steganopus tricolor.* pp. 98, 102, 118.
  Field marks: — 8½–10. This Phalarope is dark-winged (no
  wing-stripe as in the other Phalaropes) with a white rump. In
  breeding females the broad neck-stripe of *cinnamon blending into
  black* and the pale crown are the most conspicuous marks.
  Males are duller with just a wash of cinnamon on the neck.
  Fall plumage: — See below.
  Similar species: — In flight bears a striking resemblance to a
  little Yellow-legs (because of dark wings and white rump) particularly in fall. The Phalarope at that season is immaculately
  white below, with no breast-streaking, and has a thin needle-
  like bill, and greenish or straw-colored (not canary-yellow) legs.
  The swimming and spinning habit (less often indulged in than
  by other Phalaropes) is quite conclusive. (Yellow-legs occasion-

ally swim but do not spin and dab.) It is most often seen running along the margin in a very nervous manner and is first picked out among the other shore-birds by its very white breast.

Voice: — A grunting note, also a nasal *wurk*.

Range: — Breeds from s. Canadian prairies s. to Nebraska, Iowa, and nw. Indiana, rarely farther e.; rare but regular fall migrant on Atlantic Coast. Winters in s. South America.

NORTHERN PHALAROPE. *Lobipes lobatus.* pp. 98, 102, 119.

Field marks: — 6½–8. Should a 'Sanderling' be observed at sea, and should it light upon the water, then it is a Phalarope. The present species is the commonest 'Sea-Snipe' in the East, the one most likely to appear inland. Breeding females are gray above with a patch of *rufous-red on the side of the neck* and a white throat. Males are browner, with a similar pattern. In winter, both are gray above and white below, with a dark 'Phalarope-patch' through eye.

Similar species: — In full spring plumage Red Phalaropes are completely rufous below. In winter plumage, the way we usually see them (even in late summer), the two are much more similar (see Red Phalarope). The Northern Phalarope has a shorter wing-stripe than the Sanderling and flies with a deeper stroke.

Voice: — A sharp *kit*, or *whit*, similar to note of Sanderling.

Range: — Arctic; migrates chiefly offshore on coast and through prairie regions w. of Mississippi; winters in South Atlantic.

Jaegers: Stercorariidæ

THE JAEGERS are dark hawk-like or falcon-like sea-birds (their narrow wings with a pronounced angle at the joint, and slightly hooked beaks give them this look). Hawk-like they chase and plunder the Terns and Gulls. The dark immature Laughing Gull has this habit, too, so don't it a Jaeger. The plumages of Jaegers vary considerably; so we have (1) *a light phase*, with a black cap, paler back, and white under parts; (2) an *intermediate phase*, less cleanly marked, with shorter tail-feathers, barring on the sides, and a dusky breast-band; (3) *a dark phase* of uniform dark coloration. One noticeable field mark in all Jaegers is the *flash of white* in the wing created by the white wing-quills. This and the two projecting central tail-feathers immediately distinguish these birds as Jaegers. Immature Jaegers lack the projecting tail-feathers. They are heavily mottled and barred and must be given up as nigh hopeless to distinguish in the field. Ludlow Griscom writes: 'Young Parasitic Jaegers are the buffiest below and often have a pronounced cinnamon or rusty tone above. The Pomarine is *never* like this, and it is asserted that this is true of the Long-tailed also, though I am skeptical.' The rare Skua belongs to this group, but lacks the long central tail-feathers. The British call all Jaegers 'Skuas.'

POMARINE JAEGER. *Stercorarius pomarinus.* p. 7.
Field marks: — 20–23. Distinguished from other Jaegers by the central tail-feathers, which are *broad and twisted.* Although sometimes four inches long, they are usually stubby, projecting about an inch. The Pomarine is larger and heavier than the following species, usually heavily barred below, with a broad breast-band and more white in the primaries.
Similar species: — Immatures lacking the blunt central feathers can be told from immatures of the other two Jaegers when direct comparison is possible by their much heavier bill and larger size. (between that of Ring-billed and Herring Gulls); other two are closer to size of Laughing Gull.
Range: — Arctic; migrates off coast; winters off Atlantic and Gulf coasts of Southern States.

PARASITIC JAEGER. *Stercorarius parasiticus.* p. 7.
Field marks: — 16–21. A hawk-like sea-bird, the size of a Laughing Gull; chases the Terns and Gulls. It is known by its *pointed* central tail-feathers (projecting ½ to 3½ inches) and the flash of white in the wings (see illustration). It is the commonest of the three Jaegers. You must go to sea to see them (sometimes seen from shore).
Similar species: — Jaegers are very, very confusing. You will have to let many of them go by as 'just Jaegers.' Even experts do. See Jaegers (above) and Pomarine and Long-tailed Jaegers.
Range: — Arctic; migrates off coast. Winters from Florida to South America; occasional migrant inland.

LONG–TAILED JAEGER. *Stercorarius longicaudus.* p. 7.
Field marks: — 20–23. The Long-tail is much rarer than the other two Jaegers. Some birds have tail-points 9 or 10 inches long (but usually 3 to 6).
Similar species: — As the central tail-feathers of the Parasitic Jaeger vary greatly in length (up to 4 inches), only typical Long-tails with extremely attenuated points extending 6 to 10 inches can be safely identified by this character alone. Long-tails are usually much whiter on the breast than Parasitics in the same phase, and have a more clean-cut black cap, sharply defined against a broad white collar (breast and face of Parasitic are usually somewhat dingy or clouded). The back of the Long-tail is paler (in contrast to the black cap) and the yellow on the sides of the head is brighter. Look also for *blue-gray legs* (Parasitic, black), and white on two or three outer primary shafts only (Parasitic, four or five).
Range: — Arctic; in migration on open ocean and probably Great Lakes. Rarely noted. Probably winters off s. United States.

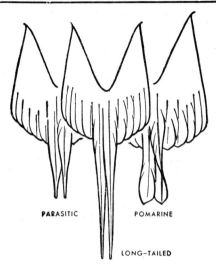

TAILS OF JAEGERS

SKUA. *Catharacta skua skua.* p. 7.
Field marks: — 20–22. A rare northern sea-bird, close to the size of a Herring Gull, but of much 'chunkier' appearance. Dark brown, with rusty under parts, a short *square-cut tail*, and *conspicuous white patches at the base of the primaries*. In air it suggests a Hawk (or a diminutive Eagle) more than a Gull. It soars only when at leisure and its beating flight is surprisingly strong and swift, a fact not fully evident until an observer notes the ease with which it overtakes other fleet-winged sea-birds and forces them to disgorge their catch.
Similar species: — Resembles a dark Jaeger but the wings are wider and rounded at the tips, not long and pointed; white wing-patches much more striking.
Range: — Fishing-banks off Newfoundland, Nova Scotia, and New England during winter.

ROBERT CUSHMAN MURPHY

Gulls: Larinæ

LONG-WINGED swimming birds with superb powers of flight. Gulls differ from Terns in averaging larger, and in having slightly hooked bills which point straight ahead in flight. Tern bills are straight and usually point downward at an angle. Most Gulls have square tails; Terns forked. Gulls are more robust with wider wings. They seldom dive, whereas Terns habitually fly above the water, then plunge into it. In Gull terminology the word *mantle* is used, meaning the upper surface of the wings and the broad strip of back separating them. The three commonest Gulls in most of the East *away from salt water* are the Herring, Ring-billed, and Bonaparte's.

GLAUCOUS GULL. *Larus hyperboreus hyperboreus.*   p. 122.
   Field marks: — 26–32. A large pale Gull *without dark wing-tips*; varying between the size of the Herring Gull and that of the Black-back. Immature birds in the first winter are pale cream-colored or pale buffy, but are recognizable by the *pale coloration and the 'frosty' primaries or wing-tips* which are even a shade lighter than the rest of the wing. Second-year birds are *extremely white* throughout. Adults, which occur less frequently, have a pale gray mantle but the *unmarked white primaries* are still conspicuous.
   Similar species: — Extremely like the Iceland Gull. Although typical Glaucous Gulls are much larger (Iceland is size of Herring Gull or smaller), they sometimes are similar in size. Then the best mark is the bill, which in the Glaucous is much longer and heavier. The wing of the Iceland is proportionately longer, extending well beyond the tip of the tail at rest. *Adult* Glaucous can be told at very close range by another mark, a narrow *yellow* ring around the eye (Iceland, red).
   Range: — Arctic, s. in winter along coast to New Jersey, occasionally farther. A few winter on Great Lakes.

ICELAND GULL. *Larus leucopterus.* Subsp.   pp. 122, 123.
   Field marks: — 23–26. A pale ghostly Gull, near size of Herring Gull. First-year birds are creamy or buffy; second-year birds are whitish throughout; adults have a pale gray mantle. All have *whitish or pure white wing-tips without any dark markings.* The Kumlien's Gull (*L. l. kumlieni*), now regarded as a sub-species of the Iceland Gull is similar but adults have *gray markings* toward the tips of the wings. For a fuller discussion see section on Subspecies.
   Similar species: — See Glaucous Gull. Race *kumlieni* sometimes approaches Thayer's Herring Gull (see Subspecies).
   Voice: — Very similar to that of Herring Gull (F. H. Allen).
   Range: — Arctic; a few wander s. in winter to Great Lakes and along coast to Maryland.

GREAT BLACK–BACKED GULL. *Larus marinus.* pp. 122, 123.
   Field marks: — 28–31. Much larger than the Herring Gull. Unmistakable. Even when so far distant that form becomes

indistinct, the dark slaty color of its back and wings stands out as a black spot superimposed on the white of its under parts. Immature birds are discussed below.

Similar species: — Young birds resemble corresponding stages of the Herring Gull, but are less brown, more contrasty, and paler on the head and under parts. The 'saddle-back' pattern, however, is quite evident, and the head and bill are noticeably larger.

Voice: — A low harsh *kyow*.

Range: — Breeds from Arctic along coast to Long Island (rarely); in winter s. to Great Lakes and Virginia; rarely Florida.

HERRING GULL. *Larus argentatus.* Subsp.   pp. 122, 123.
  Field marks: — 23–26. The common large 'Sea Gull' of much of the interior and of the coast. Acquaint yourself with this species thoroughly before attempting to recognize the others. It should be the basis of comparison. *Adult:* — The only large gray-mantled Gull that combines black wing-tips and *fresh-colored legs. Immature in first year:* — The common dusky-brown Gull one sees in such numbers. No other young Gull is quite so dark and uniform in coloration. *Immature in second year:* — Whiter. The tail-feathers are dark contrasting with the white of the rump.
  Similar species: — See Ring-billed Gull.
  Voice: — A loud *kee-ow, kee-ow,* also whining and squealing notes. A dry *gah-gah-gah* about colonies.
  Range: — Breeds from Arctic s. on coast to Long Island and to larger lakes near Canadian border of United States; winters from Gulf of St. Lawrence and Great Lakes to Gulf of Mexico.

CALIFORNIA GULL. *Larus californicus.*
  Similar species: — 20–23. Slightly smaller than Herring Gull, with *gray-green* instead of flesh-colored legs. The smaller Ring-billed Gull also has greenish legs, but this species has a *red* or *red and black* spot on the lower mandible of bill, not a complete black ring as in the adult Ring-bill. Immatures are very difficult and no attempt should be made to identify them in the area covered by this book. They are described in *A Field Guide to Western Birds.*
  Range: — Western United States; breeds e. to Stump and Devils Lakes in e. North Dakota. Probably migrates through Great Plains; winters to coast of Texas.

RING–BILLED GULL. *Larus delawarensis.*   pp. 122, 123.
  Field marks: — 18–20. *Adult:* — Almost identical in pattern with the Herring Gull; distinguished by smaller size, conspicuous *black ring* on bill, and *yellowish* or *greenish legs.*
  Similar species: — Adult Herring Gull is larger; has flesh-colored

legs. On the wing, the Ring-bill is more buoyant and dove-like and shows much more black on the *under side* of the primaries, or long wing-feathers. *Immature:* — Often confused with second-year Herring Gull, which has semblance of ring on its longer bill. In the Herring Gull the tail terminates in a *broad* band (tail-feathers dark, contrasting with the whitish rump). The band near the tip of the tail of the Ring-bill is narrower (a little over an inch wide). The leg color is not too useful in young birds as many young Ring-bills have pinkish or flesh-gray legs.

Voice: — Notes higher-pitched than Herring Gull.

Range: — Breeds from James Bay and n. shore of Gulf of St. Lawrence s. to North Dakota and Lake Ontario. Migrates throughout United States to Gulf of Mexico; winters n. to Great Lakes and New England.

BLACK-HEADED GULL. *Larus ridibundus ridibundus.* p. 123.

Similar species: — 14–15. A rare visitor from Europe. Similar to Bonaparte's Gull, with the same sequence of plumages, and found with it. *Minutely larger*, bill *noticeably longer.* *Adult:* — In breeding plumage, hood *dark brown* instead of black. *Paler gray* above, with more white on outer edge of wing in front of black tip (close range only); *under surface of primaries slate-gray to blackish*, very conspicuous; bill *dark red*, not black. Old birds have a rosy 'bloom' on the breast. *Immature:* — Very close to Bonaparte's Gull, but slightly larger; the longer bill *yellow for basal half* with a blackish tip; under surface of primaries at first white, later somewhat darker.

Range: — European. In recent years of regular occurrence at several favored spots on the coast of New England and Long Island.

LUDLOW GRISCOM

LAUGHING GULL. *Larus atricilla.* pp. 122, 123.

Field marks: — 15½–17. A little smaller than a Ring-billed Gull; larger than a Bonaparte's. Distinguished from other small Gulls by its *dark mantle* that blends into the dark wing-tips and the conspicuous *white border* that lines the hind edge of the wings. In the breeding season, the head is black; in winter white with dark markings. The immature bird is a very dark small Gull with a *white rump*. The white border on the rear edge of the wing and the dark breast are also good marks.

Similar species: — On Texas coast in migration can be confused with Franklin's Gull.

Voice: — A high strident laugh, *ha-ha-ha-ha-ha-haah-haah-haah*; also a single *kew*, lower than Common Tern's scream.

Range: — Atlantic and Gulf Coasts; breeds on grassy islands or salt marshes from Nova Scotia to Texas. Winters from South Carolina s.; casual inland.

FRANKLIN'S GULL. *Larus pipixcan.*   pp. 122, 123.
   Field marks: — 13½–15. The 'Prairie Dove' of the Great
Plains. The best mark is the *broad white band* which separates
the black wing-tips from the gray of the rest of the wing. Overhead, this white band is like a 'window,' transmitting light. In
summer the breast has a pale rosy 'bloom' (hard to see), and
the head is black. In fall and winter the bloom is gone, and
the head is white, with a dark patch extending from the eye
around the back of the nape.
   Similar species: — In actions and voice, the counterpart of the
Laughing Gull of the coast. Ordinarily found together only on
the Gulf Coast in migration and winter. The sharply zoned
black and white wing-tips easily identify the Franklin's (Laughing has dark, blended wing-tips). On the prairies the only other
small Gulls are the Bonaparte's and the Ring-bill. There is a
long triangle of white in the front edge of the Bonaparte's wing,
giving a very different effect. The Ring-bill has white spots or
'mirrors' within the black wing-tips, and pale legs (Franklin's,
dark). Immatures are quite different from young Bonaparte's
or young Ring-bills, *small dark-backed Gulls with conspicuous
white rumps*, and a dusky smudge around the back of the head.
They are so similar to some stages of the young Laughing Gull
that I do not regard it as safe to try to distinguish them. Typical
brown young Laughing Gulls with brown breasts and brown
foreheads can be distinguished, however. If your bird is seen
on the Great Lakes or farther west, it is most likely a Franklin's;
if on the Atlantic Coast, it is almost unquestionably a Laughing.
   Range: — Great Plains; breeds from s. Canadian prairies to
South Dakota and sw. Minnesota; migrates to Gulf coast of
Louisiana and Texas. Occasional on Great Lakes in fall and
becoming more frequent (usually dark immatures which are
often responsible for erroneous records of Laughing Gulls).
Accidental on Atlantic Coast.

BONAPARTE'S GULL. *Larus philadelphia.*   pp. 122, 123.
   Field marks: — 12–14. The smallest American Gull. Near size
of a Tern and often acts like one. Can be identified at a distance by the long triangle of white in the front edge of the wing
(see diagram). In breeding plumage this species has a black
head. In winter adults and immatures the head is white with a
conspicuous round black spot behind the eye. Immature birds
have a narrow black band on the tip of the tail.
   Range: — Breeds in nw. Canada; migrates through e. North
America to Florida and Gulf of Mexico. A few winter as far n.
as Great Lakes and s. New England.

LITTLE GULL. *Larus minutus.*   p. 123.
   Similar species: — 10½–11½. A rare straggler from Europe.

Similar to Bonaparte's Gull, with same sequence of plumages, and usually associating with it. Always appreciably, often *strikingly, smaller. Adult: — Wing-tip without black markings; under surface of wings smoke-gray to blackish,* in striking contrast. Bill *dark red in summer only,* otherwise black. *Immature:* — Under surface of wings *white.* With *much more black* in wings than Bonaparte's; a broad transverse bar across fore-wing meets black primaries, forming in flight a *striking zigzag pattern,* resembling young Kittiwake, and causing it to be misidentified as Sabine's Gull (*q.v.*). *Juvenile (first summer and fall):* — Almost *solid blackish above,* with a white area in wings back of black tips; Bonaparte's Gull is grayish above, extensively mottled with buffy brownish.

Range: — European. An occasional straggler: in recent years of regular occurrence at favored spots on the coast of New England, Long Island, and the Great Lakes.

LUDLOW GRISCOM

IVORY GULL. *Pagophila eburnea.*   p. 122.
Field marks: — 15–17. Pigeon-sized, with a pigeon-like look. The only all-white Gull with *black* legs. The wings are remarkably long, and in flight the bird appears as large as an Iceland Gull, but the flight is quite Tern-like. Immature birds are similar enough to be recognized but have a few dusky spots about the head, wings, and tail.
Similar species: — The other two 'white-winged' Gulls (without dark wing-tips), the Iceland and the Glaucous, are larger, with flesh-colored legs (Ivory Gull has black legs).
Range: — Very rare south of Arctic, even in winter.

KITTIWAKE. *Rissa tridactyla tridactyla.*   pp. 122, 123
Field marks: — 16–18. An open ocean Gull, seldom seen from shore. It is smaller than either the Herring or Ring-billed, which it resembles in coloration. The legs of the Kittiwake are *black.* Another good point is the wing-tips, which are *solid black* and cut *straight across,* as if they had been dipped in ink.
Similar species: — Herring and Ring-billed Gulls are larger, have white spots or 'mirrors' in the black wing-tips. Subadult Ring-bills without white spots in their black wing-tips have been called Kittiwakes by the inexperienced. Their legs are pale (Kittiwake black). The immature Kittiwake is most likely to be confused with the Bonaparte's Gull in the same plumage, but the Kittiwake has a dark bar on the back of the neck, instead of a dark spot behind the eye, and has more black in the outer primaries and the *fore border* of the wing.
Voice: — '*Keet, keet, wäck, wäck*' (R. Hoffmann).
Range: — Oceanic; breeds from Gulf of St. Lawrence to Arctic winters off coast s. to New Jersey.

SABINE'S GULL. *Xema sabini.*   pp. 122, 123.
  Field marks: — 13–14. The only Gull with a strongly *forked
  tail* (young Kittiwake is slightly forked). The jet-black outer
  primaries and the triangular white patch behind them create a
  wing-pattern that renders this rare little Gull unmistakable.
  The head is dark only in breeding plumage. The immature is
  dark grayish brown above (see diagram).
  Similar species: — Immature Kittiwake (see diagram).
  Range: — Arctic; very rare migrant in August, September, and
  May on open ocean; occasional in interior.

Terns: Sterninæ

GULL-LIKE sea-birds, more slender in build, narrower of wing, and
more graceful in flight than Gulls. The bill is slenderer and sharper-
pointed, usually held pointed downward toward the water. The
tail is usually forked. Most Terns are whitish, with black caps.
In winter this cap is imperfect, the black of the forehead being
largely replaced by white. A Tern habit is to plunge headfirst
into the water Kingfisher fashion.

GULL–BILLED TERN. *Gelochelidon nilotica aranea.* pp. 130, 134.
  Field marks: — 13–14½. The *stout*, almost gull-like *black* bill
  is the best field mark. Larger and paler than the Common or
  Forster's Tern, with tail much less forked; feet black. In winter
  the black cap is lost, the head is nearly white. It often feeds on
  insects over marshes.
  Similar species: — Young birds with their dusky head markings
  and short stubby bills look for all the world like very small Gulls
  (actually suggest winter European Little Gull but lack dusky
  wing-linings). Unless very young, the slightly notched tail gives
  away their identity.
  Voice: — A rasping, three-syllabled *za-za-za* (very katydid-like
  in quality) or *kay-weck*, *kay-weck*.
  Range: — Coastal; Maryland to Texas, breeding locally. Found
  inland in Florida (Okeechobee). Winters on Gulf Coast.

FORSTER'S TERN. *Sterna forsteri.*   pp. 130, 134.
  Field marks: — 14–15. A Tern with frosty wing-tips. Very
  similar to the Common Tern. White, with pale gray mantle
  and black cap; bill orange-red with a black tip; feet orange-red;
  tail deeply forked. *Fall and winter plumage:* — Similar, but
  without the black cap; instead, a heavy black spot, like an ear-
  cap, on the side of the whitish head. The bill at this season is
  black.
  Similar species: — Generally considered difficult to identify be-

cause of its close resemblance to the Common Tern, but with practice it becomes easy. From above, the primaries of the Forster's are *silvery* (lighter than rest of wing), in direct contrast to those of the Common, which are *dusky* (darker than rest of wing). The tail of the Common is whiter, contrasting more strikingly with the gray of the back. The bill of the Forster's is more orange. The Forster's Tern is a marsh nester; colonies of Commons are on sandy islands or beaches. In the fall, both adult and immature Forster's Terns have a black patch through the eye and ear, while in the Common Tern this same dark area extends from the eye clear around the back of the head. This ear-patch is the surest mark of all. The dusky patch on the fore part of the wing in the immature Common Tern is absent in the Forster's.

Voice: — A harsh nasal *za-a-ap* or a nasal *keer* not so drawn out as note of Common Tern.

Range: — Breeds in salt marshes along coast from Maryland to Texas and in w. prairie marshes e. to Minnesota and ne. Illinois. In late summer and fall n. to Massachusetts (a few); winters from South Carolina s.

COMMON TERN. *Sterna hirundo hirundo.* pp. 130, 134.
  Field marks: — 13–16. Terns are the small black-capped gull-like birds with the swallow-like forked tails. As the name indicates, this is the commonest species. *Adult in breeding plumage:* — White, with a light-gray mantle and black cap; bill orange-red with a black tip; feet orange-red; tail deeply forked. *Immature and winter adult:* — Similar, without complete black cap; instead, a black patch extending from the eye around the back of the head. The red bill becomes blackish.
  Similar species: — See Forster's, Arctic, and Roseate Terns.
  Voice: — A drawling *kee-arr* (downward inflection). Also, *kik-kik-kik.*
  Range: — Breeds locally on sandy beaches and small islands from Gulf of St. Lawrence and n. Manitoba s. to Great Lakes and Gulf of Mexico; winters from Florida s.

ARCTIC TERN. *Sterna paradisaea.* pp. 130, 134.
  Field marks: — 14–17. The Arctic Tern is grayer than any of the other species which it closely resembles. The bill of the breeding adult is blood-red *to the tip.*
  Similar species: — Very difficult to distinguish from the Common Tern. A fair mark is the *white streak below the black cap.* In the Common the whole face seems whiter. However, the slightly grayer coloration of the Arctic is not reliable because of the varying effects of light. The blood-red bill is the best mark: that of the Roseate Tern is largely black, and those of the Common and Forster's are orange-red, *usually* (but not always)

tipped with black. The tarsi of the Arctic Tern are shorter, so when the bird is at rest with Common Terns, it stands lower. The tail is longer and more streaming (projecting slightly beyond the wing-tips when at rest). Immature birds are indistinguishable (unless the shorter and darker legs and paler shoulder patch can be relied on). Fall adults are not safely told either, as the red bill and feet become quite dusky. Moreover, some Common Terns lose the black bill-tip for a while in late summer, accounting for the sight records of Arctics south of New England.

Voice: — Notes similar to Common Tern's; but a whistled *kee, kee*, with rising inflection is said to be characteristic.

Range: — Arctic, breeding locally on islands s. to Massachusetts. Oceanic, departing eastward across Atlantic after nesting. Sight records south of New England open to question.

ROSEATE TERN. *Sterna dougallii dougallii.* pp. 130, 134.
Field marks: — 14–17. *Adult:* — About size of Common Tern. White, with a very pale gray mantle, black cap, *black bill* (not always), and red feet; tail very deeply forked.

Similar species: — In most individuals the black bill sets it apart from similar species; Common, Forster's, and Arctic Terns all have reddish bills (except in winter). Many Roseates have some red around the base of the bill, and it is not uncommon to find birds with bills almost as red as those of Common Terns. Then the other characters must be relied on. Roseates in flight appear whiter than Common Terns (creamier under parts and pale primaries) and the wing-stroke is deeper. Close inspection reveals extremely long outer tail-feathers. At rest, the tail-tips extend far beyond the wing-tips; in the Common this is reversed.

Voice: — A rasping *ka-a-ak* and a soft two-syllabled *chu-ick* or *chivy* vaguely suggestive of the Semipalmated Plover. This last note, constantly uttered, is far more useful in identifying both adults and young in late summer than any mark.

Range: — Coastal, breeding in widely separated localities from Nova Scotia to Texas. Most common near e. Long Island and s. New England. Winters s. of United States.

SOOTY TERN. *Sterna fuscata fuscata.* p. 131.
Field marks: — 15–17. *The only Tern that is black above and white below;* cheeks and patch on the forehead white; bill and feet black. *Immature:* — Brown all over; lighter on the under parts; back spotted with white.

Similar species: — The accidental Bridled Tern is similar. See Accidentals (West Indian and Tropical Birds). See also Black Skimmer.

Voice: — Its nasal three-syllabled note has given it the nickname '*Wide-a-wake.*' Chapman renders it '*ker-wacky-wack.*'

Range: — Breeds on Dry Tortugas (Florida); sometimes carried northward by West Indian hurricanes to New England coast.

SHORE-BIRDS

WOODCOCK   p. 88.
  Long bill, barred crown; chunky.

WILSON'S SNIPE   p. 89.
  Long bill, striped crown.

DOWITCHER   p. 100.
  Spring: Snipe bill, rusty breast.
  Fall: Snipe bill, gray breast.

CURLEW SANDPIPER   p. 97.
  Spring: Decurved bill, rufous breast.

KNOT   p. 95.
  Spring: Short bill, rusty breast; chunky.

STILT SANDPIPER   p. 100.
  Spring: Barred breast, rusty ear-patch.
  Fall: Long greenish legs, white rump, eye-line (see text).

RUFF   p. 104.
  See text.

WILSON'S PHALAROPE   p. 106.
  Fall: Needle bill, white breast (see text).

SOLITARY SANDPIPER   p. 93.
  Dark back, eye-ring, dark legs.

LESSER YELLOW-LEGS   p. 95.
  Yellow legs, slim bill.

GREATER YELLOW-LEGS   p. 94.
  Yellow legs, larger bill.
  Identify by calls (see text).

WILLET   p. 94.
  Gray color, stocky bill, dark legs.

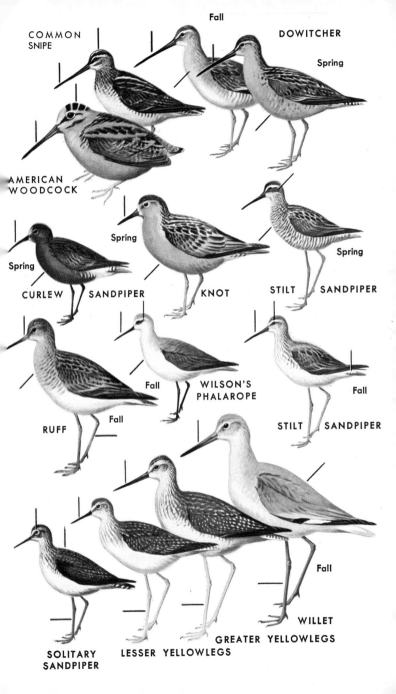

COMMON
SNIPE

Fall

DOWITCHER

Spring

AMERICAN
WOODCOCK

Spring

CURLEW SANDPIPER

Spring

KNOT

STILT SANDPIPER

Spring

RUFF

Fall

WILSON'S
PHALAROPE

STILT SANDPIPER

Fall

WILLET

Fall

SOLITARY
SANDPIPER

LESSER YELLOWLEGS

GREATER YELLOWLEGS

Fall

SPOTTED S.

Spring

RED PHALAROPE

Fall

Winter

PURPLE S.

Fall

NORTHERN
PHALAROPE

Fall

DUNLIN

Fall

CURLEW S.

Fall

SANDERLING

Fall

KNOT

SANDERLING   Spring

Fall

PECTORAL S.

WHITE-
RUMPED S.

BUFF- BREASTED S

LEAST S.

BAIRD'S S.

Fall

Spring

WESTERN S.

WHITE-RUMPED S.

Fall

SEMIPALMATED S.

Plate 32   119

SHORE-BIRDS

SPOTTED SANDPIPER   p. 93.
    Spring: Spotted breast; teeters.
    Fall: Shoulder-mark; teeters.

RED PHALAROPE   p. 106.
    Fall: Eye-patch, yellow bill, unstreaked back.

NORTHERN PHALAROPE   p. 107.
    Fall: Eye-patch, thin black bill, striped back.

RED—BACKED SANDPIPER or DUNLIN   p. 97.
    Fall: Decurved bill, grayish breast.

PURPLE SANDPIPER   p. 95.
    Portly, slaty, yellow legs; on rocks.

CURLEW SANDPIPER   p. 97.
    Fall: Decurved bill, white rump.

KNOT   p. 95.
    Fall: Chunky, gray, short bill (see text).

SANDERLING   p. 105.
    Fall: Whitish, stout bill, white wing-stripe.
    Spring: Rusty, white wing-stripe.

PECTORAL SANDPIPER   p. 96.
    Sharp division between breast and belly; striped back.

WHITE—RUMPED SANDPIPER   p. 96.
    Fall: Gray, white rump.
    Spring: Browner, white rump.

BAIRD'S SANDPIPER   p. 96.
    Buffy breast, scaly back, black legs.

BUFF—BREASTED SANDPIPER   p. 101.
    Buffy under parts, yellow legs.

LEAST SANDPIPER   p. 97.
    Small size, slim bill, yellow-green legs.

SEMIPALMATED SANDPIPER   p. 101.
    Stouter bill, black legs.

WESTERN SANDPIPER   p. 101.
    Bill longer, drooped at tip.

LEAST TERN. *Sterna albifrons.* Subsp.   pp. 131, 134.
  Field marks: — 8½–9½. A *very small* Tern with a *yellow* bill.
  Adult: — White, with a pale-gray mantle; white patch cutting
  into black cap on forehead; bill and feet *yellow. Immature:* —
  Bill darker; dark patch from eye around back of head; large
  dark areas on fore edge of wings. In the fall both adults and
  young have black bills but the legs still show some yellow (quite
  dull).
  Similar species: — May be mistaken for the fall Black Tern,
  but is smaller, paler above, with a *whitish,* instead of dark, tail.
  Young Common Terns, with their rather short tails and white
  foreheads, might possibly be mistaken for Least Terns, but the
  orange-color of the feet and wider wings help identify these
  larger birds.
  Voice: — A harsh squealing *zeek;* also *pee-dee.*
  Range: — Breeds on coast from Texas to Massachusetts, also
  in Mississippi and Missouri River systems n. to Iowa, Ohio,
  sw. Kansas, and Nebraska; winters from Louisiana s.

ROYAL TERN. *Thalasseus maximus maximus.*   pp. 130, 134
  Similar species: — 18–21. The more deeply forked tail and
  more slender *orange* or *yellow-orange* bill are the best marks by
  which to differentiate the Royal from the more heavily built
  Caspian Tern, which has a bright-red bill. (Although I have
  found bill color reliable, some observers have not, claiming that
  young and winter Caspians often have orange bills.) At rest
  the wing-tips of the Caspian extend beyond the end of the tail;
  those of most Royals barely reach the tail-tip, but this, too,
  varies, particularly in winter. Although some Royal Terns in
  spring show a solid black cap, they usually (even in the nesting
  season) have much white on the forehead, the black head-
  feathers forming a sort of crest — almost like horns standing out
  from the head. Caspians in fall or winter never have a clear
  white forehead; it is always clouded by streakings.
  Voice: — A shrill *keer,* higher than note of Caspian.
  Range: — Coast, breeds from Virginia to Texas; winters from
  South Carolina s.

CABOT'S TERN. *Thalasseus sandvicensis acuflavida.* pp. 130, 134.
  Field marks: — 14–16. The long slender black bill with its *yellow
  tip* is as good a field mark as any; it marks the Cabot's Tern
  immediately. This species, which seems to prefer the company
  of Royal Terns, is slightly larger and more slender than the
  Common Tern. It is white with a pale-gray mantle and black
  cap (white forehead later in season); feathers on back of crown
  elongated, giving a crested appearance at times; the feet are
  black. In immature birds the yellow bill-tip is often hard to see.
  Voice: — A hoarse, grating *kirr-ick.*

Range: — Coast from North Carolina to Texas; breeds locally, often in colonies of Royal Terns. Winters from Florida s.

CASPIAN TERN. *Hydroprogne caspia.*   pp. 130, 134.

Field marks: — 19–23. Almost the size of a Herring Gull, from which it may be distinguished by its black cap, *large red bill*, and forked tail.

Similar species: — The great size and large bill set the Caspian apart from all other Terns except the Royal. The Caspian occurs over most of the East as a migrant on the larger bodies of water, but the Royal is confined to the southern coasts. The tail of the Caspian is forked for only a quarter of its length; that of the Royal for fully half its length. The bill of the Royal is slenderer, *orange* rather than red. The Royal has a more *crested* look and usually has a lot of *clear white on the forehead.* The Caspian, even in winter plumage, has a clouded, streaked forehead. In mixed flocks Caspians often show much more dark in the long wing-feathers from below, very conspicuous in adults.

Voice: — A hoarse, low-pitched *kaa-uh* or *kaah.*

Range: — Breeds locally on Great Lakes, n. shore of Gulf of St. Lawrence, and along Gulf of Mexico. Has bred in Virginia and South Carolina. Occurs as a migrant on the larger bodies of water; winters from South Carolina s.

BLACK TERN. *Chlidonias nigra surinamensis.*   pp. 131, 134.

Field marks: — 9–10. The only *Black-bodied Tern. Breeding plumage:* — Head and under parts black; back and wings gray; under tail-coverts white. *Immature and adult in winter plumage:* — Head and under parts white; back and wings gray; dark markings on head, about eye, ear, and back of neck. The short tail and swooping wing-beats are good points. The winter plumage comes early; changing birds, mottled and splotched, appear in midsummer.

Similar species: — In fall the more graceful flight, grayer look, small size, and only slightly notched tail distinguish it from the Common-Forster's-Roseate group. See Least Tern.

Voice: — A sharp *keek* or *klea.*

Range: — Breeds in inland marshes from cent. Manitoba and Ontario s. to Missouri and Tennessee, and e. to w. Pennsylvania, cent. New York, and n. Vermont (a few). Migrates through Mississippi Valley and along coast and salt marshes (chiefly in summer and fall). Winters in South America.

NODDY. *Anous stolidus stolidus.*   p. 131.

Field marks: — 15. *The only brown Tern* (except immature Sooty) and the only Tern with a *rounded* tail. The *whitish cap* on a dark bird gives a reverse or 'negative' effect in contrast to the other Terns with their dark caps and light bodies.

GULLS
(Adults)

GLAUCOUS GULL   p. 110.
    Size of Black-backed Gull; white wing-tips.

ICELAND GULL   p. 110.
    Size of Herring Gull, white wing-tips.
    Bill proportionately smaller than that of Glaucous.

IVORY GULL   p. 114.
    All white, black legs.

KUMLIEN'S GULL   p. 262.
    A recognizable race of the Iceland Gull.
    Gray spots toward tips of wing.

RING–BILLED GULL   p, 111.
    Like small Herring Gull.
    Ring on bill; legs yellowish.

HERRING GULL   p. 111.
    Gray mantle, black wing-tips, pink legs.

FRANKLIN'S GULL *   p. 113.
    White 'windows' separating black on wing from gray.

KITTIWAKE   p. 114.
    'Dipped in ink' wing-tips; black legs.

LAUGHING GULL *   p. 112.
    Small size; dark wings with white border.

BONAPARTE'S GULL *   p. 113.
    Wedge of white in primaries.

GREAT BLACK–BACKED GULL   p. 110.
    Large size, black back and wings.

SABINE'S GULL *   p. 115.
    Black outer primaries, white triangle, forked tail.

    * Adults in winter lose the black heads.

GLAUCOUS

ICELAND

KUMLIEN'S

IVORY

RING–BILLED

HERRING

FRANKLIN'S

Summer

KITTIWAKE

LAUGHING

Summer

BONAPARTE'S

Summer

GREAT
BLACK–BACKED

Summer

SABINE'S

GREAT BLACK-BACKED
Immature

RING-BILLED
Immature

HERRING
First Winter

HERRING
Second Winter

HERRING

ICELAND
First Winter

LAUGHING
First Winter

FRANKLIN'S
First Winter

KITTIWAKE
Immature

SABINE'S
Immature

BONAPARTE'S
Immature

LITTLE
Immature
Adult (below)
Adult (above)

BLACK-HEADED
Adult (above)
Adult (below)

Plate 34   123

GULLS

(Immatures and two European wanderers)

GREAT BLACK–BACKED GULL   p. 110.
    Immature: More contrast between back and underparts
        than in young Herring Gull.

RING–BILLED GULL   p. 111.
    Immature: Narrow tail-band.

HERRING GULL   p. 111.
    First winter: Relatively uniform brown.
    Second winter: Whiter, with tail broadly black.

ICELAND GULL   p. 110.
    First winter: Buffy, with light wing-tips.
    Second winter: Very white throughout.
        (Glaucous Gull has same sequence of plu-
        mages.)
                                                 p. 112.

LAUGHING GULL
    First winter: Small dark Gull; white rump.

FRANKLIN'S GULL   p. 113.
    First winter: Like Laughing but breast and forehead
        whiter. (Young Laughing at a later stage
        can be almost identical.)

KITTIWAKE   p. 114.
    Immature: Dark diagonal band across wing.

SABINE'S GULL   p. 115
    Immature: Forked tail and Sabine's wing pattern.
        (Young Kittiwakes are quite similar.)

BONAPARTE'S GULL   p. 113.
    Immature: Black cheek-spot, narrow tail-band.

LITTLE GULL   p. 113.
    Adult: Blackish wing-linings, no black wing-tips.
    First winter: Wing-lining white; wings with Kittiwake
        like or Sabine-like pattern.

BLACK–HEADED GULL   p. 112.
    Adult: Like large Bonaparte's Gull, bill red.
        Wings from below show much dusky (Bonaparte's
        lacks this).

Similar species: — Young Sooty Terns are all-dark and hurricane-blown strays might be mistaken for Noddies. Look for the *forked tail* of the Sooty (Noddy has *rounded* tail, *usually* shows light forehead).

Range: — Breeds in Dry Tortugas (Florida). Like the Sooty Tern it is sometimes carried north by tropical hurricanes.

Skimmers: Rynchopidæ

BLACK SKIMMER. *Rynchops nigra nigra.*   p. 131.
Field marks: — 16–20. The remarkable scissor-like bill sets the Skimmer apart. It is a striking black and white bird, smaller and more slender than the Herring Gull, with extremely long wings. The bright red bill (tipped with black) is long and flat vertically, the lower mandible jutting out nearly a third farther than the upper. The immature bird is smaller and browner with a smaller bill, but you will know at once that it is a Skimmer. This purely maritime species skims low, dipping its long lower mandible in the salt water, cutting it like a knife. Some fishermen call it 'Shearwater.'

Voice: — Soft, short, barking notes.

Range: — Coastal; a bird of the sheltered bays; breeds from Texas to Long Island and Massachusetts (1946); winters from South Carolina and Gulf of Mexico s.

Auks, Murres, and Puffins: Alcidæ

'ALCIDS' are the nearest thing we have to Penguins in this part of the world. They are duck-like in appearance, but have short necks, and pointed or deep and compressed bills. When flying, they beat their small narrow wings in a rapid whir, and are given to much circling and veering, seldom holding the straight course of a Duck. On the rocky sea islands where some species nest in crowded colonies they stand nearly erect, Penguin-like.

Birds of this group frequent the open sea and rarely appear on fresh water. They descend to the latitude of the Northern States mainly in winter. The best time to watch for them from vantage points along the coast is during nasty weather, when a few strays are sometimes blown close inshore.

RAZOR-BILLED AUK. *Alca torda torda.*   p. 11
Field marks: — 16–18. Size of a small duck. Black above and white below; characterized by its rather heavy head, bull neck, and deep and compressed bill which is crossed midway by a

conspicuous *white* mark. On the water the *cocked wren-like tail*
of the Razor-bill is often characteristic.

Similar species: — The immature Razor-bill has a smaller bill
than the adult and it lacks the white marks (hence closely
resembles Brünnich's Murre) but the bill is still stubby and
rounded enough to suggest its parentage. (See diagram.)

Range: — Breeds on islands off coast from Arctic s. to Bay of
Fundy; winters on ocean s. to Long Island.

ATLANTIC, or COMMON, MURRE. *Uria aalge aalge.* **p. 11**
Field marks: — 16–17. Size of a small Duck with a slender
pointed bill, longer than that of any other 'Alcid.' *Breeding
plumage:* — Head, neck, back, and wings *dark*; under parts and
line on the hind edge of the wing *white*. *Winter plumage:* —
Similar, but white on the throat and side of face, and a *short
black mark extending from eye into white of face.* *'Ringed'
Murre:* — A small percentage of birds in the breeding season have a narrow white ring about the eye and a short white
line extending back from it. It is a phase of the Atlantic
Murre and not a different species.

Similar species: — Very similar to Brünnich's Murre but bill
longer and more slender. The Brünnich's Murre has a *light-
colored mark* along the base of the bill near the gape. In winter
plumage the Atlantic Murre has a narrow black line running
back from the eye into the white of the cheek — a very good
field mark.

Range: — Breeds on rocks along coast from Arctic s. to Nova
Scotia; s. in winter occasionally to Massachusetts.

BRÜNNICH'S MURRE. *Uria lomvia lomvia.* **p. 11**
Similar species: — 17–19. Usually a winter visitor. The species
with which the Brünnich's Murre is most frequently confused
within the limits of the United States is the Razor-billed Auk.
The bill of the Razor-bill is deep and flattened, whereas that
of the Brünnich's Murre is slender with a light mark near the
gape. On the water the longer tail of the Razor-bill is often
cocked up in the air. Less frequent south of the Canadian
boundary is the similar Atlantic, or Common, Murre (see above).

Range: — Breeds from Arctic s. to Gulf of St. Lawrence; winters
on ocean s. to Long Island. The only 'Alcid' one is likely to
encounter in the interior (rarely).

DOVEKIE. *Plautus alle alle.* **p. 11**
Field marks: — About size of a Starling (7½–9). Small, chubby,
and neckless. The contrasting Alcid pattern, *black above and
white below*, together with its *small size and very short stubby bill*,
render it quite unlike anything else. It is by far the smallest of
the wintering sea-birds.

Similar species: — Young of other Alcidæ are really larger (size is deceptive on ocean); all have *larger bills.*

Range: — Arctic; winters s. off coast to New York, *rarely* Florida. Occasionally driven ashore and even inland by prolonged oceanic gales.

BLACK GUILLEMOT. *Cepphus grylle.* Subsp.   p. 11.
Field marks: — About the size of our smallest Ducks (12–14). *Breeding plumage:* — A small all black duck-like bird with large *white shoulder-patches, red feet,* and a pointed bill. *Winter plumage:* — Pale with white under parts and black wings with large white patches as in summer. Immature birds are darker above than adults with dingier wing-patches. *No other 'Alcid' has white wing-patches* (although others have a narrow bar of white on the rear edge of the wings).
Similar species: — The beginner often imagines his first Guillemot will resemble a White-winged Scoter, black with white wing-patches. Guillemots, except in rare instances, are not black in winter, but are whitish birds. The Scoter is much larger with white patches placed on the rear edge of the wing, not the fore edge. They show less plainly as the bird rides the water.
Range: — Breeds on rocky islands from Arctic s. to Maine; winters s. on open ocean to Massachusetts.

ATLANTIC PUFFIN. *Fratercula arctica arctica.*   p. 11.
Field marks: — 11½–13. The most striking feature of the chunky little 'Sea Parrot' is its amazing *triangular* bill. On the wing Puffins are stubby, short-necked, thick-headed birds, with a buzzy flight. *Breeding plumage:* — Upper parts black; under parts white and cheeks pale gray; triangular bill broadly tipped with red. *Winter plumage:* — Cheeks grayer; bill smaller but still a typical Puffin bill. The immature bird has a much smaller, blackish bill, but both mandibles are distinctly curved, and the chunky shape and gray cheeks are unmistakably those of a Puffin.
Range: — Breeds on islands off coast from s. Greenland to Maine; winters s. on open sea to Massachusetts (a few).

Pigeons and Doves: Columbidæ

Two types of Pigeons occur in North America; those with fanlike tails, of which the Domestic Pigeon is the most familiar, and the smaller, brownish type with rounded or long pointed tails. The Mourning Dove is the most characteristic of the latter group.

WHITE-CROWNED PIGEON. *Columba leucocephala.* **p. 227.**
Field marks: — 13½. This stocky, obviously *wild* Pigeon is
completely dark except for a shining *white crown.*
Similar species: — Size and build of Domestic Pigeon.
Voice: — A low owl-like *wof, wof, wo, co-woo* (Maynard).
Range: — Southern tip of Florida and Florida Keys.

ROCK DOVE, or DOMESTIC PIGEON. *Columba livia.*
This bird has become feral, and in places it is as firmly estab-
lished as a wild species as the House Sparrow or the Starling.
It needs no description.

MOURNING DOVE. *Zenaidura macroura.* Subsp. **p. 135.**
Field marks: — 11–13. The common wild Dove of the East.
A small *brown* Pigeon, smaller and slimmer than a Domestic
Dove, with a *pointed,* not fan-shaped, tail which shows large
white spots when the bird flies.
Similar species: — The Passenger Pigeon has been extinct for a
generation. It was much larger, with a longer tail, longer wings
and a *blue-gray* head. The head of the Mourning Dove is buffy
brown with a *black spot* behind the eye. The wings of the Dove
produce a whistling sound; the flight of the Wild Pigeon was
silent.
Voice: — A hollow mournful *ooah, cooo, cooo, coo.* At a distance
only the three coos are audible.
Range: — Breeds from Nova Scotia, s. Maine, Ontario, and
Manitoba s. to the Gulf Coast. Winters from Massachusetts, s.
Michigan, and Iowa, s.

(EASTERN) GROUND DOVE. *Columbigallina passerina pas-*
serina. p. 135.
Field marks: — 6¾. A very small gray Dove, *not much larger
than a Sparrow* with a stubby black tail and round wings that
flash *rufous-red* in flight. It nods its head as it walks.
Voice: — A moaning *woo-oo, woo-oo, woo-oo,* etc., repeated
monotonously. At a distance sounds like one syllable, *wooo,*
with rising inflection.
Range: — Resident of coastal plain and low country from South
Carolina to Texas. Occasional in North Carolina.

Parrots: Psittacidæ

CAROLINA PAROQUET. *Conuropsis carolinensis carolinensis.*
Field marks: — 13 (tail 7). Although it is years since the last

Paroquet was authentically reported in the South, naturalists still hope that a stray individual or a flock might turn up. Adults would be about the size of a Mourning Dove, with a similar *pointed tail, bright green* with a *yellow head deepening into orange* about the base of the bill.

Similar species: — Great care must be taken not to confuse this species with exotic Paroquets, probably escapes, which have been reported in Florida and other parts of the South in recent years. A tropical species, *Aratinga holochlora* has been taken near Miami. It is similar in size to the Carolina Paroquet, but is *green all over*. Immature Carolinas would be green-headed, but with a *patch of orange* on the forehead and a suffusion of light yellow-green in the wing.

Cuckoos, Anis, Etc.: Cuculidæ

THE CUCKOOS are slim, long-tailed, sinuous-looking birds, a little longer than the Robin, dull olive-brown above and whitish below. Anis are loose-jointed and cuckoo-like in appearance, but are coal-black with deep, high-ridged bills.

MANGROVE CUCKOO. *Coccyzus minor maynardi.* p. 227.
Field marks: — 12½. Like the Yellow-billed Cuckoo, which also is found in the Florida Keys, but the under parts are a strong *yellowish buff* or *pale cinnamon*. A black ear-patch, or 'mask' extends behind the eye.
Voice: — 'A deep throaty, rather deliberately uttered *"gaw-gaw-gaw,* etc."' (James Bond). Notes of Yellow-bill are faster, ending in a deliberate *cowk-cowk-cowk*, etc.
Range: — Mangrove swamps of sw. coast of Florida and Keys.

YELLOW-BILLED CUCKOO. *Coccyzus americanus americanus.*
p. 135.
Field marks: — 11–12½. Known as a Cuckoo by the slim proportions and coloration, dull brown above and whitish below; further distinguished by the presence of *rufous* in the wings, *large* white spots at the tips of the tail-feathers, and, at close range, the *yellow* lower mandible of the bill. In flight the sinuous look and the flash of rufous in the wings are the best marks.
Similar species: — Black-billed Cuckoo is duller, has very small tail-spots, black lower mandible, and no rufous in wings.
Voice: — A rapid throaty *ka ka ka ka ka ka ka ka ka ka ka ka ka kow kow kowp-kowp-kowp-kowp* (retarded toward end). Single coos are given at intervals, independent of song.
Range: — Breeds from New Brunswick, Quebec, s. Ontario, and

North Dakota s. to Florida Keys and Mexico. Winters in South America.

BLACK-BILLED CUCKOO. *Coccyzus erythrophthalmus.* **p. 135.**
Field marks: — 11–12. Brown above, white below; bill *black*; narrow *red* ring around eye.
Similar species: — See Yellow-billed Cuckoo.
Voice: — A fast rhythmic *cu cu cu, cucucu, cucucu cucucu cucucu,* etc. The grouped rhythm (three, four, or five) is distinctive. Sometimes a series of rapid *kuks*, all on one pitch, without retarded ending of Yellow-bill. Often sings at night.
Range: — Breeds from s. Manitoba, s. Quebec, and Prince Edward Island s. to Arkansas and North Carolina, and in mountains to Georgia; winters in South America.

ROAD-RUNNER. *Geococcyx californianus.*
Field marks: — 20–24. The Cuckoo that runs on the ground. The 'Chaparral Cock' is unique; long and slender, heavily streaked, with a long expressive tail, a shaggy crest, and strong legs for running. In flight the short rounded wing shows a white crescent.
Voice: — Six or eight Dove-like *coos* descending in pitch (last note about pitch of Mourning Dove). Also a 'clackity noise made by rolling the mandibles together' (G. M. Sutton).
Range: — Western; breeds in arid country east to cent. Kansas, cent. Oklahoma, and e.-cent. Texas.

ROAD-RUNNER

TERNS

CASPIAN TERN   p. 121.
> *Winter:* Forehead streaked, tail slightly forked.
> *Spring:* Much black on under side of primaries; **tail** slightly forked.

ROYAL TERN   p. 120.
> *Winter:* Forehead white, tail deeply forked.
> *Spring:* Primaries relatively white below; tail deeply forked.

CABOT'S or SANDWICH TERN   p. 120.
> Slender black bill, yellow tip.

GULL–BILLED TERN   p. 115.
> Stout gull-like black bill.

FORSTER'S TERN   p. 115.
> *Breeding:* Pale primaries, orange bill.
> *Immature:* Black patch through eye and ear only.

ROSEATE TERN   p. 117.
> *Breeding:* Very pale; long tail feathers, blackish bill.

COMMON TERN   p. 116.
> *Breeding:* Dusky primaries, orange-red bill.
> *Immature:* Black patch extends around nape; dusky shoulder patch.

ARCTIC TERN   p. 116.
> *Breeding:* Grayer; bill blood red to tip.

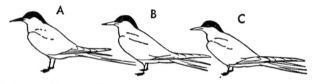

A. Roseate Tern.   Tail extends beyond wings.
B. Common Tern.   Wings extend beyond tail.
C. Arctic Tern.   Short legs.

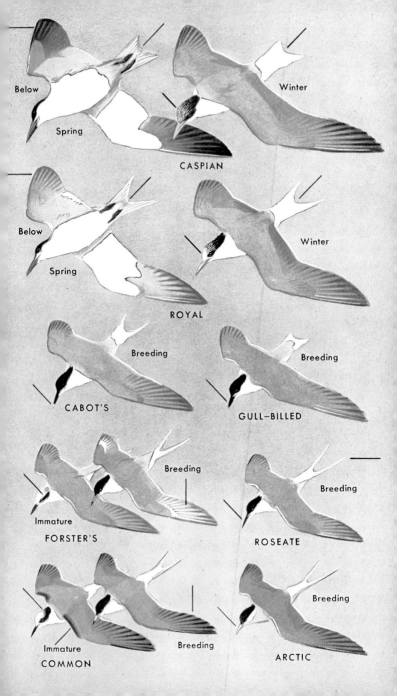

Below
Spring
Winter
CASPIAN

Below
Spring
Winter
ROYAL

Breeding
CABOT'S

Breeding
GULL-BILLED

Immature
Breeding
FORSTER'S

Breeding
ROSEATE

Immature
Breeding
COMMON

Breeding
ARCTIC

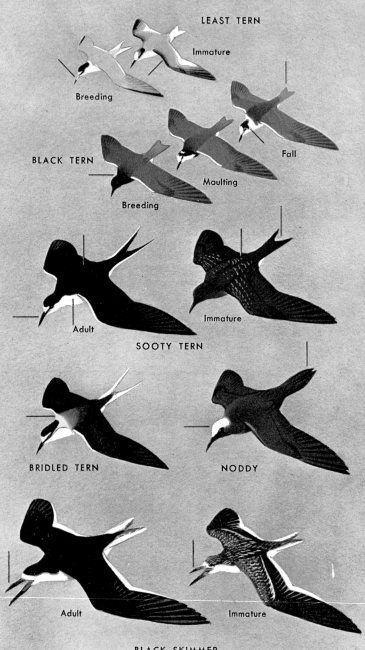

LEAST TERN

Immature

Breeding

Fall

BLACK TERN

Moulting

Breeding

SOOTY TERN

Adult

Immature

BRIDLED TERN

NODDY

BLACK SKIMMER

Adult

Immature

Plate 36   131

TERNS AND SKIMMERS

LEAST TERN   p. 120.
> *Breeding:* Small size, yellow bill.
> *Immature:* Small size, black fore-edge of wing.

BLACK TERN   p. 121.
> *Breeding:* Black body.
> *Moulting:* Patched with black and white.
> *Fall:* Pied head, dark back, gray tail.

SOOTY TERN   p. 117.
> *Adult:* Black above, white below; thin black bill.
> *Immature:* Dark body, speckled back, forked tail.

BRIDLED TERN   p. 248.
> Like Sooty, but grayer, with collar.
> See Accidentals.

NODDY   p. 121.
> Dark body, white crown, full tail.

BLACK SKIMMER   p. 124.

> *Adult:* Black upper parts; long unequal red bill.
> *Immature:* Smaller, browner, with Skimmer bill.

SMOOTH-BILLED ANI. *Crotophaga ani.*   p. 227.
   Field marks: — 12½. A coal-black cuckoo-like bird. with
loose-jointed tail, short wings (hence a weak flight), and a huge
bill with a *high, curved ridge* on the upper mandible. The peculiar bill formation gives the bird a decidedly parrot-like or
puffin-like profile.
   Similar species: — Except for the bill and strange appearance
the bird might be mistaken at first for a Grackle. The Groove-
billed Ani (*Crotophaga sulcirostris*) has occurred in Louisiana
and Florida. It is similar but has *three grooves* on the upper
mandible.
   Voice: — A long-drawn, whining whistle. 'A querulous *que-lick,*
que-lick' (James Bond).
   Range: — Occasional visitor to Louisiana and s. Florida.

Owls: Tytonidæ and Strigidæ

NOCTURNAL birds of prey, large headed with large eyes, *facial discs,*
and moth-like, noiseless flight. They seem quite neckless. Some
species have conspicuous feather-tufts, or 'horns'; others are round-
headed, devoid of these 'ears.'

BARN OWL. *Tyto alba pratincola.*   p. 150
   Field marks: — 15–20. A long-legged, light-colored Owl with
a *white heart-shaped face.* Distinguished in flight as an Owl by
the large head and light, moth-like flight; as this species, by the
whitish or pale cinnamon under parts (ghostly at night) and
buffy or rusty upper plumage.
   Similar species: — Short-eared Owl (marshes) is streaked, has
darker face and under parts, and shorter legs.
   Voice: — An eerie rasping hiss or snore: *kschh!*
   Range: — Massachusetts (occasionally), Ohio, s. Wisconsin, and
Nebraska, s. to Gulf of Mexico. Partial to old buildings, barns,
towers.

SCREECH OWL. *Otus asio.* Subsp.   p. 150.
   Field marks: — 8–10. The only *small* Owl with ear-tufts. Two
color phases occur: red-brown and gray. No other Owl is bright
rufous.
   Similar species: — See Long-eared Owl.
   Voice: — A mournful whinny, or wail, tremulous, running down
the scale. Sometimes given on a single pitch.
   Range: — Resident from New Brunswick, Maine, Ontario,
Wisconsin, and s. Manitoba s. to Florida, Texas, and Mexico.

GREAT HORNED OWL. *Bubo virginianus.* Subsp.   p. 150.
   Field marks: — 20–23. The only *large* Owl (nearly two feet in

length) with ear-tufts, or 'horns.' It has a conspicuous white throat-collar. In the more northern parts of Canada, there are very pale and dark races which are recognizable at times (see Subspecies).

Similar species: — The Long-eared Owl is much smaller (fifteen inches; crow-sized in flight), with lengthwise streakings rather than crosswise barrings, beneath. In flight the Horned Owl is larger than our largest Buteo Hawks (Red-tail, etc.), is darker, looks neckless, and is larger headed.

Voice: — The hooting of the Horned Owl is deeper and more resonant than that of the Barred Owl and consists of three, five, or six uninflected hoots (Barred Owl, eight). Usually five in this rhythm: *hoo, hoohoo, hoo, hoo.*

Range: — Resident from Labrador and Hudson Bay s. to Florida, Texas, and Mexico.

SNOWY OWL. *Nyctea scandiaca.* p. 151.
Field marks: — 20–26. A large *white* Owl with a round head. More or less flecked or barred with dusky. Some birds are much whiter than others. Day-flying: prefers marshes, meadows, shores. Perches on posts, dunes, muskrat houses, haystacks.

Similar species: — White Gyrfalcon is smaller-headed, has *pointed* wings, and flies with more vigorous strokes. The Arctic Horned Owl, a very pale race of the Horned Owl, has ear-tufts, and is a woodland, not an open-country, bird. The Barn Owl is whitish on under parts only. Young Owls of all species are whitish before feathers replace the down, and are often dubbed 'Snowy' Owls.

Range: — Arctic, wintering irregularly to Middle States. Cyclic, irrupting in numbers at about four-year intervals.

HAWK OWL. *Surnia ulula caparoch.* p. 151.
Field marks: — 15–17. A medium-sized, hawk-like day-flying Owl (smaller than a Crow), with a *long* falcon-like tail and *barred* underparts. At rest it maintains a more inclined body posture, not so upright as other Owls; often perches at the tip-top of a tree or in some other exposed situation and jerks its tail in the manner of a Sparrow Hawk. Shrike-like, it pitches from its perch, flies low and rises abruptly to its next perch. The prominent black 'sideburns' framing its face are a good mark (see illustration).

Range: — Breeds in n. Canada; winters s. to s. Canada and occasionally n. United States.

BURROWING OWL. *Speotyto cunicularia.* Subsp. p. 151.
Field marks: — 9. A small brown Owl of the prairies, often seen in the daytime sitting on the ground and on fence-posts. About the size of a Screech Owl, round-headed with *very long*

TERNS

BLACK TERN   p. 121
Breeding: Black head.
Winter: 'Pied' head (see text).

LEAST TERN   p. 120.
Breeding: Yellow bill, white forehead patch.
Immature: Small size (see text).

FORSTER'S TERN   p. 115.
Breeding: Orange bill, black tip (see text).
Winter: Black eye-patch; light or gray nape.

COMMON TERN   p. 116.
Breeding: Orange-red bill, black tip (see text).
Winter: Black patch from eye *around nape.*

ROSEATE TERN   p. 117.
Breeding: Bill mostly black.
Variant: Some have much red (see text).

ARCTIC TERN   p. 116.
Breeding: Bill blood red; no black tip.

CABOT'S or SANDWICH TERN   p. 120.
Breeding: Bill black with yellow tip.

GULL–BILLED TERN   p. 115.
Breeding: Bill gull-like, stout and black.
Immature: Very gull-like (see text).

ROYAL TERN   p. 120.
Winter: Orange bill, white forehead.
Spring: Orange bill, tufted crest.

CASPIAN TERN   p. 121.
Winter: Scarlet bill, streaked forehead.
Spring· Scarlet bill, less crest than Royal.

Winter · Summer

BLACK

Immature · Summer

LEAST

Winter · Summer

FORSTER'S

Winter · Summer

COMMON

Variant · Summer

ROSEATE

Summer

ARCTIC

Summer

CABOT'S

Immature · Summer

GULL-BILLED

Winter · **ROYAL** · Summer

Winter · **CASPIAN** · Summer

YELLOW-BILLED
CUCKOO

BLACK-BILLED
CUCKOO

GROUND DOVE

MOURNING DOVE

MEADOWLARK

WHIP-POOR-WILL ♂

NIGHTHAWK

CHUCK-WILL'S-WIDOW ♂

Plate 38   135

CUCKOOS, DOVES, MEADOWLARK, AND GOATSUCKERS

YELLOW–BILLED CUCKOO   p. 128.
    Yellow bill, rufous wings, large tail-spots.

BLACK–BILLED CUCKOO   p. 129
    Black bill, red eye-ring, small tail-spots.

GROUND DOVE   p. 127
    Small size, rufous wings, black tail.

MOURNING DOVE   p. 127
    Pointed tail.

MEADOWLARK (EASTERN)   p. 210
    Black V; white outer tail-feathers.

WHIP–POOR–WILL   p. 138
    Dead leaf pattern; wings shorter than tail.
    White tail-patches (male), black throat.

CHUCK–WILL'S–WIDOW   p. 138
    Like Whip-poor-will but larger, browner; brown throat
    (see range).

NIGHTHAWK   p. 130
    White wing-patches.
    At rest wings reach end of tail.

legs (for an Owl) and a stubby tail. Bobs and bounces when agitated.

Voice: — Commonest note a tremulous chuckling or chattering call; at night a high mellow *coo-co-hoo* or *coo-hoo* like a Mourning Dove in quality but higher.

Range: — Breeds in w. prairies e. to Manitoba, Minnesota, w. Iowa, and Louisiana; it is migratory n. of Kansas. Resident also in prairies of cent. and s. Florida.

BARRED OWL. *Strix varia.* Subsp.   p. 150.
Field marks: — 18–22. The Barred Owl is the Owl with the puffy round head, the common large gray-brown hornless Owl of the deciduous woodlands. The large liquid brown eyes (all others except the Barn Owl have yellow eyes), and the manner of the streaking and barring — barred *crosswise* on the breast and streaked *lengthwise* on the belly — identify the bird. The back is spotted with white.
Voice: — The hooting is more emphatic than that of the Great Horned Owl but not so deep. It usually consists of *eight* accented hoots (hence the nickname 'Eight Hooter'), in two groups of four: *hoohoo-hoohoo . . . hoohoo-hoohooaw.* The *aw* dropping off at the close is especially characteristic. Distorted by distance, the hooting sounds like the barking of a dog.
Range: — Resident from Newfoundland, s. Quebec, and Saskatchewan s. to Florida and Texas, particularly in wet or swampy woodlands, where it is the nocturnal counterpart of the Red-shouldered Hawk. The Great Horned Owl supplements the Red-tailed Hawk in drier woodlands, barrens, and the hills.

GREAT GRAY OWL. *Strix nebulosa nebulosa.*   p. 151.
Field marks: — 24–33. A rare Northerner. The largest of the Owls; dusky-gray, heavily striped lengthwise on the under parts. It is round-headed, without ear-tufts, and the eyes are *yellow*, not brown. The tail is very long for an Owl (about 12 inches). The facial discs are very large proportionately. It has a noticeable black chin spot.
Similar species: — Barred Owl is much smaller (18–22), browner; has *brown* eyes, smaller facial discs, shorter tail.
Voice: — 'A booming whoo-oo-oo-oo' (A. D. Henderson). 'Deep-pitched *whoo's* at regular intervals' (Grinnell and Storer).
Range: — Breeds in dense evergreen forests from tree-limit in Canada s. to Ontario and probably n. Minnesota; winters through s. Canada, irregularly to n. edge of United States.

LONG–EARED OWL. *Asio otus wilsonianus.*   p. 150.
Field marks: — 13–16. A slender crow-sized Owl of the woodlands, with long ear-tufts; much smaller than Horned Owl, streaked *lengthwise*, rather than barred crosswise, beneath. The

'ears' are closer together, toward the center of the forehead, giving this Owl a different aspect. It is usually seen 'frozen' close to the trunk of a thick evergreen.

Similar species: — Horned Owl is much larger, with ear-tufts more spread apart; seldom allows such a close approach. Larger size, longer horns, *rusty* face differentiate it from gray Screech Owl. In flight the ear-tufts are pressed flat against the head; then the large amount of gray distinguishes it from the buffier Short-eared Owl.

Voice: — 'A low moaning dove-like *hoo, hoo, hoo*. Also a cat-like whine and a slurred whistle, *wheé-you*' (Ludlow Griscom).

Range: — Breeds from Newfoundland and n. Ontario s. to Virginia and n. Texas; winters from s. Canada to Gulf of Mexico.

SHORT-EARED OWL. *Asio flammeus flammeus.*   p. 150

Field marks: — 13–17. Nearly the size of a Crow; a day-flying ground Owl of the marshes and open country. The streaked buffy-brown color and the irregular flopping flight, like that of a Nighthawk or a large moth, identify it. Large buffy wing-patches show in flight.

Similar species: — It might possibly be mistaken for a Rough-legged Hawk; both hunt by day over the same marshes, and in flight show the large black 'thumb-print' at the base of the primaries on the under surface of the wings. The Owl is much smaller, with a somewhat slovenly flight, and appears quite big-headed and neckless. See Barn Owl.

Voice: — An emphatic sneezy bark, *kee-yow!*

Range: — Breeds in marshy or open country from Arctic s. to New Jersey, n. Ohio, and s. Kansas; winters from n. United States to Gulf of Mexico.

RICHARDSON'S OWL. *Aegolius funerea richardsoni.*   p. 151

Field marks: — 9–12. A rare visitor from the North. Near size of Screech Owl, but *earless*. The facial discs of Richardson's Owl are *framed with black*, and the bill is *yellowish*. The forehead is heavily spotted with white.

Similar species: — Closely resembles commoner Saw-whet Owl (Saw-whet is smaller, has *black* bill, lacks black facial 'frames'). Hawk Owl is larger, long-tailed, and is *barred* below.

Voice: — 'Song like a soft high-pitched bell or dropping of water' (Bent). '*Ting, ting, ting,*' etc. (Seton).

Range: — Breeds in n. Canada, s. to Manitoba and Nova Scotia; winters to s. Canada, and irregularly to n. edge of United States.

SAW-WHET OWL. *Aegolius acadica acadica.*   p. 151

Field marks: — 7–8½. A tiny, absurdly tame little Owl; smaller than Screech Owl, *without* ear-tufts. Juvenile birds in

summer are very different from the streaked brown adults.
They are chocolate-brown with a *blackish* face and conspicuous
white patches or 'eyebrows' forming a broad V between the eyes.
Similar species: — See Richardson's Owl (very rare in United
States).
Voice: — 'Song,' a mellow whistled note repeated mechanically
in endless succession, often betweeen one hundred and one hundred and thirty times per minute *too, too, too, too, too, too,* etc.;
has bell-like quality in distance. Also a weak two-syllabled
rasping note.
Range: — Breeds from Nova Scotia, Quebec, and Manitoba s.
to n. Indiana and mountains of West Virginia. Winters s. to
Louisiana and Virginia.

Goatsuckers: Caprimulgidæ

THE GOATSUCKERS are ample-tailed nocturnal birds with small
bills and weak, tiny feet. During the day they rest horizontally
on some limb, or on the ground, where their mottled brown pattern
blends with the surroundings.

CHUCK–WILL'S–WIDOW. *Caprimulgus carolinensis.* p. 135.
  Field marks: — 11–13. Like the Whip-poor-will, but larger,
  very much buffier, with a *brown* throat (Whip-poor-will, *black*).
  Identify by size, brownish look, comparative lack of white,
  locality (except in migration), and voice.
  Similar species: — Chuck-will's-widow is almost universally
  called Whip-poor-will by Southerners. In most places there is
  a seasonal difference; the Chuck arrives after the Whip-poor-will
  departs, and leaves before it gets back.
  Voice: — Call, *chuck-will'-wid'ow*, less vigorous than efforts of
  Whip-poor-will; distinctly four-syllabled, *chuck* often inaudible;
  accent on second and third syllables.
  Range: — Breeds in low country and in river valleys from Florida and Gulf of Mexico n. to s. Maryland, s. Ohio, s. Indiana,
  and se. Kansas. Winters from s. Florida s.

(EASTERN) WHIP–POOR–WILL. *Caprimulgus vociferus.*
                                                    p. 135.
  Field marks: — 9–10. On summer evenings we hear the vigorous
  cry of the Whip-poor-will, repeated in endless succession. When
  we discover the bird during the day, it springs from its leafy
  hiding-place and flits away like a large brown moth. If it is a
  male, white tail-feathers flash out; if a female, it appears all
  brown.
  Similar species: — The Nighthawk shows conspicuous white

wing-patches. Perching, on the ground, or lengthwise on a limb, the pointed wings of the Nighthawk extend beyond the tip of the *forked* tail whereas the Whip-poor-will's short and rounded wings fall far short of the end of its *rounded* tail. In South see Chuck-will's-widow.

Voice: — A vigorous oft-repeated *whip'-poor-weel'*; accent on first and last syllables. Uttered at night.

Range: — Breeds in leafy woodlands from Nova Scotia, s. Quebec, and Manitoba s. to n. Georgia and n. Louisiana; winters from coastal South Carolina and Gulf Coast s.

(NUTTALL'S) POOR-WILL. *Phalænoptilus nuttallii.*
Field marks: — Best known by its night call. It is like a very small Whip-poor-will (7–8), and is grayer, with comparatively small white spots in the tail-corners. See illustration in *A Field Guide to Western Birds*.

Voice: — At night a loud, repeated *poor-will* or more exactly, *poor-jill*; when close, *poor-will-low* or *poor-jill-ip*.

Range: — Western. Breeds in arid country (west of range of Whip-poor-will) east to s. South Dakota, e. Nebraska, sw. Iowa, e. Kansas, and cent. Texas.

NIGHTHAWK. *Chordeiles minor.* Subsp.   p. 135.
Field marks: — 8½–10. The Nighthawk is the slim-winged gray bird we see flying erratically about after insects high in the air, often over the roofs of cities. It prefers dusk but also flies abroad during day. In courtship the male folds his wings and drops earthward like a dive-bomber, zooming up sharply at the end of the drop with a sudden deep whir that sounds like the well-known 'Bronx cheer.' The *broad white patch* across the wing is the Nighthawk's mark.

Similar species: — See Whip-poor-will.

Voice: — A nasal *peent* or *pee-ik.*

Range: — Breeds from Newfoundland, s. Quebec, and n. Manitoba s. to Florida Keys and Gulf of Mexico. Winters in South America.

Swifts: Apodidæ

CHIMNEY SWIFT. *Chætura pelagica.*   p. 162.
Field marks: — 5–5½. The Chimney Swift has been called a 'cigar with wings.' It is a blackish swallow-like bird with long slightly curved stiff wings and no apparent tail (occasionally it does spread its tail fan-wise). Unlike most other birds, it does not appear to beat its wings in unison, but alternately — such is the *illusion* at least (slow-motion pictures to the contrary not-

withstanding). The effect is quite batlike. Their narrow wings fairly twinkle as they fly, and they frequently sail between spurts, holding the wings *bowed like a crescent.*

Similar species: — Swallows have gliding wing-beats; they frequently perch on wires and twigs; Swifts never do. Swallows have forked, notched, or square tails.

Voice: — Loud, rapid, ticking or chippering notes.

Range: — Breeds in chimneys from Newfoundland, s. Quebec, and se. Saskatchewan s. to Gulf of Mexico. Winters in Peru.

VAUX'S SWIFT. *Chætura vauxi.*
Similar species: — Like Chimney Swift but smaller (4½) and paler, especially on throat. Probably not distinguishable, but any winter Swift on the Gulf Coast would probably be this western species.

Range: — Has been taken in Baton Rouge and believed to be rare but regular in Louisiana in winter.

Hummingbirds: Trochilidæ

RUBY-THROATED HUMMINGBIRD. *Archilochus colubris.*
Field marks: — 3–3¾. Hummingbirds hardly need a description. They are the smallest of all birds; iridescent, with long needle-like bills for sipping nectar from flowers. The wing-motion is so rapid that the wings look like blurry gauze. Ruby-throats are metallic green above; males with *glowing red throats*; females with white throats.

Similar species: — The Ruby-throat is the only eastern species

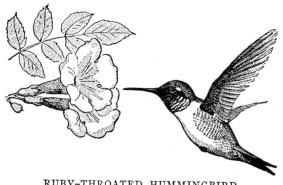

RUBY-THROATED HUMMINGBIRD

although the Rufous Hummingbird seems to turn up occasionally along the Gulf Coast in late fall.   Large Hawk Moths (Sphingidæ) might be mistaken for Hummers, but their visits to the flowers seldom take place much before dusk.
Range: — Breeds from Gulf of St. Lawrence and Saskatchewan to Gulf of Mexico; winters from Florida s.

RUFOUS HUMMINGBIRD.   *Selasphorus rufus.*
   Field marks: — 3½ in.   *Male:* — Upper parts *bright red-brown,* throat flame-red.   *Female:* — Similar to other female Hummingbirds, but has some rufous on the rump or tail-feathers.
   Similar species: — Ruby-throat shows no rufous above.
   Range: — Western.   Rare but probably regular in winter along Gulf from Louisiana to nw. Florida.

Kingfishers: Alcedinidæ

(EASTERN) BELTED KINGFISHER.   *Megaceryle alcyon alcyon.*
p. 199
   Field marks: — 11–14.   Hovering on rapidly beating wings in one spot above the water in readiness for the plunge, or flying with peculiar uneven wing-beats, rattling as it goes, the Kingfisher is easily learned by the novice.   Perched, it is big-headed and big-billed, larger than a Robin, blue-gray above, with a ragged crest and one (male) or two (female) broad breast-bands.
   Similar species: — Blue Jay has remote resemblance.
   Voice: — A loud high rattle.
   Range: — Breeds in sand-banks, river bluffs, and road cuts from s. Labrador and n. Manitoba s. to Gulf of Mexico; winters n. to Illinois, Ohio, and New England (a few).

Woodpeckers: Picidæ

CHISEL-BILLED tree-climbers.   They have stiff, spiny tails which act as props as they hitch their way up the trees.   The flight of most species is undulating, produced by several quick beats and a pause.   The males of most species have some amount of red on the head.

FLICKER.   *Colaptes auratus.*   Subsp.   p. 154
   Field marks: — 13–14.   The brown back and conspicuous *white rump*, visible as the bird flies up, is the best field mark.   Flickers are our only *brown-backed* Woodpeckers.   The flight is deeply

undulating: overhead this species flashes considerable *yellow* under the wings and tail. Close up, a wide black crescent shows across the breast, a red patch on the nape, and, in male, black 'whiskers.'

Similar species: — In Great Plains see Red-shafted Flicker.

Voice: — Song, a loud *wick wick wick wick wick*, etc.; notes, a loud *klee-yer* and a squeaky *flick-a, flick-a*, etc.

Range: — Breeds e. of Rockies from limit of trees in Canada s. to Florida and Gulf of Mexico; winters n. to Great Lakes and s. New England (a few).

RED–SHAFTED FLICKER. *Colaptes cafer collaris.*

Similar species: — 13–14. Similar to Flicker but with the yellow of the wing- and tail-linings replaced by salmon-red. The male has *red* 'whiskers' instead of black ones. Where the ranges of the two species overlap, hybrids sometimes occur, with *orange-yellow* wing-linings and spotted 'whiskers,' or with one whisker black, the other red.

Voice: — Similar to Yellow-shafted Flicker's.

Range: — Western; e. to Great Plains (South Dakota, Nebraska, and Kansas, occasionally farther).

PILEATED WOODPECKER. *Hylatomus pileatus.* Subsp.

p. 154.

Field marks: — 17–19½. A spectacular, *Crow-sized* Woodpecker with a conspicuous red *crest.* It is the only Woodpecker with a crest (except for the nearly extinct Ivory-bill). The great size, sweeping wing-beats, and flashing black-and-white coloration identify it at a distance. The diggings, large *oval* or *oblong* holes, are certain evidence of its presence.

Voice: — One common call resembles that of a Flicker, but is louder, and more hesitant — *kuk — kuk — kukkuk —— kuk-kuk*, etc. The other call is more ringing and hurried than that of a Flicker and often rises or falls slightly in pitch.

Range: — Resident of woodlands from Nova Scotia, New Brunswick, and Manitoba s. to Florida and Gulf of Mexico.

RED–BELLIED WOODPECKER. *Centurus carolinus.* Subsp.

p. 154.

Field marks: — 9–10½. The only zebra-backed Woodpecker with a *red* cap. The whole crown is red in the male; the female is red on the nape only. The young bird has no red but the combination of *brown head* and *zebra back* is safe.

Voice: — Note, *churr* or *chaw*; also *chiv, chiv*. Also a muffled flicker-like series.

Range: — Resident from Florida and Gulf of Mexico n. to Delaware, Lake Erie, se. Minnesota, and se. South Dakota.

RED-HEADED WOODPECKER. *Melanerpes erythrocephalus erythrocephalus.* p. 154.

Field marks: — 8½–9½. The only eastern Woodpecker with the *entire* head red. Many others have a *patch* of red and so are sometimes wrongly called Red-headed Woodpeckers. In flight this species shows large square white patches on the rear edge of the wing. The sexes are similar. The immature bird is dusky-headed; the large white wing-patches identify it. Perched, these patches make the lower back look white.

Voice: — A loud *querr* or *queeoh*, louder and higher-pitched than *churr* of Red-belly.

Range: — Breeds from Gulf of Mexico n. to s. New England (irregularly), w. New York, se. Ontario, s. Michigan, Minnesota, and Manitoba; migrates somewhat from n. parts of range in winter.

YELLOW-BELLIED SAPSUCKER. *Sphyrapicus varius varius.* p. 154.

Field marks: — 8–8½. The badge in all plumages is the *longitudinal white patch* or stripe on the black wing. It is our only Woodpecker with a red *forehead patch*. *Males* have red throats; *females*, white. The young bird is sooty brown, but it too has the long white wing-patch.

Voice: — A squealing cat-like or jay-like mewing note, slurring downward; sometimes sounds like Red-shouldered Hawk. The drumming of the Sapsucker is distinctive, several rapid thumps followed by several slow rhythmic ones.

Range: — Breeds from Cape Breton Island, s. Quebec, and Manitoba s. to New England, n. Ohio, Indiana, and Missouri and, in mountains, to North Carolina. Winters from Gulf of Mexico to Wisconsin, Michigan, and s. New England (occasionally).

HAIRY WOODPECKER. *Dendrocopus villosus.* Subsp. p. 154.

Field marks: — 8½–10½. Other Woodpeckers have white rumps or white bars on the back, but the Downy and the Hairy are our only *white-backed* Woodpeckers. They are almost identical in pattern, checkered and spotted with black and white; the *males* with a small red patch on the back of the head; the *females*, without. The Hairy is like a magnified Downy; it is much larger; the bill is especially large, all out of size-relation to the Downy's little 'bark-sticker.'

Similar species: — Downy Woodpecker (see above). At close range the Downy shows black bars on its white outer tail feathers. The Hairy lacks this 'ladder.' Most observers do not bother about this as the difference in bills is the quickest way to tell them.

Voice: — A kingfisher-like rattle, run together more than call of Downy. Note, a sharp *peek!*

Range: — Resident from Gulf of Mexico n. to Newfoundland, se. Quebec, and n. Manitoba.

DOWNY WOODPECKER. *Dendrocopus pubescens.* Subsp.

p. 154.

Field marks: — 6½–7. (See Hairy Woodpecker.)
Voice: — A rapid whinny of notes, descending in pitch at the end; not so run together as those of Hairy Woodpecker. Note a flat *pick*, not as sharp as Hairy's note.
Range: — Resident from Gulf of Mexico n. to Newfoundland, s. Quebec, and Manitoba.

RED–COCKADED WOODPECKER. *Dendrocopus borealis.*

Subsp.   p. 154.

Field marks: — 8½. A *zebra-backed* Woodpecker with a *black* cap; resident of open southern pine forests where Brown-headed Nuthatches are found. The *white cheek* is the most conspicuous field mark.
Similar species: — Red-bellied Woodpecker is zebra-backed but has a *red* cap. The Red-cockaded is more likely to be confused with Downy or Hairy but white cheek is a ready mark.
Voice: — A rough rasping *sripp* or *zhilp* (suggests flock note of young Starling). Sometimes a higher *tsick*, but still enough unlike Downy or Hairy to let the beginner know he is on the track of his first Red-cockaded Woodpecker.
Range: — Resident of pine woodlands of Southern States n. sparingly to se. Virginia, w. Kentucky, and s. Missouri.

ARCTIC THREE–TOED, or BLACK–BACKED, WOODPECKER.

Picoides arcticus.   p. 154.

Field marks: — 9–10. This Woodpecker can be told by the combination of heavily barred sides and *solid black* back. The male has a *yellow* crown-patch which the female lacks. The two Three-toed Woodpeckers inhabit the deep coniferous forests of the North; their presence can be detected by large patches scaled from the trunks of dead conifers.
Similar species: — See American Three-toed Woodpecker.
Voice: — 'A short sharp *cruck* or *crick*' (T. S. Roberts).
Range: — Spruce forests from n. Quebec and n. Manitoba s. to n. New England, n. New York, and n. Minnesota; occasional in winter farther south.

AMERICAN THREE–TOED WOODPECKER. *Picoides tridactylus bacatus.*

p. 154.

Field marks: — 8–9½. The males of the two Three-toed Woodpeckers are the only species of the family with *yellow* caps. The '*ladder-back*' will further distinguish this species.
Similar species: — The female lacks the yellow cap, but the *barred flanks and back* identify her. Arctic Three-toe has a

solid *black* back. Rarely aberrant immature Hairy Woodpeckers have yellowish or orange caps and so are called Three-toed Woodpeckers. (Hairy has white down the center of back.)

Voice: — Similar to that of Arctic Three-toed Woodpecker.

Range: — Spruce forests from Labrador and n. Manitoba s. to n. New England, n. New York, and n. Minnesota; occasional in winter farther south.

IVORY-BILLED WOODPECKER. *Campephilus principalis.*

p. 145.

Field marks: — 20. Close to extinction. A very large Wood-pecker, larger than a Crow; *male* with a flaming red crest; female with a *black* crest. Known by its superior size, *ivory-white bill,* and large white wing-patches *visible when the bird is at rest.*

Similar species: — Pileated Woodpecker is smaller, has dark bill. It, too, has much white in the wing, but this does not show when the bird is climbing. In flight overhead, both birds show much white. The whole *rear* edge of the Ivory-bill's wing is white; in the Pileated the white is in the lining, or *front half* of the wing.

Voice: — Call very different from Pileated, a single loud tooting note, constantly uttered as the bird forages about — a sharp nasal *kent*, suggesting to some the note of a Nuthatch. Audubon wrote it '*pait* resembling the high false note of a clarinet.'

Range: — Formerly primeval river-bottom forests of s. United States. Last reported from n. Louisiana (Singer Tract). To be looked for in Florida and South Carolina.

IVORY-BILLED WOODPECKER

The Ivory-bill shows large white wing-patches *when climbing* and white *on the rear edge* of the wing. The Pileated also has much white but it is placed differently.

Flycatchers: Tyrannidæ

FLYCATCHERS usually perch in an upright attitude on exposed twigs or branches, sallying forth at intervals to snap up passing insects. They are not so restless as most birds, but sit quite motionless save for an occasional jerk of the tail.

EASTERN KINGBIRD. *Tyrannus tyrannus.* p. 155.
Field marks: — 8½–9. When this large black and white Flycatcher flies from one perch to another, the white band at the tip of its fanlike tail leaves no doubt as to its identity. It seems to fly on the 'tips of its wings.' The red crown-mark, emphasized in many color plates, is concealed and rarely noticed.
Voice: — A rapid sputter of nervous bickering notes; also a nasal rasping *dzeeb*.
Range: — Breeds in rural country from Nova Scotia, s. Quebec, and Manitoba s. to Gulf of Mexico. Winters in tropical America.

GRAY KINGBIRD. *Tyrannus dominicensis dominicensis.* p. 227.
Field marks: — 9–9½. The other two Kingbirds have white on the tail; this species has none. Otherwise it resembles the common Kingbird, but is larger, of a *pale* washed-out gray color. The tail is conspicuously *notched*. One of the best points is the *very large bill*, which gives the bird a bull-headed look when perched at a distance on a wire.
Similar species: — Often suggests a Shrike. Eastern Kingbird is much darker, has rounded tail with white band at tip.
Voice: — A rolling *pi-teer-rrry* or *pe-cheer-ry*, less strident than call of Eastern Kingbird.
Range: — Breeds locally along both east and west coasts of Florida and rarely to South Carolina. Commonest in Keys; prefers mangroves. Winters in West Indies.

WESTERN, or ARKANSAS, KINGBIRD. *Tyrannus verticalis.* p. 155.
Field marks: — 8–9½. Smaller than a Robin, with a pale-gray head and back, and yellowish under parts. The best index to the identity of the three Kingbirds is their tails. In this species the black tail is bordered on each side with white, as in a Junco or Vesper Sparrow, but the borders are much narrower. Immature birds do not always have the white in the tail, but the grayish upper parts, lightest on the head, and the yellowish under parts are enough to identify them.
Similar species: — It looks not at all like the black and white Eastern Kingbird, reminding one more of a Crested Flycatcher. The Crested has a *rufous* tail (Arkansas Kingbird, black).

Voice: — A shrill bickering call; various shrill twittering notes; also a sharp *whit*.
Range: — West; breeds e. to w. Minnesota, w. Iowa, Kansas, and Oklahoma. Normally winters in Mexico. Each fall a few stragglers are reported at scattered localities in the East, usually near the coast.

SCISSOR-TAILED FLYCATCHER. *Muscivora forficata*. p. 155.
Field marks: — 11½–15. A beautiful bird, pale pearly gray, with an extremely long scissor-like tail. The sides and wing-linings are salmon pink. No other land bird in its range has such streaming tail-feathers. Perched, the 'scissors' are folded.
Similar species: — Immature birds with short tails resemble the Western, or Arkansas, Kingbird, but have a touch of *pinkish* on the lower belly instead of yellowish. The breast is whiter, and there is more white in the tail.
Voice: — A harsh *keck*, or *kew*; also shrill, excited kingbird-like twitterings and chatterings.
Range: — Breeds in Texas, Oklahoma, Kansas, and s. Nebraska, occasionally e. to w. Louisiana and sw. Missouri. Winters in Central America.

CRESTED FLYCATCHER. *Myiarchus crinitus*. Subsp. p. 155.
Field marks: — 8–9. A large woodland Flycatcher with a *rufous* tail, gray throat and breast, and yellow belly. No other Flycatcher has a rufous tail.
Similar species: — In Prairie States see Arkansas Kingbird.
Voice: — Note, a loud whistled *wheeeeep!* with rising inflection; also a throaty, rolling *prrrrreet!*
Range: — Breeds from New Brunswick, s. Quebec, and s. Manitoba, s. to Florida and Gulf Coast; winters in s. Florida, e. Mexico, and Central America.

EASTERN PHŒBE. *Sayornis phœbe*.   p. 155.
Field marks: — 6½–7. This gray tail-wagger has a weakness for small bridges. It is sparrow-sized, gray-brown above and whitish below, with *no* conspicuous wing-bars. This lack of wing-bars, its upright posture, and its persistent tail-wagging habit are all good points. The bill is *black*.
Similar species: — The Wood Pewee and the other small Flycatchers all have fairly conspicuous wing-bars and their bills are yellowish or whitish on the lower mandible. They do not wag their tails. Young Phœbes sometimes have dull brownish wing-bars.
Voice: — A well-enunciated *phoe-be*, or *fi-bree* (second note alternately higher or lower than first). It is not whistled like 'phœbe' song of Chickadee.
Range: — Breeds from Nova Scotia, s. Quebec, and Manitoba

LEAST FLYCATCHER

— or —
chebek chebek

Grayest of
the group

Habitat: — Farms,
orchards, groves,
open woods;
northern U.S. and
Canada

ACADIAN FLYCATCHER

spit-cheel

Greener than
Least or Alder

Habitat: — Decid-
uous woods,
wooded swamps;
fond of beech
trees; southern and
central states

Eye-ring
Wing-bars

There are four Empidonax
Flycatchers in the East.
Only the Yellow-bellied
can be told with fair certainty by appearance.
Identify the others by
voice and habitat.

**ALDER
FLYCATCHER**

wee-be-o

Brownest of
the group

Habitat: — Alder swamps and
wet thickets, usually near water;
northern states and Canada

**YELLOW–
BELLIED
FLYCATCHER**

chu-wee

Breast washed
with yellow

Habitat: — Coniferous woods,
cold bogs; Canada and northern
edge of U.S.

THE SMALL FLYCATCHERS

s. to Texas, n. Mississippi, and mountains of Georgia; winters throughout s. United States n. to Virginia and s. Missouri.

SAY'S PHŒBE. *Sayornis saya saya.*
Field marks: — 7–8. A large, pale Phœbe with pale *rusty* under parts. The black tail and rusty breast give it the look of a small Robin, but its Flycatcher habits identify it. I have seen an Eastern Phœbe so stained by red Georgia clay that it could have passed for *saya*.
Voice: — A plaintive *pee-ur*.
Range: — Western; breeds e. to central parts of Dakotas and Nebraska and to w. Kansas and w. Oklahoma.

YELLOW–BELLIED FLYCATCHER. *Empidonax flaviventris.*
pp. 148, 155.
Field marks: — 5–5½. The decidedly yellowish under parts simplify our difficulties with this *Empidonax*. Its home in the summer is the northern evergreen forest. Unlike others of its genus, it nests on the ground.
Similar species: — Others of this group have a tinge of yellow beneath, especially in fall, but none of the rest has uniform yellow from throat to belly. The eye-ring is also yellow. Many Acadians look suspiciously like Yellow-bellies in the fall, and thus it is contended by experts that these two cannot be safely distinguished in autumnal migration.
Voice: — A simple, spiritless *per-wee* or *chu-wee*, rising on second syllable; a little like Wood Pewee, but more suggestive of note of Semipalmated Plover. Also 'killic.'
Range: — Breeds in boggy coniferous regions from Newfoundland, cent. Quebec, and cent. Manitoba s. to Maine, s. New Hampshire, Pennsylvania (rarely), n. Michigan, and n. Minnesota; migrates through e. United States to Central America.

ACADIAN FLYCATCHER. *Empidonax virescens.* p. 148.
Field marks: — 5½–6¾. A small Flycatcher with a conspicuous light *eye-ring* and two white *wing-bars*. It is a greenish Empidonax with a yellowish wash on the sides, but is not safely identified except by habitat, range, and voice. It is the *only* Empidonax in most of the South; a bird of deciduous forests and wet, swampy woodlands. It is particularly fond of beech trees. Its nest is supported hammock-wise in a small fork of an overhanging branch.
Similar species: — See Least, Alder, and Yellow-bellied Flycatchers. Wood Pewee often shares same woodlands, is larger, lacks eye-ring. Even the White-eyed Vireo is sometimes mistaken for one of these small Flycatchers.
Voice: — 'Song' a sharp explosive *wee-see!* or *spit-chee!* (sharp upward inflection); also a thin *peet*.

THE COMMONER OWLS

LONG-EARED
OWL

HORNED
OWL

Gray
Phase

Red
Phase

SCREECH OWL

BARN
OWL

BARRED OWL

SHORT-EARED
OWL

SNOWY
OWL

BURROWING
OWL

Immatu

Adult

SAW—WHET
OWL

HAWK
OWL

RICHARDSON'S
OWL

GREAT GRAY OWL

Plate 40

151

OTHER OWLS

BURROWING OWL   p. 133.
    Prairies; long legs; stubby tail.

SNOWY OWL   p. 133.
    Large, white.

SAW–WHET OWL   p. 137.
    Adult: Very small, brown, earless.
    Juvenile: Chocolate brown, white eyebrows.

HAWK OWL   p. 133.
    Long tail, barred breast, heavy face-marks.

GREAT GRAY OWL   p. 136.
    Very large, gray; yellow eyes, black chin-spot.

RICHARDSON'S OWL   p. 137.
    From Saw-whet by yellow bill, spotted forehead, black
    facial 'frames.'

Range: — Southeastern United States, breeding from Florida and Gulf of Mexico n. to Nebraska, Iowa, s. Michigan, Lake Erie, w. New York, and s. New England (rarely or formerly). Winters in n. South America.

ALDER, or TRAILL'S, FLYCATCHER. *Empidonax traillii traillii.*
p. 148.

Field marks: — 5¼–6. A small Flycatcher with a dark back and light breast, light *eye-ring* and two white *wing-bars*. It inhabits slashings and willow and alder thickets at the edges of streams and swamps. (In Mid-West often scrubby pastures.)

Similar species: — Like Least and Acadian Flycatchers, but browner. It is a bit larger and has a whiter throat but these are not safe field characters. (Rely only on the habitat and voice.) The nest is also determinative (usually in a bush).

Voice: — Voice descriptions vary. The regular song in New York and New England is a three-syllabled *wee-be'-o* with a hoarse burry quality, the accent on the middle syllable. The Ohio bird contracts this into a sneezy *fitz-bew* or '*witch-brew*' as distinctly different as that of any other two species of the genus. Possibly collecting would prove that subspecific differences existed. The common note is a low *pep* or *pit*.

Range: — Breeds in swampy thickets from n. Manitoba, n. Ontario, and Newfoundland s. to cent. Arkansas, Kentucky, n. New Jersey, and Connecticut, and in mountains to West Virginia. Migrates mostly through Mississippi Valley; winters in Central America.

LEAST FLYCATCHER. *Empidonax minimus.*
pp. 148, 155.

Field marks: — 5–5¾. A small Flycatcher, smaller than Wood Pewee or Phœbe, dark above and light below, with a conspicuous white *eye-ring* and two white *wing-bars*. Inhabits rural areas, orchards, groves, and woodland edges.

Similar species: — Wood Pewee is larger, has no eye-ring. Two other Empidonaces, the Alder and the Acadian, are almost identical; it is very risky to try to tell them apart by mere variations in color. During a 'wave' of these small birds in May, we let most of them go as 'Empidonax' Flycatchers, but during the breeding season their calls are characteristic, and their haunts are a clue. Ludlow Griscom writes: 'Collecting has proved that it is *impossible* to be certain in separating the Acadian, Alder, and Least Flycatchers by color characters even in the spring. In the fall, it is out of the question, the determination of museum skins often being very critical. The songs of all three species are easily recognizable. However, in migration they rarely sing their names.' The Least Flycatcher is grayer above and whiter below than the others. Its wing-bars are whiter, and its lower mandible brownish (other Empidonaces, whitish or flesh-colored). These are comparative characteristics of little value in the field. Its voice, and the northern groves, orchards, and open woodlands it inhabits, identify it. It saddles its nest to a horizontal branch.

Voice: — A sharply snapped dry *che-bek'*, accent on the second syllable; very emphatic. The 'K' sound is distinctive.

Range: — Breeds from cent. Manitoba, s. Quebec, and Cape Breton Island s. to Oklahoma, Missouri, Indiana, n. New Jersey, and, in mountains, to North Carolina; winters in Central America.

WOOD PEWEE. *Contopus virens.* p. 155.

Field marks: — 6–6½. A sparrow-sized Flycatcher, dusky olive-brown above and whitish below. It has *two conspicuous wing-bars* but *no eye-ring*. The lower mandible of the bill is *yellow*.

Similar species: — It is most like the Phœbe but has conspicuous wing-bars and does not wag its tail. It does not have the conspicuous eye-ring of the smaller and paler *Empidonax* Flycatchers. The wing is much longer than that of the Phœbe or the other small Flycatchers, reaching halfway down the tail.

Voice: — A plaintive drawling whistle *pee-a-wee*, slurring down in the middle, then up. Also *pee-ur*, slurring downward.

Range: — Breeds in woodlands, orchards, and groves from n. Florida and Gulf of Mexico n. to Prince Edward Island, s. Quebec, and s. Manitoba; winters in Central and South America.

OLIVE-SIDED FLYCATCHER. *Nuttallornis borealis.* p. 155.

Field marks: — 7¼–8. A rather large, stout bull-headed Flycatcher, usually seen perched at the extreme tip of a dead tree or exposed branch, from which it makes wide sallies after passing insects. It resembles the smaller Wood Pewee but the distinctive points are its large bill, white throat, *dark chest-patches* separated or nearly separated by a narrow strip of white (suggests a 'dark jacket unbuttoned down the front'). It also has *two tufts of white* which sometimes poke out from behind the wings near the back.

Similar species: — See Wood Pewee.

Voice: — Note a trebled *pep-pep-pep*. Song, a spirited whistle, *hip-three-cheers!* or *whip whee wheer!* the middle note highest, the last slurring down.

Range: — Breeds near brushy slashings in coniferous forests from Gulf of St. Lawrence, n. Ontario, and cent. Manitoba s. to n. Minnesota, n. Michigan, New York, Massachusetts, and, in mountains, to North Carolina. Migrates through United States to winter home in nw. South America.

VERMILION FLYCATCHER. *Pyrocephalus rubinus mexicanus.*
p. 155.

Field marks: — 5½–6½. *Male:* — *Head and under parts, flam-*

WOODPECKERS

NOTE: The birds shown opposite are males unless noted other-
     wise.

FLICKER or **YELLOW-SHAFTED FLICKER**   p. 141.
     Brown back, white rump.

HAIRY WOODPECKER   p. 143.
     White back, large bill.

DOWNY WOODPECKER   p. 144.
     White back, small bill.

RED-BELLIED WOODPECKER   p. 142.
     Adult: Zebra back, red cap.
     Immature: Zebra back, brown head.

SAPSUCKER (YELLOW-BELLIED)   p. 143.
     Adult: Long white wing-stripe.
     Immature: Brown; long wing-stripe.

PILEATED WOODPECKER   p. 142.
     Large size, red crest.

RED-COCKADED WOODPECKER   p. 144.
     Zebra back, white cheek.

RED-HEADED WOODPECKER   p. 143.
     Adult: Red head, broad wing-patch.
     Immature: Brown head, broad wing-patch.

AMERICAN THREE-TOED WOODPECKER   p. 144
     Ladder back, ladder sides; male with yellow cap.

ARCTIC THREE-TOED or **BLACK-BACKED WOODPECKER**   p. 144.
     Black back, ladder sides; male with yellow cap.

FLICKER

HAIRY

DOWNY

Immature

RED-BELLIED

Immature

SAPSUCKER

PILEATED

Immature

RED-COCKADED

RED-HEADED

♀

AMERICAN THREE-TOED

ARCTIC THREE-TOED

SCISSOR-
TAILED
FLYCATCHER

♂

VERMILION
FLYCATCH

♀

CRESTED
FLYCATCHER

WESTERN
KINGBIRD

EASTERN
KINGBIRD

OLIVE-SIDED
FLYCATCHER

WOOD
PEWEE

PHOEBE

LEAST
FLYCATCHER

YELLOW-BELLIED
FLYCATCHER

Note: Acadian Flycatcher and Alder
Flycatcher are almost identical to Least
Flycatcher

Plate 42   155

FLYCATCHERS

Flycatchers perch in an upright attitude and often sit quite motionless.

CRESTED FLYCATCHER   p. 147.
  Yellow belly, rufous tail.

SCISSOR–TAILED FLYCATCHER   p. 147.
  Long forked tail.

VERMILION FLYCATCHER   p. 153.
  Male: Vermilion breast, black back.
  Female: Streaks, pinkish belly.
  Some young females have yellowish bellies.

WESTERN or ARKANSAS KINGBIRD   p. 146.
  Yellow belly, black tail.

EASTERN KINGBIRD   p. 146.
  White band on tip of tail.

OLIVE–SIDED FLYCATCHER   p. 153.
  Dark 'vest,' unbuttoned down front; white tufts.

WOOD PEWEE   p. 153.
  Conspicuous wing-bars, no eye-ring.
  Also yellow on bill.

PHOEBE   p. 147.
  No wing-bars (or dull ones), no eye-ring.

YELLOW–BELLIED FLYCATCHER   p. 149.
  Wing-bars, eye-ring, yellowish under parts.

**LEAST FLYCATCHER ***   p. 152.
  Wing-bars, eye-ring, whitish under parts.

* Acadian Flycatcher and Alder Flycatcher are almost identical with Least Flycatcher. Identify by voice and habitat. See schematic illustration of these small Flycatchers on page 148.

ing vermilion-red: tail and upper parts blackish. *Female:* — Upper parts dark brown; breast white, narrowly streaked with dusky; belly and under tail-coverts *pinkish.* Immature females have yellowish bellies.

Similar species: — Male Scarlet Tanager has scarlet back.

Voice: — A twittering Phœbe-like *zi-breee* or *p-p-pit-zeee.*

Range: — Rare but regular in winter along Gulf Coast from Texas to w. Florida (more frequent westward).

Larks: Alaudidæ

HORNED LARK. *Eremophila alpestris.* Subsp. p. 226.
   Field marks:— 7–8. A brown ground bird, larger than a Sparrow, with black 'whiskers' and a contrasting head pattern. It has two small black *horns* (not always noticeable), and a black collar, or ring, below the light throat; *walks,* does not hop; frequents plains, prairies, fields, golf-courses, and shores; flying overhead, looks light-bellied with a *black* tail; folds its wings tightly after each beat. Females and immature birds are duller, but show the Horned Lark pattern. The Northern and Prairie subspecies are often distinguishable (see Subspecies).

Similar species: — See Pipit, Longspurs.

Voice: — Song, tinkling, irregular and high-pitched, often long-sustained, and sometimes given high in air in the manner of European Skylark. Note, *tee-ee* or *tee-titi.*

Range: — Breeds from Arctic s. to North Carolina, West Virginia, Missouri, and Kansas; also coast of Texas. Winters s. to Gulf Coast, Georgia, and Florida (rarely).

Swallows: Hirundinidæ

SPARROW-SIZED birds with long, slim wings and graceful flight. They can be identified by flight. Although the voices of Swallows are distinctive, once learned, they are not well adapted to description.

TREE SWALLOW. *Iridoprocne bicolor.* p. 162.
   Field marks: — 5–6. Steely blue-black or green-black above and *clear white* below; no other Swallow has such immaculate white under parts.

Similar species: — Immatures in late summer are sometimes confusing. (See Rough-winged Swallow.)

Voice: — Note, *cheet* or *chi-veet,* also a liquid 'song.'

Range: — Breeds mostly in open wooded swamps and near water from Quebec and n. Manitoba s. to Virginia, ne. Arkansas, and Kansas. Winters along coast from North Carolina to Florida and Gulf of Mexico (rarely n. to Long Island).

BANK SWALLOW. *Riparia riparia riparia.*   p. 162.
   Field marks: — 5–5½. A small *brown-backed* Swallow with a *distinct dark band* across the white breast.
   Similar species: — The other Brown-backed Swallow, the larger Rough-wing, lacks this band, has a *dusky throat.* The Bank Swallow is colonial, the Rough-wing more solitary. In the late summer brownish young Tree Swallows sometimes seem to have a faint breast-band.
   Voice: — A short dry buzz or rattle, *brrt* or *bjjt.*
   Range: — Breeds in sand-banks and road-cuts from Quebec and Alaska s. to Virginia, n. Alabama, Louisiana (probably), and Texas; winters in South America.

ROUGH-WINGED SWALLOW. *Stelgidopteryx ruficollis serripennis.*   p. 162.
   Field marks: — 5–5¾. A *brown-backed* Swallow, larger and lighter brown than the Bank Swallow; no breast-band. The light under parts shade into a dingy color toward the throat.
   Similar species: — Bank Swallow has dark band across breast. Immature Tree Swallows in late summer are sooty brownish and might be mistaken for this species, except for their white throats and more snowy-white under parts.
   Voice: — Rougher than Bank Swallow's; *trit-trit* (F. H. Allen).
   Range: — Breeds in banks or masonry near water from Gulf of Mexico n. to Massachusetts, New York, se. Ontario, Minnesota, and North Dakota. Winters in Central America.

BARN SWALLOW. *Hirundo rustica erythrogaster.*   p. 162.
   Field marks: — 6–7½. This is the only native Swallow that is really 'swallow-tailed,' and the only one with white spots in the tail. Pinkish or cinnamon-buff below, with a blue-black back; males brighter than females.
   Voice: — A soft *wit* or *kvik-kvik, wit-wit* (W. M. Tyler). About nest a harsh irritated *ee-tee.*
   Range: — Breeds about barns and building from cent. Quebec and s. Manitoba s. to North Carolina, n. Alabama, Tennessee, and Arkansas (also locally on Gulf Coast). Winters from Mexico to Brazil.

(NORTHERN) CLIFF SWALLOW. *Petrochelidon pyrrhonota albifrons.*   p. 162.
   Field marks: — 5–6. Look for the pale rusty or *buffy* rump; it quickly marks the Cliff Swallow. Overhead it appears *square-tailed* with a *dark* throat-patch.

Similar species: — Cliff Swallows nest in gourdlike mud nests plastered against cliffs, under bridges, or beneath the eaves on the *outside* of barns. Barn Swallows build open nests, *usually*, but not always, on the *inside* of barns.

Voice: — More squeaky and husky than Barn Swallow.

Range: — Breeds about barns (sometimes cliffs) from Gulf of St. Lawrence, n. Ontario, and n. Manitoba s. locally to w. Virginia, n. Alabama, and Texas. Migrates through s. United States; winters in s. South America.

PURPLE MARTIN. *Progne subis subis.* p. 162.
Field marks: — 7½–8½. Our largest Swallow. The male is uniformly blue-black *above and below*. No other Swallow is black-bellied. The female is light-bellied, sometimes with a faint collar around the back of the neck.

Similar species: — The female may be known from the much smaller Tree Swallow by her size and the dingy grayness of the throat and breast.

Voice: — Throaty and rich, *tchew-wew*, etc.

Range: — Breeds in bird-houses and about buildings from Gulf of Mexico n. to Nova Scotia, nw. Ontario, and s. Manitoba. Winters in Brazil.

Crows and Jays: Corvidæ

CANADA JAY. *Perisoreus canadensis.* Subsp. p. 199.
Field marks: — 11–13. A large *gray* bird of the cool north woods; larger than a Robin, with a *black cap* set on the back of its head, and a *white forehead*; suggests a huge, overgrown Chickadee. Juvenile birds (first summer) are dark slate-colored, almost blackish around the head.

Voice: — A soft *whee-ah*, also many other notes, some harsh.

Range: — Resident of spruce forests from n. New England, n. New York, n. Michigan, and n. Minnesota n. to limit of evergreens.

BLUE JAY. *Cyanocitta cristata.* Subsp. p. 199.
Field marks: — 11–12. A *large* bright blue bird, larger than a Robin; blue above, whitish below, and *crested*.

Similar species: — The dissimilar Bluebird is much smaller, not much larger than a Sparrow, with a *reddish* breast. (See Kingfisher.) In Florida see Florida Jay.

Voice: — A harsh slurring *jeeah* or *'jay'*; also many other notes, some musical. Imitates Red-shouldered and Red-tailed Hawks.

Range: — Resident from Gulf of St. Lawrence and n. Manitoba

AMERICAN MAGPIE

to s. Florida and Gulf of Mexico. There is some migration from n. part of range.

FLORIDA, or SCRUB, JAY. *Aphelocoma cœrulescens cœrulescens.*
p. 227.
Field marks: — 11½. Look for this *crestless* Jay *only* in the stretches of 'scrub' in Florida. The wings and tail are solid blue with no white markings. Easily tamed.
Similar species: — The Florida race of the Blue Jay is often present in the same locality, but has a *crest*, and has white markings on the wings and tail.
Voice: — A rough rasping note: *kwesh . . . kwesh.* Also a low rasping *zhreek* or *zhrink.*
Range: — Local in scrub oak regions of Florida Peninsula. The most essentially Floridian bird. Never recorded out of the State.

AMERICAN MAGPIE. *Pica pica hudsonia.* p. 159.
Field marks: — 17½–21½, tail 9½–12. Larger than a Jay or a Grackle; the only large *black and white* land bird with a *long wedge-shaped* tail. In flight the iridescent tail streams out behind and large white patches flash in the wing.
Voice: — A rapid *cheg cheg cheg cheg.* Also a nasal querulous *maaag?* or *maa—maa?*
Range: — Western North America; a few wander e. in winter to Minnesota and Nebraska; occasionally farther.

RAVEN. *Corvus corax.* Subsp. p. 160.
Field marks: — 21½–26½. Although a Raven is nearly twice the bulk of a Crow, field comparison is not always possible. Watch, then, the flight. Hawk-like, the Raven alternates flap-

SILHOUETTES OF CORVIDÆ

Note the Raven's shaggy throat, heavy bill, wedge-shaped tail. Identify the Fish Crow by voice.

ping with soaring. It soars on horizontal wings; the Crow and the Turkey Vulture with wings 'bent upward.' The ample tail, seen from below, is distinctly *wedge-shaped*. Perched, at not too great a distance, the shaggy throat-feathers are evident.
Voice: — Raven croaks: *cr-r-ruck* or *pruk*. (Crow caws.)
Range: — Resident of wild regions from n. Canada s. to Maine, Michigan, and Minnesota and locally in Appalachians to Georgia; occasional along coast from New Jersey to North Carolina.

CROW. *Corvus brachyrhynchos.* Subsp.   p. 160.
Field marks: — 17–21. Much larger than any of the Blackbirds, this chunky, ebony-hued bird needs no description.
Similar species: — See Fish Crow, Raven, Grackles.
Voice: — A loud *caw* or *cah*, easily imitated by voice.
Range: — Breeds from Newfoundland and n. Manitoba s. to Florida and Texas. Winters n. to Great Lakes and s. Maine.

FISH CROW. *Corvus ossifragus.*   p. 160.
Field marks: — 16–20. Along tidewater listen for this small Crow. Go by voice, not by size, unless both Crows are together.
Voice: — A short, nasal *car* or *că*. Sometimes a two-syllabled *că-hă*. (Common Crows utter an honest-to-goodness *caw*.) In late spring and summer, certain of the calls of young Crows are much like those of the Fish Crow.
Range: — Seldom far from tidewater; from s. New England to Florida and along Gulf to e. Texas. Found throughout Florida

and quite far up rivers influenced by tide (Hudson, Delaware, Potomac, etc.). Withdraws from n. part of range in winter.

Titmice: Paridæ

SMALL GRAY BIRDS, smaller than most Sparrows, with proportionately longer tails and small stubby bills; extremely active, hanging upside down as well as right side up in their busy search for insects.

BLACK–CAPPED CHICKADEE. *Parus atricapillus.* Subsp.
p. 163.
Field marks: — 4¾–5½. Chickadees are the only small birds with the combination of *black cap, black bib,* and *white cheeks.* These small tame acrobats are smaller than Sparrows.
Similar species: — See Carolina and Brown-capped Chickadees.
Voice: — A clearly enunciated *chick-a-dee-dee-dee* or *dee-dee-dee.* In spring a clear whistle *fee-bee* or *fee-bee-ee* the first note higher. The Phœbe Flycatcher does not whistle, but says its name simply — *phœbe.*
Range: — Resident from n. Ontario and Newfoundland s. to Kansas, Missouri, Illinois, Ohio, Pennsylvania, n. New Jersey, and, in mountains, to North Carolina.

CAROLINA CHICKADEE. *Parus carolinensis.* Subsp. p. 163
Field marks: — 4¼–4¾. Nearly identical with the Black-cap, but noticeably smaller, without so much white in the wing created by the white feather-edgings.
Similar species: — Replaces Black-cap in southern United States. The two are best identified by the localities where found and by voice (below). The slight differences in the wings are not reliable because of season, wear, angle of light, etc. Moreover the two intergrade where their ranges meet.
Voice: — The 'Chickadee' call of this species is higher-pitched and more rapid than that of the Black-cap. The two-noted whistle is replaced by a four-syllabled song, *fee-bee, fee-bay.*
Range: — Resident from where range of Black-cap ends, from New Jersey, Ohio, Missouri, and Oklahoma s. to Florida and Gulf of Mexico. Check your local publication for more exact range if you live in a borderline state.

BROWN–CAPPED CHICKADEE. *Parus hudsonicus.* Subsp.
p. 163.
Field marks: — 5–5½. The small size and black bib proclaim it a Chickadee; the general color of the bird is *brown* rather than gray, and it has a *dark brown* cap.
Similar species: — Black-cap is grayer, has black cap.

SWALLOWS AND SWIFT

PURPLE MARTIN   p. 158.
    Male: Black breast.
    Female: Grayish breast.

BARN SWALLOW   p. 157.
    Deeply forked tail.

CLIFF SWALLOW   p. 157.
    Pale rump, square tail.

BANK SWALLOW   p. 157.
    Brown back, breast-band.

ROUGH-WINGED SWALLOW   p. 157.
    Brown back, dingy throat.

TREE SWALLOW   p. 156.
    Adult: Back blue-black; breast snow white.
    Immature: Brownish back, white throat, no breast-band.

CHIMNEY SWIFT   p. 139.
    Sooty; 'a cigar with wings.'

Martin	Barn	Cliff	Bank	Rough-	Tree
(Male)	Swallow	Swallow	Swallow	winged	Swallow
				Swallow	

SWALLOWS ON A WIRE

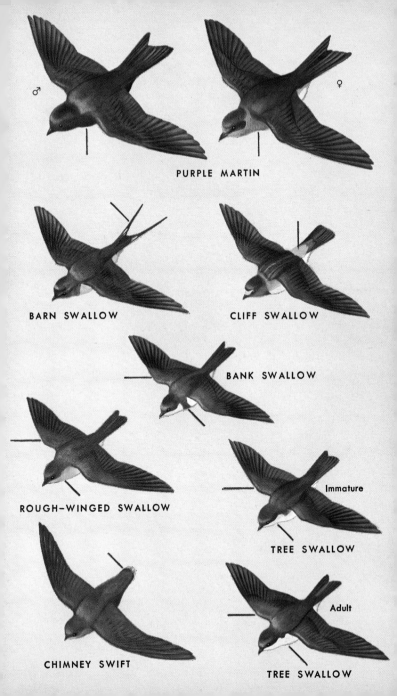

PURPLE MARTIN

BARN SWALLOW

CLIFF SWALLOW

BANK SWALLOW

ROUGH-WINGED SWALLOW

Immature

TREE SWALLOW

CHIMNEY SWIFT

Adult

TREE SWALLOW

GOLDEN-
CROWNED
KINGLET

♀ ♂

RUBY-
CROWNED
KINGLET

♀ ♂

BLACK-CAPPED
CHICKADEE

CAROLINA
CHICKADEE

BROWN-CAPPED
CHICKADEE

BROWN
CREEPER

TUFTED
TITMOUSE

BLUE-GRAY
GNATCATCHER

RED-BREASTED
NUTHATCH

WHITE-BREASTED
NUTHATCH

BROWN-HEADED
NUTHATCH

Plate 44   163

KINGLETS, TITMICE, CREEPER,
GNATCATCHER AND NUTHATCHES

GOLDEN–CROWNED KINGLET   p. 174
    Male: Eye-stripe, orange crown.
    Female: Eye-stripe, yellow crown.

RUBY–CROWNED KINGLET   p. 175
    Male: Broken eye-ring, red crown.
    Female: Broken eye-ring, stubby tail.

BLACK–CAPPED CHICKADEE   p. 161
    Black cap, black bib.

CAROLINA CHICKADEE   p. 161
    Less white in feather edges (not safe).
    Use voice and range (see text).

BROWN–CAPPED CHICKADEE   p. 161
    Brown cap, black bib.

BROWN CREEPER   p. 165
    Slender curved bill, creeping posture.

TUFTED TITMOUSE   p. 164
    Gray back, tufted head.

BLUE–GRAY GNATCATCHER   p. 174
    Long tail, white eye-ring, white under parts.

RED–BREASTED NUTHATCH   p. 164
    Black line through eye.

WHITE–BREASTED NUTHATCH   p. 164
    Black eye on white cheek.

BROWN–HEADED NUTHATCH   p. 165
    Brown cap to eye.

Voice: — The notes are slower and more drawling than those of the Black-cap; instead of a lively *chick-a-dee-dee-dee,* it utters a wheezy *chick — che — day — day.*

Range: — Resident in spruce forests from mountains of n. New England, n. New York, n. Michigan, and n. Minnesota n. to limit of trees in Canada. In winter *casually* to n. New Jersey and n. Pennsylvania.

TUFTED TITMOUSE. *Parus bicolor.* p. 163.
  Field marks: — 6–6½. No other small *gray,* mouse-colored bird has a tufted crest. Its flanks are rusty.
  Voice: — A clear whistled chant: *peter, peter, peter* or *here, here, here, here.* Other notes, similar to chickadee notes of Chickadee but more drawling; nasal, wheezy, and complaining.
  Range: — Resident in s. United States from Florida and Gulf n. to n. New Jersey, Lake Erie, Illinois, Iowa, and Nebraska.

Nuthatches: Sittidæ

SMALL, CHUBBY tree-climbers; smaller than a Sparrow, with a long bill and a stubby tail that is never braced against the tree wood-pecker-like as an aid in climbing. No other tree-climbers attempt to go down tree-trunks *headfirst,* as these little birds habitually do.

WHITE-BREASTED NUTHATCH. *Sitta carolinensis.* Subsp.
p. 163.
  Field marks: — 5–6. Nuthatches are the 'upside-down birds.' The White-breasted Nuthatch is known by its black cap and its beady black eye on a white cheek.
  Similar species: — Red-breasted Nuthatch has eye-stripe. Chickadees have black bibs.
  Voice: — Spring song, a series of low, rather nasal, whistled notes all on same pitch, *whǐ, whǐ, whǐ, whǐ, whǐ, whǐ, whǐ, whǐ,* or *who who who,* etc. Note, a nasal *yank* or *hank.* Also an abrupt nasal *tootoo* (double-noted).
  Range: — Resident of woodlands, village trees, orchards, from s. Quebec and n. Minnesota s. to Florida and Gulf Coast.

RED-BREASTED NUTHATCH. *Sitta canadensis.* p. 163.
  Field marks: — 4¼–4¾. Smaller than the White-breast; rustier below, with a *broad black line* through the eye.
  Similar species: — White-breast has white cheeks, no eye line.
  Voice: — The call corresponding to the *yank-yank* of the White-breast is higher and more nasal, like a 'baby' Nuthatch or a 'tiny tin horn.'
  Range: — Prefers evergreens. Breeds from limit of spruce trees

in Canada s. to n. Minnesota, Michigan, and n. New England
and in Appalachians to North Carolina. Migrates irregularly
(occasionally to Gulf States).

BROWN-HEADED NUTHATCH. *Sitta pusilla.* Subsp. p. 163.
   Field marks: — 4–5. This dwarf Nuthatch loves the southern
   pinelands. Smaller than the other two species, with a *brown* cap
   coming down to the eye and a white spot on the nape.
   Similar species: — White-breast has *black cap*; Red-breast has
   black eye-stripe.
   Voice: — Un-nutha ch-like, a rapid, high *kit-kit-kit*; also a
   squeaky, piping *ki-day* or *ki-dee-dee* constantly repeated, sometimes becoming an excited twitter or chatter.
   Range: — Resident of open pine woods from Florida and Gulf of
   Mexico n. to coastal Delaware and s. Missouri.

Creepers: Certhiidæ

BROWN CREEPER. *Certhia familiaris.* Subsp.   p. 163.
   Field marks: — 5–5¾. The name Creeper fits. It is a slim well-
   camouflaged brown bird, much smaller than a Sparrow, with a
   slender curved bill and a rather stiff tail used as a prop when
   climbing. It climbs a tree like a spiral staircase, then flies to the
   base of the next tree.
   Voice: — Note, a single long thin *seeee*, similar to quick trebled
   note (*see-see-see*) of Golden-crowned Kinglet. Song, weak, clear
   notes, *see-ti-wee-tu-wee*, or *see-see-see-ti-ti-see*, the high *see* notes
   resembling the thin call-note.
   Range: — Woodlands; breeds from s. Quebec, cent. Ontario, and
   s. Manitoba s. to n. parts of United States and, in mountains, to
   North Carolina; winters to Texas and Florida.

Wrens: Troglodytidæ

ENERGETIC brown birds, smaller than Sparrows, plump and stumpy
with slender bills; tails often cocked over back.

HOUSE WREN. *Troglodytes aëdon.* Subsp.   p. 182.
   Field marks: — 4½–5¼. A Wren of the orchards, farmyards,
   etc.; recognized as a Wren by the small size, brown coloration,
   energetic actions, and habit of cocking its tail over its back; distinguished from the others by its grayer-brown color and the
   lack of any evident facial stripings.
   Similar species: — See Bewick's Wren and Carolina Wren (all
   three nest in bird-boxes). See also Winter Wren.

THRUSHES

EASTERN BLUEBIRD   p. 173.
   Adult: Blue back, rusty breast.
   Juvenile: Speckled breast, blue in wing.

ROBIN   p. 171.
   Rusty breast, gray back.

WOOD THRUSH   p. 171.
   Rufous head, large spots.

HERMIT THRUSH   p. 172.
   Rufous tail.

VEERY   p. 173.
   Tawny from head to tail; little spotting.

GRAY-CHEEKED THRUSH   p. 172.
   Dull gray-brown above, no rusty.
   Gray cheeks, inconspicuous eye-ring.

OLIVE-BACKED THRUSH   p. 172.
   Dull gray-brown above, no rusty.
   Buffy cheeks, conspicuous eye-ring.

Juvenile

BLUEBIRD

♂

ROBIN

♂

WOOD THRUSH

HERMIT THRUSH

VEERY

GRAY-CHEEKED THRUSH

OLIVE-BACKED THRUSH

CATBIRD

BROWN THRASHER

MOCKINGBIRD

LOGGERHEAD SHRIKE
Adult

Adult
NORTHERN SHRIKE

Immature
NORTHERN SHRIKE

Juvenile   Adult
CEDAR WAXWING   BOHEMIAN WAXWING

Plate 46   167

MIMIC THRUSHES, SHRIKES AND WAXWINGS

BROWN THRASHER   p. 170.
  Rufous; long tail, stripes, wing-bars.

CATBIRD   p. 170.
  Slaty; black crown, rusty under tail-coverts.

MOCKINGBIRD   p. 170.
  White wing and tail-patches, no mask.
  Shrikes (below) have black masks.

NORTHERN SHRIKE   p. 176.
  Adult: Light lower mandible, faintly barred breast.
  Immature: Brownish; lightly barred breast.

LOGGERHEAD SHRIKE   p. 177.
  Bill all black; mask meets over bill.

CEDAR WAXWING   p. 176.
  Adult: Yellow band on tail, crest.
  Juvenile: Soft streakings.

BOHEMIAN WAXWING   p. 176.
  White wing-patches, rusty under tail-coverts.

Voice: — A stuttering, gurgling song, rising in a musical burst, then falling at the end.

Range: — Breeds from New Brunswick, s. Quebec, s. Ontario, and s. Manitoba s. to Virginia, Kentucky, s. Missouri, and cent.-w. Texas; winters in s. Atlantic and Gulf States.

WINTER WREN. *Troglodytes troglodytes.* Subsp.   p. 182.
Field marks: — 4–4¼. A very small round dark Wren, smaller than a House Wren; has a *much stubbier tail* than that species, a light line over the eye and a *brownish, heavily barred belly*; often bobs its head; frequents mossy tangles, brush-piles, ravines, roots along stream-banks, etc.
Similar species: — See House Wren.
Voice: — Song, a rapid succession of high tinkling warbles and trills, long sustained and often ending on a *very high* light trill. Note, a hard two-syllabled *kip kip*, suggestive of Song Sparrow's *chip*.
Range: — Breeds from s. Manitoba, n. Ontario, and Gulf of St. Lawrence s. to Minnesota, New York, and, in mountains, to n. Georgia; winters s. to Texas and Florida.

BEWICK'S WREN. *Thryomanes bewickii.* Subsp.   p. 182.
Field marks: — 5–5½. The long tail with *white spots* in the corners (not always easy to see) is the most characteristic thing about this bird. No other eastern Wren has this. It has a white stripe over the eye.
Similar species: — House Wren lacks the white eye-stripe and white tail-spots. Bewick's Wren often nests in bird-boxes and to many people in the central Mississippi Valley is their 'House' Wren. Carolina Wren is larger, bright rusty, and lacks the tail-spots.
Voice: — Song variable; usually suggests that of a Song Sparrow, but thinner, starting on two or three high notes, dropping lower, and then ending on a thin trill.
Range: — Mississippi Valley and southern Appalachian Plateau from cent. Pennsylvania, s. Michigan, n. Illinois, and s. Nebraska s. to cent. Georgia, Alabama, Mississippi, and Arkansas. Winters throughout most of range to Gulf of Mexico.

CAROLINA WREN. *Thryothorus ludovicianus.* Subsp.   p. 182.
Field marks: — 5½–6. The largest and reddest of the Wrens; as large as a small Sparrow; *rufous red* above and buffy below, with a conspicuous *white stripe* over the eye. Prefers tangles and brushy undergrowth.
Similar species: — The Long-billed Marsh Wren has a white eye-line, but that bird is striped on the back; the Carolina is unmarked. The Bewick's Wren is grayer, and has white tail-corners.

Voice: — A clear chanting whistle. Variable; *chirpity, chirpity, chirpity, chirp,* or *tea-kettle, tea-kettle, tea-kettle, tea.* Usually tri-syllabic but sometimes two-syllabled, for example: *wheedle, wheedle, wheedle.*

Range: — Resident from Rhode Island (local), lower Hudson River, Pennsylvania, Ohio, s. Iowa, and se. Nebraska, s. to Florida, Gulf Coast, and Texas.

LONG-BILLED MARSH WREN. *Telmatodytes palustris.* Subsp.
p. 182.

Field marks: — 4½–5½. The Wren of the cattail marsh; brown, with a conspicuous white line over the eye; known from the other small Wrens with white eye-stripes by the *black and white stripes on the back.*

Similar species: — See Short-billed Marsh Wren. Bewick's and Carolina Wrens have eye-stripes but no marks on the back.

Voice: — Song, reedy and gurgling, running into a guttural rattle: *cut-cut-turrrrrrrrr-ur;* often heard at night.

Range: — Breeds from Massachusetts, n. Vermont, Ontario, and Saskatchewan s. to Florida and Gulf Coast; winters in s. United States (a few north to New York).

SHORT-BILLED MARSH WREN. *Cistothorus platensis stellaris.*
p. 182.

Field marks: — 4–4½. The Wren of the wet meadows and *grassy* marshes. Under parts very buffy; crown *streaked.*

Similar species: — Long-bill has more contrastingly marked upper parts, a conspicuous white line over the eye, a *solid* un-streaked crown and, when the tail is cocked over the back, whiter under tail-coverts. The Long-bill prefers cattails rather than grass and sedges except in those parts of its range where it lives in salt marshes.

Voice: — Song, a dry staccato chattering — *chap chap chap chap chap chap chapper-rrrrr.* The call-note is of the same quality: a single *chick* or *chap.*

Range: — Breeds from s. Maine, s. Ontario, and Manitoba s. to n. Delaware, Indiana, Missouri, and e. Kansas; winters from New Jersey and s. Illinois to Gulf of Mexico.

ROCK WREN. *Salpintces obsoletus obsoletus.*

Field marks: — 5¼–6¼. Western. Inhabits rocky slopes and canyons. A gray Wren showing *whitish or buffy* patches at end of tail. Distinguished from Bewick's Wren (which also shows tail-spots) by pale back and *finely streaked breast.* See illustration in *A Field Guide to Western Birds.*

Voice: — Song, a harsh chant, *tew, tew, tew, tew* or *chr-wee chr-wee, chr-wee;* call, a loud dry trill; also a clear *ti-keer.*

Range: — Breeds e. to or almost to the 100th meridian in the central parts of the Dakotas, Nebraska, and Kansas.

Mockingbirds and Thrashers: Mimidæ

(EASTERN) MOCKINGBIRD. *Mimus polyglottos̄ polyglottos.*
p. 167.
Field marks: — 9–11. As large as a Robin, but more slender and longer-tailed; gray above and white below, with *large white patches* on the wings and tail, conspicuous in flight.
Similar species: — Shrikes have black facial masks and show less white in the wings and tail. See Loggerhead Shrike.
Voice: — Song, a long-continued succession of notes and phrases of great variety. The Mockingbird rapidly repeats each phrase a half-dozen times or more in succession before going on to the next one. (Thrasher usually repeats once; Catbird does not repeat.) Many Mockingbirds are excellent mimics, adeptly imitating a score or more of the other species found in the neighborhood. Often sings at night. Note, a loud *tchack*.
Range: — Resident of towns, rural country, edges, from Maryland, Ohio, Illinois, s. Iowa, and Nebraska s. to the Gulf of Mexico. A few n. to Massachusetts and Great Lakes.

CATBIRD. *Dumetella carolinensis.* p. 167.
Field marks: — 8½–9¼. Smaller and slimmer than a Robin; *slaty-gray* with a black cap, and with *chestnut-red* under tail-coverts (these are seldom noticed in the field).
Similar species: — The other uniformly dark gray song-birds — the juvenile Starling, female Cowbird, female Rusty Blackbird, and (in prairies) female Brewer's Blackbird — are shorter-tailed, and lack the black cap and rusty under tail-coverts.
Voice: — Catlike mewing note, distinctive. Song, a disjointed succession of notes and phrases, some musical. Notes not repeated as in songs of Thrasher and Mockingbird.
Range: — Prefers thickets; breeds from Nova Scotia, s. Quebec, and s. Manitoba s. to n. Florida, Louisiana, and se. Texas; winters in s. United States, n. rarely to s. New England.

(EASTERN) BROWN THRASHER. *Toxostoma rufum rufum.*
p. 167.
Field marks: — 10½–12. A slim rufous bird. Slightly longer than a Robin; bright *rufous-red* above, *heavily striped* below. Has *wing-bars*, a curved bill, and a long tail.
Similar species: — Differs from the Thrushes in possessing a much longer tail and in being *streaked*, rather than spotted, below. The eye is yellow (Thrushes brown). Thrushes do not have wing-bars.
Voice: — Song, a succession of deliberate notes and short

phrases, resembling Catbird's song, but more musical and each phrase usually in *pairs*. Note, a harsh *chack*.

Range: — Breeds in thickets and shrubbery from Maine, se. Quebec, n. Michigan, and s. Manitoba s. to Gulf of Mexico; winters in s. United States, rarely to Massachusetts.

Thrushes, Robins, Bluebirds, Etc.: Turdidæ

THE FIVE eastern species that bear the name 'Thrush' are brown-backed birds with *spotted* breasts. Robins and Bluebirds, though entirely unlike the other Thrushes in color, betray relationship to this group through their speckle-breasted young. The family has rather long legs for songbirds, large eyes, and moderately slender bills.

ROBIN. *Turdus migratorius.* Subsp.   p. 166.
    Field marks: — 8½–10½. One of the most familiar of all birds; easily recognized by its gray back and *brick-red* breast. In the male, the head and tail are blackish; in the female, paler. The bill is *yellow*. Young Robins have speckled breasts, but the gray back and rusty under parts identify them.
    Voice: — Song, a clear, whistled caroling, often long continued, made up of short phrases of two or three notes.
    Range: — Breeds from limit of trees in Canada s. to w. South Carolina, n. Georgia, n. Mississippi, and n. Louisiana; winters in s. United States n. to Ohio Valley and New England Coast.

WOOD THRUSH. *Hylocichla mustelina.*   p. 166.
    Field marks: — 7½–8½. *Rusty-headed.* Smaller than a Robin; breast and sides heavily spotted. Plumper than the other Thrushes; distinguished from them by the deepening redness *about the head* and the larger, more numerous *round* spots.
    Similar species: — Brown Thrasher is longer-tailed, has wing-bars, and is streaked, not spotted. (See Hermit Thrush.)
    Voice: — Song, flute-like; phrases rounder than those of other Thrushes. Listen for a flute-like *ee-o-lay*. Guttural notes occasionally interspersed are distinctive. Call, a rapid *pip-pip-pip-pip*.
    Range: — Deciduous woodlands; breeds from cent. New Hampshire, se. Ontario, cent. Minnesota, and South Dakota almost to Gulf of Mexico. Winters from Florida s.

(EASTERN) HERMIT THRUSH. *Hylocichla guttata faxoni.*

p. 166.

Field marks: — 6½–7½. *Rusty-tailed.* Larger than a Sparrow, a brown-backed bird with a slender bill and spotted breast. The *reddish tail*, conspicuous as the bird flies away, is the Hermit Thrush's mark. At rest the Hermit has a trick of cocking its tail at an angle and dropping it slowly.

Similar species: — Three of the five brown Thrushes are tinged with some rufous. The Veery is *uniformly* colored above, the Wood Thrush is reddest *about the head*, and the Hermit reddest *on the tail.* The Fox Sparrow is also reddish-tailed, but the under parts are heavily streaked, not spotted. The bill of the Sparrow is short and conical.

Voice: — Song, clear and flute-like. Four or five phrases in *different pitches*, each introduced by a *long introductory or key note.* Each phrase is given in turn after a deliberate pause. The pure key note is diagnostic. Note, a low *chuck* or *quilp*; also a scolding *tuk-tuk-tuk* and a harsh *pay*.

Range: — Breeds in mixed evergreen-hardwood forests from n. Manitoba and s. Quebec s. to cent. Minnesota, n. Michigan, Massachusetts, Long Island (a few), New Jersey (a few), and, in mountains, to Virginia; winters throughout s. United States to Ohio Valley and s. New England (a few).

OLIVE-BACKED THRUSH. *Hylocichla ustulata.* p. 166.

Field marks: — 6½–7½. When we come upon a Thrush that lacks any warmth of color in its plumage and is uniformly gray-brown or olive-brown above, then we have found one of two species. If the bird also has a conspicuous *buffy eye-ring* and *buffy cheeks*, it is the Olive-backed Thrush.

Similar species: — If the cheeks are gray and the eye-ring indistinct or lacking, then it is the Gray-cheek (but see them well and be cautious, especially in the fall).

Voice: — Song, melodious, breezy flute-like phrases; distinguished by tendency of each phrase to climb *upwards* (like a Veery in reverse). Note, *whit.* Migrants at night, a short *heep.*

Range: — Breeds in spruce belt from n. Manitoba and Newfoundland s. to n. Michigan, New York, n. New England, and, in Appalachians, to West Virginia. Migrates through s. United States; winters in Central and South America.

GRAY-CHEEKED THRUSH. *Hylocichla minima.* Subsp.

p. 166.

Field marks: — 6¼–8. An olive-brown or gray-brown Thrush. It is identified, when seen very well, by its *grayish cheeks* and by its inconspicuous eye-ring.

Similar species: — The only other Thrush which is olive-brown or gray-brown above without any hint of rusty is the Olive-backed Thrush. It is very similar but has *buffy cheeks* and a conspicuous *buffy eye-ring*. Its breast is also suffused with buff. Study your bird very carefully. In fall migration it is sometimes not safe to try to distinguish them.

Voice: — Song, thin and nasal; resembles slightly that of Veery, but often rises abruptly at close (Veery goes down); *whee-wheeoo-tili-whee* (F. H. Allen). Note, *vee-a* or *quee-a* higher and more nasal than Veery's note; uttered by migrants at night.

Range: — Breeds in spruce forests from near limit of trees in Newfoundland, cent. Quebec, and n. Manitoba s., in higher mountains (Bicknell's Thrush), to nw. Massachusetts (Mt. Greylock) and New York (Catskills). Winters in South America.

VEERY. *Hylocichla fuscescens.* Subsp. p. 166.
  Field marks: — 6½–7½. A Thrush *uniformly* cinnamon-brown or tawny above is quite certainly a Veery. Of all the Thrushes this is the least spotted; the spots are *indistinct*, often giving a clear-breasted appearance at a distance.
  Similar species: — The Gray-cheek and Olive-back are dull *gray-brown* above; Wood Thrush is reddish *about the head*; Hermit reddish *on the tail.*
  Voice: — A liquid breezy whistle, wheeling *downward*: *vee-ur, vee-ur, veer, veer.* Distinctive. Note, *phew* or *view.*
  Range: — Moist woods and bottomland forests, breeding from Newfoundland and s. Manitoba to cent. Iowa, n. Indiana, n. Ohio, New Jersey, and, in mountains, to n. Georgia. Migrates through s. United States; winters in South America.

EASTERN BLUEBIRD. *Sialia sialis.* Subsp. p. 166.
  Field marks: — 6½–7½. A little larger than a Sparrow; the only *blue* bird with a *red* breast; appears round-shouldered when perching. Females are paler and duller than males; young birds are speckle-breasted, grayish, devoid of red, but there is always some telltale blue in the wings and tail.
  Similar species: — Blue Jay is large, has *white* breast; Indigo Bunting has *dark blue* breast.
  Voice: — Note, a simple musical *chur-wĭ.* Song, three or four soft gurgling notes.
  Range: — Breeds in semi-open country from Newfoundland, s. Quebec, and s. Manitoba s. to Florida and Gulf of Mexico; winters n. to Ohio Valley and Middle States, less commonly to New England (along coast), and occasionally to Great Lakes.

(GREENLAND) WHEATEAR. *Œnanthe œnanthe leucorhoa.*
p. 226.
  Field marks: — 6¼. A perky, dapper ground bird of the open country, barrens, etc., shaped a little like a Bluebird, but smaller. In winter plumage, both adults and young are brownish with light unstreaked *cinnamon-brown* under parts. The Wheatear is

best recognized by the *white rump and base of tail* contrasting
with the *broad black inverted* T (see illustration) of the latter.
No other small bird of similar habits has a white rump. It
stands rather upright, but is seldom still, restlessly spreading its
tail, bobbing, and moving on the ground with quick hops.
Range: — Breeds in Greenland and Arctic America e. to n.
Ungava and Boothia Peninsula. Migrates to Europe. Casual
or accidental in migration or winter in Ontario, Quebec, New
Brunswick, Massachusetts, New York, Pennsylvania, Michigan,
Nebraska, and Louisiana.

Gnatcatchers and Kinglets: Sylviidæ

BLUE–GRAY GNATCATCHER.   *Polioptila cærulea cærulea.*
                                                      p. 163.
Field marks: — 4½–5. Looks like a miniature Mockingbird.
A very tiny, slender mite, smaller even than a Chickadee, blue-
gray above and whitish below, with a narrow white eye-ring and
a *long, contrastingly colored tail* (black in the center, white on
the sides, often cocked like a Wren's tail).
Similar species: — The Cerulean Warbler might be mistaken
for it, but that bird is shorter-tailed, lacks the eye-ring, and has
a *narrow black ring* across the breast.
Voice: — Note a thin peevish *zpee*. Song, a thin squeaky,
wheezy series of notes, easily overlooked.
Range: — Breeds in woodlands from s. New Jersey, sw. Pennsylvania, extreme s. Ontario, s. Michigan, and Iowa s. to Gulf
of Mexico; winters from coastal South Carolina, s. Mississippi,
and s. Texas s.

(EASTERN) GOLDEN–CROWNED KINGLET.   *Regulus satrapa satrapa.*
                                                      p. 163.
Field marks: — 3½–4. Kinglets are tiny mites of birds, smaller
than Warblers. Their diminutive proportions and somber olive-
gray backs make them difficult to discern among the thick
branches of the evergreens through which they forage. The
present species, except for summer juveniles always shows a
conspicuous bright crown, yellow in the female, orange in the
male. Another point (if it be needed) is that the Golden-crown
has a *white stripe* over the eye.
Similar species: — See Ruby-crowned Kinglet.
Voice: — Call note, a high wiry *see-see-see* (similar to the Creeper's single *seee*). Song, a series of high thin notes (like the
ordinary call-notes) rising up the scale then dropping into a
chickadee-like chatter.

Range: — Breeds in spruce belt from cent. Manitoba and Gulf of St. Lawrence s. to Minnesota, Michigan, New York, and, in higher mountains, to North Carolina; winters from s. Canada to Gulf of Mexico.

(EASTERN) RUBY-CROWNED KINGLET. *Regulus calendula calendula.* pp. 163, 194.

Field marks: — 3¾–4½. A tiny short-tailed bird; olive-gray above with two pale wing-bars; male with a *scarlet* crown-patch (usually concealed). Occasional males have yellow crowns. The best recognition mark is the conspicuous *broken white eye-ring*, which gives the bird a big-eyed appearance. Any Kinglet not showing a conspicuous crown-patch is of this species. The stubbier tail distinguishes it at once from any of the Warblers, and so does the dark bar bordering the rear wing-bar. Kinglets have a habit of nervously fluttering their wings.

Similar species: — See Golden-crowned Kinglet.

Voice: — Note, a husky *ji-dit*. Song, remarkable for so small a bird, starting with three or four high *tees*, then several low *tews*, and ending in a repetitious chant, thus: *tee tee tee tew tew tew tew, ti-dadee, ti-dadee, ti-dadee.* Variable.

Range: — Breeds in cold spruce belt across Canada from nw. Alaska to New Brunswick and Nova Scotia; winters in s. United States n. to Iowa and Virginia (occasionally farther).

Pipits: Motacillidæ

AMERICAN PIPIT. *Anthus spinoletta rubescens.* p. 226.

Field marks: — 6–7. A brown, tail-wagging ground bird. Near the size of a Sparrow, but with a *slender* bill; under parts *buffy* with streakings; *outer tail-feathers white*; frequents open country, plowed fields, shores, etc. Learn the note — you will hear many more Pipits flying over than you will see on the ground.

Similar species: — It may be known from the Vesper Sparrow, which also shows white outer tail-feathers, by the buffy under parts and the habits of *constantly wagging its tail*, of *walking* instead of hopping, and of dipping up and down when in flight.

Voice: — Note, a thin *jee-eet* or, by a stretch of the imagination, *pĭ-pit*, thinner than note of Horned Lark.

Range: — Breeds in Arctic; winters in open country from New Jersey and Ohio s. to Gulf of Mexico.

SPRAGUE'S PIPIT. *Anthus spragueii.* p. 226.

Field marks: — 6¼–7. A buffy sparrow-like bird with a striped back and white outer tail-feathers. It looks like a Vesper Sparrow with a thin warbler-like bill. The upper parts, *streaked* conspicuously with *buff and black* are the best marks.

Similar species: — The American Pipit wags its tail more, has a solid dark back (not striped), a darker breast, and *dark* legs (Sprague's, *yellowish* or *straw-colored*). The thin Pipit bill will distinguish either Pipit from the Longspurs or the Vesper Sparrow. The habit of *walking* and the manner of singing further distinguish this species from the Vesper Sparrow.

Voice: — Sings high in the air like Horned Lark, a series of sweet thin notes that descend in pitch. Flight note, a soft *chur-r*, suggesting Bluebird.

Range: — Breeds on Plains from cent. Saskatchewan and s. Manitoba s. to North Dakota and nw. Minnesota; migrates through prairies to Gulf Coast. Occasional in South Carolina, Georgia, and Florida.

Waxwings: Bombycillidæ

BOHEMIAN WAXWING. *Bombycilla garrulus pallidiceps.*
p. 167.
Similar species: — 7½–8½. Resembles the Cedar Waxwing closely, but is larger, has some *white in the wing*, is grayer, and has *chestnut-red* under tail-coverts instead of white.

Voice: — A low *zreee*, rougher than note of Cedar Waxwing.

Range: — Breeds in w. Canada; winters irregularly to n.-cent. states and rarely to ne. states.

CEDAR WAXWING. *Bombycilla cedrorum.* p. 167.
Field marks: — 6½–8. Between the size of a Sparrow and a Robin; a sleek, *crested*, brown bird with a broad *yellow* band at the tip of the tail. It is the only sleek *brown* bird with a long crest.

Similar species: — See Bohemian Waxwing.

Voice: — A high thin lisp or *zeee*. Sometimes slightly trilled.

Range: — Breeds from Gulf of St. Lawrence and cent. Manitoba s. to North Carolina, n. Georgia, and Kansas; winters irregularly throughout e. United States.

Shrikes: Laniidæ

NORTHERN SHRIKE. *Lanius excubitor borealis.* p. 167.
Field marks: — 9–10½. In the Northern States during the winter a robin-sized bird, sitting *alone* in the *tip-top* of a tree in open country is likely to be a Sparrow Hawk or a Northern Shrike. If it is the latter, closer inspection shows it to be light gray above and white below, with a *black mask* through the eyes.

On taking flight it drops low, and, progressing with a rapid wing-motion on a beeline course, rises suddenly to its tree-top perch. **Similar species:** — This species can be told from the very similar Loggerhead (or Migrant) Shrike by its slightly larger size and *finely barred* breast. At close range, the bill of the Loggerhead is solid black; the basal portion of the lower mandible of the present species is *pale-colored* (except in late spring). The Loggerhead's black mask meets over the base of the bill. Generally speaking, winter Shrikes in the colder parts of the United States are Northerns, summer Shrikes, Loggerheads. Young Northern Shrikes are much browner and are recognizable by this alone and by the fine vermiculations on the breast. The young Loggerhead is finely barred on the breast in late summer, but is a *gray*, not a brown, bird.
Voice: — Song, a long-continued thrasher-like succession of phrases, harsher on the whole than the Thrasher's song.
Range: — Breeds from limit of trees s. to s. Ontario and s. Quebec; winters s. irregularly to Kentucky and Virginia.

LOGGERHEAD SHRIKE. *Lanius ludovicianus.* Subsp. p. 167.
Field marks: — 9. Slightly smaller than a Robin; big-headed and slim-tailed; gray above and white below, with a conspicuous *black mask* through the eyes. To many Northerners, the sub-specific name, Migrant Shrike, is more familiar.
Similar species: — See Northern Shrike. Also confused with Mockingbird because of coloration and white patches in the wing, but Mockingbird is slimmer, longer-tailed, has larger wing-patches, and lacks the mask through the eyes. Perched on a wire the Shrike scans the ground; looks short-legged, heavy-headed (Mocker is longer-legged, alert-looking). The flight of the Shrike is flickering; that of the Mockingbird more 'like strokes of the oars of an old rowboat.'
Voice: — Song, half-hearted notes and phrases; repeated mock-ingbird-like, but deliberate, with long pauses (*queedle*; *queedle*; over and over, or *tsurp-see, tsurp-see*, etc.).
Range: — Breeds locally from New Brunswick, s. Quebec, and se. Manitoba s. to Florida and Gulf Coast; winters n. occasionally to New England, New York, and Ohio.

Starlings: Sturnidæ

STARLING. *Sturnus vulgaris vulgaris.*   p. 198.
Field marks: — 7½–8½. The Starling, like the Crow, English Sparrow, and Robin, should need no introduction, yet it is sur-prising that some people do not know the bird. It is a *short-tailed* 'Blackbird,' with somewhat the shape of a Meadowlark. In

spring it is glossed with purple and green (visible at close range), and the bill is *yellow*. In winter the Starling is heavily speckled with light dots. The bill is dark, changing to yellow as spring approaches. No other 'Blackbird' has a *yellow* bill. In flight, Starlings have a triangular look, flying swiftly and direct, not rising and falling like most Blackbirds.

Similar species: — The Starling is the *short-tailed* 'Blackbird'; the Grackle, the long-tailed; and the Red-wing, Rusty, and Cowbird are the in-betweens. Young birds are dark dusky-gray, a little like the female Cowbird, but the tail is shorter, and the bill longer and more spike-like, not stout and conical. See Meadowlark for comparison of flight.

Voice: — The male Starling sings from the tree-top, house-gutter, or chimney. Many of the whistled notes are musical; other sounds are harsh and rasping. Some Starlings give very good imitations of other species, but they are never as adept mimics as the Mockingbird. Note: *feee-u*, high-pitched and descending.

Range: — Most abundant in ne. United States, but now found w. to Rockies, n. to Gulf of St. Lawrence, and s. to Gulf of Mexico.

Vireos: Vireonidæ

SMALL OLIVE or gray-backed birds; much like the Warblers, but with somewhat heavier bills (with a more curved ridge), and less active, slowly searching for insects under the leaves instead of flitting about. Because of their white wing-bars and eye-rings, some species might be confused with the small *Empidonax* Fly-catchers, but they do not sit in the typical upright Flycatcher posture, and the eye-rings join a light spot between the eye and bill, giving more the appearance of spectacles. Of the six most widespread species, three — the Yellow-throated, Blue-headed, and White-eyed Vireos — have wing-bars; the Philadelphia, Warbling, and Red-eyed have none. This is a helpful thing to remember, as the rest of the identification becomes easier through elimination.

BLACK-CAPPED VIREO. *Vireo atricapillus.* p. 179.
  Field marks: — 4½–4¾. A small, sprightly Vireo with *top and sides of head glossy black* in male, slaty gray in female. It has conspicuous white 'spectacles' formed by the eye-ring and loral patch (between eye and bill) and two distinct wing-bars, which are pale yellow in male, white in female. Its custom of hanging head downward an instant before fluttering to a lower branch is characteristic.
  Voice: — Song hurried, harsh; composed of phrases and syllables

BLACK–CAPPED˙ VIREO

remarkable for variety and restless, almost angry quality. Alarm note, a harsh *chit-ah*, not unlike that of Ruby-crowned Kinglet.
Range: — Breeds mainly in cent. Texas and sw. Oklahoma but also in cent. and ne. Oklahoma and s. Kansas. Local, favoring gullies with wild plum, blackberry, etc., or canyons lined with oak, cedar, dogwood, and other 'scrub.'

GEORGE MIKSCH SUTTON.

WHITE–EYED VIREO. *Vireo griseus.* Subsp.   p. 182.
  Field marks: — 4½–5½. A small Vireo of the shrubbery and undergrowth. Know it by the combination of *yellowish 'spectacles'* and *whitish throat*. It is an olive-colored bird, with wing-bars, yellowish sides, and *white eyes*.
  Similar species: — The Blue-headed Vireo is often mistaken for it because of its white *eye-ring*. The only other Vireo with yellow spectacles is the easy-to-tell Yellow-throated Vireo. Because of its size, markings, and un-vireo-like song the White-eye can be mistaken for one of the small Flycatchers.
  Voice: — Song, un-vireo-like, a sharply enunciated *chick'-a-per-weeoo-chick'*. Variable, but a sharp *chick* at the beginning or end is distinctive. Some birds introduce notes that resemble those of the Crested Flycatcher or Summer Tanager.
  Range: — Breeds from Florida and Gulf of Mexico n. to Massachusetts, New York, Ohio, and s. Wisconsin; winters along coast from Gulf n. to South Carolina.

BELL'S VIREO. *Vireo bellii bellii.*   p. 182.
  Similar species: — 4¾–5. A small grayish Vireo with wing-bars and pale yellowish-washed sides; perhaps the most nondescript of the Vireos. Distinguished from the Warbling Vireo by the light wing-bars and narrow light eye-ring. Most like the White-eyed Vireo, but has a *dark eye* and lacks the yellow spectacles. Immature White-eyes have dark eyes but always show *yellow* in the loral spot and eye-ring.
  Voice: — Song, low, husky, unmusical phrases at short intervals; sounds like *cheedle cheedle chee? cheedle cheedle chew!* The first phrase ends in a rising inflection; the second phrase, which is given more frequently, has a downward inflection and sounds as if the bird were answering its own question.

Range: — Breeds in willows and bushes along streams, chiefly w. of Mississippi River, from Texas n. to nw. Indiana, n. Illinois, and s. South Dakota.

YELLOW-THROATED VIREO. *Vireo flavifrons.* pp. 182, 194.
Field marks: — 5–6. Olive-green above, with white wing-bars, yellow 'spectacles,' and a *bright yellow throat and breast.*
Similar species: — Other Vireos are washed with yellowish on the sides but this is the only Vireo possessing *bright* yellow. The similarly colored Yellow-breasted Chat is larger, has *no* wing-bars, and has *white* 'spectacles'. This Vireo might easily be confused with the Pine Warbler. (Pine Warbler has more slender bill, dusky streaks on the sides and large white spots in the tail — and it lives in pines.)
Voice: — Song, similar to Red-eyed Vireo's, but more musical, lower-pitched and with a *burr in the notes.* There is a longer pause between phrases. One phrase which sounds like *ee-yay* or *three-eight* is distinctive.
Range: — Breeds in deciduous woodlands and shade-trees from s. Maine, sw. Quebec, and s. Manitoba s. to n. Florida and Gulf Coast; winters from s. Mexico into South America.

BLUE-HEADED VIREO. *Vireo solitarius.* Subsp. p. 182.
Field marks: — 5–6. A Vireo with white wing-bars. Look for the *blue-gray* head, *white eye-ring,* and *snowy-white* throat. The earliest Vireo in the spring.
Similar species: — The other two common Vireos with wing-bars are the White-eyed and Yellow-throated Vireos.
Voice: — Song, a series of short whistled phrases, with a rising and falling inflection, rendered with a short wait between phrases. Similar to Red-eyed Vireo's song, but higher and *sweeter* with sweeping slurs. The phrases are not repeated as many times in a minute.
Range: — Breeds in mixed evergreen-deciduous woodlands from Manitoba and Gulf of St. Lawrence s. to North Dakota, Minnesota, Michigan, and n. New Jersey, and, in Appalachians, to n. Georgia; winters in Gulf States and along coast n. to South Carolina.

BLACK-WHISKERED VIREO. *Vireo altiloquus barbatulus.*
p. 227.
Field marks: — This Vireo has a narrow black streak, or 'whisker' mark, on each side of the throat.
Similar species: — Almost identical with the Red-eyed Vireo except for the 'whiskers.'
Voice: — Song very similar to that of Red-eyed Vireo.
Range: — Breeds chiefly in Mangroves in s. Florida (Keys, s. tip, sw. coast to Tampa Bay); winters in South America.

RED-EYED VIREO. *Vireo olivaceus.*   p. 182.
   Field marks: — 5½–6½. Olive-green above, white below, *no wing-bars*; characterized by the *gray cap* and the *black-bordered white stripe* over the eye. The red eye is of little aid.
   Similar species: — Warbling Vireo is paler, more uniformly colored above, without such contrasting facial striping. The songs of these two birds are absolutely unlike.
   Voice: — Song a monotonous series of short abrupt phrases of robin-like character. These phrases, separated by deliberate pauses, are repeated as often as forty times in a minute, all through the day. Learn this song well, so as to compare with other Vireos. Note, a nasal whining *chway.*
   Range: — Breeds in deciduous woodlands from Gulf of St. Lawrence and cent. Manitoba s. to cent. Florida and Gulf Coast; winters in South America.

PHILADELPHIA VIREO. *Vireo philadelphicus.*   pp. 182, 195
   Field marks: — 4½–5. The only Vireo that combines the characters of *unbarred* wings and *yellow-tinged* under parts (particularly across the breast).
   Similar species: — The Warbling Vireo is similar. It is paler-backed, and usually lacks the yellow, although some birds have a strong tinge on the sides. If in doubt, a good mark at close range is a dark spot between eye and bill (lores) in the Philadelphia. The Orange-crowned Warbler is similar, but the more restless actions, and dingier, more uniform coloration help identify it. The fall Tennessee Warbler is similar but has a more needle-like bill and in many individuals (but not all), *clear-white* under tail-coverts. However, anyone unable to tell a Vireo from a Warbler is hardly ready to recognize this species. The Vireo is chubbier and less active; its bill is thicker, with a curved ridge (Warbler's bill is more needle-like). See female Black-throated Blue Warbler.
   Voice: — Song similar to Red-eyed Vireo but phrases less frequent and higher in pitch. As Bradford Torrey wrote, 'it looks like one Vireo and sings like another.'
   Range: — Breeds in deciduous second growth and edges of clearings from n. Ontario and s. Manitoba s. to n. New England, n. Michigan, and n. North Dakota; winters in Central America.

(EASTERN) WARBLING VIREO. *Vireo gilvus gilvus.*   p. 182.
   Field marks: — 5–6. Three common species of Vireos have *no* wing-bars. If the head is *inconspicuously* striped and the breast is whitish, then it is this species.
   Similar species: — The Philadelphia Vireo is very similar but is darker and more olive above and extensively tinged with yellow below (particularly on the breast). The Red-eyed Vireo has a more contrastingly striped head.

WRENS

WINTER WREN   p. 168.
　Stubby tail, dark barred belly.

SHORT–BILLED MARSH WREN   p. 169.
　Buffy; streaked crown, streaked back.

LONG–BILLED MARSH WREN   p. 169.
　Eye stripe, back stripes.

HOUSE WREN   p. 165.
　No facial striping; grayer.

BEWICK'S WREN   p. 168.
　Eye stripe, white in tail.

CAROLINA WREN   p. 168
　Eye stripe, rusty coloration.

VIREOS

Without Wing-bars

RED–EYED VIREO   p. 181.
　Gray crown, black and white eyebrow stripes.

WARBLING VIREO   p. 181
　Light eyebrow line, whitish breast.

PHILADELPHIA VIREO   p. 181.
　Light eyebrow line, yellowish breast.

With Wing-bars

BLUE–HEADED VIREO   p. 180.
　Spectacles, gray head, white throat.

YELLOW–THROATED VIREO   p. 180.
　Bright yellow throat.

WHITE–EYED VIREO   p. 179
　Yellow spectacles, whitish throat.

BELL'S VIREO   p. 179
　Like White-eyed Vireo but eye dark and spectacles with
　no yellow.

WINTER

SHORT-BILLED MARSH

LONG-BILLED MARSH

HOUSE

BEWICK'S

CAROLINA

WRENS

RED-EYED

WARBLING

PHILADELPHIA

Without wing-bars

BLUE-HEADED

WHITE-EYED

With wing-bars

YELLOW-THROATED

BELL'S

VIREOS

WORM-EATING

SWAINSON'S

TENNESSEE ♂

ORANGE-   CROWNED

YELLOW-BREASTED CHAT

♀

PARULA ♂

♀

CERULEAN ♂

BLACK-THROATED BLUE ♂

♀

BLACKBURNIAN ♀ ♂

♀ REDSTART ♂

OVEN-BIRD

LOUISIANA WATER-THRUSH

NORTHERN WATER-THRUSH

Plate 48   183

SPRING WARBLERS

WORM–EATING WARBLER   p. 185.
    Black stripes on buffy head.

SWAINSON'S WARBLER   p. 185.
    Brown crown, white stripe over eye.

TENNESSEE WARBLER   p. 189.
    Gray crown, white eye-stripe, white breast.

ORANGE–CROWNED WARBLER   p. 190.
    Dingy greenish, faintly streaked; no wing-bars.

YELLOW–BREASTED CHAT   p. 207.
    Large; white spectacles, yellow breast.

PARULA WARBLER   p. 191.
    Blue and yellow; white wing-bars.
    Male with dark breast-band.

BLACK–THROATED BLUE WARBLER   p. 193
    Male: Blue-gray back, black throat.
    Female: White wing-spot.

CERULEAN WARBLER   p. 196
    Male: Blue back, black line across breast.
    Female: See text.

BLACKBURNIAN WARBLER   p. 197.
    Male: Orange throat.
    Female: Paler.

REDSTART   p. 208.
    Male: Orange tail-patches.
    Female: Yellow tail-patches.

OVEN–BIRD   p. 204.
    Eye-ring, dull orange crown.

LOUISIANA WATER–THRUSH   p. 205.
    White eye-stripe, unstreaked throat.

NORTHERN WATER–THRUSH   p. 204.
    Yellowish eye-stripe, streaked throat.

Voice: — Song, a single languid warble unlike the broken phraseology of the other Vireos; resembles slightly the Purple Finch's song but less spirited and with a burry undertone and an upward turn at the end. A characteristic call-note is a wheezy querulous *twee*.

Range: — Breeds in tall shade-trees from Nova Scotia, cent. Ontario, and s. Manitoba s. to North Carolina, s. Louisiana, and nw. Texas; winters in Tropics.

Wood Warblers: Parulidæ

THESE are the 'butterflies' of the bird world — bright-colored mites, smaller than Sparrows (except the Chat), with thin bills. Vireos are similar, but their bills are heavier and their movements when foraging among the leaves and twigs are rather sluggish, unlike the active flittings of the Warblers.

In the fall of the year there is a preponderance of olive-yellow species — adults that have changed their plumage, immature birds, etc. In the earlier editions of the *Field Guide* I gave a list or brief key, separating these into two groups — those with wing-bars and those without. I have now replaced these lists with two color plates. One shows species which either have *wing-bars* or are *streaked* (although in immature Prairie, Yellow, and Palm Warblers the wing-bars are obscure or lacking). On the other plate are grouped those which are *devoid of both wing-bars and streaks* (although Tennessee shows a tendency toward a wing-bar and the immature Canada and sometimes the Orange-crown are faintly streaked).

You will note I have titled these plates *Confusing Fall Warblers*. Such obvious birds as Redstarts, Kentuckys, Yellow-throated Warblers, Black and Whites, and others that are much the same in the fall as in the spring are not included. In addition to the Warblers I have added several birds like the Ruby-crowned Kinglet, Philadelphia Vireo, and Yellow-throated Vireo which are often mistaken for fall Warblers.

These two plates show the trouble-makers. You should not attempt to do much with them until you have mastered the spring Warblers. If at the end of ten years of field work you can say you know the fall Warblers you are doing very well.

BLACK AND WHITE WARBLER. *Mniotilta varia.*   p. 186.
  Field marks: — 5–5½. *Striped with black and white*; *creeps* along trunks and branches. Female has whiter underparts.
  Similar species: — The Black-poll Warbler is the only one that at all resembles it, but that species has a *solid black cap*; the present species has a *striped* crown.

Voice: — Song, a thin *weesee weesee weesee weesee weesee weesee weesee* (two-note phrases, with second note lower; repeated); suggests one of Redstart's songs but is higher-pitched and longer (*weesee* usually repeated at least seven times). A second sibilant song is similar, but in the middle several notes drop to a lower pitch, returning at the end.

Range: — Breeds in leafy woodlands from Gulf of St. Lawrence and cent. Manitoba s. to n. parts of Gulf States; winters from Florida s. into tropics.

PROTHONOTARY WARBLER. *Protonotaria citrea.*

pp. 187, 195.

Field marks: — 5½. A golden bird of the wooded swamps. Entire head and breast *deep yellow*, almost orange; wings *blue-gray*; sexes similar, but female duller.

Similar species: — The Yellow Warbler and the Blue-wing are often misidentified by the beginner as this species. The Yellow Warbler has *yellowish* wings; the Blue-wing, *white wing-bars* and a black mark through the eye.

Voice: — Emphatic *tweet tweet tweet tweet tweet* on one pitch.

Range: — Breeds in river swamps from se. Minnesota, s. Michigan, w. New York (local) and s. New Jersey (rarely) s. to cent. Florida and Gulf Coast; winters in Central and n. South America.

SWAINSON'S WARBLER. *Limnothlypis swainsonii.* p. 183.

Field marks: — 5. Very hard to see; 'a voice in the swamp.' Both sexes are *olive-brown* above and dingy white below, with a conspicuous *whitish stripe* over the eye.

Similar species: — The Worm-eating Warbler differs in having *black stripes* on the crown; the Water-Thrush, in possessing heavily *streaked* under parts.

Voice: — Song similar to that of Louisiana Water-Thrush but shorter (five notes); opens with two slurred notes, then two lower notes and a higher one.

Range: — Breeds in wooded swamps *where there is a growth of cane* from Maryland (probably), s. Virginia, s. Indiana, and Oklahoma s. to n. Florida and Louisiana. Found locally in rhododendron-hemlock tangles in central Alleghenies (West Virginia, etc.). Winters in Jamaica and Yucatan.

WORM-EATING WARBLER. *Helmitheros vermivorus.* p. 183.

Field marks: — 5-5½. Dull olive, with *black stripes* on a *buffy* head. Sexes similar. Inhabits woodland hillsides, shady ravines, etc.

Voice: — Song, a thin buzz; resembles rattle of Chipping Sparrow but is thinner, more rapid and insect-like (Chipping Sparrow would not be in the dry woodland).

Range: — Breeds in deciduous woodland slopes from Connecti-

SPRING WARBLERS

(Most of these have streaked under parts.)

YELLOW-THROATED WARBLER p. 197.
 Gray back, yellow bib, striped sides.

MYRTLE WARBLER p. 193.
 Yellow rump, dark breast, yellow patches.

MAGNOLIA WARBLER p. 192.
 White tail-band, heavy stripes.

SUTTON'S WARBLER (After drawing by G. M. Sutton) p. 197.
 West Virginia; possibly a hybrid. Like Yellow-throated
 Warbler but no side stripes (see text).

CANADA WARBLER p. 208.
 Necklace of streaks; no wing-bars.

KIRTLAND'S WARBLER p. 202.
 Striped gray back, spotted sides, wags tail; Michigan.

BAY-BREASTED WARBLER p. 200.
 Chestnut breast, pale neck spot.

CHESTNUT-SIDED WARBLER p. 200.
 Chestnut sides, yellow crown.

CAPE MAY WARBLER p. 192.
 Male: Chestnut cheek.
 Female: Yellow neck spot.

BLACK AND WHITE WARBLER p. 184.
 Black and white crown stripes.

BLACK-POLL WARBLER p. 201.
 Male: Black cap, white cheek.
 Female: See text.

BLACK-THROATED GREEN WARBLER p. 196.
 Black throat, yellow cheek.

PINE WARBLER p. 201.
 Yellow throat, dull streaks, wing-bars.

PALM WARBLER p. 203.
 Chestnut cap, wags tail.
 (*a*) WESTERN PALM WARBLER: Whitish belly.
 (*b*) YELLOW PALM WARBLER: Yellow belly.

PRAIRIE WARBLER p. 203.
 Striped face, striped sides; wags tail.

ELLOW-THROATED

MYRTLE

MAGNOLIA

SUTTON'S

CANADA

KIRTLAND'S

BAY-BREASTED

CHESTNUT-SIDED

CAPE MAY

BLACK AND WHITE

BLACKPOLL

BLACK-THROATED
GREEN

PINE

PALM

PRAIRIE

MOURNING

CONNECTICUT

NASHVILLE

KENTUCKY

HOODED

WILSON'S

♂

♀

♂

YELLOW-THROAT

LAWRENCE'S

♂

BACHMAN'S

♂

GOLDEN— WINGED

BREWSTER'S

♂

BLUE— WINGED

♂

PROTHONOTARY

♀

♂

YELLOW

Plate 50   **187**

SPRING WARBLERS

(Most of these have unstreaked breasts.)

MOURNING WARBLER   p. 206.
    Gray hood, black throat (male).

CONNECTICUT WARBLER   p. 205
    Gray hood, white eye-ring.

NASHVILLE WARBLER   p. 191.
    Yellow throat, white eye-ring.

KENTUCKY WARBLER   **p. 205.**
    Black sideburns, yellow spectacles.

HOODED WARBLER   **p. 207.**
    Male: Black hood, yellow face.
    Female: See text.

WILSON'S WARBLER   **p. 207.**
    Male: Round black cap.
    Female: See text.

YELLOW-THROAT   p. 206.
    Male: Black mask.
    Female: Yellow throat, white belly.

BACHMAN'S WARBLER   p. 189.
    Male: Black cap, black bib; Southern, rare.
    Female: See text.

LAWRENCE'S WARBLER (Hybrid)   p. 189.
    Black bib, black cheek, yellow belly.

GOLDEN-WINGED WARBLER   p. 188.
    Black bib, black cheek, white belly.

BREWSTER'S WARBLER (Hybrid)   p. 188.
    Like Blue-wing with some white below.

BLUE-WINGED WARBLER   p. 188.
    Black eye-line, yellow under parts.

PROTHONOTARY WARBLER   p. 185.
    Golden head, bluish wings.

YELLOW WARBLER   p. 191.
    Yellowish back, yellow tail-spots.
    Reddish breast streaks (male).

cut, n. Illinois, and s. Iowa s. to n. Georgia and Missouri.
Winters in Florida (rarely), West Indies, and Central America.

GOLDEN-WINGED WARBLER.   *Vermivora chrysoptera.*

p. 187.

Field marks: — 5–5¼. No other Warbler has the combined
characters of *yellow wing-patch and black throat*. It is gray above
and white below, with a yellow forehead-patch, broad yellow
wing-patch, black patch through eye, and black throat. In
females the black is replaced by gray.

Voice: — Song unlike that of any other Warbler, except the
Blue-wing — *beee-bz-bz-bz* (one buzzy note followed by three in
a lower pitch). The Blue-wing sounds similar but *usually* has
but one lower buzz — *beee-bzzz*. (Both species occasionally sing
the song of the other.)

Range: — Breeds in openings and bushy edges from Minnesota,
se. Ontario, and Massachusetts s. to Iowa, n. Indiana, n. New
Jersey, and, in mountains, to Georgia. Migrates *via* Gulf States
(avoiding South Atlantic coast) to tropical America.

BLUE-WINGED WARBLER.   *Vermivora pinus.*   p. 187.

Field marks: — 4½–5. Face and under parts yellow; *black mark
through eye*; wings with two *white* bars. Sexes similar.

Similar species: — The narrow black eye-mark distinguishes it
from any other largely yellowish Warbler (Yellow Warbler,
Prothonotary, etc.).

Voice: — *Beee-bzzz* (inhale and exhale).

Range: — Breeds in bushy swamps and wet woodland edges
from se. Minnesota, s. Michigan, and s. New England s. to
Kansas, Missouri, Delaware, and, in uplands, to Georgia.
Migrates *via* Gulf States to Central America.

BREWSTER'S WARBLER.   *Vermivora leucobronchialis.*   p. 187.

Field marks: — The Golden-winged and Blue-winged Warblers
commonly hybridize where their ranges overlap. Two distinct
types are produced, the Lawrence's Warbler and the Brewster's,
which occurs the more commonly of the two. Typical Brewster's
are like Golden-wings without the black throat, or, putting it
differently, like Blue-wings with whitish under parts. There is
a good deal of variation; some individuals have white wing-bars,
others yellow, and some birds are tinged with yellow below.
The thin black eye-mark, as in the Blue-wing, and the white or
largely white, instead of solid yellow, under parts are diagnostic.
The most outstanding factor to consider between the two hybrids is the black throat, which the Lawrence's must have and
the Brewster's must lack.

Voice: — Like either Golden-wing or Blue-wing.

LAWRENCE'S WARBLER. *Vermivora lawrencei.* p. 187.
  Field marks: — The recessive hybrid of the Blue-wing-Golden-wing combination. Yellowish with white wing-bars; like Blue-wing, but with black face-pattern of Golden-wing. The only yellow-bellied Warbler with both a black bib and a black ear-patch (the very rare Bachman's Warbler of the southern river swamps also has a black bib). Most examples of this rare hybrid conform fairly closely with the type shown in the color plate.
  Voice: — Like either Golden-wing or Blue-wing.

BACHMAN'S WARBLER. *Vermivora bachmanii.* p. 187.
  Field marks: — 4¼. A very rare denizen of southern river swamps, perhaps the rarest North American songbird today. *Male:* — Olive-green above; face and under parts yellow; *throat-patch and crown-patch black* (suggests a small Hooded Warbler with an incomplete hood). *Female:* — Obscure; lacks black throat; upper parts olive-green; forehead and under parts yellow; crown grayish.
  Similar species: — The only other Warbler with the combination of black bib and yellow under parts is Lawrence's Warbler, which has two broad *white wing-bars*, a broad black patch through the eye, and *none* on the crown. In the Hooded Warbler the black completely encircles the neck. Two other Warblers look much like the female — the female Hooded and the female Wilson's. They are solid yellow below, olive-green above and lack wing-bars. All have yellowish foreheads, but the face-pattern of the Bachman's is different — *blue-gray crown and cheeks* set off by a *yellow eye-ring.* The yellowish bend in the wing of the female Bachman's is said to be an aid. The female Hooded is much larger, with white tail-spots.
  Voice: — Song, a wiry buzzing trill; resembles that of Parula Warbler but is rendered all on one pitch. Has also been likened to Worm-eating Warbler.
  Range: — Breeds in wooded thicket-grown river swamps; bred, formerly at least, in se. Missouri, ne. Arkansas, w. Kentucky, n. Alabama, and South Carolina. Migrates through Gulf States and Florida; winters in Cuba.

TENNESSEE WARBLER. *Vermivora peregrina.* pp. 183, 195.
  Field marks: — 4½–5. *Adult male in spring:* — Very plain, unmarked save for a *conspicuous white stripe over the eye*; head gray, contrasting with olive-green back; under parts white. *Adult female in spring:* — Similar to the male, but head less gray and under parts slightly yellowish. The eye-line is the best mark. *Adults and immature in autumn:* — Greenish above, pale dingy yellow below; known by the combined characters of *unstreaked* yellowish breast and *conspicuous* yellowish line over the eye.

Similar species: — The bird in spring plumage, with the white eye-stripe, is much like the Red-eyed and Warbling Vireos, but the smaller size, the Warbler actions, and the thin, fine-pointed bill identify it. Autumn birds resemble the Orange-crowned Warbler but the under tail-coverts are *white* in typical Tennessees (but many immature Tennessees show a tinge of yellow). Other shades of difference are: (1) Tennessee has more conspicuous eye-stripe; (2) is *greener* and has paler under parts with no suggestion of faint streaking; (3) almost invariably shows *trace of a light wing-bar*; (4) Tennessee occurs in early fall, Orange-crown later. See also Philadelphia Vireo.

Voice: — Song, a staccato two-part affair (sometimes three-parted) — *tizip-tizip-tizip-tizip-tizip-tizip, zitzitzitzitzizizizizi.* The second part of the song is like an emphatic Chipping Sparrow but gets louder at the end. In pattern the whole song suggests the Nashville Warbler's, but is very loud and more repetitious, one song quickly following the preceding one.

Range: — Breeds in spruce and tamarack swamps from Gulf of St. Lawrence and n. Manitoba s. to n. New England, n. New York, n. Michigan, and n. Minnesota. Migrates mainly through Mississippi Valley, rare near coast, especially in spring; winters in South and Central America.

ORANGE–CROWNED WARBLER.   *Vermivora celata celata.*

pp. 183, 195.

Field marks: — 5. The dingiest of all warblers. Has no wing-bars or other distinctive marks; olive-green above, greenish yellow below; *under parts faintly streaked;* 'orange crown' seldom visible (Nashville also has a veiled crown-patch); sexes similar. The points to remember are the greenish-yellow under parts, faint, blurry streakings, and the lack of wing-bars. In the *autumn immature*, the plumage most frequently observed in the Northeast, the bird is greenish drab throughout — barely paler on the under parts. Some birds are decidedly gray (see color plate).

Similar species: — The most similar birds are (1) the autumn Tennessee Warbler, which lacks the faint breast-streakings, has a trace of a wing-bar, and usually (but not always) has *white* under tail-coverts, not yellow; (2) the Philadelphia Vireo, which has a more noticeable light stripe over the eye and a thicker Vireo bill, and lacks the streakings. The Vireo is sluggish; the Warbler, active. The Orange-crown is usually found in brushy places *after* October 1, after the main fall flight of Tennessees and Philadelphia Vireos has passed through. Early in the fall many Tennessees are misidentified as Orange-crowns.

Voice: — Song, a weak, colorless trill, dropping in pitch and energy at the end; sometimes rises then drops.

Range: — Breeds in Canada w. of Hudson Bay; migrates mainly through Mississippi Valley; winters in s. Atlantic and Gulf States, occasionally as far n. as New England.

NASHVILLE WARBLER. *Vermivora ruficapilla ruficapilla.*

pp. 187, 195.

Field marks: — 4½–5. The *white eye-ring* in conjunction with the bright *yellow* throat is the best mark. A small, rather plain Warbler; throat and under parts yellow; *head gray*, contrasting with the olive-green back; sexes similar.

Similar species: — Connecticut Warbler has a white eye-ring but its throat is *grayish*. More confusing in the fall, but the brownish breast-stain of the Connecticut, its size and sluggish actions set it apart. Immature Magnolia Warblers in fall have a yellow throat, gray head, and an eye-ring, but you can tell them by the *wing-bars, yellow rump,* and *white tail-band*.

Voice: — Song, two-parted: *seebit, seebit, seebit seebit, titititititititi* (first part measured like Black and White Warbler, last part run together like Chipping Sparrow).

Range: — Breeds in slashings and edges of bogs from Gulf of St. Lawrence and cent. Ontario s. to Connecticut, n. New Jersey, West Virginia, n. Illinois, and Nebraska. Migrates *via* Gulf States; winters in Central America (rarely Florida).

PARULA WARBLER. *Parula americana.* Subsp. pp. 183, 194.

Field marks: — 4¼–4¾. The only *bluish* Warbler with a *yellow* throat and breast. Two white wing-bars are conspicuous. A suffused greenish patch on the back is a clinching point, if it can be seen. In the male the most useful mark, visible from below, is a *dark band* crossing the yellow of the breast. In the female this band is indistinct or lacking. Tell her by the general blue and yellow color and white wing-bars.

Voice: — Commonest song, a buzzy trill or rattle which climbs the scale and snaps over at the top, *zeeeeeeeee-up*; also a series of buzzy notes which ends in the familiar rising trill: *zh-zh-zh-zheeeeee*.

Range: — Breeds mainly in humid woodlands where usnea (bearded) moss or Spanish moss hangs from the trees (but also in some regions where neither is found), from the Gulf of St. Lawrence, central Ontario, and Minnesota s. to Florida, Gulf Coast, and Texas; winters in Florida and the tropics.

YELLOW WARBLER. *Dendroica petechia.* Subsp. pp. 187, 194.

Field marks: — 5. No other small bird appears in the field to be *all yellow*. Many other Warblers are yellow below, but none is so yellow on the back, wings, and tail. Many Warblers have white spots in the tail; this is the only species with *yellow* spots (with exception of female Redstart). At close range the male shows chestnut-red breast-streakings. In the female these are faint or lacking.

Similar species: — The Goldfinch shares the nickname 'Yellow-bird,' but has *black* wings and a *black* tail. In fall, female and young Yellow Warblers might be mistaken for other species but this is the only one with *yellowish tail-spots*. There is also at least *a trace of yellow feather-edging in the wings*. The female Wilson's has no tail-spots. Some dull autumn Yellow Warblers, especially examples of the Alaskan race, look almost as dingy as Orange-crowns. *Look for the tail-spots.*

Voice: — Learn this song well so as to learn other *Dendroicas* by comparison; a cheerful, bright *tsee-tsee-tsee-tsee-ti-ti-wee* or *weet weet weet weet tsee tsee.*

Range: — Breeds in small willows near water, and in towns and farms from tree-limit in Canada s. to n. Georgia, s. Missouri, and Oklahoma. Also in Mangroves in Florida Keys (Cuban Yellow Warbler — see Subspecies). Winters in tropics.

MAGNOLIA WARBLER. *Dendroica magnolia.*   pp. 186, 194.
Field marks: — 4½–5. The Magnolia's old name, 'Black and Yellow Warbler,' well describes it. The upper parts are blackish, with large white patches on the wings and tail; the under parts yellow with heavy black stripings. From below, the tail appears white with a *wide black terminal band*. In *fall*, Magnolias are quite brown above and yellow below, the stripings reduced to a few sparse marks on the flanks. The *black tail, crossed midway by a very broad white band*, is the best mark.

Similar species: — Three other spring Warblers with bright yellow under parts are striped with black beneath — the Canada, Cape May, and Prairie — but none has the black and white coloration of the upper plumage. Immature birds in the fall are sometimes called Nashville Warblers because of their yellow throat, gray crown, and white eye-ring, but the *wing-bars, yellow rump*, and *white tail-band* identify them.

Voice: — Song suggests Yellow Warbler's but is shorter: *weeta weeta weetee* (last note rising) or *weeta weeta weeto* (last note dropping). Yellow Warbler would not be heard singing in ever-green woods. See Hooded Warbler. Note, an unwarblerlike *tizic* (F. H. Allen).

Range: — Breeds in young evergreen growth from Manitoba and Newfoundland s. to Minnesota, n. Michigan, n. Massachusetts, and, in Appalachians, to Virginia. Winters in Central America.

CAPE MAY WARBLER. *Dendroica tigrina.*   pp. 186, 194.
Field marks: — 5–5½. *Male:* — Patterned tiger-like; under parts yellow narrowly striped with black; rump yellow; crown black; cheek-patch chestnut; *the only Warbler with chestnut*

cheeks. Females and immature birds lack the chestnut cheeks and are duller. They are often very nondescript; the breast is often almost white, lined with dusky streaks (a little like a female Myrtle, without the yellow areas). A good point, if it can be observed, is a *dim, suffused patch of yellow behind the ear.*
Similar species: — Obscure autumn birds are perhaps the most heavily streaked of all the fall nondescripts. Some are peculiarly gray and the light yellow spot behind the ear is often absent. The two most similar birds are (1) Myrtle Warbler, which is *brown* above with a more *conspicuous* yellow rump-spot; (2) Palm Warbler, which is brown, has bright *yellow* under tail-coverts, and *wags its tail.* Both have streaked backs (Cape May plain). Nondescript Pine Warblers are another source of confusion, but darker breast-streaks and yellowish rump distinguish the Cape May.
Voice: — Song, a very high thin *seet seet seet seet* repeated four or more times. Most easily confused with song of Bay-breast.
Range: — Breeds in spruce forests from s. Mackenzie e. across Canada to Nova Scotia and s. to Maine and New Hampshire. Migrates through e. United States; winters in West Indies.

BLACK-THROATED BLUE WARBLER. *Dendroica cœrulescens.* Subsp. pp. 183, 195.
Field marks: — 5–5½. *Male:* — Very clean-cut; *blue, black, and white*; upper parts blue-gray; throat and sides black; breast and belly white. *Females* are very plain, brown-backed with a light line over the eye and a small *white wing-spot* (not always visible).
Similar species: — Fall immatures and females often lack the white wing-spot. They are buffy-breasted and dark-backed and suggest Philadelphia Vireo or Tennessee Warbler but *the dark-cheeked look* (see color plate) is a good mark.
Voice: — Song, a husky, lazy *zur, zur, zur, zreee* or *I am la-zy* (with a rising inflection). Sometimes only two or three notes are given: *zur, zreee.*
Range: — Breeds in undergrowth of deciduous and mixed woodlands from n. Minnesota and s. Quebec s. to cent. Minnesota, s. Ontario, and Massachusetts, and, in mountains, to Georgia. Winters at Key West (a few) and in West Indies.

MYRTLE WARBLER. *Dendroica coronata coronata.* pp. 186, 194.
Field marks: — 5–6. The Myrtle Warbler can be identified in any plumage by its *bright yellow rump*, in conjunction with its note, a loud *check. Male in spring:* — Blue-gray above; white below, with a heavy inverted U of black on the breast and sides, and a patch of yellow on the crown and one in front of each wing. *Female in spring:* — Brown instead of bluish, but pattern similar. *Winter adults and young:* — Brownish above; white below, streaked with dark; rump yellow.

CONFUSING FALL WARBLERS

(Most of these have streaks or wing-bars.)

* RUBY–CROWNED KINGLET   p. 175.
  Broken eye-ring, dark wing-bar.

CHESTNUT–SIDED WARBLER   p. 200.
  Immature: Yellow-green above, whitish below.

* YELLOW–THROATED VIREO   p. 180.
  Bright yellow breast, yellow spectacles.

BAY–BREASTED WARBLER   p. 200.
  Dark legs, buffy under tail (see text).

BLACK-POLL WARBLER   p. 201.
  Pale legs, white under tail (see text).

PINE WARBLER   p. 201.
  From preceding two by unstreaked back (see text).

PARULA WARBLER   p. 191.
  Immature: Bluish and yellow; wing bars.

MAGNOLIA WARBLER   p. 192.
  Immature: White band across tail.

PRAIRIE WARBLER   p. 203.
  Immature: Neck spot, side stripes; wags tail.

YELLOW WARBLER   p. 191.
  Yellow tail spots.

BLACKBURNIAN WARBLER   p. 197.
  Immature: Yellow throat, dark cheek, striped back.

BLACK–THROATED GREEN WARBLER   p. 196.
  Immature: Dusky streaks framing yellow cheek.

PALM WARBLER   p. 203.
  Brownish back; wags tail.

MYRTLE WARBLER   p. 193.
  Immature: Bright yellow rump.

CAPE MAY WARBLER   p. 192.
  Immature: Heavy streaks, neck spot (see text).

  * Not a Warbler, but often mistaken for one.

RUBY-CROWNED KINGLET

Immature

CHESTNUT-SIDED

YELLOW-THROATED
VIREO

♂
Adult

Immature

BLACKPOLL

Immature

♂ Adult

PINE

BAY-BREASTED

Immature

PARULA

Immature

MAGNOLIA

Immature

PRAIRIE

Immature
(Alaskan)

Immature

YELLOW

Immature

BLACKBURNIAN

Immature

BLACK-
THROATED
GREEN

PALM

Immature

MYRTLE

Immature

CAPE MAY

PHILADELPHIA
VIREO

TENNESSEE

Immature

ORANGE-CROWNED

Immature

BLACK-THROATED BLUE
♀

HOODED
Immature

WILSON'S
Immature

CONNECTICUT
Immature

MOURNING
Immature

NASHVILLE

YELLOW-THROAT
♀

PROTHONOTARY
♀

CANADA
Immature

Plate 52   195

CONFUSING FALL WARBLERS

(Most of these have no streaks or wing-bars.)

* PHILADELPHIA VIREO   p. 181.
    Vireo bill; actions (see text).

TENNESSEE WARBLER   p. 189.
    Trace of wing-bar; white under tail.

ORANGE–CROWNED WARBLER   p. 190.
    Dingy breast, yellow under tail.

BLACK–THROATED BLUE WARBLER   p. 193.
    Dark-cheeked look, white wing-spot.
    Some young birds lack the wing-spot.

HOODED WARBLER   p. 207.
    Immature: Yellow eye-stripe, white tail-spots.

WILSON'S WARBLER   p. 207
    Immature: Like small Hooded; no white in tail.

CONNECTICUT WARBLER   p. 205.
    Immature: Suggestion of hood, complete eye-ring.

MOURNING WARBLER   p. 206.
    Immature: Suggestion of hood, broken eye-ring.

NASHVILLE WARBLER   p. 191.
    Yellow throat, eye-ring.

YELLOW–THROAT   p. 206.
    Female: Yellow throat, brownish sides, white belly.

PROTHONOTARY WARBLER   p. 185.
    Female: Golden head, gray wings.

CANADA WARBLER   p. 208.
    Immature: Spectacles; trace of necklace.

   * Not a Warbler, but often mistaken for one.

Similar species: — The white throat and under parts distinguish it from the Cape May and Magnolia Warblers, the only other species that possess contrasting yellow rump-patches.
Voice: — Summer song, a loose junco-like trill, but rising in pitch, or dropping. Spring song more primitive; weak, colorless, and irregular. Note, a loud *check*.
Range: — Breeds in coniferous belt from tree-limit in Canada s. to n. Minnesota, n. Michigan, New York (mountains), and Massachusetts; winters in s. United States, n. locally where bayberries are found to Lake Erie and Massachusetts.

BLACK-THROATED GREEN WARBLER. *Dendroica virens.*
Subsp. pp. 186, 194.
Field marks: — 4½–5¼. *Male:* — The bright *yellow face* framed by the *black throat* and olive-green crown and back is the best mark. *Female:* — Recognized by the yellow face-patch, but with much less black on the throat and under parts.
Similar species: — The young and the female in autumn have virtually no black on the throat and upper breast. Hence they suggest the Pine Warbler or even the immature Blackburnian, but there is always enough of dusky at the edge of the throat to act as a frame for the bright yellow cheeks, and this leaves no doubt that they are Black-throated Green Warblers.
Voice: — A lisping dreamy *zoo zee zoo zoo zee* or *zee zee zee zee zoo zee*, the *zee* note on same pitch, the *zoo* notes lower.
Range: — Breeds in evergreen woods from s. Manitoba and s. Labrador s. to s. Minnesota, n. Ohio, New Jersey, Long Island, and, in mountains, to n. Georgia. Also in cypress swamps near coast from Dismal Swamp, Virginia, to South Carolina (*D. v. waynei*). Winters in Mexico and Central America.

CERULEAN WARBLER. *Dendroica cerulea.* p. 183.
Field marks: — 4–5. *Male:* — Blue above, white below. It usually forages too high in the trees to reveal the azure-blue back. Then the *narrow black ring* crossing the upper breast is the best mark. No other white-breasted Warbler is so marked. *Female:* — Blue-gray and olive-green above and whitish below, with two white wing-bars and a white line over the eye.
Similar species: — The female suggests the Tennessee Warbler, but the Tennessee has no wing-bars. It resembles closely the autumn Black-poll but is greener above, whiter below and has a more conspicuous eye-stripe. See Blue-gray Gnatcatcher.
Voice: — Song suggests song of Parula Warbler; rapid buzzy notes on same pitch followed by a longer note on a higher pitch: *zray zray zray zray zreeeee*. Also has the quality of the Black-throated Blue but rapid, not lazy.
Range: — Breeds in deciduous forests, particularly in river valleys, from cent. New York (local), s. Ontario, s. Michigan, se.

Minnesota, and se. Nebraska s. to n. parts of Gulf States, chiefly w. of the Appalachians. Migrates through Gulf States (rare on Atlantic slope); winters in South America.

BLACKBURNIAN WARBLER. *Dendroica fusca.* pp. 183, 194.
Field marks: — 5-5½. The 'fire-throat.' *Male in spring:* — Black and white with *flaming orange* about the head and throat; unmistakable. *Female:* — Paler, but still orange enough on the throat to be recognized as a Blackburnian. *Autumn birds:* — Color-pattern similar, but paler, the orange more yellowish. The clean-cut yellow head-stripings are distinctive.
Similar species: — The differently patterned Redstart is the only other small bird of similar color to the male Blackburnian. Young birds in autumn suggest young Black-throated Green Warblers except: (1) the throat is strongly *yellow*, (2) dark ear-patch, (3) light stripes on back.
Voice: — The most distinctive song begins with several well-measured *zip* notes on the same pitch and ends on an extremely high thin slurred note: *zip zip zip zip titi tseeeeee.* This wiry end note is diagnostic if your ears can catch it. Another song is more like Nashville's, a two-parted affair: *tizip tizip tizip tizip, zizizizizizizizi.*
Range: — Breeds in evergreen woods from cent. Manitoba and Gulf of St. Lawrence s. to Minnesota, n. Michigan, and s. New England, and, in Appalachians, to n. Georgia. Migrates through e. United States; winters in South America.

YELLOW–THROATED WARBLER. *Dendroica dominica.* Subsp. p. 186.
Field marks: — 5-5½. *A gray-backed Warbler with a yellow bib.* White stripe over the eye, two white wing-bars, and black stripes on the sides; sexes similar; creeps about the branches of trees. The Sycamore race of the Mississippi Valley (see Subspecies) can be told at close range by the *white* instead of yellow lores (between eye and bill).
Similar species: — The female Blackburnian (a migrant in the South) is slightly similar, but is *broadly striped with yellow* over the eye and through the center of the crown.
Voice: — Song, a series of clear slurred notes dropping slightly in pitch, *tee-ew, tew, tew, tew, tew, tew wi* (last note picking up); slightly suggestive of Louisiana Water-Thrush.
Range: — Breeds along Atlantic coastal plain from Florida to Maryland and s. New Jersey (probably) ... (prefers Southern pines, live oaks), also in Mississippi Valley from Gulf States n. to s. Michigan and s. Wisconsin (where it prefers sycamores). Winters from s. Georgia and Florida into tropics.

SUTTON'S WARBLER. *Dendroica potomac.* p. 186
Field marks: — Known from only two specimens, both taken in

BLACKBIRDS AND STARLING

BOAT–TAILED GRACKLE   p. 213
    Male: Very large; long creased tail.
    Female: Smaller; brown.

PURPLE GRACKLE   p. 213.
    Male: Plain dull purple back.

BRONZED GRACKLE   p. 216.
    Male: Plain bronzy back.
    Intergrades between Bronzed and Purple
    Grackles have broken iridescent bars on the back and are
    known as 'Ridgeway's Grackles' (see text).

RUSTY BLACKBIRD   p. 212.
    Male in spring: Black; yellow eye. medium tail.
    Female in spring: Gray; yellow eye.
    Immature in fall: Rusty; barred breast.

BREWER'S BLACKBIRD   p. 213.
    Male: Purplish head, medium tail.
    Female: Gray, dark eye.

RED–WING (RED–WINGED BLACKBIRD)   p. 211
    Male: Red 'epaulettes.'
    Female: Heavily striped.

COWBIRD   p. 210.
    Male: Brown head, short bill.
    Female: Gray, short bill.

YELLOW–HEADED BLACKBIRD   p. 210.
    Male: Yellow head.
    Female: Yellow throat.

STARLING   p. 177.
    Male in spring: Yellow bill, short tail.
    Juvenile: Gray or gray-brown; short tail.

PURPLE GRACKLE

BRONZED GRACKLE ♂

♂

♀

BOAT-TAILED GRACKLE

♀ Spring

♂ Spring

BREWER'S BLACKBIRD

Autumn Immature

RUSTY BLACKBIRD

♀

♂

♀

♂

RED-WING

♀

♂

COWBIRD

♂

♂ Spring

♀

Juvenile

YELLOW-HEADED BLACKBIRD

STARLING

CANADA JAY

KINGFISHER ♀

BLUE JAY

BOBOLINK ♀   ♂ Breeding

BALTIMORE ORIOLE   ♀   ♂ Adult

Adult ♂

Immature ♂

♀ ORCHARD ORIOLE

SCARLET TANAGER   Moulting   ♀   ♂ Breeding

♂ Breeding

♀ WESTERN TANAGER

SUMMER TANAGER ♀   ♂ Breeding

Plate 54   199

KINGFISHER, JAYS, BOBOLINK, ORIOLES AND TANAGERS

BELTED KINGFISHER   p. 141.
    Large bill, bushy crest, banded breast.

CANADA JAY   p. 158.
    Gray; white forehead, black nape.

BLUE JAY   p. 158.
    Bright blue, with crest.

BOBOLINK   p. 209.
    Male: Black belly, white patches above.
    Female: Striped head, buffy breast.

BALTIMORE ORIOLE   p. 211.
    Male: Orange; black head.
    Female: Yellow-orange; wing-bars.

ORCHARD ORIOLE   p. 211.
    Adult male: Deep rusty breast and rump.
    Immature male: Black throat-patch.
    Female: Yellow-green; wing-bars.

SCARLET TANAGER   p. 217
    Breeding Male: Scarlet, with black wings.
    Moulting Male: Red patches.
    Female: Yellow green; dusky wings.

SUMMER TANAGER   p. 220
    Breeding Male: Red all over, no crest.
    Female: Deeper yellow than Scarlet Tanager.

WESTERN TANAGER   p. 217
    Breeding Male: Red face, black back.
    Female: Wing-bars, Tanager bill.

the eastern panhandle of West Virginia; also one or two good
sight records from the same area. It is a question whether it is
a very rare species, newly discovered, a well-marked subspecies
of limited range, or a chance hybrid between the Yellow-throated
and the Parula Warblers. It looks like a Yellow-throated Warbler but *lacks the black stripes on the sides* and has the suffused
greenish back of the Parula. Its song is like the buzzy trill of
the Parula, doubled by repetition: *zeeeeeee-up, zeeeeeee-up.* Sexes
similar.

CHESTNUT-SIDED WARBLER. *Dendroica pensylvanica.*

pp. 186, 194.

Field marks: — 5. *Adults in spring:* — Easily identified by the
yellow crown and the *chestnut* sides. *Autumn* birds are quite
different — greenish above and white below, with a white eye-
ring and two wing-bars. Adults usually retain some of the
chestnut. The lemon-colored shade of green, in connection with
the white under parts, is sufficient for recognition.
Similar species: — The only other Warbler with chestnut sides,
the Bay-breast, has a chestnut throat and a *dark crown,* thus
appearing quite dark-headed.
Voice: — Most characteristic song similar to one of the Yellow
Warbler's but more emphatic; can be interpreted '*I wish to see
Miss Beecher,*' or '*please please please ta meetcha*' the last note
dropping abruptly. If the song comes from a streamside, a
town, or a farmyard, it is the Yellow Warbler. If it comes from
a dry, bushy clearing it is the Chestnut-side. A second, more
rambling song is given in the summer.
Range: — Breeds in shrubby deciduous slashings and bushy
pastures from cent. Manitoba and Gulf of St. Lawrence s. to
Nebraska, Illinois, n. Ohio, n. New Jersey, and, in uplands, to
Tennessee and w. South Carolina; winters in Central America.

BAY-BREASTED WARBLER. *Dendroica castanea.*

pp. 186, 194.

Field marks: — 5-6. *Male in spring:* — A dark-looking Warbler with *chestnut throat, upper breast,* and sides, and a *large spot
of pale buff* on the side of the neck. *Female in spring:* — Similar
in general pattern to the male, but paler and more washed out.
Autumn birds: — Totally different; olive-green above with two
white wing-bars, dingy buff below. Some individuals have
traces of bay on the sides.
Similar species: — The Chestnut-sided Warbler is much lighter
colored than the breeding Bay-breast, with a *yellow* crown and
white throat. One of the most challenging field problems is to
distinguish the fall Black-poll from the fall Bay-breast: (1) Black-
poll is tinged with greenish-yellow below and is noticeably
streaked (Bay-breast is buffier, with breast streakings very in-

distinct or wanting); (2) Black-poll has *white* under tail-coverts (Bay-breast *buff*); (3) Some Bay-breasts have a touch of bay on flanks — these individuals are easy; (4) Black-poll has *pale yellowish legs* (Bay-breast, *blackish*). This is the most useful field mark of all. See also Pine Warbler.

Voice: — A high sibilant *teesi teesi teesi*; resembles song of Black and White but thinner, shorter, and more on one pitch.

Range: — Breeds in mature spruce forests from Gulf of St. Lawrence and cent. Manitoba s. to Adirondacks and n. New England; migrates through e. United States but rare on s coastal plain. Winters in Panama and Colombia.

BLACK-POLL WARBLER. *Dendroica striata.* pp. 186, 194
Field marks: — 5–5½. *Male in spring:* — A striped gray Warbler with *a solid black cap*; reminds the beginner of a Chickadee. *Female in spring:* — Less heavily streaked, lacking the black crown-patch; a plain, black-streaked Warbler, greenish-gray above and white below. *Autumn birds:* — Olive-green above, with two white wing-bars; dingy yellow below, faintly streaked. These are the common greenish-looking fall Warblers with white wing-bars, the ones which cause the field student so much trouble.

Similar species: — Spring males suggest the Chickadee but lack the black throat. They might be confused with the Black and White Warbler, which has a *striped* crown. Females are also known from the Black and White by the lack of these head-stripings, and from the female Myrtle by the absence of yellow in the plumage. Fall Black-polls are much more tricky (see fall Bay-breasted Warbler and Pine Warbler).

Voice: — Song, a thin deliberate, mechanical *zǐ-zǐ-zǐ-zǐ-zǐ-zǐ-zǐ* on one pitch, becoming slightly louder and more emphatic in the middle and diminishing toward the end (crescendo and diminuendo). Another song is a very rapid variation of this with the notes almost run together.

Range: — Breeds in stunted spruces from timberline in Canada s. to n. Michigan, n. Maine, and mountains of New York, Vermont, and New Hampshire; migrates through e. United States; winters in South America.

PINE WARBLER. *Dendroica pinus.* Subsp. pp. 186, 194.
Field marks: — 5–5½. No other *bright* yellow-breasted Warbler, without other conspicuous field marks, has white wing-bars. *Male:* — Olive-green above with two white wing-bars; under parts lemon yellow, brightest on the throat; breast dimly streaked. *Female:* — Like a dull-colored male; rather nondescript. *Immature and autumn female:* — Very obscure; grayish or brownish above, with *two white wing-bars*; under parts dull whitish with a dull buffy wash across the breast; best identified by the 'boiling-down' system of elimination (see following).

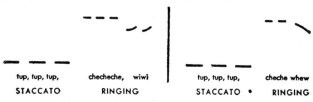

tup, tup, tup,   checheche,   wiwi   tup, tup, tup,   cheche whew
STACCATO   RINGING   STACCATO •   RINGING

TWO TYPICAL SONGS OF KIRTLAND'S WARBLER (R.T.P.)

Similar species: — The Yellow-throated Vireo is similar to the male, but has a thicker Vireo bill, lacks the breast-streaks, and does not show white spots in the tail. *Autumn* Black-polls and Bay-breasts are very similar to female and immature Pine Warblers — dingy dull-colored Warblers with white wing-bars. The plain, *unstreaked* back of the Pine Warbler, if it can be seen, at once eliminates either of those two. In addition, the Bay-breast has *buffy* under tail-coverts (Pine, white); Black-polls have *pale yellowish* legs (Pine, black). Some female Pine Warblers can be easily told because the breast is such a strong yellow but many immatures are plain grayish or brownish birds with a buffy wash across the breast, probably best identified by their lack of streaking. As James Boswell Young puts it, 'a museum tray of Pine Warblers looks like a catch-all for the museum's ratty, discarded Warbler skins.'
Voice: — Song, a trill, like that of Chipping Sparrow but looser, more musical, and slower in tempo.
Range: — Breeds in open pine woods from New Brunswick, s. Quebec, n. Michigan, and n. Manitoba s. to s. Florida and Gulf States; winters in s. United States n. to s. Illinois and Virginia (occasionally to New England near coast).

KIRTLAND'S WARBLER. *Dendroica kirtlandii.* pp. 186, 202.
Field marks: — 5¾. Bluish-gray above, with conspicuous black streaks on the back. Male has black 'mask.' Pale lemon-yellow below, with bold dark streaks or spots on flanks and sides of breast (sometimes also across the breast). The female is duller, grayer, and lacks the mask. In fall plumage, the face, sides, and whole upper parts (except rump and upper tail-coverts) are heavily obscured with brown. It persistently jerks ('wags') the tail up and down like a Palm Warbler; no other gray-backed Warbler has this habit.
Similar species: — May be known from the Canada Warbler by the habit of 'tail-wagging,' by the presence of wing-bars and of streaks on the back, by the dark (instead of light) legs, and by the interrupted white eye-ring (instead of yellow 'spectacles'). Female and immature Magnolia Warblers have been mistaken for Kirtland's, but they are much smaller and have a yellow rump and a broad white central band across the tail.

Voice: — Song, loud and low-pitched for a Dendroica, resembles that of the Northern Water-Thrush; in some individuals is rather like the House Wren's. A typical song starts with three or four low staccato notes, continues with some rapid ringing notes on a higher pitch, and ends abruptly.

Range: — Nests in loose colonies in an area about 100 miles long and 60 miles wide, in the n.-cent. part of the lower peninsula of Michigan, i.e., n. to Montmorency County (Clear Lake); e. to Alpena County (sw. of Alpena) and Iosco County (w. of Oscoda); s. to Ogemaw County (w. of Rose City) and Clare County (nw. of Harrison); w. to Wexford County (n. of Manton) and Kalkaska County (ne. of Kalkaska). The habitat is groves of young jack pines 5 to 18 feet high with ground cover of blueberry, bearberry, or sweet fern. Winters in Bahamas.

J. VAN TYNE

PRAIRIE WARBLER. *Dendroica discolor.* Subsp. pp. 186, 194.
   Field marks: — 4½–5. This Warbler *wags its tail* (so does Palm Warbler). It is the only common Warbler with yellow under parts striped with black in which the stripings are *confined to the sides. Two black face-marks,* one through the eye and one below, are conclusive. At close range, in good light, some *chestnut markings* can be seen on the back of the male; no other Warbler shares this feature (they are reduced to a trace in females; otherwise the sexes are similar). Immature birds in late summer and fall are nondescript *without* wing-bars; pale yellow below with indistinct streaking. Note the *tail-wagging* and the *dark neck-mark* (see color plate).

   Voice: — Song, a thin *zee zee zee zee zee zee zee zee,* going up the chromatic scale. Parula ascends, too, but notes of Prairie are clear and distinctly separated (Parula buzzes up).

   Range: — Dry bushy slashings and burns; is particularly fond of scrubby pine and oak barrens. In Florida it prefers mangroves. Breeds from Florida and Gulf States (locally) n. to Massachusetts, s. New York, s. Ohio, and e. Nebraska (and locally in s. New Hampshire, s. Ontario, and s. Michigan); winters from cent. Florida to West Indies.

PALM WARBLER. *Dendroica palmarum.* Subsp. pp. 186. 194.
   Field marks: — 5–5½. This Warbler spends most of its time on the ground. Brown above; whitish or yellowish below, with a *chestnut-red* crown (obscure in fall and winter); *constantly flicks its tail up and down.* This tail-wagging habit will often identify the species when no color or markings can be discerned. The sexes are similar. The two races of the Palm Warbler can be distinguished in the field (see Subspecies).

   Similar species: — Other tail-wagging Warblers are Prairie Warbler and Kirtland's Warbler (rare-Michigan). The Water-Thrushes *teeter,* more like a Spotted Sandpiper.

Voice: — Song, a chippy-like series of weak notes *thĭ thĭ thĭ thĭ thĭ thĭ*, etc.

Range: — Breeds in spruce and tamarack bogs from Gulf of St. Lawrence and n. Manitoba s. to Maine and n. Minnesota; migrates throughout e. United States; winters from Louisiana to Florida and occasionally n. along coast to Massachusetts.

OVEN–BIRD. *Seiurus aurocapillus.* Subsp.   p. 183.

Field marks: — 5½–6½. A voice in the woods. A sparrow-sized ground Warbler of the leafy woodlands; has somewhat the appearance of a small Thrush — olive-brown above, but *striped* rather than spotted, beneath. A *light orange patch* on the top of the head is visible at close range. The bird is usually seen *walking* on pale *pinkish* legs over the leaves or along some log. It is *heard* a dozen times to each time seen.

Voice: — The song is an emphatic *teach'er*, TEACH'ER, T E A C H'-ER, etc., repeated rapidly, louder and louder, till the air rings with the vibrant accents (to be more exact the accent is really on the *second* syllable, thus: *chertea'*, CHERTEA', C H E R T E A', etc.) In some parts of the Oven-bird's range (western Virginia, for example) its song is almost monosyllabic with little change of emphasis *T E A C H, T E A C H, T E A C H,* etc.

Range: — Breeds on leafy ground of deciduous woodlands (preferably) from Gulf of St. Lawrence and nw. Canada s. to e. North Carolina, n. Georgia, Arkansas, and Kansas; winters from Florida and s. Louisiana into tropics.

NORTHERN WATER–THRUSH. *Seiurus noveboracensis.* Subsp.
                                                                p. 183.

Field marks: — 5–6. The Water-Thrushes are brown-backed birds about the size of a Sparrow, with a *conspicuous light stripe over the eye, and heavily striped under parts.* Though Warblers, they act ridiculously like little Sandpipers; when not walking along the water's edge like mechanical toys they are constantly *teetering* up and down in much the manner of the 'Spotty' of the shore. In the present species the light under parts are strongly tinged with yellowish or buffy. The stripe over the eye is also *yellowish.*

Similar species: — The Louisiana Water-Thrush, a larger, grayer bird, is usually *whitish* below but may sometimes be slightly tinged with yellow. The eye-stripe is always *pure white.* Some Northern Water-Thrushes in fall, particularly the western race (Grinnell's Water-Thrush) have eye-lines that are quite white. Know them by the small spots on the throat (Louisiana has unspotted white throat). The preferred habitat of the two Water-Thrushes differs (see Range).

Voice: — The two Water-Thrushes are distinguished easily by song. In this species the song ends in a diagnostic *chew-chew-chew* (*twit twit twit twee twee twee chew chew chew* — rapid, dropping in pitch at the end).

Range: — Breeds in wooded swamps and swampy edges of slug-gish streams from limit of trees in w. Canada and n. Quebec s. to nw. Nebraska, n. Minnesota, nw. Michigan, ne. Ohio, New York, and mountains of West Virginia. Migrates through s. United States; winters from Florida into tropics.

LOUISIANA WATER-THRUSH. *Seiurus motacilla.*   p. 183
Field marks: — 6¼. See Northern Water-Thrush.
Voice: — The song is musical and ringing, starting with *three clear slurred whistles*, followed by a jumble of twittering notes dropping in pitch.
Range: — Prefers leafy ravines, small streams, and clear moun-tain brooks, but in some places is found in wooded swamps. Breeds from w. New England, s. Ontario, se. Minnesota, and e. Nebraska s. to cent. South Carolina, n. Georgia, n. Louisiana, and ne. Texas; winters in Central America.

KENTUCKY WARBLER. *Oporornis formosus.*   p. 187
Field marks: — 5½. The outstanding mark is the *broad black* 'sideburns,' or 'whiskers,' extending from the eye down the side of the yellow throat. The bird also has a yellow eye-ring, or 'spectacles.' The sexes are similar. Learn the song; ten Ken-tuckys are heard for every one seen.
Similar species: — The Yellow-throat has a black face-patch but lacks the yellow 'spectacles' and is whitish on the belly. The Canada Warbler has similar 'spectacles' but is *gray above*, not olive, usually shows some trace of its dark necklace mark-ings, and has *white* under tail-coverts.
Voice: — Song, a rapid, rolling chant *tory-tory-tory-tory* or *churry-churry-churry-churry*. Very suggestive of song of Carolina Wren but less musical, and two-syllabled rather than trisyllabic.
Range: — A bird of deciduous woodland thickets and glades, especially moist spots. Breeds from the Gulf States n. to se. Nebraska, s. Wisconsin, n. Ohio, and lower Hudson Valley (rare); winters in Mexico and Central America.

CONNECTICUT WARBLER. *Oporornis agilis.*   pp. 187, 195
Field marks: — 5¼-6. This species and the Mourning Warbler, both thicket birds, possess a gray *hood*, contrasting with the yellow and olive of their body-plumage. This species is at once recognized by the *round white eye-ring. Fall females and young* are duller, with no gray, but there is always an obvious suggestion of a hood (like a *brownish* stain across the yellow of the under parts). The eye-ring is always present.
Similar species: — The Nashville Warbler is of a similar color scheme, white eye-ring and all, but the throat is *yellow*, not gray. The Mourning Warbler in breeding plumage *lacks* the eye-ring, but it often has one in the fall. The yellow under tail-coverts

reach nearly to the end of the tail in the Connecticut and but halfway in the Mourning.

Voice: — Song, an oven-bird-like *beecher beecher beecher beecher beech* without the change of emphasis.

Range: — Breeds in tamarack and spruce bogs from Manitoba s. to cent. Minnesota and n. Michigan; migrates through Mississippi Valley in spring, along Atlantic Coast in autumn; winters in South America.

MOURNING WARBLER. *Oporornis philadelphia.* pp. 187, 195.
Field marks: — 5–5¾. Olive above, yellow below, with a *gray hood* completely encircling the head and neck; *male* with an apron of *black crape* on the upper breast where the hood meets the yellow. Skulks in thickets.

Similar species: — Neither sex in the breeding season has the conspicuous white eye-ring of the Connecticut. The male Connecticut never has the black crape. *Female and immature* Mourning Warblers in the fall often have an eye-ring, but it is broken in front of the eye, *not complete.* The Mourning is brighter yellow below and smaller.

Voice: — Song, *chirry chirry, chorry chorry,* the voice falling on the last two notes. There is considerable variation, but, as with all members of the genus *Oporornis,* the ringing, Carolina-wren-like 'turtling' is evident.

Range: — Breeds in swampy thickets and dry brushy clearings from Manitoba and Gulf of St. Lawrence s. to cent. Minnesota, Michigan, New York, and, in mountains, to West Virginia. Migrates chiefly w. of Appalachians; winters in Central and South America.

YELLOW-THROAT. *Geothlypis trichas.* Subsp. pp. 187, 195.
Field marks: — 4½–5½. We easily learn the *male* with his *black mask,* or 'domino.' *Females and immature birds* are plain olive-brown with a rich yellow throat, buffy yellow breast, and *white belly.* The black mask is absent. The habitat is low vegetation in swamps, stream-beds, marshes, and clearings. The bird's actions are very wren-like.

Similar species: — The only Warbler that suggests the male is the Kentucky. Females and immatures may be distinguished from similar Warblers by the *whitish belly* (the others are solid yellow below) and by the sort of place where they are found. Some fall birds have much brownish on the sides.

Voice: — Song, very distinctive, a rapid, well-enunciated *witchity-witchity-whitchity-witch,* or *witchity-ta-witchity-ta-witchity-ta-witch.* Note, a husky *tchep,* distinctive.

Range: — Breeds from s. Labrador, Quebec, and Alberta to Florida and Gulf Coast; winters from Louisiana and Florida n. along coast to North Carolina (occasionally farther).

YELLOW-BREASTED CHAT. *Icteria virens virens.* p. 183.
 Field marks: — 7–7½. Except for its color, the Chat seems
more like a Catbird or a Mocker than a Warbler. Its superior
size (larger than a Sparrow), its rather long tail, its eccentric
song and actions, and its brushy habitat, all suggest those larger
birds. Both sexes are plain olive-green above, with white 'spectacles'; the throat and breast are bright yellow; the belly, white.
 Similar species: — The Yellow-throated Vireo is colored similarly, but is smaller, with two white wing-bars.
 Voice: — An odd song made up of clear repeated whistles, alternated with harsh notes and soft crow-like *caws*. Even gives
imitations at times (suggests Mockingbird) but repertoire more
limited and much longer pauses between phrases. Single notes,
such as *whoit* or *kook*, are distinctive (Mockingbird does not do
this). The Chat often sings on the wing, with dangling legs,
and, like the Mocker, frequently sings at night.
 Range: — Breeds in brier thickets and bushy clearings from
Massachusetts (local), cent. New York, s. Ontario, Michigan,
and s. Minnesota s. to Florida and Gulf of Mexico; winters in
Central America.

HOODED WARBLER. *Wilsonia citrina.* pp. 187, 195.
 Field marks: — 5–5¾. The black 'hood' of the *male* completely
encircles the yellow face and forehead, which stand out as a
bright spot superimposed on the black. *Females*, both adult and
young, are plain olive above and bright yellow on the *forehead*
and under parts. Aside from large white spots in the tail, the
bird is *without streaks, wing-bars, or distinctive marks of any kind.*
 Similar species: — The female is almost identical with the
female Wilson's except for the larger size. The best mark is
the *white tail-spots* visible as the Hooded nervously flicks its tail
open and shut. The Wilson's has no white.
 Voice: — Song, a loud whistled *weeta wee-tee-o* (next to last note
higher). There are other arrangements but the slurred *tee-o* is a
clue. It is similar to Magnolia Warbler's song but more ringing.
Rarely do the two birds overlap except in migration. Note, a
metallic *chink*.
 Range: — Breeds in undergrowth of deciduous woodlands, laurel
thickets, and heavily wooded swamps from Rhode Island, cent.
New York, s. Michigan, n. Iowa, and se. Nebraska s. to Gulf of
Mexico; winters in Central America.

WILSON'S WARBLER. *Wilsonia pusilla pusilla.* pp. 187, 195.
 Field marks: — 4½–5. *Male:* — A yellow Warbler with a *round
black cap. Females* sometimes do, and *immature birds* do not,
show traces of the black cap. If they do not, they appear as
small, plain Warblers, olive-green above and bright yellow below,
with *no streaks, wing-bars,* or outstanding marks of any kind.

They are golden-looking with a yellow eyebrow stripe above the beady black eye.

Similar species: — Female Hooded has white spots in tail; Yellow Warbler, yellow spots. Wilson's has no tail-spots.

Voice: — Song, a thin rapid little chatter dropping in pitch at the end; *chi chi chi chi chi chet chet*.

Range: — Breeds in brushy northern bogs and swampy spots from n. Quebec and n. Manitoba s. to n. Maine, n. New Hampshire, and n. Minnesota; winters in Central America.

CANADA WARBLER. *Wilsonia canadensis.*   pp. 186, 195.

Field marks: — 5–5¾. The 'Necklaced Warbler.' Plain gray above, bright yellow below; male with a *necklace of short black stripes* across the breast. *Females and immature birds* are similar, but the necklace is fainter, sometimes nearly wanting. All have *yellow 'spectacles.'* In any plumage the *gray* color of the upper parts in connection with the *total lack of white in the wings and tail* is conclusive.

Voice: — A jumble of emphatic musical notes, no two on same pitch. Hard to describe; lacks distinctive pattern, but often ends in an emphatic *wip*.

Range: — Breeds in woodland undergrowth, usually near water, from cent. Manitoba and the Gulf of St. Lawrence s. to Minnesota, Michigan, New York, n. New Jersey, and, in mountains, to n. Georgia; winters in South America.

AMERICAN REDSTART. *Setophaga ruticilla.*   p. 183

Field marks: — 4½–5½. The Redstart is one of the most butterfly-like of birds. It is constantly flitting about, drooping its wings and spreading fanwise its tail. *Male:* — Largely black with *bright orange patches on the wings and tail*; belly white. *Female:* — Chiefly olive-brown above, white below, with large *yellow* flash-patches on the wings and tail. *Immature male:* — Considerable variation; much like the female; yellow often tinged with orange. The Redstart pattern is obvious in any plumage.

Similar species: — The only other small bird similarly colored is the male Blackburnian Warbler, which, however, has the orange confined to the head, throat, and upper breast.

Voice: — Three commonest songs *tsee tsee tsee tsee tseet* (last note higher), *tsee tsee tsee tsee tsee-o* (with drop on last syllable), and *teetsa teetsa teetsa teetsa teet* (double-noted). The songs are often alternated, an excellent field aid.

Range: — Breeds in medium deciduous forest growth (second growth saplings, etc.) from Gulf of St. Lawrence and cent. Manitoba s. to North Carolina, n. Georgia, s. Alabama, Louisiana, and Oklahoma; winters in West Indies and Central and South America.

Weaver Finches: Ploceidæ

HOUSE, or ENGLISH SPARROW. *Passer domesticus domesticus.* p. 215.
  Field marks: — 5–6¼. A species with which everybody is familiar. City birds are usually so sooty that more than one beginner has thought he had discovered something good when he first saw a clean country male with its black throat, white cheeks, and chestnut nape. Females are dull brown above and dingy white below without distinctive marks.
  Range: — Distributed widely about civilization; about cities, towns, and farms throughout the United States and Canada.

EUROPEAN TREE SPARROW. *Passer montanus montanus.* p. 215.
  Field marks: — An introduced species, resident about St. Louis, Missouri, and in near-by Illinois. Both sexes resemble the male House Sparrow with the black throat-patch, but are smaller and trimmer and are marked with a *large black spot* behind the eye. The crown is *chocolate*, not gray.
  Voice: — 'A rather hoarse, hard *teck, teck*' (B. W. Tucker).

Meadowlarks, Blackbirds, and Orioles: Icteridæ

As MEMBERS of this group are so vastly different, it is difficult to make any generalizations for use in the field, except that they have conical, sharp-pointed bills and rather flat profiles. They are best characterized under their various species.

BOBOLINK. *Dolichonyx oryzivorus.* p. 199.
  Field marks: — 6½–8. *Male in spring:* — The only songbird that is *black below and largely white above*, like a dress suit on backwards, a reversal of the normal tone-pattern of other birds, which are almost invariably lighter below. *Female and autumn birds:* — These are the 'Reedbirds' of the southern marshes; somewhat larger than Sparrows, largely yellowish-buff with dark stripings on the crown and upper parts.
  Similar species: — The male Lark Bunting of the Western Plains resembles the male Bobolink somewhat but has its white *confined to the wings*. Female Red-wings are duskier, have a longer bill and have heavy stripings on the breast.
  Voice: — Song, reedy and bubbling, starting with low melodious notes and rollicking upward in pitch; given on the wing. Flight

note, *pink*; unlike any other bird note (heard overhead in late summer and fall).

Range: — Breeds in meadows from s. Quebec and s. Manitoba s. to New Jersey, West Virginia, Illinois, and n. Missouri; migrates through se. United States; winters in s. South America.

MEADOWLARK. *Sturnella magna.* Subsp. p. 135.
Field marks: — 9–11. As we cross an extensive field or meadow this chunky brown bird flushes from the grass, showing a conspicuous patch of *white* on each side of the short, wide tail. Should it perch on some distant fence-post, our glass reveals a bright yellow breast crossed by a black V, or gorget.
Similar species: — The Flicker is similarly sized and brown above, but has a white *rump* instead of white sides to the tail, and it flies in a very different, *bounding* manner. On the ground the Flicker hops awkwardly; the Meadowlark walks. When with flocks of Starlings, the Meadowlark can be picked out by the different flight — several short, rapid wing-beats alternating with short periods of sailing. The other ground birds that show similar white outer tail-feathers (Pipit, Vesper Sparrow, and Junco) all are very much smaller, with the slimmer proportions of Sparrows. See Western Meadowlark.
Voice: — Song, two clear slurred whistles, musical and pulled out: *tee-yah, tee-yair* (last note 'skewy' and descending).
Range: — Breeds in meadows and prairies from New Brunswick, s. Quebec, and e. Minnesota s. to Florida and s. Texas, and e. to Nebraska and Kansas; winters in s. United States (a few north to Great Lakes and coastal New England).

WESTERN MEADOWLARK. *Sturnella neglecta.*
Similar species: — 8–10. Nearly identical with the Eastern Meadowlark, but paler, and yellow of throat edging a trifle farther onto cheek; best recognized by its song (below).
Voice: — A variable song of seven to ten notes, flute-like, gurgling, and double-noted; very unlike clear slurred whistles of Eastern Meadowlark.
Range: — Breeds in prairies of w. United States from s. Manitoba to cent. Texas and e. to Wisconsin and Illinois; winters from Iowa s. to Mexico. The ranges of the two Meadowlarks broadly overlap, and often both kinds may be heard singing in the same field in the Prairie States.

YELLOW–HEADED BLACKBIRD. *Xanthocephalus xanthocephalus.* p. 198.
Field marks: — 9–11. The name identifies it. A robin-sized Blackbird with a *yellow* head; shows a conspicuous white patch in the wing in flight. Females are smaller and browner with most of the yellow confined to the throat and chest; the breast is streaked with white. Inhabits marshes.

Voice: — Note, a low *krick* or *kack*. Song, low hoarse rasping notes produced with much effort; 'like rusty hinges.'

Range: — Breeds in marshes from cent. Manitoba, Hudson Bay (e. side), and n. Minnesota s. and e. locally to Nebraska, Iowa, s. Wisconsin, and n. Indiana; winters from w. Louisiana to Mexico; occasional in migration e. of Mississippi River.

RED-WING. *Agelaius phœniceus.* Subsp. p. 198.

Field marks: — 7½–9½. *Male:* — Black, with *red epaulets* or patches at the bend of the wings. Absolutely unmistakable. Often, when at rest, the scarlet is concealed, only the buffy or yellowish margin of the red patch being visible. *Immature male:* — Dusky-brown, but with the scarlet patches of the adult male. *Female and young:* — Brownish; identified by the sharp-pointed bill, Blackbird appearance, and *well-defined stripings below.*

Similar species: — Bobolinks frequent marshes in the fall but are yellowish, without the heavily streaked under parts. In fact, no female Blackbirds except Red-wings have these stripings.

Voice: — Song, a gurgling *konk-la-reeee* or *o-ka-leeee*, the last note high and quavering. Notes, a loud *check* and a high, slurred *tee-err.*

Range: — Breeds in marshes and swampy spots from Nova Scotia, Quebec, and Ontario s. to Florida and Texas; winters in s. United States (occasionally n. to Great Lakes and s. New England).

ORCHARD ORIOLE. *Icterus spurius.* p. 199.

Field marks: — 6–7¼. Smaller than a Robin. *Adult male:* — *Chestnut and black*; head, neck, back, wings, and tail black; rump and belly deep chestnut. *Immature male:* — Greenish above, yellow below, with a *black throat.* (Some female Baltimore Orioles have black throats, but such birds appear more orange than green.) *Females and young:* — Olive above, yellow below, with two white wing-bars.

Similar species: — The male Baltimore Oriole is fiery orange and black. Females and young of the Baltimore Oriole are not as green-looking as those of this species. See female Tanagers.

Voice: — Song, unlike clear abrupt piping whistles of Baltimore Oriole; a fast-moving joyous outburst interspersed with piping whistles and guttural notes. Suggests Purple Finch's song. A strident slurred *what-cheeer!* or *wheeer!* at or near the end is distinctive.

Range: — Breeds in rural country from Gulf of Mexico n. to s. New England, cent. New York, se. Ontario, Michigan, nw. Minnesota, and North Dakota; winters in Central America.

BALTIMORE ORIOLE. *Icterus galbula.* p. 199.

Field marks: — 7–8. Smaller than a Robin. *Male:* — *Fiery* *orange and black. Female and young:* — Oiive above, yellow below, with two wing-bars. Some females are quite orange, with 'some black around the head, thereby resembling males.

Similar species: — The male Redstart and the Blackburnian Warbler, the only other species with such intense orange, are both smaller than Sparrows. Females and young are very similar to the female Orchard Oriole, and are decidedly more orange-yellow. Female Orioles resemble female Tanagers in general coloration, but the latter birds show no wing-bars (except the accidental Western Tanager).

Voice: — Song, a series of rich, piping whistled notes. Note, a low whistled *hew-li.* Young birds just out of the nest give an incessant plaintive *tee-deedee.*

Range: — Breeds in groves and shade-trees (particularly elms) from Nova Scotia, Ontario, and s. Manitoba to n. Georgia, Louisiana, and s. Texas (absent on se. coastal plain); winters in Central America.

BULLOCK'S ORIOLE. *Icterus bullockii bullockii.*
   Field marks: — 7½–8½. The western counterpart of the Balti-more. The *male* is fiery orange and black, with *orange cheeks,* and large *white wing-patches. Female:* — See below.
   Similar species: — The male Baltimore has a *black head* and less white in the wing. Along the western edge of the Plains, where the ranges overlap, puzzling hybrids occur. Females and young have grayer backs and whiter bellies than Baltimores. See illustration in *A Field Guide to Western Birds.*
   Voice: — A series of accented double notes with one or two piping notes thrown in.
   Range: — Breeds in w. United States e. to South Dakota, cent. Nebraska, w. Kansas, and w. Oklahoma; winters in Mexico.

RUSTY BLACKBIRD. *Euphagus carolinus.*   p. 198.
   Field marks: — 8½–9½. The Rusty Blackbird is 'rusty' only in the fall, and usually suggests a short-tailed Grackle. *Male in spring:* — A robin-sized Blackbird with a whitish eye; frequents wet places, woodland swamps, etc. *Female in spring:* — Slate-colored. *Adults and young in autumn and winter:* — More or less tinged with rusty; closely *barred* beneath.
   Similar species: — Grackles are the long-tailed Blackbirds, Starlings the short; the Red-wing, Cowbird, and Rusty are of more average proportions. The Grackles, like the Rusty, have whitish eyes, but the larger size, ample *rounded* or *keel-shaped* tail, and, in strong light, the bright iridescence, identify them. Male Red-wings have red epaulets; females, heavy black stripings beneath. Cowbirds are smaller, *dark-eyed and short-billed.* In prairies, see Brewer's Blackbird.
   Voice: — Note, a loud *chack.* The 'song' is a split creak like a rusty hinge (*koo-a-lee*), rather penetrating.

Range: — Breeds in swampy woodlands from limit of trees in Canada, s. to cent. Ontario, n. New York, and n. New England; winters chiefly in s. United States (occasionally to Lake Erie and s. New England).

BREWER'S BLACKBIRD. *Euphagus cyanocephalus.* p. 198.
Field marks: — 8–9½. A prairie Blackbird that suggests a short-tailed Grackle. *Male:* — Has a white eye; shows *purplish* reflections on head and greenish reflections on body in strong light. Looks all black at a distance. *Female:* — Brownish-gray with *dark* eyes.
Similar species: — Rusty Blackbird has *dull greenish* head reflections, and the iridescence is almost lacking, not noticeable as in Brewer's Blackbird or Grackle. Female Rusty has *light* eyes, not dark. Where both birds occur, they tend to separate out, the Brewer's preferring fields and barnyards, and the Rusty, wet brushy places and swampy woodlands.
Voice: — Note, a harsh *check.* Song, a harsh wheezy *que-ee* or *ksh-eee* like the creaking of a rusty hinge.
Range: — Breeds in grassy prairies and meadows of w. United States e. to Minnesota, Wisconsin, n. Illinois, and Kansas; winters from Wisconsin and Kansas to Central America; a regular winter visitor recently to most southeastern states, where it probably has been overlooked.

BOAT–TAILED GRACKLE. *Cassidix mexicanus.* Subsp.
p. 198.
Field marks: — ♂ 16–17. ♀ 12–13. The Boat-tail, or 'Jackdaw,' is a very large Blackbird, *well over a foot long*, with a long, wide *keel-shaped* tail. Females are brown, not black, and are *much* smaller than the males.
Similar species: — The Boat-tail is not much smaller than a Fish Crow, but the long, creased tail is a good mark. The other Grackles are much smaller, hardly larger than Robins, and are less frequent around salt water.
Voice: — A harsh *check check check,* also a variety of harsh whistles and clucks.
Range: — Resident near salt water along coast (with a partiality for marshes) from Delaware and Chesapeake s. to Florida Keys and w. to Texas; also inland throughout Florida.

PURPLE GRACKLE. *Quiscalus quiscula.* Subsp. p. 198.
Field marks: — 11–13. Grackles are the familiar large iridescent Blackbirds, larger than Robins, with the *long wedge-shaped tails*. A crease in the center often gives the tail a *keel-shaped appearance* particularly in the spring. The line of flight is more even, not as undulating as that of other Blackbirds. Females are smaller than males and less iridescent.

FINCHES

(Most of these are 'Winter Finches.')

PURPLE FINCH   p. 223.
　　Male: Rosy, size of Sparrow.
　　Female: Light eye-stripe, dark jaw-stripe.

PINE GROSBEAK   p. 224.
　　Male: Large, rosy; wing-bars, stubby bill.
　　Female: Gray; dull yellow crown and rump.

WHITE-WINGED CROSSBILL   p. 228.
　　Male: Pink; wing-bars, crossed bill.
　　Female: Olive; wing-bars, streaks.

RED CROSSBILL   p. 228.
　　Male: Dull red, black wings.
　　Female: Dull olive; dark wings.

REDPOLL   p. 225.
　　Red forehead, black chin.
　　Male with pink breast.

CARDINAL   p. 220.
　　Male: Red; crest, black face.
　　Female: Brownish; red bill and crest.

EVENING GROSBEAK   p. 223.
　　Male: Dull yellow; black and white wings.
　　Female: Silver gray and yellow; large bill.

EUROPEAN GOLDFINCH   p. 224.
　　Red face, yellow wing-patch.

COMMON GOLDFINCH   p. 225.
　　Male in summer: Yellow body, black wings.
　　Female: Yellow-olive; Finch bill, unstreaked.

PINE SISKIN   p. 225.
　　Streaked; yellow patch in wings and tail.

PURPLE FINCH
♀ ♂

PINE GROSBEAK
♀ ♂

WHITE-WINGED
CROSSBILL
♀ ♂

RED CROSSBILL
♀

REDPOLL
♀ ♂

CARDINAL
♀ ♂

EVENING GROSBEAK
♀ ♂

EUROPEAN GOLDFINCH
♂

AMERICAN
GOLDFINCH
♀ ♂

PINE SISKIN
♂

BLUE GROSBEAK ♀

PAINTED BUNTING ♂

INDIGO BUNTING ♂ ♀

TOWHEE ♀ ♂

ROSE-BREASTED GROSBEAK ♀ ♂

DICKCISSEL ♀ ♂

SLATE-COLORED JUNCO ♂

OREGON JUNCO ♂

HOUSE SPARROW ♀ ♂

EUROPEAN TREE SPARROW

Sexes alike

Plate 56   215

FINCHES AND WEAVER FINCHES

BLUE GROSBEAK   p. 221.
    Male: Blue; tan wing-bars, large bill.
    Female: Brown; tan wing-bars, large bill.

PAINTED BUNTING   p. 222.
    Male: Red breast, purple head, green back.
    Female: Only green Finch.

INDIGO BUNTING   p. 222.
    Male: Blue all over.
    Female: Brown; no distinctive marks.

TOWHEE (EASTERN)   p. 229.
    Male: Rusty sides, white tail-spots.
    Female: Similar, but brown.

ROSE-BREASTED GROSBEAK   p. 221.
    Male: Rose breast-patch.
    Female: Striped head, large bill.

DICKCISSEL   p. 223.
    Male: 'Like little Meadowlark.'
    Female: See text.

SLATE-COLORED JUNCO   p. 234.
    Slate gray; white outer tail-feathers.

OREGON JUNCO   p. 234.
    Brown back and sides, black hood.

HOUSE SPARROW   p. 209.
    Male: Black throat, gray crown.
    Female: Plain dingy breast, dull eye-stripe.

EUROPEAN TREE SPARROW   p. 209.
    Black cheek-spot, chocolate crown.
    Sexes alike.

Similar species: — Like the Rusty Blackbird, this species has a white eye, but the larger size, heavier bill, more iridescent coloring, and longer, somewhat *wedge-shaped* tail are good marks. The Rusty is about the size of a Red-wing; this species, considerably larger. Along southern coast see Boat-tailed Grackle. In New England and west of Appalachians see Bronzed Grackle.

Voice: — Note, *chuck*; 'song,' a split rasping note that is both husky and squeaky.

Range: — Breeds from s. New England (intergrades between *Q. q. stonei* and *Q. versicolor*, often called 'Ridgway's Grackle') and extreme s. New York s. in a belt between the Appalachians and the coast to Florida and s. Louisiana; winters in s. United States n. to New Jersey.

BRONZED GRACKLE. *Quiscalus versicolor.* p. 198.

Similar species: — The Grackle of New England and the Mississippi Valley. At present this bird is officially called a full species — distinct from the Purple Grackle. It was long considered just a subspecies of that bird and might be again reduced to that rank. Typical birds have a *plain bronzy back.* Typical Purple Grackles (*Q. q. stonei*) have a *plain dull-purplish back.* Florida Purple Grackles (*Q. q. quiscula*) have dull-greenish backs. Where the ranges of the Purple and Bronzed Grackles meet (along Appalachians, s. New York, and s. New England) they intergrade, producing birds that can be seen in good sunlight to have *broken iridescent bars* on the back. These intergrades, formerly called 'Purple Grackles' by students in New York City and southern New England and now unofficially known as 'Ridgway's Grackles,' are the main reason why some of us believe it is a mistake to give the two Grackles full specific rank.

Range: — Breeds from Gulf of St. Lawrence and n. Manitoba s. to Massachusetts and w. of Appalachians (throughout Mississippi Valley and plains) to Louisiana and Texas. Winters n. to Ohio and New York.

(EASTERN) COWBIRD. *Molothrus ater ater.* p. 198.

Field marks: — 7–8. A rather small Blackbird with a short, conical sparrow-like bill. The *male* is the only black bird with a *brown* head. The *female* is uniformly gray. The finch-like bill is always a good mark.

Similar species: — The female can be told from the female Red-wing by lack of streakings and from the female Rusty and Brewer's Blackbirds by the *shorter bill* and smaller size. Besides the latter two, the only other all gray birds are the Catbird, which is slimmer, with *chestnut* under tail-coverts, and the young Starling, which is chunkier, shorter-tailed, and longer-billed. The young Cowbird is paler than the female, buffy-gray with soft breast-streakings; often seen fed by smaller birds. When with other Blackbirds, Cowbirds are obviously smaller and walk about with their tails lifted high.

Voice: — Note, *chuck*. Flight note, *weeee-titi* (a high whistle followed by two lower notes). Courtship song, bubbly and creaky, *glug-glug-gleeee* (last note thin, on high pitch).

Range: — Breeds from Nova Scotia, s. Quebec, and s. Manitoba s. to Virginia, Kentucky, Tennessee, Louisiana, and cent. Texas; winters chiefly in s. United States (a few n. to Great Lakes and s. New England).

Tanagers: Thraupidæ

MALE TANAGERS are brilliant-colored birds, the species found in the East possessing more or less bright red. Females are duller, green above and yellow below, a little like large Warblers or Vireos; somewhat larger than House Sparrows. Female Tanagers are most likely to be confused with Orioles, but are sluggish, much less active, and do not have such sharp-pointed bills. The dark of the crown comes down on the cheeks farther — nearly to the throat.

WESTERN TANAGER. *Piranga ludoviciana.* p. 199.
   Field marks: — 6¼–7. *Breeding male:* — Yellow with black wings and *red face.* Males lose red in autumn. *Female:* — Yellowish below and dull greenish above with white or yellowish wing-bars.
   Similar species: — Both sexes can be told from the two Eastern Tanagers by the broad *yellow wing-bars.* The only other bird with a red face is the British Goldfinch, but the yellow and black coloration identifies the Tanager. The female Western Tanager can be confused with female Orioles, but the sides of the face are darker. The bill is shorter and not so sharply pointed.
   Range: — Western. Accidental, but as there are a score of records from Maine to Louisiana, it should be watched for. A Tanager in winter might be this species.

SCARLET TANAGER. *Piranga olivacea.* p. 199.
   Field marks: — 6½–7½. *Male:* — A bright scarlet bird with *black* wings and tail. *Female, immature, and winter male:* — Dull green above and yellowish below, with brownish or blackish wings. Males changing from summer to winter plumage, or *vice versa*, are more or less patched with scarlet, yellowish, and green.
   Similar species: — The male Summer Tanager and the Cardinal are more extensively red, wings and tail included. Sluggish actions and large size (larger than House Sparrow) distinguish females, young and winter males from the Warblers and Vireos; the lack of wing-bars and greener coloration. from female Orioles.

SPARROWS

(Most of these have *streaked* breasts.)

FOX SPARROW
Rufous tail, heavily striped breast.
p. 237.

SONG SPARROW
Streaked breast, with large central spot.
p. 239.

VESPER SPARROW
White outer tail-feathers.
p. 233.

IPSWICH SPARROW
Ocean dunes; like large pale Savannah.
p. 229.

SAVANNAH SPARROW
Like Song; striped crown, short notched tail.
p. 230.

LINCOLN'S SPARROW
Like Song; buffy breast, fine black streaks.
p. 238.

GRASSHOPPER SPARROW
Clear buffy breast, striped crown.
p. 230.

HENSLOW'S SPARROW
Olive head, rufous wings.
p. 231.

BAIRD'S SPARROW
Ochre crown-stripe, necklace of streaks.
p. 230.

SEASIDE SPARROW
Dingy; yellow eye-spot, white jaw line.
p. 232.

LECONTE'S SPARROW
Buffy breast, streaked sides, white crown-stripe, reddish nape.
p. 231.

SHARP–TAILED SPARROW
Ochre face pattern, gray ear-patch.
The following are recognizable subspecies:
COMMON SHARP-TAILED SPARROW
Sharp breast-streakings
ACADIAN SHARP-TAILED SPARROW
Pale; washed-out, blurry breast-streaks
NELSON'S SHARP-TAILED SPARROW
Buffy breast with few streaks, sharply striped back.
p. 231.
p. 271.
p. 271.
p. 271.

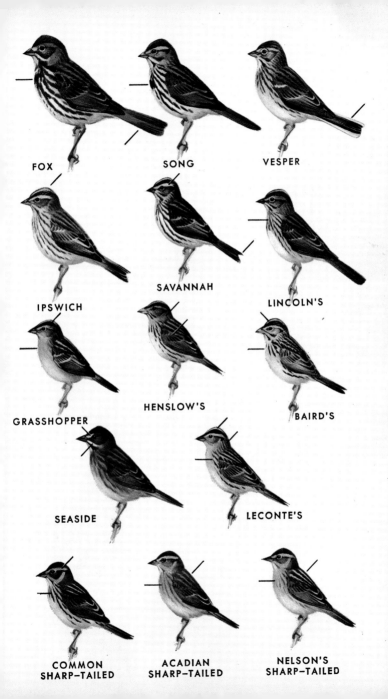

FOX

SONG

VESPER

IPSWICH

SAVANNAH

LINCOLN'S

GRASSHOPPER

HENSLOW'S

BAIRD'S

SEASIDE

LECONTE'S

COMMON
SHARP-TAILED

ACADIAN
SHARP-TAILED

NELSON'S
SHARP-TAILED

WHITE-
THROATED   Adult

WHITE-CROWNED   Adult

HARRIS'S   Adult

WHITE-THROATED   Immature

WHITE-CROWNED   Immature

HARRIS'S   Immature

PINE-WOODS

LARK

TREE

SWAMP   Immature   Adult

FIELD

CHIPPING   Immature   Adult

CLAY-COLORED   Immature   Adult

Plate 58   219

SPARROWS

(Most of these have *unstreaked* breasts.)

WHITE–THROATED SPARROW   p. 237.
 Adult: Striped crown, white throat.
 Immature: Striped crown, white throat.

WHITE–CROWNED SPARROW   p. 237.
 Adult: Striped crown, grayish throat.
 Immature: Brown and buff head-stripes, pink bill.

HARRIS'S SPARROW   p. 236.
 Adult: Black face, black bib.
 Immature: Buffy face, dark breast splotch.

PINE WOODS SPARROW   p. 233.
 Dull buffy breast, brown back stripes.

LARK SPARROW   p. 233.
 'Quail' head-pattern, 'stickpin,' white in tail.

TREE SPARROW   p. 235.
 Rusty cap, black 'stickpin.'

SWAMP SPARROW   p. 238.
 Adult: Rusty cap, gray breast, white throat.
 Immature: Dull breast-streaking (see text).

FIELD SPARROW   p. 236.
 Rusty cap, pink bill.

CHIPPING SPARROW   p. 235.
 Adult: Rusty cap, white eyebrow stripe.
 Immature: Gray rump (see text).

CLAY-COLORED SPARROW   p. 235.
 Adult: Striped crown, brown cheek-patch.
 Immature: Buffy rump (see text).

Voice: — Note, a low *chip-burr*. Song, four or five short, nasal phrases, robin-like in form but hoarse (like a Robin with a sore throat).

Range: — Breeds in woodlands and groves (*preferably oak*) from Nova Scotia, s. Quebec, and s. Manitoba s. to w. South Carolina, n. Georgia, n. Alabama, and Kansas; winters in South America.

SUMMER TANAGER. *Piranga rubra rubra.*   p. 199.
   Field marks: — 7–7½. *Male:* — Bright rose-red *all over*, no crest. *Female:* — Olive above, deep yellow below.
   Similar species: — The male Scarlet Tanager has *black wings and tail*; the Cardinal, a *crest* and a black face. In the female the wings are not dusky or blackish as in the female Scarlet Tanager, and the under parts are more orange. The bird is of much the color of a female Oriole but lacks the wing-bars. *Immature males* acquiring the adult plumage may be patched with red and green, but do not possess the black wings of the similarly plumaged Scarlet Tanager.
   Voice: — Note, a staccato *pi-tuck or pik-i-tuck-i-tuck*; song, robin-like phrases, less nasal and resonant than those of Scarlet Tanager and usually more sustained.
   Range: — Breeds in woodlands and groves (*preferably oak*) from Florida and Gulf of Mexico n. to Delaware, cent. Ohio, s. Wisconsin, s. Iowa, and se. Nebraska; winters in Central and South America.

Grosbeaks, Finches, Sparrows, and Buntings: Fringillidæ

THE BEST CHARACTER by which this family can be recognized is the bill, which is short and stout, adapted for seed-cracking. The two birds not belonging to this group which are most likely to be mistaken for *Fringillidae*, because of their stout, conical bills, are the Cowbird and the Bobolink. Three types of bills exist within the group: that of the Grosbeak, extremely large, thick, and rounded in outline; the more ordinary canary-like bill, possessed by most of the Finches, Sparrows, and Buntings; and that of the Crossbill, the mandibles of which are crossed, somewhat like pruning-shears, at the tips. Many of the Grosbeaks, Finches, and Buntings are highly colored, in contrast to the Sparrows, which are, for the most part, plain, streaked with brown.

CARDINAL. *Richmondena cardinalis.* Subsp.   p. 214.
   Field marks: — *The only all-red bird with a crest.* Smaller than Robin (8–9). *Male:* — All red except for black patch at base of

bill. *Female:* — Yellowish-brown, with a touch of red; at once recognizable by its crest and heavy red bill.

Similar species: — Summer Tanager (no crest); Scarlet Tanager (black wings).

Voice: — Song, a series of clear, slurred whistles diminishing in pitch. Several variations: *what-cheer cheer cheer*, etc.; *whoit whoit whoit*, etc. Note, a short thin chip.

Range: — United States e. of Plains and n. to s. New York, Lake Erie (s. Ontario), s. Minnesota, and se. South Dakota; towns, farms, roadsides, edges, swamps, etc. Non-migratory.

ROSE-BREASTED GROSBEAK. *Pheucticus ludovicianus.*

p. 215.

Field marks: — 7–8½. *Male:* — Black and white, with large triangular patch of *rose-red* on breast. In flight, ring of white flashes across black upper plumage. *Female:* — Very different; streaked, like a large Sparrow; recognized by large Grosbeak bill, broad white wing-bars, and conspicuous white line over eye.

Similar species: — Female resembles in pattern female Purple Finch.

Voice: — Song resembles Robin's but mellower, given with more feeling; note a sharp metallic *kick*, or *eek*.

Range: — Breeds in moist deciduous second-growth from cent. Manitoba, cent. Ontario, and s. Quebec s. to Kansas, s. Missouri, cent. Ohio, cent. New Jersey, and, in mountains, to n. Georgia; winters in Central and South America.

BLACK-HEADED GROSBEAK. *Pheucticus melanocephalus papago.*

Field marks: — 6½–7¾. Western. *Male:* — Unmistakable. Size of Rose-breasted Grosbeak. Breast dull robin-red, head and back blackish. Wings boldly marked with white bars and spots. Female like female Rose-breasted Grosbeak but breast browner, nearly devoid of streaking.

Voice: — Song and notes similar to Rose-breasted Grosbeak.

Range: — Western; breeds e. to w. Dakotas and cent. Nebraska. Hybrids with Rose-breast occur where ranges meet.

(EASTERN) BLUE GROSBEAK. *Guiraca cærulea cærulea.*

p. 215.

Field marks: — 6½–7½. *Male:* — Deep dull blue, with a large bill and two *rusty* wing-bars. *Female:* — Larger than a Sparrow, or about size of Cowbird; brown, lighter below, with two *buffy* wing-bars. Immature males are a mixture of brown and blue.

Similar species: — The male appears black at a distance, then resembling a Cowbird. The only other *all-blue* bird is the Indigo Bunting. The Bunting is smaller with a much smaller bill, and lacks the tan wing-bars. (See immature male Indigo Bunting.)

The female Indigo Bunting likewise is smaller than the female of this species and lacks the wing-bars and the Grosbeak bill.

Voice: — Song, a rapid finch-like warble with short phrases rising and falling; suggests Orchard Oriole but lower and more guttural without the clear whistled notes. Pairing of notes suggests Indigo Bunting but song is more run together.

Range: — Breeds locally in brushy edges, scrub, and willow thickets from Gulf States n. to Maryland, s. Illinois, and Nebraska; winters in Central America.

INDIGO BUNTING. *Passerina cyanea.*   p. 215.
Field marks: — 5¼–5¾. Smaller than House Sparrow. *Male:* — Deep, rich blue *all over*. In autumn the male becomes more like the brown female, but there is always enough blue in the wings and tail to identify it.
Female: — Plain brown, under parts paler with indistinct streakings; *the only small brown Finch devoid of obvious stripings, wing-bars, or other distinctive marks.*
Similar species: — Immature or changing males are brown and blue; resemble Blue Grosbeaks but are much smaller (slightly larger than Chipping Sparrow), with a smaller, sparrow-like bill.
Voice: — A lively Finch-song, high and strident, with well-measured phrases at different pitches. *The notes are usually in twos: sweet-sweet, chew-chew,* etc. Note, a sharp thin *spit.*
Range: — Breeds in open brushy places, roadsides, and edges from s. New Brunswick, s. Ontario, and North Dakota s. to central parts of Gulf States; winters in Cuba and Central America.

LAZULI BUNTING. *Passerina amœna.*
Field marks: — 5–5½. Male a small bright-blue Finch. Head and upper parts *turquoise blue*; band across breast and sides *cinnamon*; wing-bars white. Distinguished from Bluebird by small size, Finch bill, and *white wing-bars.* Female nondescript — a small brown Finch with white wing-bars. Distinguished from Sparrows by lack of streakings above or below; from female Indigo Bunting by *white wing-bars.* See illustration in *A Field Guide to Western Birds.*
Voice: — Similar to Indigo Bunting.
Range: — Western; breeds e. to w.-cent. North Dakota, w. Nebraska, and extreme w. Oklahoma.

(EASTERN) PAINTED BUNTING. *Passerina ciris ciris.*
                                                        p. 215.
Field marks: — 5¼. The most gaudily colored American bird. *Male:* — A little chippy-sized Finch, a patchwork of *bright red, green, and indigo* — blue-violet on head, green on back, red on rump and under parts. *Female:* — Very plain — greenish above, paling to lemon-green below; *no other small Finch is green.*

Voice: — Song, a bright pleasing warble; resembles song of Warbling Vireo but more wiry; note, a sharp *chip*.

Range: — Breeds in Southern towns, thickets, and brushy edges from Gulf States n. to se. North Carolina, n. Mississippi, cent. Arkansas, and s. Kansas; winters from cent. Florida and s. Louisiana (occasionally) into tropics.

DICKCISSEL. *Spiza americana.*   p. 215.

   Field marks: — 6–7. The Dickcissel is midwestern, a grassland bird with a fondness for alfalfa fields. It is about the size of a House Sparrow but a bit slimmer.

   Male: — Suggestive of tiny Meadowlark, with yellow breast and black bib. In the fall the black of throat is obscured or lacking.

   Female: — Very much like female House Sparrow, but paler, with much whiter stripe over eye, touch of yellow on breast, and bluish bill. Chestnut bend of wing is also an aid.

   Similar species: — Often looks a lot like House Sparrow (above). Female might be confused with female Bobolink.

   Voice: — Song, a staccato rendition of its name: *Dick-ciss-ciss-ciss* or *'chup-chup-klip-klip-klip'* (P. A. Taverner).

   Range: — Breeds in Prairie States e. to s. Michigan, w. Ohio, and se. Ontario, and s. to Texas and Alabama; winters in n. South America.

(EASTERN) EVENING GROSBEAK. *Hesperiphona vespertina vespertina.*   p. 214.

   Field marks: — 7½–8½. A large, chunky, short-tailed Finch, nearly size of Starling. The dusky, dull yellowish color, and extremely large, conical, whitish bill distinguish it at once. Awing, recognized as a Finch by the characteristic undulating flight and distinguished from Pine Grosbeak, only winter Finch of similar size, by shorter tail. The large white wing-patches show at a great distance in flight. *Male:* — Largely dull yellow, with black and white wings, suggesting an overgrown Goldfinch. *Female:* — Silvery-gray, but with just enough of the yellow and the black and white to be recognizable.

   Similar species: — The Snow Bunting is the only other Northern Finch showing so much white in the wing. The female Pine Grosbeak is slimmer than the female Evening, with a smaller, *dark* bill, much less white in the wing, *none in the tail*.

   Voice: — Song, a short uneven warble; note, a ringing finch-like chirp, *cleer* or *clee — ip*. (Suggests glorified House Sparrow.)

   Range: — Breeds in spruce belt of nw. Canada e. to n. Michigan; winters erratically s. and e. to Missouri, Kentucky, Ohio, Virginia (rarely), and New England.

(EASTERN) PURPLE FINCH. *Carpodacus purpureus purpureus.*   p. 214.

   Field marks: — 5½–6¼. Purple is hardly the word; raspberry or old-rose is more like it. *Male:* — About size of House Sparrow, rosy-red, brightest on head and rump ('like a Sparrow dipped in raspberry juice'). *Female:* — A heavily striped brown sparrow-like bird with a broad, whitish line over eye. The large, stout bill distinguishes it from the streaked Sparrows. *Immature male:* — Resembles female.

Similar species: — The male Pine Grosbeak is similarly colored, but is much larger, nearer the size of Robin. Redpolls are red only on forehead, not on entire head.

Voice: — Song, a fast, lively warble; note, distinctive, a dull metallic *tick*, or *pit*.

Range: — Breeds in small evergreens from n. Ontario and Newfoundland s. to North Dakota, cent. Minnesota, n. Illinois, n. New Jersey, Long Island, and, in mountains, to Maryland; winters from s. Ontario and s. New England to Gulf of Mexico.

(CANADIAN) PINE GROSBEAK.   *Pinicola enucleator leucura.*
                                                            p. 214.
Field marks: — 9–9¾. A robin-sized winter Finch with a moderately long tail is quite surely this species, the largest of the Finches. It is often quite tame. *Male:* — Rosy-red with two white wing-bars. *Female:* — Gray with two wing-bars; head and rump tinged with dull yellow. *Immature male:* — Similar to female but with touch of reddish on head and rump. Most Finches rise and fall in flight; this one in particular.

Similar species: — The White-winged Crossbill is rosy-red with white wing-bars, but is smaller, about size of House Sparrow, with slender cross-tipped bill. The Evening Grosbeak is shorter-tailed, with chunkier proportions. See also Purple Finch.

Voice: — Most characteristic call a clear three-syllabled whistle: *tee-tee-tew*, remarkably like cry of Greater Yellow-legs but with a more *finch-like* quality.

Range: — Breeds in cold spruce forests of Canada s. to mountains of n. New England; winters erratically into Northern States.

EUROPEAN GOLDFINCH.   *Carduelis carduelis britannica.* p. 214.
Field marks: — 5½. Slightly larger than American Goldfinch; tawny-brown with *bright red* patch about base of bill and *broad yellow band* crossing wing. Sexes similar.

Similar species: — See Western Tanager.

Voice: — Song, liquid, suggesting Canary; 'more twittering than American Goldfinch's song' (John Elliott); note, a liquid *swit-wit-wit*.

Range: — Naturalized in Bermuda; small colonies established on se. Long Island (Seaford, Garden City, Massapequa, etc.).

HOARY REDPOLL.   *Acanthus hornemanni exilipes.*
Similar species: — 4½–5½. Among the Redpolls look for a

smaller, frostier-looking bird. If it has an immaculate white rump, *devoid of streakings*, it is this species.

Range: — Subarctic; winters south occasionally to n. United States.

REDPOLL. *Acanthus flammea.* Subsp.   p. 214.

Field marks: — 5–5½. In notes, size, shape, and actions Redpolls resemble Goldfinches and Siskins; little streaked, gray-brown birds that may be known by a *bright red cap* on the forehead and a *black chin. Males* are pink-breasted.

Similar species: — Purple Finches are larger and redder than Redpolls (*entire head* and much of back are reddish); Siskins are darker with more heavily striped under parts.

Voice: — In flight a rattling *chut-chut-chut-chut.*

Range: — Subarctic, wandering s. irregularly to Northern States in winter. Prefers open country, weedy edges.

PINE SISKIN. *Spinus pinus pinus.*   p. 214.

Field marks: — 4½–5. A small dark, *heavily streaked* Finch with a *flash of yellow* in wing and tail. In size and actions resembles Goldfinch. Learn the calls. Most Siskins are spotted as they fly high overhead, uttering their characteristic notes.

Similar species: — Winter Goldfinches are unstreaked; Redpolls are paler, without the heavy streakings across front of breast; female Purple Finch is larger (size of House Sparrow) with larger bill. None of these show any yellow in either wings or tail, nor do they have the Siskin's pointed face and bill.

Voice: — Song, similar to Goldfinch's, but more coarse and wheezy; call, a loud *clee-ip* or *chlee-ip*, also a light *tit-i-tit* and a long buzzy *shreeeee* — latter unique among bird-notes.

Range: — Breeds chiefly in evergreen forests from timber line in Canada s. to n. Minnesota and n. New England, and in mountains of North Carolina; winters erratically throughout United States s. very rarely to Florida and Gulf States.

COMMON GOLDFINCH. *Spinus tristis tristis.*   p. 214.

Field marks: — 5–5½. Smaller than a House Sparrow. Flight extremely undulating. *Male in summer:* — *The only small yellow bird with black wings. Female in summer:* — Dull olive-yellow with blackish wings and conspicuous wing-bars; distinguished from any other small olive-yellow bird (Warblers, etc.) by its stout Finch bill. *Winter birds:* — Much like the summer female. This eastern race is called the Eastern Goldfinch.

Similar species: — The Yellow Warbler, which shares with this bird the nickname 'Yellow-bird,' is yellow all over. The only two similar small winter Finches, the Redpoll and the Siskin, are *streaked*; the winter Goldfinch is unstreaked above and below.

Voice: — Song, long-sustained, clear, light, and canary-like. In flight, each dip is often punctuated by a simple *ti-dee-di-di.*

GROUND BIRDS OF OPEN COUNTRY
(Fields, Prairies, Shores)

SNOW BUNTING   p. 241.
    Wings largely white.

LARK BUNTING   p. 229.
    Male: Black body, white wing-patches.
    Female: Striped; some white in wing.

HORNED LARK   p. 156,
    Adult: 'Horns,' face-patch, breast splotch.
    Immature: Suggestion of adult pattern.
    NORTHERN HORNED LARK: Yellowish eye-stripe.
    PRAIRIE HORNED LARK: Whitish eye-stripe.

WHEATEAR   p. 173.
    White rump, black tail-pattern.

AMERICAN or WATER PIPIT   p. 175.
SPRAGUE'S PIPIT   p. 175.
    Both Pipits: Thin bill, white outer tail-feathers.
    AMERICAN PIPIT: Dark back, black legs.
    SPRAGUE'S PIPIT: Striped back, yellowish legs.

LAPLAND LONGSPUR   p. 239.
    Male in spring: Black throat, rusty collar.
    Winter: Smudge on breast, rusty nape.
    Tail pattern below (No. 1).

McCOWN'S LONGSPUR   p. 239.
    Male in spring: Black breast splotch, black cap.
    Winter: Rusty shoulders; tail pattern below (No. 4).

CHESTNUT–COLLARED LONGSPUR   p. 240.
    Male in spring: Black below; rusty collar.
    Winter: Tail pattern below (No. 3).

SMITH'S LONGSPUR   p. 240.
    Male in spring: Black and white ear-patch.
    Winter: Buffy; tail pattern below (No. 2).

TAILS OF LONGSPURS

♀

♂

SNOW BUNTING

♀

♂ Breeding

LARK BUNTING

Immature

♂

NORTHERN HORNED LARK

♂

PRAIRIE HORNED LARK

Winter

WHEATEAR

♂ Summer

Winter

LAPLAND LONGSPUR

Winter

AMERICAN PIPIT

SPRAGUE'S PIPIT

♂ Summer

Winter

McCOWN'S LONGSPUR

♂ Summer

Winter

CHESTNUT-COLLARED LONGSPUR

♂ Summer

Winter

SMITH'S LONGSPUR

MANGROVE
CUCKOO

WHITE-CROWNED
PIGEON

ANI

FLORIDA or
SCRUB JAY

BAHAMA
SWALLOW

BAHAMA
BANANAQUIT

GRAY KINGBIRD

BLACK-WHISKERED VIREO

CAPE SABLE
SEASIDE SPARROW

DUSKY SEASIDE SPARROW

Plate 60   227

SOME FLORIDA SPECIALTIES

WHITE–CROWNED PIGEON   p. 127.
Dark body, white crown.

MANGROVE CUCKOO   p. 128.
Buffy breast.

ANI (SMOOTH–BILLED)   p. 132.
Occasional; high ridged bill, long loose tail.

FLORIDA or SCRUB JAY   p. 159.
No crest, no white tail-spots.

BAHAMA SWALLOW   p. 250.
Accidental; like Tree Swallow, tail deeply forked.

GRAY KINGBIRD   p. 146.
Gray, large bill; tail notched, no white.

BAHAMA BANANAQUIT   p. 250
Accidental; black back, yellow breast, white eyebrow.

BLACK–WHISKERED VIREO   p. 180.
Black whisker mark.

CAPE SABLE SEASIDE SPARROW   p. 232.
Only Seaside Sparrow in southern Florida.

DUSKY SEASIDE SPARROW   p. 232.
Dusky; found only near Titusville.

Range: — Breeds from Newfoundland, s. Quebec, and s. Manitoba s. to n. Georgia, n. Alabama, cent. Arkansas, and s. Oklahoma; winters from s. Canada to Gulf Coast.

RED CROSSBILL. *Loxia curvirostra.* Subsp. p. 214.

Field marks: — 5¼–6½. Size near that of House Sparrow. The sound made by the cracking open of the cones of evergreen trees often betrays their presence. They act like small Parrots as they dangle around the cones. The crossed, pruning-shear mandibles are distinctive; at a distance, when crossed tips are not visible, the comparative length of the bill is obvious. *Male:* — *Brick-red,* brighter on the rump; wings and tail dusky. Several other Northern Finches are *rosy-red,* but this is only brick-red bird of group. Young males are more or less orange. *Female:* — Dull olive-gray; yellowish on the rump and under parts. See Subspecies.

Similar species: — The plain dark wings distinguish this species from White-winged Crossbill. Juvenile birds, striped above and below, look like large Pine Siskins. The larger bill and absence of yellow in the wings are the points to look for.

Voice: — Note, a hard *jip-jip* or *pip-pip-pip.* Song, finch-like warbled passages: '*chip-chip-chip-jee-jee-jee,* first notes delivered like a trill, following ones loud and creaking' (J. W. Bond, R. J. Ussher).

Range: — Breeds in spruce belt of Canada s. to n. edge of United States and thought to breed locally in s. Appalachians (w. North Carolina, n. Georgia, etc.); winters erratically s. to Southern States.

WHITE-WINGED CROSSBILL. *Loxia leucoptera leucoptera.*
p. 214.

Field marks: — 6–6¾. *Male:* — Size of House Sparrow; *rosy-pink* with black wings and tail and *two broad white wing-bars.* *Female and young:* — Olive-gray with yellowish rump, like Red Crossbill, but with *two broad white wing-bars.* The wing-bars are often quite evident in flight and help in picking out this species from mixed flocks of Crossbills. Both Crossbills are usually found in conifers.

Similar species: — Pine Grosbeak is rosy, with wing-bars, but is much larger (near size of Robin). See Red Crossbill.

Voice: — The common notes of the White-wing are a sweet *peet* and a dry *chif-chif.* The note corresponding to the *chif-chif* in the Red Crossbill is a hard *jip* or *jip-jip.* Song of White-winged Crossbill, a succession of loud trills on different pitches.

Range: — Breeds in spruce belt from limit of trees in Canada to n. edge of United States; winters occasionally to Central States.

TOWHEE: CHEWINK. *Pipilo erythrophthalmus.* Subsp.

p. 215.

Field marks: — 7½–8¾. Smaller and more slender than Robin, which it remotely resembles; *reddish confined to the sides.* Frequents brushy places; often detected by noisy rummaging among dead leaves. *Male:* — Entire head and upper parts black; *sides robin-red;* belly white. In flight, looks black, with large white spots showing toward outer tips of ample tail. *Female:* — Similar, but dusky brown where male is black. Juvenile birds in summer are streaked below like large slender Sparrows but have the telltale Chewink wing and tail pattern. In winter in the South, the white and red-eyed races can be distinguished by voice, eyes, and appearance. See Subspecies.

Voice: — Song, *drink-your teeeeeee,* the last syllable higher, drawn out and wavering. Call, a loud, easily recognized *chewink!* Note of southern birds (White-eyed Towhee) has southern drawl: a slurred *shrink* or *zreee;* typical song, *cheet cheet cheeeeee* (last note lower in pitch).

Range: — Breeds in open brushy places, barrens, slashings, and edges from s. Maine, s. Ontario, and s. Manitoba s. to Florida and Gulf Coast. Winters from Gulf n. to Wisconsin, Lake Erie, and Potomac (rarely Massachusetts).

LARK BUNTING. *Calamospiza melanocorys.* p. 226.

Field marks: — 5½–7½. A prairie bird. *Male in spring:* — Like a small Blackbird (about House Sparrow size) *with large white wing-patches. Females, young,* and *autumn males* are brown with stripings on breast; usually some members of the flock show white or buffy wing-patches.

Similar species: — Male Bobolink has white *on back* as well as on wings. Striped brown Lark Buntings slightly resemble female Purple Finches except for the whitish wing-patches.

Voice: — Song, a series of sweet trills. Note, a soft *hoo-ee.*

Range: — Breeds on dry upland plains and prairie bluffs of West, e. to w. Minnesota and e. Nebraska; occasional farther e. in migration; winters mostly in Mexico.

IPSWICH SPARROW. *Passerculus princeps.* p. 218.

Field marks: — 6–6¼. Look for this large pale *sandy-colored* Sparrow in the coarse beach grass among the dunes along the ocean. In spring it has a pale yellow line over the eye.

Similar species: — In pattern it resembles a Savannah Sparrow, but is so much larger and paler that it would not be confused with it. (Some taxonomists consider it only a well-marked subspecies of the Savannah Sparrow.) Superficially it is more like a Vesper Sparrow, but has a white stripe through the crown and lacks the white outer tail-feathers.

Voice: — Similar to Savannah Sparrow.

Range: — Breeds on Sable Island, Nova Scotia; winters in dunes and at edge of salt marshes along coast s. to Georgia.

SAVANNAH SPARROW. *Passerculus sandwichensis.* Subsp.
p. 218.

Field marks: — 5¼–6. A streaked open-country Sparrow; suggests a *short-tailed* Song Sparrow with a *yellowish stripe* over the eye and a whitish stripe through the crown.

Similar species: — The tail of a Savannah is slightly forked, not rounded like that of the Song Sparrow. This obvious notch is an aid to the observer flushing Sparrows from the salt meadow where both Savannahs and Sharp-tails are common.

Voice: — Song, a dreamy lisping *tsit-tsit-tsit, tseeeee-tsaaay* (last note lower). At a distance only the two long notes can be heard.

Range: — Breeds in meadows and prairies from Labrador and Hudson Bay s. to n. Iowa, n. Indiana, Pennsylvania, Long Island, and New Jersey coast (local); winters from Long Island and s. Indiana s. to Florida and Gulf Coast.

GRASSHOPPER SPARROW. *Ammodramus savannarum.* Subsp.
p. 218.

Field marks: — 5–5¼. A *short-tailed* flat-headed little Sparrow of the open fields; crown with a pale stripe through the center. Differs from other Sparrows of the open fields in having an *unstreaked* dingy breast. The conspicuously striped back, very short tail, and unstreaked buffy breast are best marks.

Similar species: — Young birds in late summer with streaked breasts complicate matters. They resemble the adult Henslow's Sparrow, but are not so reddish on the wings as that bird.

Voice: — Two songs: (1) a long, sizzling insect-like tumble of notes; (2) two low introductory notes and a thin dry buzz, *pi-tup zeeeeeeeeeeee* (at a distance the introductory notes are inaudible).

Range: — Breeds in meadows and prairies from s. New Hampshire, s. Ontario, Minnesota, and North Dakota s. to n. Georgia, s. Louisiana, and Texas; also prairies of cent. Florida. Winters from North Carolina and s. Illinois s. to Gulf.

BAIRD'S SPARROW. *Ammodramus bairdii.* p. 218.

Field marks: — 5–5½. A prairie Sparrow with a light breast crossed by a *narrow band of fine black streaks*. Head *yellow-brown* streaked with black. The best mark is the *very broad center stripe on the crown,* which is conspicuously *ochre.* The habitat of the Baird's Sparrow is dry upland prairies where the native grass is long.

Similar species: — The Savannah Sparrow has more extensive streakings on the under parts. The light stripe through the crown is much narrower (*whitish,* not yellow-brown).

Voice: — Song often begins with three or four musical zips and ends with a trill on a lower pitch; more musical than insect-like efforts of Savannah; variable.

Range: — Breeds in dry upland prairies from sw. Saskatchewan and Manitoba to North Dakota and nw. Minnesota; migrates through plains to Mexico.

LECONTE'S SPARROW. *Passerherbulus caudacutus.* p. 218.

Field marks: — 5. A sharp-tailed Sparrow of the prairie marshes, characterized by the *bright buffy-ochre* of the eye-line, throat and breast, and the wide *pinkish-brown collar* on the nape of the adult.

Similar species: — The ochre of the under parts distinguishes it from the Henslow's Sparrow; the streaked sides from the Grass-hopper Sparrow; and the *white stripe* through the crown, from the Sharp-tail. Bright buffy juvenile Sharp-tails in early fall are sometimes called Leconte's.

Voice: — Song, two extremely thin grasshopper-like *hisses,* first note barely audible.

Range: — Breeds in prairie marshes from Great Slave Lake s. to s. Minnesota and North Dakota; migrates se. to South Carolina, Florida, Louisiana, and Texas.

HENSLOW'S SPARROW. *Passerherbulus henslowii.* Subsp. p. 218.

Field marks: — 4¾–5¼. Short-tailed and flat-headed with a big pale bill; finely streaked below. The striped olive-colored head in conjunction with reddish wings identify it. Its flight is low and jerky with a twisting motion of the tail.

Similar species: — In most of the East, the only other 'sharp-tailed' Sparrow of the open meadow (not salt marsh) is the Grasshopper Sparrow, which is clear-breasted. In late summer young Grasshopper Sparrows are streaked and resemble adult Henslow's; young Henslow's are practically without breast-streakings, thus resembling the adult Grasshopper Sparrow. The Henslow's always has more or less russet on the wing.

Voice: — The Henslow's perches atop a weed, from which it utters one of the poorest vocal efforts of any bird; throwing back its head, it ejects a hiccoughing *tsi-lick.* As if to practice this 'song' so that it might not always remain at the bottom of the list, it often hiccoughs all night long.

Range: — Breeds in poor weedy meadows from s. New Hamp-shire, New York, s. Ontario, and South Dakota s. to n. North Carolina, West Virginia, and n. Texas; winters in se. United States.

SHARP-TAILED SPARROW. *Ammospiza caudacuta.* Subsp. p. 218.

Field marks: — 5–6. Sharp-tails are marsh Sparrows. They are identified by the *ochre yellow of the face*, which completely surrounds the gray of the ear-patch. The Sharp-tails of the coast have *streaked* breasts; those of the inland prairies (*A. c. nelsoni*) are buffier, almost devoid of breast-streaking. It is often possible for an experienced field man to distinguish the various races of the Sharp-tail, but it is not a thing for the beginner to experiment with. See Subspecies.

Similar species: — The Savannah Sparrow, often seen in the salt marsh, has a *notched* tail. This is evident when the bird flushes and flies ahead. It also has a striped crown. See Seaside Sparrow (often lives with Sharp-tails).

Voice: — Song, a gasping buzz, *tuptup-sheeeeeeeee*; more hissing than husky, accented song of Seaside.

Range: — Breeds in salt marshes along coast from Virginia to Gulf of St. Lawrence and locally in upper St. Lawrence River and s. James Bay; also in inland prairie marshes from Minnesota and South Dakota to Great Slave Lake. Winters along Atlantic and Gulf Coasts from Long Island to Florida and Texas.

SEASIDE SPARROW. *Ammospiza maritima.* Subsp. p. 218.
Field marks: — 5½–6½. Very dingy-looking. A dark, olive-gray, sharp-tailed Sparrow of the salt marsh, with a short yellow line *before the eye* and a white streak along the jaw.
Similar species: — The Seaside is dingier than the Sharp-tailed Sparrow, without the conspicuous ochre head-markings.
Voice: — Song, *cutcut, zhe'-eeeeeeee*; very similar to Sharp-tailed Sparrow but usually with a stronger accent (*zhe'*) in middle of song. Note, *chack* (like a little Red-wing).
Range: — Breeds in salt marshes along coast from Massachusetts (a few) to Florida and along Gulf to Texas; a few winter n. occasionally to Long Island.

DUSKY SEASIDE SPARROW. *Ammospiza nigrescens.* p. 227.
Field marks: — About size of Seaside Sparrow, but *upper parts blackish*, and under parts heavily streaked with black. (Local name: 'Black Shore Finch.') Remember, any Seaside Sparrow seen in the Titusville area in summer is this species. (It might be regarded some day as only a race of *A. maritima*.)
Voice: — A buzzy *cut-a-zheeeeee* (like *maritima*) vaguely suggestive of Florida Red-wing in pattern, but not in quality.
Range: — Salt marshes around Merritt Island in vicinity of Titusville, Florida. You will find it across the bridge.

CAPE SABLE SEASIDE SPARROW. *Ammospiza mirabilis.*
p. 227.
Field marks: — *The only Seaside Sparrow in southern Florida;*

greener above and whiter below than any race of *maritima.*
Range: — Coastal prairie near Cape Sable, Florida. Very local.

(EASTERN) VESPER SPARROW. *Pocœcetes gramineus grami-*
neus.   p. 218.
    Field marks: — 5½–6½. The *white outer tail-feathers* flashing
conspicuously as the bird flies make the best mark. Perched,
it looks like a grayish Song Sparrow, but seems to have a *whitish
eye-ring.* A *chestnut-colored patch* at the bend of the wing is
determinative.
    Similar species: — Several other open-country birds have white
outer tail-feathers: the Meadowlark, which is much larger and
chunkier; the Juncos, which are slate-gray; the Longspurs and
the Pipits. The Pipits are the most similar, but they are thin-
billed, *walk* instead of hop, and frequently *bob their tails.* The
Lark Sparrow has large white spots in the *corners of the tail,* in
addition to the white edges.
    Voice: — Song, throatier and more minor in quality than that
of Song Sparrow, and beginning with *two* low clear whistled notes
followed by two higher ones (Song Sparrow begins with *three or
four* repetitious notes on the same pitch).
    Range: — Breeds in meadows, fields, and prairies from Gulf of
St. Lawrence, cent. Ontario, and s. Saskatchewan s. to North
Carolina, Kentucky, Missouri, and Nebraska; winters from s.
part of breeding range to Florida and Gulf Coast.

(EASTERN) LARK SPARROW. *Chondestes grammacus gram-*
macus.   p. 219.
    Field marks: — 5½–6½. The best mark on this open-country
Sparrow is the *black fan-shaped tail with much white in the outside
corners* (somewhat as in Towhee — not as in Vesper Sparrow).
It also has *chestnut* ear-patches, a striped crown, and a white
breast with a single dark central spot. Young birds are finely
streaked on the breast and lack the central spot, but are otherwise quite recognizable.
    Similar species: — See Vesper Sparrow.
    Voice: — A broken song consisting of clear notes and trills with
pauses in between; best characterized by buzzing and churring
passages interspersed here and there.
    Range: — Breeds in weedy fields and poor pastures and on open
knolls of Mississippi Valley from s. Ontario, Minnesota, and s.
Saskatchewan s. to Texas and Louisiana and e. to Ohio and nw.
West Virginia; winters in Gulf States.

PINE WOODS SPARROW. *Aimophila œstivalis.* Subsp.
                                                                                        p. 219.
    Field marks: — 5¾. In the open pine woods of the South,
especially where scrub palmetto covers the ground, this shy

Sparrow is found. It flushes reluctantly, and drops back into the undergrowth, where it plays hide-and-seek. A glimpse shows it to be a brown-backed bird with a wash of *dingy buff* across its unstreaked breast.

Similar species: — Resembles the better known Field Sparrow, but is less rusty, with a larger bill which is *not pink*. It also suggests the Grasshopper Sparrow, which lives in meadows, has a light crown-stripe, and a tail only half as long. Juvenile birds have eye-rings and buffy breasts with streakings. They suggest the Lincoln's Sparrow, which has a more distinctly striped crown and of course would not be found in the South in the summer months.

Voice: — Song, variable. Usually a clear liquid whistle followed by a loose trill or warble on a different pitch. For example, *seeeeee, slipslipslipslipslip*. This melodious arrangement — a key-note followed by a passage in a different pitch — vaguely suggests the Hermit Thrush's pattern of song.

Range: — Breeds in open pine country from Florida, Gulf Coast, and Texas n. locally to Maryland, sw. Pennsylvania, s. Ohio, cent. Illinois, and se. Iowa. Winters n. to North Carolina.

SLATE–COLORED JUNCO. *Junco hyemalis.* Subsp. p. 215.
Field marks: — 6–6½. Smaller than House Sparrow; dark *slate-gray* with a hood and *conspicuous white outer tail-feathers*; belly white.

Similar species: — The Vesper Sparrow also shows a V of white formed by the outer tail-feathers, but is buffy brown, not blackish. Streaked young Juncos in summer may be told from Vespers by their dusky color and their woodland habitat. For field distinction of Carolina Junco see Subspecies.

Voice: — Song, a loose quavering trill suggestive of Chipping Sparrow's song but slower and more musical; note a light smack or click; also twittering notes.

Range: — Breeds in coniferous country from tree-limit s. to n. Minnesota, n. Michigan, Maine, and, in higher Appalachians, to n. Georgia; winters from s. Canada to Gulf of Mexico.

OREGON JUNCO. *Junco oreganus.* p. 215.
Field marks: — 5–6. Male resembles Slate-colored Junco but with back *red-brown*, contrasting sharply with black head; sides yellowish or rusty. Females have grayer heads, and the rusty of the back is not so sharply defined, but the 'pink' or tan sides are always sharply separated from the gray of the hood (a good way to tell them from immature Slate-colored Juncos which occasionally show 'pinkish'). The specific status of the Juncos is still disputed by museum men. The Western ones intergrade and mongrels between *oreganus* and the Slate-color are frequent, especially in the Plains. Just call them Juncos.

Range: — Rare, but one or more turn up almost every winter in the Northeast. Look for it at your feed-tray.

(EASTERN) TREE SPARROW. *Spizella arborea arborea.*

p. 219.

Field marks: — 6–6½. The single *round black spot* or 'stickpin' in the center of the breast, and the bright *red-brown cap* are the only marks necessary to identify the 'Winter Chippy.' Two conspicuous white wing-bars are also characteristic. Another good mark is the bill, dark above, yellow below.

Similar species: — See Field Sparrow and Chipping Sparrow.

Voice: — Song, sweet and variable, beginning with one or two high, sweet, clear notes. Note, a distinct *tseet*; feeding note a musical *teeler* or *teelwit*.

Range: — Breeds beyond limit of trees in Canada (Hudson Bay, Newfoundland, etc.); s. in winter to Kansas, Arkansas, and South Carolina; prefers weedy open country, roadsides, edges, brushy marshes.

(EASTERN) CHIPPING SPARROW. *Spizella passerina passerina.*

p. 219.

Field marks: — 5–5½. A very small clear gray-breasted Sparrow with a bright *rufous cap*, a *black line* through the eye, and a *white line* over it. *Young birds* in late summer are finely streaked below, but are recognized by their small size and moderately long forked tail. Immature birds in winter look like adults, but are buffier, with a striped crown. *Winter adults* are browner, not so gray-breasted.

Similar species: — See Field Sparrow and Clay-colored Sparrow.

Voice: — Song, a dry chipping rattle or trill all on one pitch. (Birds with similar songs are Junco, Swamp Sparrow, Pine Warbler, Worm-eating Warbler.) Note, a short chip.

Range: — Breeds from s. Quebec and Manitoba s. to n. parts of Gulf States; winters in s. United States, n. rarely to New Jersey; prefers towns and farms, also conifers in parts of range.

CLAY-COLORED SPARROW. *Spizella pallida.*

p. 219.

Field marks: — 5–5½. A small pale sparrow of the Prairie States; clear-breasted like Field Sparrow and Chippy, but with a *light stripe* through center of crown and a *sharply outlined brown ear-patch.*

Similar species: — Fall birds and immatures are much like Chippies in the same plumage. Somehow the idea got started that Chippies with brown ear patches are Clay-colored Sparrows. Both birds possess them. The patch in the Clay-colored adult is *outlined* above and below by black lines; the fall Chippy lacks them. The only sure point in immature birds is the rump, which is *buffy-brown*; that of the Chippy is gray.

Voice: — Song, unbird-like; three or four low flat buzzes, *bzzzz, bzzzz, bzzzz* (slow tempo).

Range: — Interior; breeds iñ brushy country (prairies, pine barrens, and woodland openings) from Great Slave Lake s. to n. Nebraska, nw. Illinois, and n.-cent. Michigan; winters mainly in Mexico.

(EASTERN) FIELD SPARROW. *Spizella pusilla pusilla.*

p. 219.

Field marks: — 5¼–6. The *pink bill* identifies the Field Sparrow. It has reddish upper parts and a clear breast. 'Pasture Sparrow' would be a better name for it, as it does not live in open fields.

Similar species: — Except for the pink bill, it resembles the Tree Sparrow and the Chippy. It has less noticeable facial striping; this and the *eye-ring* give the bird a blank expression. Young birds in summer are finely streaked below like young Chippies, but lack the well-marked head-stripings.

Voice: — Song, a clear, sweet series of notes starting with deliberate slurring notes and speeding into a hurried trill (which ascends, descends, or stays on same pitch). Note, *tseee*, has querulous quality.

Range: — Breeds in brushy pastures, clearings, and edges, from s. Maine, s. Quebec, s. Minnesota, and s. North Dakota s. to n. parts of Gulf States; winters in s. United States n, to s. New York and Illinois.

HARRIS'S SPARROW. *Zonotrichia querula.* p. 219.

Field marks: — 7–7¾. A sturdy Sparrow, longer than Fox Sparrow. Sexes alike. In breeding plumage recognizable instantly by *black crown, face, and bib encircling pink bill.* In winter adults, black crown is veiled with gray. Young birds in first winter are *white on throat,* less black on crown, buffy brown on rest of head, and blotched and streaked on breast. Birds in second winter plumage are black *on the chin.*

Similar species: — In breeding plumage wholly unlike other species (save possibly male House Sparrow). In behavior like White-crowned and White-throated Sparrows, but when disturbed flies up into the trees rather than down into the underbrush.

Voice: — Song has delicate, quavering quality of White-throated Sparrow's, a series of clear whistles, all on same pitch, or first one or two at one pitch, rest at a slightly higher or lower pitch, *the general effect being minor.* Winter songs interspersed with chuckling sounds. Alarm note, a loud *weenk* or *wink.*

Range: — Summers among stunted spruces at edge of barren grounds w. of Hudson Bay, where it nests among Labrador tea and arctic bearberry. Migrates through Prairie States e. to sw.

Ohio, e. Illinois, and Michigan. Winters from s. Nebraska and w. Missouri s. well into Texas. In fall and winter inhabits brush and weed-patches in open woodland.

GEORGE MIKSCH SUTTON

WHITE-CROWNED SPARROW. *Zonotrichia leucophrys.* Subsp.

p. 219.

Field marks: — 6½–7½. *Adult:* — A clear pearly-gray breast and a high and puffy crown *striped with bands of black and white* makes this one of the handsomest of all the Sparrows. *Immature:* — Buffier, with head-stripings of dark red-brown and light buffy-brown; *bill pinkish.* For field identification of western race, Gambel's Sparrow (*Z. l. gambelii*), see Subspecies.

Similar species: — The White-throated Sparrow is also striped on the crown, but has in addition, (1) a conspicuous white throat, (2) a yellow spot before the eye. It is, on the whole, a much browner-looking bird. Young White-throats, though duller, always look like White-throats.

Voice: — Song, begins with a clear plaintive whistle like that of a White-throat but ends with a husky trilled whistle.

Range: — Breeds near limit of tree in Canada; migrates mainly through Mississippi Valley; less commonly along coast, chiefly in fall; winters mainly w. of Appalachians from Ohio Valley to Gulf of Mexico. Prefers brushy edges, tangles.

WHITE-THROATED SPARROW. *Zonotrichia albicollis.*

p. 219.

Field marks: — 6½–7. *Adult:* — Gray-breasted with *white throat-patch, striped black and white crown,* and *yellow* spot between bill and eye. *Immature:* — Duller, but with same essential recognition-marks.

Similar species: — The White-crown has a striped head but *lacks* the clean-cut white throat. The Swamp Sparrow has a white throat, but a *reddish* crown.

Voice: — Song, several clear, pensive whistles easily imitated; opens on one or two clear notes and follows with three quavering notes on a different pitch. New Englanders interpret it as 'Old Sam Peabody, Peabody, Peabody,' and call the singer the Peabody Bird. Note, a hard *chink*, also a slurred *tseet.*

Range: — Breeds in spruce belt from cent. Quebec and Newfoundland s. to cent. Minnesota, s. Ontario, n. New England, and, in mountains, to ne. Pennsylvania; winters from Ohio Valley and Massachusetts s. to Gulf of Mexico. Prefers brushy edges, thickets.

(EASTERN) FOX SPARROW. *Passerella iliaca iliaca.* p. 218.

Field marks: — 6¾–7½. Large for a Sparrow, larger than a House Sparrow, with a *bright rufous-red tail,* conspicuous when the bird flies. The rich rusty gives the bird its 'foxy' look. Its

breast is more heavily streaked than that of any other Sparrow.
Similar species: — The Hermit Thrush flashes a similar red tail
in flight, but is more olive-brown on the back, thin-billed, and
spotted on the breast, not *streaked.*
Voice: — Song, melodious; a variable arrangement of short
clear notes and sliding whistles.
Range: — Breeds in spruce belt from tree-limit in Canada s. to
Gulf of St. Lawrence and n. Manitoba; winters from Massachu-
setts (a few) and Ohio Valley to Gulf of Mexico (very rarely).
Prefers edges, woodland tangles, thickets.

LINCOLN'S SPARROW. *Melospiza lincolnii lincolnii.*   p. 218.
Field marks: — 5¼–6. The Lincoln's Sparrow is a skulker,
'afraid of its own shadow' and often hard to glimpse. Like
Song Sparrow, with shorter tail; streakings on under parts *much
finer* and often not aggregated into a central spot; best identified
by broad band of *creamy buff* across breast.
Similar species: — The buffy band and fine breast-streakings
distinguish it from most Sparrows except the immature Swamp
and Song Sparrows. It is grayer-backed than either, with a
more contrastingly striped crown. A narrow *eye-ring* is also
quite characteristic. The immature Swamp Sparrow in spring
migration is continually misidentified as the Lincoln's Sparrow,
but its breast is duller with dull blurry streaks (Lincoln's fine
and sharp). In the South the juvenile Pine Woods Sparrow can
easily be mistaken for Lincoln's.
Voice: — Song, sweet and gurgling; suggests both House Wren
and Purple Finch, starting with low passages, rising abruptly
in pitch, then dropping at the end.
Range: — Breeds in tamarack swamps and boggy spots from
Newfoundland and n. Quebec s. to Maine, n. New York, n.
Michigan, and Minnesota; winters from n. Mississippi and s.
Oklahoma s. to Gulf; casual along Atlantic Coast s. of Washington, D.C. Likes wet brushy places, swamp edges, boggy
spots.

SWAMP SPARROW. *Melospiza georgiana.* Subsp.   p. 219.
Field marks: — 5–5¾. A rather stout, dark Sparrow, with
clear-gray breast, white throat, and *reddish cap*; frequents cattail
marshes, bushy swamps, etc. *Immature* birds in the first winter
resemble adults but are streaked and have no red on the crown.
Similar species: — The Chipping Sparrow is clear-breasted with
a red cap, but is less robust and shows a white stripe over the eye.
Field and Tree Sparrows both show prominent wing-bars.
Immature Swamp Sparrows in spring migration are continually
misidentified as the Lincoln's Sparrow. *Juvenile* Swamp Sparrows in summer are buffy with fine breast-streakings. They are
difficult to distinguish from young Song Sparrows, but are usually
darker on the back and redder on the wings.

Song: — A trill, similar to Chipping Sparrow's but slower, sweeter and stronger, sometimes sung on two pitches simultaneously. *Note,* a hard *chink* similar to White-throat's.

Range: — Breeds in marshes from Newfoundland, s. Quebec, and n. Manitoba s. to New Jersey, West Virginia, n. Missouri, and n. Nebraska; winters from s. New England (occasionally) and Lake Erie (a few) s. to Gulf of Mexico.

SONG SPARROW. *Melospiza melodia.* Subsp.   p. 218.

Field marks: — 5–6¾. Breast heavily streaked, the streaks confluent into a *large central spot*; pumps its tail as it flies.

Similar species: — The Savannah Sparrow, though streaked similarly below, shows yellow over the eye, and has a shorter, *forked* tail. The tail of the Song Sparrow is not noticeably notched. *Young* birds are more finely streaked, often without the central spot. (See Lincoln's Sparrow and young Swamp Sparrow.)

Voice: — Song variable, familiar to everyone; musical, usually starting with three or four bright repetitious notes *sweet sweet sweet,* etc. Call note, a low nasal *tchap* or *tcheck.*

Range: — Breeds from Gulf of St. Lawrence and Great Slave Lake s. to coastal North Carolina, s. Virginia, n. Georgia (in mountains), s. Illinois, and Missouri; winters from Massachusetts, Lake Erie, and Iowa s. to Gulf of Mexico.

McCOWN'S LONGSPUR. *Rhynchophanes mccownii.*   p. 226.

Field marks: — 6. *Spring male:* — Forehead and patch on breast black; tail largely white. The hind-neck is *gray,* not brown or chestnut as in other Longspurs. *Female and winter plumages:* — See Chestnut-collared Longspur.

Similar species: — Male Chestnut-collared Longspur in spring has chestnut collar and black belly. Horned Lark has similar breast-splotch but has thin bill, black face-patch.

Voice: — Flight song, clear sweet warbles, of 'much the same character as Lark Bunting' (R. J. Niedrach).

Range: — Breeds in Great Plains from Saskatchewan s. to North Dakota and w. Minnesota (formerly); winters in plains from Kansas to Texas.

LAPLAND LONGSPUR. *Calcarius lapponicus lapponicus.*
      p. 226.

Field marks: — 6–7. Longspurs, like Snow Buntings and Horned Larks, are cold-weather birds of the beaches, fields, plains, and barren grounds; like those two they often *run* (but occasionally take big hops). The Lapland Longspur is the only common Longspur east of the plains. It appears a trifle like a House Sparrow. Two white wing-bars, some black streakings on the sides, and a varying amount of reddish on the nape of the neck (in males) are distinctive points. There is often a smudge of streaks across the upper breast. In the spring both sexes acquire a black throat.

Similar species: — With Snow Buntings it appears as a smaller, house-sparrow-like bird, with *dark wings*; when with Horned Larks it can be recognized by the short, sparrow bill, and the lack of an outlined yellow throat, and on the wing, by the *smaller tail* and more undulating flight. It has much less white on the outer tail-feathers than the other Longspurs. On Plains see other Longspurs.

Voice: — Note, a dry rattle or a rattling sound followed by a whistle: '*ticky-tick-teu*' (L. S. V. Venables).

Range: — Arctic tundra; s. in winter to Texas, n. Louisiana, and, rarely, South Caroïina.

SMITH'S LONGSPUR. *Calcarius pictus.* p. 226.

Field marks: — 6½. A *buffy* Longspur; a little like the Lapland, but with warm buff on entire under surface. The tail is edged with white as in a Vesper Sparrow (no terminal band). Male in spring is marked on cheek with a white spot strikingly outlined with triangle of black (black ear-patch with white spot in center); no other bi d is marked similarly.

Similar species: — Lapland Longspur, Vesper Sparrow, Sprague's Pipit.

Voice: — Similar to Lapland Longspur.

Range: — Arctic; migrates s. through plains to Texas; in migration e. to sw. Indiana.

CHESTNUT–COLLARED LONGSPUR. *Calcarius ornatus.*

p. 226.

Field marks: — 5½–6½. Smallest of the Lonspurs — smaller than a House Sparrow. *Male in breeding plumage:* — *Solid black below* except on throat; nape of neck, chestnut. *Female and winter male:* — Sparrow-like, known from other Longspurs (except McCown's) by large amonut of white on sides of tail.

Similar species: — Vesper Sparrow and the Pipits have straight white sides of tail to tip; Chestnut-collared and McCown's Longspurs have *dark band across end of tail*. In Chestnut-collar the dark central tail-feathers *curve* into the terminal band, fanwise; in McCown's, the band is more angular, forming a T with the dark central feathers (see diagram). This is about the only way to distinguish females and winter birds.

Voice: — Song, short, feeble, but musical, 'suggestive of Western Meadowlark in melody' (R. J. Niedrach).

Range: — Interior Plains; breeds from s. Saskatchewan and Manitoba s. to Kansas and w. Minnesota; winters from Nebraska and Iowa s. to Mexico.

SNOW BUNTING.   *Plectrophenax nivalis nivalis.*   p. 226.
   Field marks: — 6–7¼. No other song-bird shows so much
white. Some individuals look quite brown as they run about,
but when they fly the large white wing-patches flash forth.
Overhead, they look almost entirely white (Pipits and Horned
Larks are both black-tailed). They often travel in large flocks,
drifting over a field like snowflakes.
   Voice: — Note, a high clear whistled *teer* or *tew*; also a musical
purring note and a rough *bzzt*.
   Range: — Breeds in Arctic tundra; winters in open country s. to
n. United States and along coast to North Carolina.

Shore Silhouettes

1 COMMON TERN
2 BLACK TERN
3 HERRING GULL
4 CORMORANT
5 BLACK SKIMMER
6 GREAT BLUE HERON
7 BLACK DUCK
8 PIED–BILLED GREBE
9 MARBLED GODWIT
10 GREATER YELLOW–LEGS
11 DOWITCHER
12 CLAPPER RAIL
13 HUDSONIAN CURLEW
14 BLACK–BELLIED PLOVER
15 RUDDY TURNSTONE
16 NIGHT HERON
17 PHALAROPE
18 LEAST SANDPIPER
19 SEMIPALMATED PLOVER
20 SANDERLING
21 SPOTTED SANDPIPER
22 KILLDEER
23 GREEN HERON

Appendix I

ACCIDENTALS

THE GREAT HOPE of every field man is to see rare birds. Rarities are discovered at best a few times a year; most trips yield lists devoid of them. However, a bird that is rare in your region might be common in the next state or even the next county. It is a term that is hard to define.

Accidentals are the rarest of the rarities — those birds that should not occur in your region at all. They turn up but few times in the lifetime of most ornithologists. I suppose Ludlow Griscom of Cambridge, Massachusetts, has discovered more accidentals in the East than any other man I know. This term, too, is an arbitrary one. Boobies, for example, are accidental along the Atlantic Coast of the United States, except in the Dry Tortugas, where one can reasonably expect to see one or more almost any day in the summer.

I have defined *accidentals* as those birds that have occurred less than twenty times in eastern North America. Some species might eventually turn up with more frequency, as the European Teal, Black-headed Gull, and Little Gull of Europe recently have done. All three are now reported almost every year from the northeast. Their records run into scores, so I have given them a place in the main text of this book. Those with less than twenty occurrences are listed in the following pages. Many of them have been recorded only once or twice. The list is not exhaustive and there are probably omissions. I predict that hardly a year will pass without an additional species being added to our Eastern avifauna.

If you see an accidental bird, study it with extreme care. Check your notes against the study skins in your nearest large museum. The tradition amongst ornithologists has been to accept sight records only if a specimen has previously been taken in the state. If there are no previous state records, the bird might be collected, but of course this is usually not possible; more than likely you do not have a collecting permit or the bird is in some place where shooting is prohibited. Try, then, to show the bird to other reliable observers for their corroboration. In that way your bird will at least win a place on the hypothetical list of the birds of your state. Some records have been authenticated by photographs.

Remember, it is the 'second look' that turns up the rarities and the accidentals. In New England, the amateur takes for granted that the Oriole he sees is a Baltimore. Griscom takes a second look — for a Bullock's. One day he really did see one, but he has never put it on record, except in his own notes.

Oceanic Birds

When hurricanes sweep up the coast, leveling all before them, they often leave in their wake sea-birds, dead or exhausted. Sooty Terns from the West Indies or our own Dry Tortugas are the most frequent, but now and then someone picks up a stranger, an unknown Petrel or Shearwater from some distant part of the world. Sooner or later it reaches a museum and is identified. In this way a dozen or more pelagic species have been added to our North American list.

Most of the following birds have occurred only once, twice, or half a dozen times. Some may never occur again. They hardly constitute a field problem. Some observers would probably class the Yellow-billed Tropic-bird, Blue-faced Booby, and White-bellied Booby as accidentals. True, they are accidental along most of the coast — but it now appears they are fairly regular off the Florida Keys, particularly in the Dry Tortugas. I have described them earlier in the book. The standard handbook on oceanic birds is *Birds of the Ocean*, by W. B. Alexander. *Oceanic Birds of South America*, by R. C. Murphy, covers many species.

YELLOW-NOSED ALBATROSS. *Diomedea chlororhynchos.* Accidental in Gulf of St. Lawrence and Me. Much larger than any Gull with tremendously long saber-like wings (spread 7 feet). Glides and banks like Shearwater. Back suggests Black-backed Gull. From below, white with black border on both edges of wing. Bill very large, black with yellow upper ridge.

MANX SHEARWATER. *Puffinus puffinus puffinus.* Accidental in N.Y. and Me. A 'capped' Shearwater black above and white below. Smaller than Greater Shearwater and *lacking white rump-patch*. Larger than Audubon's Shearwater, which it resembles but feet *pink* (dark in Audubon's). Flies more like the larger Shearwaters (Audubon's flaps much more).

ALLIED SHEARWATER. *Puffinus assimilis barolii.* Accidental in Nova Scotia and S.C. (Called Madeiran Little Shearwater by British and regarded by some as a race of same species as Audubon's Shearwater.) Similar to Audubon's probably not safely distinguishable in field, but under side of tail (coverts) *white* in this species, black in Audubon's Shearwater.

BLACK-CAPPED PETREL. *Pterodroma hasitata.* Accidental in Fla., Va., Ky., O., N.Y., N.H., Ont. Extremely rare or on verge of extinction even in West Indies. Larger than Audubon's Shearwater; could be mistaken for it or Greater Shearwater. (Dark above, white below), but *forehead white*, and black cap separated from back by *whitish collar*. Rump-patch *white* (Audubon's Shearwater lacks this, but Greater Shearwater shows it).

SOUTH TRINIDAD PETREL. *Pterodroma arminjoniana.* The one specimen (N.Y.), found after a storm, is in the black phase and looks like an undersized Sooty Shearwater with a very stubby bill. The wing-linings are black, whereas in the Sooty they are pale. This species has light phases and intermediate phases but as it is so extremely local and unlikely the reader is referred to Murphy's *Oceanic Birds of South America*.

SCALED, or PEALE'S, PETREL. *Pterodroma inexpectata.* Once in N.Y. State. Large as a small Shearwater. Upper parts dark gray, under parts white. Head light. From below its wings are white with a narrow black border all around. A small dark patch around the eye and a large dark patch on the lower belly are the best marks.

PINTADO PETREL. *Daption capensis.* Accidental in Maine. Size of a small Shearwater, boldly pied and spotted; back *checkered*; cap black; *two large round white patches on each wing.*

MADEIRA PETREL. *Oceanodroma castro castro.* Accidental in Ont., Pa., Ind., and D.C. Distinguished from Wilson's Petrel by forked tail and longer wings; from Leach's by less deeply forked tail and even band of white across rump. This white patch surrounds base of tail and is visible from below too. (At close range Leach's shows gray feathers dividing the white rump-patch down the middle.) Although there are these differences, Doctor R. C. Murphy says he cannot distinguish the two in the field.

STORM PETREL. *Hydrobates pelagicus.* Has been recorded accidentally at Ungava Bay, Labrador. Distinguished from Leach's Petrel by very small size (6 in.) and square tail; from Wilson's Petrel by much shorter legs and *black* feet. (In flight *yellow-webbed* feet of Wilson's Petrel project *half* an inch beyond the tail.)

BLACK-BELLIED STORM PETREL. *Fregetta tropica.* One Fla. record. Head and upper parts sooty black; under parts white with a narrow black strip running down the belly from breast to tail, separating the white into two large areas, one on each side.

WHITE-FACED, or FRIGATE, PETREL. *Pelagodroma marina hypoleuca.* Recorded off Mass. and 400 miles off coast of N.J. A long-legged Petrel with white face and under parts (8 in.). Identified by black patch through eye and broad white stripe over eye.

RED-BILLED TROPIC-BIRD. *Phaëthon æthereus æsonauta.* Accidental on Newfoundland Banks. Resembles Yellow-billed Tropic Bird but upper parts finely barred with black, and much less black on wings. The best field mark is, of course, the *bright red bill.*

RED-FOOTED BOOBY. *Sula sula sula.* A record for La. and a doubtful one off Fla. A small Gannet with *bright red feet.* Resembles Blue-faced Booby but distinguished by red feet and white tail. Black in wings restricted to primaries (entire rear edge of wing black in Blue-faced Booby).

LESSER BLACK-BACKED GULL. *Larus fuscus.* Although there are a handful of sight records of this European Gull, there is no specimen for North America. In Europe the standard way to distinguish adults from the Great Black-backed Gull is by the smaller size (size of Herring Gull) and *yellow* instead of flesh-colored feet. A further distinction is made between the two races: Scandinavian Lesser Black-backed Gull (*L. f. fuscus*), black back; and British Lesser Black-backed Gull (*L. f. grællsii*), slate-gray back. Even so, birds that look like Lesser Black-backs can be other things, as was proved when the one specimen from Greenland (*Fourth A.O.U. Check-List*) turned out to be a Herring Gull. Griscom points out that the Lesser Black-back looks quite like several other things: the

Western Gull (*Larus occidentalis*), the Slaty-backed Gull (*Larus schistisagus*), of ne. Asia, and, also, possible hybrids between Herring and Great Black-backed Gulls. However, the overwhelming chances are that any such bird with *yellow* feet would be the Lesser Black-back. The above birds all have flesh-colored feet except for a race of the Western Gull known as the Yellow-footed Gull (*L. o. livens*), a bird found in the Gulf of California, which would be far less likely than a trans-Atlantic visitor.

SHORT-BILLED. or, MEW GULL. *Larus canus.* Has been seen in Mass. and L.I. Adult, greenish legs. Smaller than Ring-billed Gull with small, *unmarked* greenish-yellow bill. Shows more white in wing-tips than Ring-bill. Immature difficult (see *Field Guide to Western Birds*). It is a question when this bird is seen whether it is the race of w. North America (*L. c. brachyrhynchus*) or the Common, or Mew, Gull of Europe (*L. c. canus*).

BRIDLED TERN. *Sterna anœthetus.* (p. 131.) This West Indian bird should be looked for after tropical storms. Undoubtedly it has occurred more often on the s. Atlantic Coast than the few records would indicate. (Fla., Ga., S.C., N.Y., and Mass.) It resembles the Sooty Tern — dusky above and white below, but has a wide *whitish collar* separating the black of the cap from the dark of the back. It is slightly smaller than the Sooty, has a grayer back, and the white forehead-patch extends in a point *behind the eye.* (In Sooty white extends *to eye.*) Could be confused with Black Tern in fall plumage but larger, with a very long bill, and a deeply forked tail. (Black has small bill, slightly notched tail.) The Bridled Tern has a black stripe joining the eye and the bill.

West Indian and Tropical Birds

Most of the tropical strays on our North American list have been picked up in southern Florida or along the Gulf Coast. Occasional birds such as the Fork-tailed Flycatcher have even reached New England. Probably the best spot to look for waifs from the West Indies would be Key West, particularly after storms. The standard handbook on West Indian birds is *Birds of the West Indies,* by James Bond.

SCARLET IBIS. *Guara rubra.* A small bright-scarlet Ibis, accidental on Gulf Coast. Pink birds are probably escapes, as zoo birds lose color.

BLACK-BELLIED TREE DUCK. *Dendrocygna autumnalis autumnalis.* Ill. Suspected but not authenticated in La. and Fla. See *Field Guide to Western Birds.*

BAHAMA PINTAIL. *Anas bahamensis bahamensis.* Accidental in Fla., Va., and Wis. Does not look like Pintail. A mottled cinnamon-brown duck smaller than a Pintail with *white cheeks and throat,* a dark cap, and a *red or orange bill.*

MASKED DUCK. *Erismatura dominica.* Accidental in La., Md., Mass., Vt., and Wis. Suggests a small Ruddy Duck. **Male:** — Rusty with white wing-patches and a black face. **Female:** — Like Ruddy, but with *two* black stripes crossing each cheek instead of one.

KING VULTURE. *Sarcoramphus papa.* Found by William Bartram in Florida, 1774 or 1775. A huge white or pink-bodied Vulture with black and white wings, and a black tail. Head highly colored (red, yellow, etc.).

JACANA. *Jacana spinosa.* Accidental in Fla. A marsh-dweller; like a shore-bird with *extremely long toes.* Head and neck blackish, body deep rusty. The best marks are the conspicuous yellow *shield* on the forehead and large *pale-yellow wing-patches.* Immature resembles fall Wilson's Phalarope, gray-brown above with white under parts and a broad white stripe over the eye. The extremely long toes, short rounded wings, notes, and habitat identify it.

SCALED PIGEON. *Columba squamosa.* Twice at Key West. Larger than Domestic or White-crowned Pigeons; slate-colored; feathers of neck purplish, with dark maroon edgings, giving the appearance of scales. At close range neck of White-crowned Pigeon has appearance of scales too, but lacks the purplish or maroon luster. The crown of this species is *dark* (even young White-crowns show some white, at least on forehead).

ZENAIDA DOVE. *Zenaida aurita zenaida.* Formerly Fla. Keys; would be accidental now. Like Mourning Dove, but tail square, broadly tipped with pearl-gray; wing with *white stripe on hind edge.* Do not confuse with white-winged Dove which has a large white patch *in the center* of each wing. In this species the white is like a bar on the rear edge of the wing.

WHITE-WINGED DOVE. *Zenaida asiatica asiatica.* Occasional in Fla. and La.; accidental on L.I. Like a Mourning Dove but heavier, with a *rounded* tail which is tipped with a broad white band. The best field mark is a large *white patch* diagonally crossing each wing.

KEY WEST QUAIL DOVE. *Oreopeleia chrysia.* Formerly Key West. None for years. Slightly larger than Mourning Dove, with rounded tail. Purple-rufous above, whitish below. Best mark is *broad white stripe below eye.*

RUDDY QUAIL DOVE. *Oreopeleia montana montana.* Twice at Key West. Smaller than Mourning Dove; short rounded tail. Dark rufous throughout, paler on belly. No outstanding marks — a small all-red Dove.

GROOVE-BILLED ANI. *Crotophaga sulcirostris sulcirostris.* Like the Smooth-billed Ani, but with *three grooves* on the upper mandible. Occasional in La. and Fla.

CUBAN EMERALD HUMMINGBIRD. *Riccordia ricordii.* Accidental near Miami. Male unmistakable. *Green above and below;* looks black at distance. Throat iridescent *emerald-green;* base of bill pink. Female has whitish throat; can be told from female Ruby-throat by pink on bill and deeply forked tail. (Female Ruby-throat has *rounded* tail showing *white spots.*)

LICHTENSTEIN'S KINGBIRD. *Tyrannus melancholicus chloronotus.* Central America. Accidental in Maine. A race of the Mexican Kingbird, of which Couch's Kingbird of the Lower Rio Grande Valley is also a race. Very similar to Western or Arkansas, Kingbird, but tail more deeply forked, brownish without hint of black, and *without white edgings.*

FORK-TAILED FLYCATCHER. *Muscivora tyrannus.* Central America. Accidental in Miss., Ky., N.J., Mass., and Me. Gray-backed with *black cap* and *extremely long forked tail* (much longer than body). Scissor-tailed Fly-catcher is much whiter with *whitish* head and crimson on sides.

BAHAMA SWALLOW. *Callichelidon cyaneoviridis.* (p. 227.) Occasional' in s. Fla. Like a small Tree Swallow, steely green above and white below, but tail much more deeply forked (about one inch of its length — tail of Tree Swallow is forked about one third inch).

CAVE, or CUBAN, CLIFF SWALLOW. *Petrochelidon fulva cavicola.* Accidental on Dry Tortugas. Like Cliff Swallow but forehead *deep chestnut* (Cliff, whitish); throat and breast *evenly rusty* (Cliff Swallow has dark throat sharply separated from light breast).

BAHAMA HONEY CREEPER or BANANAQUIT. *Coereba bahamensis.* (p. 227.) Occasional in s. Fla.; about size of House Wren, bill *decurved.* The upper parts are *black*, the breast and rump *yellow*; the belly is *white*, and the bird has a white line over the eye.

TAWNY-SHOULDERED BLACKBIRD. *Agelaius humeralis.* Recorded from Key West. Like a very small male Red-wing with *buffy-orange* or *tawny* shoulder patches (many Florida Red-wings have their red epaulettes broadly *edged* with this color). Unlike Red-wing sexes are similar.

BAHAMA, or BLACK-FACED, GRASSQUIT. *Tiaris bicolor bicolor.* Accidental in Fla. A very small short-tailed black Finch, smaller than a Goldfinch. *Appears all black at a distance*, but at close range back is lighter, tinged with olive. The female is a short-tailed gray finch with an unstreaked breast and a darker, almost olive back.

CUBAN or MELODIOUS GRASSQUIT. *Tiaris canora.* Accidental in Fla. Keys. A very dark little finch smaller than a Goldfinch; olive above, dusky below. The face and breast are black with a *broad bright-yellow ruff on each side of the neck.* The female is paler (face brown, breast gray) but the conspicuous yellow neck-patches, though duller, identify her.

European Birds

More birds have flown from America to Europe than have reached us from the other side. The prevailing winds are in favor of our birds, as they were in favor of American aviators when the first transatlantic flights were made. The few European species that have reached us are strong fliers, mostly waterfowl. The occasional Greenland Wheatears probably come from the American Arctic, where some of them nest. Normally this species migrates to Europe.

I am omitting from this list several species like the European Coot, Great Snipe, and European Jack Snipe, which have been recorded accidentally only in sub-arctic America. Other birds such as the European Teal, European Widgeon, Curlew Sandpiper, Black-headed Gull, and Little Gull occur with enough frequency on this side so that experienced field students now look for them. Borderline cases are the Barnacle Goose, Ruff, and Wheatear. All these are described and figured earlier in the book. The best source of detailed information on European birds is *The Handbook of British Birds* (Witherby, Jourdain, Ticehurst, and Tucker).

ACCIDENTALS

GRAY LAG GOOSE. *Anser anser anser.* Accidental in Mass. Like a gray barnyard Goose, or like a White-front; with *pink* legs (White-front, orange) and *bright orange bill* (White-fronted Goose, pink; Pink-footed Goose, black with a pink band).

PINK-FOOTED GOOSE. *Anser brachyrhynchus.* Accidental in Mass. A pale gray goose with dark head and neck. Feet bright-*pink*; bill black crossed by pink band. Immature Blue Goose has dark bill and dark feet. Immature White-front has yellow or orange feet and (usually) yellow bill.

SHELD-DUCK. *Tadorna tadorna.* Accidental in Mass. A large Duck with goose-like posture. Boldly patterned with white, black, and chestnut. Male has bright-red bill with knob at forehead, black head, and large white wing-patches. The best mark is the *broad band of rufous* which completely encircles the forepart of the bird's white body (across the back and around the breast). Female similar, but lacks knob on bill.

RUDDY SHELD-DUCK. *Casarca ferruginea.* Accidental in N.J. and N.C. Shaped like a small goose; *orange-brown with a pale, almost whitish head.* Tail black and wings black with large white patches. The male has a narrow black ring on the neck.

RUFOUS-CRESTED DUCK. *Netta rufina.* An old record, presumably from L.I. Resembles male Red-head (head rufous, chest black) but bill *crimson red.* Female resembles female American Scoter (pale cheek, dark crown) but has white wing-patch. Under parts paler, tip of bill reddish-brown.

GRAY SEA EAGLE. *Haliæetus albicilla.* Twice in Mass. Adult like a pale Bald Eagle with only the tail white. A bird like a Bald Eagle with a *light brown head* and yellow bill would be this straggler. (A light brown head and *black bill* would most likely be an aberrant immature Bald Eagle. Immature: — Paler than most Bald Eagles above, but not safely distinguishable as some immature Bald Eagles have similar buffy upper parts.

EUROPEAN KESTREL. *Falco tinnunculus tinnunculus.* Accidental in Mass. Male resembles Sparrow Hawk; rufous but *head and tail blue gray.* Tail has black band near tip. Female similar to female Sparrow Hawk; rufous above, barred with black; paler below, streaked. European Kestrel lacks black-and-white face-pattern of female Sparrow Hawk, or 'American Kestrel.'

CORN CRAKE. *Crex crex.* At least fifteen records on this side of Atlantic, but only one or two in past 40 years. An upland field Rail of the *short-billed* Sora type but larger; *yellowish-buff* with conspicuous *rufous-red wings.*

LAPWING. *Vanellus vanellus.* N.C., N.Y., Me., e. Can. A very large Plover, larger than Killdeer (13 in.). Black and white; chest crossed by one very wide black band; tail white with broad black band, head with long wispy crest. *No native shore-bird has a crest.* It has *broad rounded wings* unusual for a shore-bird and flies with slow flapping action.

EUROPEAN WOODCOCK. *Scolopax rusticola.* Va., Pa., N.J., N.Y., R.I., Mass. Much larger than our native Woodcock (13½ in.); *under parts thickly barred* with narrow dark lines.

EUROPEAN CURLEW. *Numenius arquata arquata.* If you see a Curlew with a *white rump* it is one of two European forms. Both have occurred on L.I. If the bird suggests a Long-billed Curlew (long bill, no head-stripings) it is this species. If it suggests the Hudsonian Curlew (shorter bill, distinct head-stripings) it is the **WHIMBREL** (*Numenius phæopus phæopus*), now regarded as the European subspecies of our Hudsonian Curlew.

BAR-TAILED GODWIT. *Limosa lapponica lapponica.* If you see a white-rumped Godwit that looks like a Hudsonian but with *whitish* instead of the usual blackish wing-linings, it is one of two European species. If the tail forms a broad black band like that of the Hudsonian, it is the **BLACK-TAILED GODWIT** (*Limosa limosa*), which has once been reported seen (N.J.?) and should be looked for. If the tail lacks the broad band and is *barred* with short dusky bars and spots, it is the **BAR-TAILED GODWIT** (*Limosa lapponica lapponica*), which has been recorded twice in Mass.

WHITE-WINGED TERN. *Chlidonias leucoptera.* Once, Wis. Like Black Tern but tail *white* and under wing-linings *black* (breeding season). Pale wings contrast strikingly with black back. Immature and winter birds resemble Black Terns, but lack the dark smudges at side of breast. The rump is whitish.

Western Birds

The greatest source of strays will always be the West. There are no oceans to act as barriers to birds 'off-beam.' They can rest when they choose, then wander onward — until finally stopped by the Atlantic or Gulf Coasts.

The ranges of birds do not conform to political boundaries. A line had to be drawn somewhere between the East and the West in planning this guide. I drew that line through the center of the Great Plains States (North Dakota, South Dakota, Nebraska, Kansas, and Oklahoma). West of the one hundredth meridian the bird life takes on an increasingly Western flavor; the Eastern species tend to follow the river valleys westward, and the Western species appear on the ridges and in the more arid sections. The result is that Nebraska has a state list of 473 (388 species and 85 additional races). This is exceeded by only two or three other States. At least forty typical Western birds have been recorded in Nebraska. Although this Guide will be useful in the Plains states, observers in the western parts of those states will also require *A Field Guide to Western Birds* to cover their regions adequately.

I have been somewhat arbitrary as to what birds occurring in the Great Plains States should be included in this book. I have included only those that breed up to or east of the one hundredth meridian. Strays that cross that invisible line in migration are many.

Sooner or later a large percentage of Western species will be recorded from these borderline states. There is also a strong tendency in fall for Western birds to drift toward the southeast, and many strays wind up along the Gulf in Louisiana or even

Florida. As we go east these records thin out. The coast is better than adjacent inland localities for Western strays because it is the last barrier to lost travelers.

Some of the strays that have been detected *east of the Mississippi* are listed below. (A few, such as the Black-headed Grosbeak and Bullock's Oriole, that breed up to or almost to the one hundredth meridian in the central parts of the Plains States have been described earlier in the book.)

WHITE-TAILED KITE. *Elanus leucurus majusculus.* Accidental in se. states today. See main text.

HARRIS'S HAWK. *Parabuteo unicinctus harrisi.* S. Tex., occasional in La. and Miss. Accidental in O. A black Buteo with a white rump and white tail crossed by a very wide black band. Harris's Hawk perched close shows chestnut-colored areas on the body and a white band *at the end* of the tail, marks of distinction from other black or melanistic Buteos.

MOUNTAIN PLOVER. *Eupoda montana.* Mass. and Fla. (Occurs on w. parts of Great Plains.) Like a small Killdeer (8–9½) with no breast-rings. May be told from winter Golden and Black-bellied Plovers by smaller size and even coloration of back, *devoid of mottling.*

ANCIENT MURRELET. *Synthliboramphus antiquus.* Minn., Wis., Ont., Que., Lake Erie. In winter plumage like a large Dovekie but back *gray* contrasting with black crown. Chin usually black.

VAUX'S SWIFT. *Chætura vauxi.* Occasional along Gulf in winter. Taken at Baton Rouge, La. See main text.

WHITE-THROATED SWIFT. *Aëronautes saxatalis.* Recorded from Mich. Known as a Swift by its long, narrow, stiff wings and characteristic twinkling and gliding flight; and from Chimney Swift by the contrasting pattern (white face and breast, black patches on sides).

RUFOUS HUMMINGBIRD. *Selasphorus rufus.* Rare but probably regular along Gulf Coast in winter. See main text.

LEWIS'S WOODPECKER. *Asyndesmus lewis.* Accidental in R.I. A large dark, black-backed Woodpecker with a *rose-red belly* (only woodpecker so marked, wide gray collar around breast and neck, and red face-patch).

SAY'S PHŒBE. *Sayornis saya saya.* Wis., Ill., Mich., N.Y., Conn., and Mass. See main text.

ASH-THROATED FLYCATCHER. *Myiarchus cinerascens cinerascens.* Fla. and La. Like a small Crested Flycatcher (8–8½); yellow of under parts paler, back grayer; notes different. The best mark is the white throat.

OLIVACEOUS FLYCATCHER. *Myiarchus tuberculifer olivascens.* One hypothetical record for S.C. A small pale Flycatcher of the Crested Flycatcher type; hardly larger than a Phœbe (7¼), known from the Ash-throated Flycatcher by its still smaller size and gray instead of white throat.

VERMILION FLYCATCHER. *Pyrocephalus rubinus mexicanus.* Rare but regular in winter along Gulf Coast (La. to Fla.). See main text.

VIOLET-GREEN SWALLOW. *Tachycineta thalassina lepida.* Ill. Like Tree Swallow but greener, with two *white rump patches* that almost meet above the base of the tail.

MAGPIE. *Pica pica hudsonia.* Straggler in Wis., Ill., Mich., W. Va., N.J., N.Y., Ont., and Que. See main text.

CLARKE'S NUTCRACKER. *Nucifraga columbiana.* Casual ♀. to Minn., Wis., Mo., Mich., Ia. Built like a small crow, with a *light-gray* body and conspicuous *white patches* in black wings and tail (Canada Jays do not have white patches).

PALMER'S (CURVE-BILLED) THRASHER. *Toxostoma redivivum redivivum.* Fla. A dull gray-brown Thrasher with pale-cinnamon belly and under tail-coverts; bill *sickle-shaped.*

SAGE THRASHER. *Oreoscoptes montanus.* N.Y. Smaller than Brown Thrasher, shorter tail, straight slender bill, gray back, streaked breast, white spots at tip of tail.

VARIED THRUSH. *Ixoreus nævius.* N.J., N.Y., Mass., Que. Similar to Robin but with an *orange eye-stripe, orange wing-bars,* and a *black* or *gray band* across the rusty breast.

TOWNSEND'S SOLITAIRE. *Myadestes townsendi.* Minn., Ill., N.Y. Smaller and slimmer than Robin, gray with white *eye-ring,* white sides of tail, and tawny patch in the center of the wing. A confusing bird. Resembles Mockingbird somewhat, but darker breast, white eye-ring, and tawny instead of white wing-patch distinguish it from that species.

AUDUBON'S WARBLER. *Dendroica auduboni.* Minn., O., Pa., Mass. Like Myrtle Warbler with *yellow* instead of white throat. Adult males have a large white wing-patch instead of two narrow white wing-bars. Hybrids occur.

BLACK-THROATED GRAY WARBLER. *Dendroica nigrescens.* Mass., S.C., Fla. Black throat of male and black cheek-patch suggest Golden-winged Warbler but readily distinguished by *white* wing-bars, *black* crown, and black stripes on sides. Black and White Warbler has *striped* crown. Male Black-poll has *white cheeks.* Female Black-throated Gray lacks black throat, but combination of black cheek-patch and *solid* black crown identify her.

TOWNSEND'S WARBLER. *Dendroica townsendi.* Miss., Pa., L.I. Male has yellow under parts and black-and-yellow face-pattern. Black throat and black cheek-patch suggest Lawrence's Warbler, from which it may be distinguished by *black crown* and *black stripes* on sides. Female duller.

MACGILLIVRAY'S WARBLER. *Oporornis tolmiei.* Neb., Ill., and Ind. Like a Mourning Warbler with an eye-ring. Not safe to try to distinguish from Connecticut and Mourning Warblers. (Mourning often has eye-ring in fall.)

BULLOCK'S ORIOLE. *Icterus bullockii bullockii.* Me., Mass. See main text.

WESTERN TANAGER. *Piranga ludoviciana.* Wis., La., N.J., N.Y., Conn.. Mass., and Me. See main text.

BLACK-HEADED GROSBEAK. *Pheucticus melanocephalus papago.* Mass. and N.Y. See main text.

ROSY FINCH. *Leucosticte tephrocotis.* Minn. and Me. A sparrow-sized winter finch. *Dark-brown body* with *pinkish wash* on wings and rump. The dark-brown breast and light-gray patch on the back of the head distinguish this species from other rose-colored Finches (Purple Finch, Redpoll, Crossbills, etc.). Females are duller than males.

GREEN-TAILED TOWHEE. *Chlorura chlorura.* S.C., Va., N.J., Mass., and Mo. Slightly larger than House Sparrow. A ground Finch with a *rufous* crown and conspicuous *white* throat; breast gray. Suggests Swamp Sparrow but has *unstreaked olive-green back.*

SPOTTED, or ARCTIC, TOWHEE. *Pipilo maculatus arcticus.* Similar to Eastern Towhee, but *rows of white spots* on back and scapulars. Breeds e. to w. N.D. and w. Neb.; wanders farther e. in winter. Casual e. to n. Ill.

WHITE-WINGED JUNCO. *Junco aikeni.* Like Slate-colored Junco, but larger and paler, with two white wing-bars and a greater amount of white in the tail. All supposed White-winged Juncos taken in the East have proved to be aberrant Slate-colored Juncos (*Junco hyemalis*).

OREGON JUNCO. *Junco oreganus.* Frequent enough in East in winter to be regarded as rare rather than accidental. See main text.

BREWER'S SPARROW. *Spizella breweri.* Mass. A small pale Sparrow; resembles Chipping Sparrow, but slimmer, sandier-colored, and with *crown finely streaked*; no rufous. Young Chipping Sparrows in fall are similar, but the crown is browner and often divided by a pale median line.

GOLDEN-CROWNED SPARROW. *Zonotrichia coronata.* La., Wis., Ill., N.J., Mass. Adult like White-crowned Sparrow with *no white line over eye* and a *golden-yellow* stripe through center of crown. Immature White-crowns have center of crown buffy and resemble Golden-crown, but have broad buffy lines over eyes. Immatures look like large female House Sparrows, but are browner and sometimes have a dull-yellowish suffusion on the crown.

Appendix II

SUBSPECIES

THE PROBLEM of subspecies is complex. In earlier editions I listed under each species all subspecies and their ranges. Several leaders of ornithological thought who work on taxonomic problems urged that subspecies be left out unless they can be identified in the field. There are many good reasons for following such a plan. One of the simpler explanations of a subspecies is that it is a geographical race that blends with other races of the same species. To illustrate, the Song Sparrows of the coast from New Jersey to North Carolina differ from those inland in being grayer, so they are called by a different name (Atlantic Song Sparrow). The differences between subspecies are sometimes well marked, but often can only be determined by experts after careful examination in the hand and comparison with museum series. It is such a subtle and critical thing that ornithologists often disagree as to which subspecies a bird belongs, or even whether a certain subspecies is well marked enough to be worthy of recognition at all.

Whereas two subspecies of the same species are fundamentally the same bird and capable of interbreeding, species are reproductively isolated. They will not under ordinary circumstances hybridize. A Song Sparrow will not mate with a Chippy. It was recently stated by Doctor Ernst Mayr that at least ninety-four of the 755 full species of North American birds will be considered by some authors to be merely subspecies of other species. This is not because of disagreement about the species concept but because more information or more study is needed to clarify things. A few examples are the Ipswich and Savannah Sparrows; Seaside and Dusky Seaside Sparrows; Clapper and King Rails, etc. However, we need not concern ourselves with this theoretical question, as most of these examples are quite distinguishable in the field.

Another angle is that the various races of many birds *intergrade* where their ranges come together. The Downy Woodpecker is a good example of a *Cline*; which means that it changes *gradually* from South to North so that at no point could you say the Southern Downy stops and the Northern Downy starts without being very arbitrary. The taxonomists who describe races and the *A.O U. Check-List* Committee, which later passes on the validity of them, have of necessity been arbitrary. They have broken the species into *three* races in the East: Southern Downy, Northern Downy, and Nelson's Downy. But theoretically there could just as well be six races as three, depending on where the lines are to be drawn or how fine the splitting is to be. The point I am driving at is that if the problem is so specialized, it is not one for the average field student. It is better that he use only the name Downy Woodpecker, the accepted species name. Subspecies have a meaning to the student of bird distribution and evolution, and are of practical value to conservation and wild-life management practices, but they should not concern the field amateur. Doctor George Miksch Sutton writes:

'One of the worst problems of present-day field bird study, as I see it, is this desire to use trinomials. I asked my students to turn in a field notebook last year, and every one of them listed trinomials wherever he possibly could, without bothering himself to discover what specimens had actually been collected and identified, what the characters of certain races were, etc. They all were willing to take someone else's word on the subspecies — to use the name that seemed to fit geographically, to employ what I call *fake* accuracy. In other words, *Turdus migratorius migratorius*, Eastern Robin, looked more thoroughgoing to them than simply *Turdus migratorius*, Robin. The use of the trinomial very often is a sort of four-flushing.'

In the main text I have given only the ranges of *each species as a whole*. The amateur need not wade through the range of each subspecies to see whether his territory falls within it. If subspecies ranges were outlined prominently in the body of the text, the student would be encouraged to use the vernacular subspecific names, which is seldom a good idea.

The *A.O.U. Check-List*, which initiated the use of vernacular names for subspecies, has often been misleading by not always indicating in the name to which species a subspecies belongs. All Song Sparrows are called Song Sparrows; i. e., Atlantic Song Sparrow, Mississippi Song Sparrow, etc. This is fine, but on the other hand, the races of the Canada Jay are designated by such unrelated names as Canada Jay, Labrador Jay, and Anticosti Jay. Nothing in these names indicates whether the bird is a race of the Canada Jay or the Blue Jay. The inference might even be drawn that they are all distinct species.

In most cases it is quite easy to settle on an inclusive species name. However, the vernacular names of some subspecies have already gained such a foothold that many people prefer to use them instead; for instance, Ward's Heron (a race of the Great Blue) and *Florida* Cormorant (a race of the Double-crested). Many vernacular subspecies names are of recent manufacture, but if every bird book that came out gave them full importance, it would not take long before these names were as firmly intrenched in usage as Ward's Heron and Florida Cormorant.

Doctor Alden H. Miller in *The Distribution of the Birds of California* (1944) took a bold step by attempting to put the vernacular names of California birds into a sort of trinomial system which would give a clear idea of each bird's relationship, so that a subspecific name would modify a specific name instead of stand alone. For example, California Great Blue Heron instead of California Heron. This idea is sensible, but the critics, who would perpetuate the existing confusion, point to the occasional cases where the plan results in a ponderous or absurd name. This need be no excuse for discarding the whole idea. True, it would be incongruous to call the Florida race of the Carolina Wren the Florida Carolina Wren, but there is no reason why Ward's Great Blue Heron and Florida Double-crested Cormorant should not make better sense than Ward's Heron or Florida Cormorant. The only thing in favor of the latter names is their brevity.

I am adopting this plan partially, except for the hard nuts, which I'll leave for others to crack. Doctor Alexander Wetmore, with whom I have exchanged ideas on this, informs me that the *A.O.U. Check-List Committee*, of which he is chairman, is now contemplating a similar course. The fifth edition of the *Check-List* will also use species headings for the first time.

To be really consistent about adopting an over-all English name for each species, we would be forced to give up many appropriate and long cherished names for the older ones to which Great Britain justly has a prior claim. The Loons would be called Divers; the Dowitchers, Red-breasted Snipe, and the Bank Swallow, Sand Martin. Although there has been recent talk of it, we are probably not ready for such a standardization of names yet — not until we become 'one world.' Up to the present we have been isolationists and have stuck to New World usage. The scientific names, after all, are the international names.

This book is primarily for amateurs who merely wish to attach a name or a 'handle' to the creature before them. They will range from those who know little to those who have spent years of study and who will wish to use the book in areas unfamiliar to them. It is in deference to some students, who will feel the book is incomplete if the ranges of subspecies are omitted, that I have decided to include these ranges, but to de-emphasize them, and relegate them to this section in the back of the book. For a more extended account of these ranges refer to the *A.O.U. Check-List*. It is true that a few subspecies are identifiable in the field and constitute field problems. These of course are discussed.

On the Great Plains there is a great deal of spilling over in migration and winter of subspecies that breed farther to the west. There is also a southeasterly drift of many of these to the Gulf Coast. As determination of these would depend on collecting, and as our knowledge of their occurrence is still so spotty, most of them are left out. All races known to breed east of the one hundredth meridian are listed.

If subspecific names are used at all, call birds by these names only on their breeding-grounds, and not when indistinguishable migrants of other races might be present.

COMMON LOON. *Gavia immer:* (1) Greater Common Loon, *G. i. immer*; breeds from n. edge of U.S. n. to Lab. and N.F. (2) Lesser Common Loon, *G. i. elasson*; w. U.S.; breeds e. to N.D. and Wis. Both races mingle in winter.

CORY'S SHEARWATER. *Puffinus diomedea:* (1) Cory's Shearwater, *P. d. borealis*; off Atlantic Coast from N.C. to N.F. (2) Mediterranean Shearwater, *P. d. diomedea*; a smaller European form that has been recorded on L.I. Characterized by white on inner webs of outer primaries. Not distinguishable in the field.

DOUBLE-CRESTED CORMORANT. *Phalacrocorax auritus:* (1) Northern Double-crested Cormorant, *P. a. auritus*; breeds from James Bay and Gulf of St. Lawrence s. to coast of Me. and Mass.; in interior to n. Neb. and locally along Miss. River to La.; migrates s. to Gulf of Mex. (2) Florida Double-crested Cormorant, *P. a. floridanus*; slightly smaller. Breeds along coast from N.C. to Fla., and w. along Gulf to se. La.

GREAT BLUE HERON. *Ardea herodias:* (1) Eastern Great Blue Heron, *A. h. herodias*; breeds s. to Neb., Ia., and S.C.; winters to Gulf of Mex. (2) Ward's Great Blue Heron, *A. h. wardi*; larger and paler, with greenish instead of black legs and a much whiter head. Breeds from se. S.C., s. Ala., se. Ill., and se. Ia. s. to Gulf and Fla. Keys.

CANADA GOOSE. *Branta canadensis:* (1) Common Canada Goose, *B. c. canadensis*; breeds in coastal region of Que., N.F., and Lab., occasionally to N.E. (the birds of the n. Prairie States are probably referable to the proposed race *B. c. moffitti*, Basin Canada Goose). Winters from Great Lakes, s. N.E., and N.S. s. to Gulf of Mex. (2) Ungava Canada Goose, *B. c. interior*. Darker above and below than *canadensis*. Breeds on coasts of Hudson Bay and James Bay, formerly s. to Minn.; in migration to s. Atlantic and Gulf Coasts. (3) Lesser Canada Goose, *B. c. leucopareia*; breeds nw. of Hudson Bay; migrates through Miss. Valley to Gulf of Mex.; occasional along Atlantic and formerly wrongly called Hutchins's Goose. Much smaller than Common Canada or about size of Snow or Blue Geese, with which it often associates. Neck shorter, bill smaller, and voice higher than Common Canada. (4) Hutchins's, or Richardson's, Canada Goose, *B. c. hutchinsi*; a Canada Goose in miniature, hardly larger than Mallard; smaller, stubbier-necked, and stubbier-billed even than Lesser Canada. The flight notes are a high-pitched yelping. Some authorities believe this is a distinct species and should not be called a race of *canadensis*. Breeds n. of Hudson Bay; migrates through Prairie States to coasts of Tex. sw. La. (p. 18).

BRANT. *Branta bernicla:* (1) American Brant, *B. b. hrota*; winters along coast s. to N.C. (2) Black Brant, *B. b. nigricans*; Pacific Coast; accidental on Atlantic. Under parts blackish to the under tail-coverts instead of showing the sharp contrast of black breast and light belly. It probably cannot be identified on the water as the sides are quite light, much as in the Eastern bird. The name 'Black Brant' is confusingly used by gunners in Maryland for *B. b. hrota* to distinguish it from the Snow Goose, or 'White Brant.'

SNOW GOOSE. *Chen hyperborea:* (1) Lesser Snow Goose, *C. h. hyperborea*; (23–30) migrates through Miss. Valley and Plains; winters on Gulf Coast. (2) Greater Snow Goose, *A. h. atlantica*; (30–38) larger, not distinguishable in field. More eastern; stops in migration on St. Lawrence R. near city of Quebec; winters near coast from Del. Bay to N.C.

MOTTLED DUCK. *Anas fulvigula:* (1) Florida Mottled Duck, *A. f. fulvigula*; breeds in cent. and s. Fla. (2) Louisiana Mottled Duck, *A. f. maculosa*; a darker race found along Gulf Coast in La. and Tex.

EIDER. *Somateria mollissima:* (1) American Eider, *S. m. dresseri*; breeds from Lab. s to Me. coast; winters to Mass. and L.I. (rarely). (2) Northern Eider, *S. m. borealis*; Arctic, a straggler on coast of n. U.S. Hardly safe to distinguish in field. The yellow bill of the male American Eider has a frontal process that is wide and *rounded* where it terminates in front of the eye. It ends in a *narrow point* in the northern race. (3) Hudson Bay Eider, *S. m. sedentaria.* Hudson Bay from Cape Fullerton s. into James Bay.

TURKEY VULTURE. *Cathartes aura:* (1) Eastern Turkey Vulture, *C. a. septentrionalis*; breeds from Gulf of Mex. n. to Conn. and s. N.Y. and w. to range of following race. (2) Western Turkey Vulture, *C. a. teter*; from s. Man. and Sask. s. through Neb., Kans., and Tex. (occurs e. to s. Mich.(?)); range imperfectly known. (3) Mexican Turkey Vulture, *C. a. aura*; from Cent. America and W. Indies to s. Tex. and s. Fla.

RED-TAILED HAWK. *Buteo jamaicensis:* (1) Eastern Red-tailed Hawk, *B. j. borealis*; breeds from Sask., n. Ont., s. Que., and N.F. s. to cent. Tex., Ark., Ala., and n. Fla. (2) Florida Red-tailed Hawk, *B. j. umbrinus*; s. Fla., darker, with a broad black band (nearly an inch wide) at the tip of the tail. (3) Krider's Red-tailed Hawk, *B. j. krideri*; in appearance a partially albinistic Red-tail; birds vary from almost normal to almost white, but pale white or 'pinkish' tail is the best mark. Occasionally white Red-tails are seen in the East, but these are probably true albinos, rather than this prairie race. Interior, from Sask. and s. Man. s. through plains in winter to La. and Miss. (p. 54). (4) Western Red-tailed Hawk, *B. j. calurus*; not too safe to try to tell in field but much rusty-red on the body both above and below. At close range thigh feathers barred with rusty. Migrates e. to Plains States and s. to La.

RED-SHOULDERED HAWK. *Buteo lineatus:* (1) Northern Red-shouldered Hawk, *B. l. lineatus*; breeds from N. S., s. Que., and Ont. s. to range of Florida Red-shoulder. (2) Florida Red-shouldered Hawk, *B. l. alleni*; smaller and whiter-headed, breeding from S.C., Ala., and Okla. s. (3) Insular Red-shouldered Hawk, *B. l. extimus*; Fla. Keys; the smallest and palest of all the Red-shoulders. (4) Texas Red-shouldered Hawk, *B. l. texanus*; from s.-cent. Tex. into Mex.

BALD EAGLE. *Haliæetus leucocephalus.* The ranges of the two races have long been described thus: (1) Southern Bald Eagle, *H. l. leucocephalus*; from Gulf of Mex. n. to n. edge of U.S. (2) Northern Bald Eagle, *H. l. washingtoniensis*; from Arctic s. to Great Lakes (to s. N.E. in winter). A. C. Bent believes that the Southern Bald Eagle should be limited as a breeding bird to the southern lowlands from the Gulf and Fla. n. to the Carolinas. He is probably right, and the presence of numerous specimens of Southern Bald Eagles from the Northern States can be easily accounted for by post-breeding wanderers. C. L. Broley has banded hundreds of Eagles in Fla. and has had numerous returns after the nesting season from the Northern States, and even the Gulf of St. Lawrence.

SPARROW HAWK. *Falco sparverius:* (1) Eastern Sparrow Hawk, *F. s. sparverius*; breeds from N.F., s. Que., and Sask. s. to Ga. and n. parts of Gulf States. (2) Little Sparrow Hawk, *F. s. paulus*; breeds in Fla. and s. parts of Gulf States.

SPRUCE GROUSE. *Canachites canadensis:* (1) Hudsonian Spruce Grouse, *C. c. canadensis*; boreal forests from Alb. to Lab. (2) Canada Spruce Grouse, *C. c. canace*; from s. Man., s. Que., and s. N.S. s. to n. Minn., n. Mich., n. N.Y., and n. N.E.

RUFFED GROUSE. *Bonasa umbellus.* The races of the Ruffed Grouse are still subject to much discussion and the following differentiations are far from the last word. (1) Eastern Ruffed Grouse, *B. u. umbellus*; Mass., R.I., Conn., s. N.Y., N.J., and e. Pa.; also s. Minn., s. Wis., s. Mich., and locally in O., s. Ind., and Mo. (2) Canada Ruffed Grouse, *B. u. togata*; s. shore of Gulf of St. Lawrence, N.B., n. New England, n. N.Y., n. Great Lakes region, and s. Can. w. to ne. Minn. and s. in Appalachians to n. Ga. (3) Nova Scotia Ruffed Grouse, *B. u. thayeri*; Nova Scotia. (4) Gray Ruffed Grouse, *B. u. umbelloides*; the northern edge of the range of the species from s. Lab. and n. shore of Gulf of St. Lawrence w. across Can. past s. James Bay to Alb. (5) Hoary Ruffed Grouse, *B. u. incanus*; N.D., S.D., and w. Neb.

WILLOW PTARMIGAN. *Lagopus lagopus:* (1) Canadian Willow Ptarmigan, *L. l. albus*; Arctic, s. to s. Sask., cent. Ont., and s. Que. except where following races are found. (2) Ungava Willow Ptarmigan, *L. l. ungavus*; n. Que. (Ungava). (3) Allen's Willow Ptarmigan, *L. l. alleni*; N.F. (4) White-shafted Willow Ptarmigan, *L. l. leucopterus*; Arctic Ids. from Southampton Id. and Baffin Id. n.

ROCK PTARMIGAN. *Lagopus mutus:* (1) Canadian Rock Ptarmigan, *L. m. rupestris*; Arctic s. to Ungava Peninsula. (2) Welch's Rock Ptarmigan, *L. m. welchi*; N.F.

PRAIRIE CHICKEN. *Tympanuchus cupido:* (1) Greater Prairie Chicken, *T. c. pinnatus*; from s. Sask. and s. Man. s. to e. Colo. and Ark. Occurs e. to Mich. (locally) and nw. O. (very rarely). (2) Attwater's Prairie Chicken, *T. c. attwateri*: coastal Tex. and sw. La.

SHARP-TAILED GROUSE. *Pediœcetes phasianellus:* (1) Northern Sharp-tailed Grouse, *P. p. phasianellus*; a dark form found in the more open sections of w. Can. (e. to Lake Superior and Ungava). (2) Prairie Sharp-tailed Grouse, *P. p. campestris*; Interior Plains from s. Man. s. to Nev. and e. to Minn. and w. Wis.

BOB-WHITE. *Colinus virgianus:* (1) Eastern Bob-white, *C. v. virginianus*; from Gulf of Mex. n. to S.D., s. Minn., s. Ont., and sw. Me. (2) Florida Bob-white, *C. v. floridanus*; peninsular Fla. (3) Texas Bob-.white, *C. v. texanus*; s. Tex., introduced in many eastern localities.

TURKEY. *Meleagris gallopavo:* (1) Eastern Turkey, *M. g. silvestris*; from Pa., e. Ky., and se. Mo. s. to Gulf of Mex. (2) Florida Turkey, *M. g. osceola*; Fla. Peninsula. (3) Rio Grande Turkey, *M. g. intermedia*; from n.-cent. Tex. s. into Mex.

SANDHILL CRANE. *Grus canadensis:* (1) Greater Sandhill Crane, *G. c. tabida*; breeds from Sask. s. to Wis. and Mich. Migrates to La. and Tex. (2) Florida Sandhill Crane, *G. c. pratensis*; Fla. and s. Ga. (p. 86).

CLAPPER RAIL. *Rallus longirostris:* (1) Northern Clapper Rail, *R. l. crepitans*; Conn. to N.C. (2) Wayne's Clapper Rail, *R. l. waynei*; se. N.C. to midway down

e. coast of Fla. (3) Florida Clapper Rail, *R. l. scotti*; w. coast of Fla. and lower
e. coast at Palm Beach and Jupiter Inlet. (4) Mangrove Clapper Rail, *R. l.
insularum*; Fla. Keys. (5) Louisiana Clapper Rail, *R. l. saturatus*; Gulf Coast
from Ala. to Tex.

PIPING PLOVER. *Charadrius melodus:* (1) Eastern Piping Plover, *C. m.
melodus*; breeds from Gulf of St. Lawrence and s. Can. s. to Great Lakes and
along coast to N.C.; winters from S.C. to Fla. (2) Belted Piping Plover, *C. m.
circumcincta*; black on breast forms a *complete band* across front (Eastern Piping
has black confined to sides of breast). Breeds in Mo. Valley; migrates along Atlantic Coast with preceding race. Winters on Gulf Coast. Breeding birds farther
east (Great Lakes region and Maritime Canada) show intergradation between the
two races.

WILLET. *Catoptrophorus semipalmatus:* (1) Eastern Willet, *C. s. semipalmatus*;
breeds along coast in N.S. and from N.J. and Del. to Tex. (2) Western Willet,
C. s. inornatus; breeds inland from Sask. and s. Man. s. to Neb. and n. Ia. Along
the Atlantic Coast the Western Willet is a common migrant in the fall. It is
larger and paler and has a noticeably longer bill.

RED-BACKED SANDPIPER. *Erolia alpina:* (1) Red-backed Sandpiper, *E. a.
pacifica*; American Arctic; migrates through Great Lakes and along coast to Gulf
of Mex.; winters n. to N.J. (2) Greenland Dunlin, *E. a. arctica*; accidental in
N.A. Typical birds in breeding plumage are smaller than Red-backs with heavier breast-streakings passing without as abrupt contrast into black abdominal
patch. Back more heavily streaked with black; very little rufous. Winter birds
not distinguishable. As one or two other similar European races are possible,
suspicious-looking early 'Dunlins' could be subspecifically recorded only if collected.

DOWITCHER. *Limnodromus griseus:* Eastern Dowitcher, *L. g. griseus*; breeds
from cent. Alb. to w. side of Hudson Bay and n.; migrates through U.S. (2)
Long-billed Dowitcher, *L. g. scolopaceus*; breeds in nw. Can. and Alaska. Less
common on the North Atlantic Coast in migration than Eastern Dowitcher.
Commoner in w. Miss. Valley and along coasts of Southern States. Most late
Dowitchers on the Atlantic Coast (September to November) seem to be Long-
bills. The bill measurements overlap, but extreme long-billed birds of this subspecies can probably be safely recognized. The rusty tinge on the under parts of
Long-bills in breeding plumage extends farther down on the belly, often to the
under tail-coverts. There is said to be a difference in the notes but this needs
further study and testing. The call of the Eastern Dowitcher is a trebled *tū-tū-tū*,
metallic and slightly *Yellow-legs-like*. The common note ascribed to the Long-
bill is a single thin *keek*, occasionally trebled. As there is much talk of a third
intermediate race, it is probably safer to call them all Dowitchers and forget the
splitting.

ICELAND GULL. *Larus leucopterus:* (1) Iceland Gull, *L. l. leucopterus*; Arctic,
wandering s. to N.J. and Great Lakes (a few). (2) Kumlien's Gull, *L. l. kumlieni*; Arctic, se. in winter to N.J. and Great Lakes. Once regarded as a hybrid
between Herring and Iceland Gulls, it is now believed to be a race of the latter.
Its paleness approaches that of the Iceland Gull, but it has *gray* markings toward
the tips of the wings (not black with white 'mirrors' as in Herring Gull). Immature Gulls that are paler than Herring Gulls of the same stage, but with darker

primaries than Iceland Gulls are supposed to be immature *kumlieni*. It is possible that many immature Kumlien's would be passed by as Icelands. Much is still to be learned about the plumages of these Gulls (p. 122).

HERRING GULL. *Larus argentatus:* (1) American Herring Gull, *L. a. smithsonianus*; breeds from L.I. and larger lakes near Canadian border of U.S. n. to s. Baffin Id. and s.-cent. Alaska; winters s. to Gulf of Mex. (2) Thayer's Herring Gull, *L. a. thayeri*; breeds on Arctic Coasts of N.A. and Arctic Ids. s. to Baffin Id. Casual in winter to n. U.S. Usually looks like American Herring Gull but black in primaries *sometimes* replaced by *gray* darker than that of *kumlieni*. *Thayeri* presumably can be told from Kumlien's Gull by white spots or 'mirrors' in the dark wing-tips as in American Herring Gull, but as some individuals come so close to *kumlieni*, it is a question exactly what they are. Thayer's Herring Gull is very rare in ne. U.S. and is probably not safe to identify without collecting. Adults of *thayeri* have been reported to have a *pale brown iris* (Brooks, 1937; Shortt, 1939; Shortt and Peters, 1942).

LEAST TERN. *Sterna albifrons:* (1)Eastern Least Tern, *S. a. antillarum*; breeds along coast from Mass. to Tex. (2) Interior Least Tern, *S. a. athalassos*; lower Miss. and Mo. Riv. Valley System n. to Ia., O., sw. Kans., and Neb.

BLACK GUILLEMOT. *Cepphus grylle:* (1) Southern Black Guillemot, *C. g. grylle*; breeds from cent. Lab. s. to Me.; winters s. along coast to Mass. (2) Mandt's Black Guillemot, *C. g. mandti*; Arctic coasts and islands except where following race is found; casual to s. Que. and Lake Ontario in winter. (3) Northern Black Guillemot, *C. g. arcticus*; from Greenland and se. Baffin Id. s. to Hamilton Inlet, Lab.

MOURNING DOVE. *Zenaidura macroura:* (1) Eastern Mourning Dove, *Z. m. carolinensis*; e. N.A.; breeds from N.S., s. Me., Ont., and Wis. s. to Fla. and Gulf Coast and w. to e. Kans. and Ia. (2) Western Mourning Dove, *Z. m. marginella*; w. N.A.; breeds e. to Man., Minn., Neb., and Okla.

SCREECH OWL. *Otus asio:* (1) Eastern Screech Owl, *O. a. nævius*; e. of Great Plains from N.B., Me., Ont., Wis., and Minn. s. to highlands of Ga., Ala., and e. Okla. (2) Southern Screech Owl, *O. a. asio*; lowlands of South from Va. to Ga. and w. to La.; n. in Miss. Valley to s. Ill. and se. Kans. (3) Florida Screech Owl, *O. a. floridanus*; Fla. (4) Texas Screech Owl, *O. a. mccalli*; s. Tex. n. to Bexar and Comal Cos. (5) Hasbrouck's Screech Owl, *O. a. hasbroucki*; cent. Tex. from Travis Co. to Palo Pinto and Dallas Cos. (6) Nebraska Screech Owl, *O. a. Swenki*; Great Plains from s. Man. s. through Dakotas and Neb. to cent. Kans. and w. Okla.

HORNED OWL. *Bubo virginianus:* (1) Great Horned Owl, *B. v. virginianus*; from Ont., Que., and N.B. s. to Gulf of Mex. and w. to e. Minn., se. S.D., and e. Tex. (2) Montana Horned Owl, *B. v. occidentalis*; w. U.S. e. to Minn., S.D., Neb., and Kans.; in winter to Ia. (3) Arctic Horned Owl, *B. v. wapacuthu*; like the Great Horned Owl, but grayer; some birds are almost as white as Snowy Owls. The facial discs are *pale gray*, not chestnut brown as in the common form. Breeds from Hudson Bay s. to sw. Sask. and n. Ont.; in winter to Neb. (rare) and occasionally N.Y. and Mass. (4) Labrador Horned Owl, *B. v. heterocnemis*; like the Great Horned Owl but darker and more heavily barred beneath. The barring often obliterates the white markings, giving a black-breasted appearance. Breeds in n. Ungava, Lab., N.F., and N.S.; winters to Ont. and n. N.E.

BURROWING OWL. *Speotyto cunicularia:* (1) Western Burrowing Owl, *S. c. hypugæa*; w. N.A. e. to Man., Minn., w. Ia., and coastal La. (2) Florida Burrowing Owl, *S. c. floridana*; prairies of cent. and s. Fla.

BARRED OWL. *Strix varia:* (1) Northern Barred Owl, *S. v. varia*; from Sask., s. Que., and N.F. s. to Ark., Tenn., and n. Ga. (2) Florida Barred Owl, *S. v. georgica*; Southern States, n. to cent. N.C. and n. Ala., w. to Ark. and e. Tex. (3) Texas Barred Owl, *S. v. helveola*; s.-cent. Tex.; Gulf Coast to Lee and Bexar Cos.

NIGHTHAWK. *Chordeiles minor:* (1) Eastern Nighthawk, *C. m. minor.* Breeds from n. Man., s. Que., and N.F. s. to n. Ark., s. Ill., s. Va., and uplands of Ga. and w. to edge of Great Plains (Minn. to ne. Okla.). (2) Florida Nighthawk, *C. m. chapmani*; breeds in low country of South Atlantic and Gulf States from N.C. s., and n. along Miss. Valley to s. Ill. (3) Sennett's Nighthawk, *C. m. sennetti*; n. Great Plains, breeding from n. N.D. and ne. Mont. s. to nw. Ia. and n. Neb.; migrates through Okla. and Tex. (4) Cuban Nighthawk, *C. m. gundlachii*; apparently the breeding form at Key West where Earle Greene and the author first discovered it in June, 1941. The note, entirely unlike that of any other North American race is described by Bond as a 'Katydid-like *pity-pit-pit*' (responsible for local name of *Killykadick*).

FLICKER. *Colaptes auratus:* (1) Northern Flicker, *C. a. luteus*; breeds from limit of trees in Can. s. to Kans., cent. Mo., s. Ill., N.C., and, in mts., to Ga. (2) Southern Flicker, *C. a. auratus*; s. U.S., breeding from N.C. and s. Ill. s. except in higher mts. (3) Boreal Flicker, *C. a. borealis*; breeds from Lab. and e. Wyo. n. to limit of trees; s. in winter in Miss. Valley.

PILEATED WOODPECKER. *Hylatomus pileatus:* (1) Northern Pileated Woodpecker, *H. p. abieticola*; from Man., N.B., and N.S. s. to Minn., Ia., Ind., and Pa.; farther s. in mts. (2) Southern Pileated Woodpecker, *H. p. pileatus*; from se. Pa., Ill., and Okla. s. to n. Fla. and Gulf Coast. (3) Florida Pileated Woodpecker, *H. p. floridanus*; Fla., n. to Orange Co.

RED-BELLIED WOODPECKER. *Centurus carolinus:* (1) Eastern Red-bellied Woodpecker, *C. c. carolinus*; lowlands of s. Atlantic States from N.C. to Fla. (2) Western Red-bellied Woodpecker, *C. c. zebra*; Miss. Valley from Gulf of Mex. n. to se. S.D., se. Minn., Lake Erie, and w. N.Y. (occasional), and in Middle Atlantic States (Va., Md., Del.). (3) Florida Red-bellied Woodpecker, *C. c. perplexus*; s. Fla. and Fla. Keys.

HAIRY WOODPECKER. *Dendrocopos villosus:* (1) Eastern Hairy Woodpecker, *D. v. villosus*; ne. U.S. and s. Can.; from Man., s. Ont., s. Que., and Gulf of St. Lawrence s. to w. N.C. (mts.) and w. to e. Col. (2) Northern Hairy Woodpecker, *D. v. septentrionalis*; larger, with more white; breeds from cent. Ont. n. (3) Newfoundland Hairy Woodpecker, *D. v. terrænovæ*; larger and blacker; N.F. (4) Southern Hairy Woodpecker, *D. v. auduboni*; dingier breast; from se. Va. and s. Ill. s. to Gulf of Mex.

DOWNY WOODPECKER. *Dendrocopos pubescens:* (1) Northern Downy Woodpecker, *D. p. medianus*; from Man., s. Ungava, and N.F. s. to Kans., Tenn., and Va. (2) Southern Downy Woodpecker, *D. p. pubescens*; smaller and dingier on the under parts. Se. U.S. from Okla. and N.C. s. to Gulf. (3) Nelson's Downy Woodpecker, *D. p. nelsoni*; nw. Can.; occasional in winter to n. N.E. Larger, but not safely identifiable without collecting.

RED-COCKADED WOODPECKER. *Dendrocopos borealis:* (1) Northern Red-cockaded Woodpecker, *D. b. borealis*; se. U.S., n. to se. Va., w. Ky., Tenn., and s. Mo.; (2) Southern Red-cockaded Woodpecker, *D. b. hylonomus*; cent. and s. Fla.

CRESTED FLYCATCHER. *Myiarchus crinitus:* (1) Northern Crested Flycatcher, *M. c. boreus*; breeds from s. Man., s. Que., and N.B. s. to s. Tex., La., and Ga. (2) Southern Crested Flycatcher, *M. c. crinitus*; from Fla. n. on coastal plain to s. S.C., and w. to se. La.

HORNED LARK. *Eremophila alpestris:* (1) Northern Horned Lark, *E. a. alpestris*; breeds from Arctic s. to Gaspe; winters s. to Ga. (2) Prairie Horned Lark, *E. a. praticola*; like preceding but smaller and *paler* above, not so pinkish-brown; line over the eye *white*, not yellow; throat white or whitish, but in some individuals tinged with yellow — then the color of the eye-stripe is the surest mark (from Northern; almost indistinguishable from Hoyt's). Breeds from s. Man. and s. Que. s. to e. Kans., Mo., O., Md., and s. N.Y.; winters to Tex. and Ga. (3) Hoyt's Horned Lark, *E. a. hoyti* not certainly distinguishable in the field from the Prairie (has white eye-line but is larger, with a darker back). Many migrant Hoyt's have probably been called Prairies — another good example why it is poor ornithology to become too deeply engrossed in subspecies unless backed by collecting. Breeds in nw. Can.; winters eastward to Kans. and Great Lakes. (4) Texas Horned Lark, *E. a. giraudi*; coast of Tex. e. to Galveston Bay. (5) Saskatchewan Horned Lark, *E. a. enthymia*; Great Plains, breeding from cent. Sask. through Dakotas and Neb. to cent. Kans.

CANADA JAY. *Perisoreus canadensis:* (1) Canada Jay, *P. c. canadensis*; resident from n. Minn., n. Mich., n. N.Y., and n. N.E. n. to limit of evergreens in Canada, except where following races are found. (2) Labrador Jay, *P. c. nigricapillus*; Lab. and N.F. (3) Anticosti Jay, *P. c. barbouri*; Anticosti Id., Que.

BLUE JAY. *Cyanocitta cristata:* (1) Northern Blue Jay, *C. c. bromia*; breeds from n. Man. and Gulf of St. Lawrence s. to cent. Ill., Tenn., and Va. (2) Florida Blue Jay, *C. c. cristata*; resident along Atlantic Coast from N.C. s. to Everglades and w. along Gulf to La. (3) Semple's Blue Jay, *C. c. semplei*; s. Fla. from the Everglades s. (4) Western Blue Jay, *C. c. cyanotephra*; Neb., Kans., n. Okla., and Tex. panhandle.

RAVEN. *Corvus corax:* (1) Northern Raven, *C. c. principalis*; n. Can. s. to Minn., Mich., and Me. A few in mts. s. to Ga.; occasional on coasts of N.J. and Va. (2) American Raven, *C. c. sinuatus*; w. U.S. e. to N.D. and probably Mo., Ill., and Ind.

CROW. *Corvus brachyrhynchos.* (1) Eastern Crow, *C. b. brachyrhynchos*; breeds from n. Man., s. Que., and N.F. s. to Md. and the n. parts of the Gulf States. (2) Southern Crow, *C. b. paulus*; breeds from lower Potomac and Ohio valleys s. to Ga. and Gulf Coast (except Fla.). (3) Florida Crow, *C. b. pascuus*; Fla. peninsula.

BLACK-CAPPED CHICKADEE. *Parus atricapillus:* (1) Eastern Black-capped Chickadee, *P. a. atricapillus*; from n. Ont., c. Que., N.B., and N.S. s. to Mo., Ill., O., Pa., and n. N.J. (2) Long-tailed Black-capped Chickadee, *P. a. septentrionalis*; w. N.A., e. to w. Minn., w. Ia., and e. Kans. (3) Appalachian Black-capped Chickadee, *P. a. practicus*; e. O. to sw. Pa. and s., in mts., to N.C. (4) Newfoundland Black-capped Chickadee, *P. a. bartletti*; N.F.

CAROLINA CHICKADEE. *Parus carolinensis:* (1) Northern Carolina Chickadee, *P. c. extimus*; range roughly from that of Black-cap in N.J., O., and cent. Mo. s. to n. N.C. and Tenn. (2) Southern Carolina Chickadee, *P. c. carolinensis*; N.C., S.C., Ga., Ala., Miss., La., and Ark. (3) Florida Chickadee, *P. c. impiger*; s. Ga. and Fla. Plumbeous Carolina Chickadee, *P. c. agilis*; from Tex. (Refugio and Kendall Cos.) n. to n. Okla.

BROWN-CAPPED CHICKADEE. *Parus hudsonicus:* (1) Hudsonian Brown-capped Chickadee, *P. h. hudsonicus*; W. Can. from cent. Ont. w. to Alaska. (2) Acadian Brown-capped Chickadee, *P. h. littoralis*; e. Can. from tree-limit in Lab., N.F., and cent. Que. s. to mts. of n. N.E. and n. N.Y. and coast of Me.

WHITE-BREASTED NUTHATCH. *Sitta carolinensis:* (1) Northern White-breasted Nuthatch, *S. c. cookei*; resident from n. Minn., cent. Ont. and s. Que. s. to n. Tex., cent. Ill., and S.C. (2) Florida White-breasted Nuthatch, *S. c. carolinensis*; Fla., n. along coast to N.C., also Gulf Coast and Miss. Valley n. to s. Ill.

BROWN-HEADED NUTHATCH. *Sitta pusilla:* (1) Brown-headed Nuthatch, *S. p. pusilla*; s. U.S. from s. Del. and s. Mo. s. to Gulf of Mex. (except Fla.). (2) Gray-headed Nuthatch, *S. p. caniceps*; Fla. peninsula.

BROWN CREEPER. *Certhia familiaris:* (1) Northern Brown Creeper, *C. f. americana*; breeds in Can. from s. Man., cent. Ont., and s. Que. s. to n. parts of U.S. (to n. Neb., n. Ind., n. N.J., Pa.). (2) Southern Brown Creeper, *C. f. nigrescens*; mts. from W. Va. to N.C. and Tenn.

HOUSE WREN. *Troglodytes aëdon:* (1) Eastern House Wren, *T. a. aëdon*; breeds in Atlantic States and Provinces e. of Appalachian divide from N.B. s. to Va. (2) Ohio House Wren, *T. a. baldwini*; St. Lawrence Valley, e. Great Lakes region, O. Valley, and s. Appalachians from Va. to S.C. (3) Western House Wren, *T. a. parkmani*; breeds from w. U.S. through Miss. Valley to n. Mich. and w. Ind. and s. to s. Mo. and sw. Ky.

WINTER WREN. *Troglodytes troglodytes:* (1) Eastern Winter Wren, *T. t. hiemalis*; breeds from s. Man., n. Ont., and Gulf of St. Lawrence s. to Minn., N.Y., Pa., and N.E. (2) Southern Winter Wren, *T. t. pullus*; s. Appalachians from W. Va. and w. Va. to n. Ga.

BEWICK'S WREN. *Thryomanes bewickii:* (1) Mississippi Bewick's Wren, *T. b. bewickii*; Miss. Valley breeding from s. Neb., n. Ill., and s. Mich. s. to Ark. and Miss. (2) Appalachian Bewick's Wren, *T. b. altus*; mainly Appalachian district from cent. Pa. and cent. O. to Ala. and n. Ga.

CAROLINA WREN. *Thryothorus ludovicianus:* (1) Northern Carolina Wren, *T. l. ludovicianus*; resident in e. U.S. from se. Neb., O., Pa., lower Hudson River, and (sparingly) s. N.E. s. to ranges of following races. (2) Florida Wren, *T. l. miamensis*; Fla. n. to Levy and Putnam Cos. (3) Burleigh's Carolina Wren, *T. l. burleighi*; Cat, Ship, and Horn Ids., Miss. (4) Lomita Carolina Wren, *T. l. lomitensis*; Lower Rio Grande Valley, Tex.

LONG-BILLED MARSH WREN. *Telmatodytes palustris:* (1) Long-billed Marsh Wren, *T. p. palustris*; breeds along Atlantic slope from R.I. to coast of Va. and Potomac. (2) Prairie Marsh Wren, *T. p. iliacus*; breeds from Great

Plains, prairies, and cent. and n. Miss. Valley e. to Ont., N.Y., and N.E. (3) Wayne's Marsh Wren, *T. p. waynei*; breeds on coast of N.C. (4) Worthington's Marsh Wren, *T. p. griseus*; easily recognized by its grayness; breeds along coast from S.C. to n. Fla. (5) Marian's Marsh Wren, *T. p. marianæ*; a small, dark Marsh Wren; breast *shaded or speckled with drab*. Resident along the Gulf from Old Tampa Bay, Fla., to Miss. (6) Louisiana Marsh Wren, *T. p. thryophilus*; coast of La. and Tex.

ROBIN. *Turdus migratorius:* (1) Eastern Robin, *T. m. migratorius*; breeds from limit of trees in Can. s. to Kans., Ill., O., Pa., and N.J.; winters in s. U.S. n. to O. Valley and N.E. coast. (2) Southern Robin, *T. m. achrusterus*; breeds from Md. and s. Ill. to w. S.C., n. Ga., cent. Ala., and n. Miss. (3) Black-backed Robin, *T. m. nigrideus*; breeds in N.F., Lab., and n. Que.; in winter to e. Can. and e. U.S. Noticeably darker backed; probably distinguishable in spring only; does not show contrast between head and upper back.

OLIVE-BACKED THRUSH. *Hylocichla ustulata:* (1) Eastern Olive-backed Thrush, *H. u. swainsoni*; breeds from N.F. and se. Can. s. to n. Mich., N.Y., n. N.E., and, in mts., to W. Va. (2) Western Olive-backed Thrush, *H. u. almæ*; Rocky Mt. region, breeding across Can. to Gulf of St. Lawrence (n. of *swainsoni* in e. Can.). Both migrate throughout e. U.S.

GRAY-CHEEKED THRUSH. *Hylocichla minima:* (1) Northern Gray-cheeked Thrush, *H. m. minima*; breeds in belt near limit of trees from n. Man. to cent. Que. and in N.F.; migrates through e. U.S. (2) Bicknell's Gray-cheeked Thrush, *H. m. bicknelli*; breeds in N.S. and mts. of n. N.E. and N.Y. s. to Catskills. There is a difference in size between *minima* (8 in. largest) and *bicknelli* (6¾ in. smallest), but as they often overlap (neighborhood of 7¼ and 7½ in.), field recognition is not encouraged.

VEERY. *Hylocichla fuscescens:* (1) Eastern Veery, *H. f. fuscescens*; breeds from Gulf of St. Lawrence w. to ne. O. and s. Que. and s. to N.J. and, in mts., to n. Ga. (2) Willow Veery, or Willow Thrush, *H. f. salicicola*; Western; breeding e. to nw. O., Mich., and se. Ont. (3) Newfoundland Veery, *H. f. fuliginosa*; breeds in N.F.

EASTERN BLUEBIRD. *Sialia sialis:* (1) Eastern Bluebird, *S. s. sialis*; breeds from s. Man., s. Que., and N.F. s. to Gulf of Mex.; winters n. to Ohio Valley, N.J., and s. N.E. (a few along coast). (2) Florida Bluebird, *S. s. grata*; s. half of Fla.

LOGGERHEAD SHRIKE. *Lanius ludovicianus:* (1) Southern Loggerhead Shrike, *L. l. ludovicianus*; Atlantic Coast from s. N.C. to Fla. and w. through Ga., Ala., and Miss. to e. and s. La. (2) Migrant Loggerhead Shrike, *L. l. migrans*; breeds from se. Man., s. Que., and N.B. s. to ne. Tex., cent. La., Mo., and s. Ill., and w. N.C.; winters irregularly to n. states.

WHITE-EYED VIREO. *Vireo griseus:* (1) Northern White-eyed Vireo, *V. g. noveboracensis*; breeds from Mass., N.Y., O., s. Wis., Ia., and se. Neb. s. to uplands of Ga. and w. to Tex. (2) Southern White-eyed Vireo, *V. g. griseus*; breeds on coastal plain from N.C. to Fla., and w. along Gulf to Tex. (3) Key West White-eyed Vireo, *V. g. maynardi*; Fla. Keys. (4) Rio Grande White-eyed Vireo, *V. g. micrus*; Rio Grande Valley.

BLUE-HEADED VIREO. *Vireo solitarius:* (1) Northern Blue-headed Vireo, *V. s. solitarius*; breeds from cent. Man. and Gulf of St. Lawrence s. to N.D., Minn., Mich., s. Pa., and n. N.J. (2) Mountain Blue-headed Vireo, *V. s. alticola*; breeds in mts. from w. Md. and W. Va. to n. Ga.

PARULA WARBLER. *Parula americana:* (1) Northern Parula Warbler, *P. a. pusilla*; breeds from Gulf of St. Lawrence and cent. Ont. s. to Md. and W. Va., and locally in Miss. Valley from e. Neb. and n. Minn. s. to Tex. and La. (2) Southern Parula Warbler, *P. a. americana*; breeds along seaboard from e. Va. to Fla.; winters in Fla..

YELLOW WARBLER. *Dendroica petechia:* (1) Eastern Yellow Warbler, *D. p. æstiva*; breeds from s. Can. s. to n. S.C., n. Ga., n. Ala., s. Mo., and n. N.M. (2) Newfoundland Yellow Warbler, *D. p. amnicola*; breeds from N.S. and N.F. w. across Can. to Alaska. (3) Alaskan Yellow Warbler, *D. p. rubiginosa*; darker and greener above in breeding plumage with yellow more restricted. Immatures in fall are so dusky that they are likely to be taken for Orange-crowns. This race migrates to some extent through e. U.S., particularly the Gulf States. (4) Cuban Yellow Warbler (Golden Warbler), *D. p. gundlachi*; found breeding on the Bay Keys off Key West, Fla., by Earle Greene and the author. Formerly these mangrove-loving birds of the tropics were considered a distinct species. A Yellow Warbler on the Keys in the breeding season would be this race. Similar to Eastern Yellow Warbler; song similar in quality but end dropping in pitch, suggesting Water-thrush. Southbound Yellow Warblers, *D. p. æstiva*, arrive in the Keys in July, so confusion is possible.

BLACK-THROATED BLUE WARBLER. *Dendroica cærulescens:* (1) Northern Black-throated Blue Warbler, *D. c. cærulescens*; breeds from n. Minn. and s. Que. s. to cent. Minn., s. Ont., Pa., and n. N.J. (2) Cairns's Black-throated Blue Warbler, *D. c. cairnsi*; breeds in mts. from Md. and W. Va. to Ga.

BLACK-THROATED GREEN WARBLER. *Dendroica virens:* (1) Northern Black-throated Green Warbler, *D. v. virens*; breeds from s. Man., cent. Ont., cent. Que., and N.F. s. to s. Minn., s. Wis., n. O., N.J., and L.I., and, in mts., to n. Ga. and n. Ala.; migrates through s. U.S. (rare on Atlantic slope). (2) Wayne's Black-throated Green Warbler, *D. v. waynei*; breeds locally in cypress swamps near coast from S.C. to se. Va.

YELLOW-THROATED WARBLER. *Dendroica dominica:* (1) Eastern Yellow-throated Warbler, *D. d. dominica*; breeds along Atlantic slope from s. N.J. (probably), Del., and Md. to Fla. (2) Sycamore Yellow-throated Warbler, *D. d. albilora*. Typical birds can be distinguished at very short range from the preceding race by the lack of any yellow between the eye and the bill (lores). In these the eye-stripe is entirely white. This is not a constant character, as some individuals have distinctly yellow lores. Breeds in Miss. Valley from s. Wis. and s. Mich. s. to Tex. and La.

PINE WARBLER. *Dendroica pinus:* (1) Northern Pine Warbler, *D. p. pinus*; breeds from n. Man., n. Mich., s. Que., and N.B. s. to Gulf States. (2) Florida Pine Warbler, *D. p. florida*; resident in s. Fla. south of lat. 29° (Volusia, Lake, and Citrus Cos.).

PRAIRIE WARBLER. *Dendroica discolor:* (1) Northern Prairie Warbler, *D. d. discolor*; breeds from e. Neb., s. O., s. N.Y., and Mass. (and locally in

s. N.H., s. Ont., and s. Mich.) s. to La., n. Miss., s. Ala., and cent. Ga. (rare and local in Gulf States). (2) Florida Prairie Warbler, *D. d. collinsi*; Fla., commonest along coast.

PALM WARBLER. *Dendroica palmarum:* (1) Western Palm Warbler, *D. p. palmarum*; breeds from n. Man. s. and e. to n. Minn.; migrates chiefly w. of Appalachian Mts. to Fla. and Bahamas. Occurs on Atlantic slope in autumn. (2) Yellow Palm Warbler, *D. p. hypochrysea*; similar to the preceding, but much brighter yellow below; the Western Palm is dingier, *bright* yellow only on the under tail-coverts. In fall and winter the eye-stripe of the Western Palm Warbler is *whitish*, that of the Yellow Palm, yellow. Breeds from Ont. and Gulf of St. Lawrence s. to Me.; chiefly coastal in migration; winters from Fla. to La. and occasionally as far n. along coast as Mass.

OVEN-BIRD. *Seiurus aurocapillus:* (1) Eastern Oven-bird, *S. a. aurocapillus*; breeds from n. Ont. s. to Kans., Ark., n. Ga., and e. N.C. (2) Newfoundland Oven-bird, *S. a. furvior*; breeds in N.F.

WATER-THRUSH. *Seiurus noveboracensis:* (1) Northern Water-Thrush, *S. n. noveboracensis*; breeds from n. Ont. and Gulf of St. Lawrence s. to s. Ont., N.Y., and, in mts., to W. Va. (2) Grinnell's Water-Thrush, *S. n. notabilis*; breeds from limit of trees in w. Can. s. to nw. Neb., n. Minn., and nw. Mich., and e. to ne. O., nw. Pa., and probably w. N.Y.

YELLOW-THROAT. *Geothlypis trichas:* (1) Maryland Yellow-throat, *G. t. trichas*; breeds from s. Pa. and s. Ill. s. to e. Tex., w. and n. La., cent. Miss., n. Ala., and n. Ga. except where following races are found. (2) Northern Yellow-throat, *G. t. brachidactyla*; breeds from N.F. s. to n. N.J., W. Va., and O. and w. to Ont. and Great Plains (Dakotas, Neb., etc.). (3) Athens Yellow-throat, *G. t. typhicola*; breeds in coastal plain from se. Va. to Ga. and w. to cent. Ala. (4) Florida Yellow-throat, *G. t. ignota*; breeds in Fla. and along Gulf to se. La.

MEADOWLARK. *Sturnella magna:* (1) Eastern Meadowlark, *S. m. magna*; breeds from N.B. and s. Que. s. to N.C. and Mo. and w. to nw. Tex., Kans., w. Neb., e. Ia., and e. Minn. (2) Southern Meadowlark, *S. m. argutula*; breeds from s. Ill. and S.C. s. to Gulf of Mex. (3) Rio Grande Meadowlark, *S. m. hoopesi*; s. Tex.

RED-WING. *Agelaius phœniceus:* (1) Eastern Red-wing, *A. p. phœniceus*; breeds from Ont., Que., and N.S. s. to n. parts of Gulf States and w. to Great Plains except where following races are found. (2) Giant Red-wing, *A. p. arctolegus*; breeds from w. Can. s. to N.D., Minn., Wis., and n. Mich. (3) Florida Red-wing, *A. p. mearnsi*; from Okeefinokee Swamp, Ga., s. through Fla. except where following two races occur. (4) Maynard's Red-wing, *A. p. floridanus*; s. Fla. s. of Lake Okeechobee. (5) Gulf Coast Red-wing, *A. p. littoralis*; Gulf Coast from Choctawatchee Bay, Fla., w. to Galveston, Tex. (6) Rio Grande Red-wing, *A. p. megapotamus*; s. coast of Tex. and Rio Grande Valley.

BOAT-TAILED GRACKLE. *Cassidix mexicanus:* (1) Eastern Boat-tailed Grackle, *C. m. major*; resident along coast from s. Del. and Chesapeake s. to Fla. Keys and w. to e. Tex. (2) Mesquite Boat-tailed Grackle, *C. m. prosopidicola*; s. coast of Tex.

PURPLE GRACKLE. *Quiscalus quiscula:* (1) Florida Purple Grackle, *Q. q. quiscula*; Fla.; n. along coast to se. N.C. and w. along Gulf to s. La. (2) Stone's Purple Grackle, *Q. q. stonei*; belt between Appalachians and coast. from s. N.Y.

s. to n. Fla. and La. (except s. coastal strip where preceding race is found); at n. and w. borders of range (s. N.E., s. N.Y., and Appalachians) the Purple Grackle seems to intergrade with the Bronzed Grackle, *Quiscalus versicolor*. See main text under Bronzed Grackle.

CARDINAL. *Richmondena cardinalis:* (1) Eastern Cardinal, *R. c. cardinalis*; s. U.S. e. of Great Plains and n. to s. Ia., n. Ind., Lake Erie (s. Ont.), and s. N.Y. (2) Florida Cardinal, *R. c. floridana*; Fla. (3) Louisiana Cardinal, *R. c. magnirostris*; s. La. (4) Gray-tailed Cardinal, *R. c. canicauda*; cent. and s. Tex.

REDPOLL. *Acanthis flammea:* (1) Common Redpoll, *A. f. linaria*; sub-Arctic, visiting n. U.S. irregularly in winter. (2) Greater Redpoll, *A. f. rostrata*; somewhat larger (5½–6); darker and larger-billed than Common Redpoll. Difference fairly obvious when the two birds are together in the same flock (much less frequent than preceding).

RED CROSSBILL. *Loxia curvirostra:* (1) Eastern Red Crossbill, *L. c. minor*; evergreen forests of Can. and n. U.S.; wanders s. occasionally to Southern States. (2) Newfoundland Red Crossbill, *L. c. pusilla*; N.F. and N.S.; it is possible to identify typical individuals in the field, if one is well acquainted with *L. c. minor*. It is larger, especially the bill; the comparison is a little like that of the bills of Downy and Hairy Woodpeckers. Males are darker, with the red rump more glowing; females are also darker, hence the yellow rump shows to better advantage; in brief, it is a Red Crossbill intensified. Extremes are recognizable, but many specimens can be determined only by collecting. During those occasional years when it enters the U.S. it is most likely (though not always) to be found at coastal points where pitch pines are numerous. (3) Sitka Red Crossbill, *L. c. sitkensis*; breeds on nw. Pacific Coast, at rare intervals invading the East, and has reached coast. Small with a very stumpy bill — males tend to be much more dull brick-red or orange than the typical Eastern race.

EASTERN TOWHEE. *Pipilo erythrophthalmus:* (1) Red-eyed Towhee, *P. e. erythrophthalmus*; breeds e. of Great Plains from s. Me., s. Ont., s. Man., and s. Sask. s. to n. Ga. and cent. Kans. (2) Alabama Towhee, *P. e. canaster*; La., Miss., Ala., cent. Ga., and n. Fla. w. of peninsula. Iris usually red or orange. (3) White-eyed Towhee, *P. e. alleni*; the breeding Towhee of s. Atlantic Coast from N.C. to and incl. Fla. peninsula. The iris is *white*. The call, corresponding to the clearly enunciated *chewink* of the Northern bird, is a higher-pitched, wheezy *zree*. The paler flanks and smaller areas of white in wings and tail of the two Southern forms permit field recognition of Northern birds in winter in s. U.S.

SAVANNAH SPARROW. *Passerculus sandwichensis:* (1) Eastern Savannah Sparrow, *P. s. savanna*; breeds from s. shore of Gulf of St. Lawrence and s. Ont. s. to coast of N.J., Pa., W. Va., O., n. Ind. and n. Ill., w. to Ia. and Minn. (2) Labrador Savannah Sparrow, *P. s. labradorius*; breeds in Lab. and N.F.; migrates s. to Fla. and Gulf Coast. This race averages darker, and is more heavily streaked on the breast than the Eastern Savannah Sparrow. Observers in New England and New York blithely try to identify it in the field, but of this Griscom says: 'while it is quite possible to observe slightly darker and paler Savannah Sparrows among our migrants in the East in life, only critical comparison of such birds in the hand can settle whether the darker bird was really a *labradorius* or a dark extreme or more worn specimen of *savanna*.' This bit of caution applies even more in many Midwestern States where three or four races are possible in migration. (3) Churchill Savannah Sparrow, *P. s. oblitus*; Can., breeding from w. side of Hudson Bay (e. of prairies) to n. Minn. and e. to cent. Que. (Lake St. John). Winters on Gulf Coast. Lacks buff or rusty of *savanna*. Blacker than *labradorius*. (4) Nevada Savannah Sparrow, *P. s. nevadensis*; breeds e. to N.D.; migrates through Great Plains and occasionally to O. and Miss. Valley.

GRASSHOPPER SPARROW. *Ammodramus savannarum:* (1) Eastern Grasshopper Sparrow, *A. s. pratensis*; breeds e. of Great Plains from s. N.H., s. Ont., and s. Wis. s. to s. La., n. Ga., and n. S.C.; winters in s. U.S. (2) Western Grasshopper Sparrow, *A. s. bimaculatus*; Western; breeds e. in prairie regions to s. Minn., Neb., and s. Tex. (3) Florida Grasshopper Sparrow, *A. s. floridanus*; breeds in prairie regions of cent. Fla.; stripes on upper parts blacker with little or no brown.

HENSLOW'S SPARROW. *Passerherbulus henslowii:* (1) Eastern Henslow's Sparrow, *P. h. susurrans*, mainly e. of Appalachians; breeds from N.Y. and s. N.H. s. to n. Va. (2) Western Henslow's Sparrow, *P. h. henslowii*; breeds from n. Tex. n. to S.D. and Ont., and e. to O. and W. Va.

SHARP-TAILED SPARROW. *Ammospiza caudacuta:* For a long time three races of the Sharp-tailed Sparrow were recognized by the *A.O.U.*; the race on the Eastern seaboard (*caudacuta*), the Northern form (*subvirgata*) and the inland form (*nelsoni*). Almost yearly the Linnaean Society of New York held seminars devoted to the field identification of these three Sharp-tails so that its members could add them to their lists. Now, after the museum men have been hard at work making further discoveries which demonstrate the facts of geographical variation, we find we have *five* races, not three, and it is obvious that many misidentifications were made in the past. This points up clearly the folly of being too concerned with subspecies, at least during this period in taxonomic development. The distinctions between races are often quite arbitrary and the sifting out of the facts will undoubtedly continue for a while. Although I would recommend that a Sharp-tail be called just a Sharp-tail, a few experienced field men will find interest in the following analysis — but I suggest they also study the skins in their museum. (1) Common Sharp-tailed Sparrow, *A. c. caudacuta*; the race that breeds from N.H. to N.J. known from the more northern and inland races by the *sharply defined dark breast-streakings*. (2) Nelson's Sharp-tailed Sparrow, *A. c. nelsoni*; breeds in prairie provinces of Can. and s. to S.D. and w. Minn.; in migration to Atlantic Coast of s. U.S. Inland, about fresh marshes, the Nelson's and the James Bay Sharp-tails are the two which would occur. The Acadian and Common Sharp-tails are strictly coastal. The Nelson's is best distinguished by its *bright ochre-buff breast, almost devoid of streakings* (or with indistinct streakings). It has a contrastingly marked back like the Common Sharp-tail, while those of the Acadian and James Bay birds are more washed out. (3) Acadian Sharp-tailed Sparrow, *A. c. subvirgata*; breeds from Me. to Gulf of St. Lawrence; in winter to Fla. In migration when Sharp-tails throng in the coastal marshes, a decidedly pale or gray individual will often flush from the grass. In the early days Audubon noticed this, but did not recognize these as a different race. Some individuals appear almost bluish as they fly up. Besides being paler and more washed out on the back, this subspecies, the Acadian, is less buffy and the streakings on the breast are pale and *blurry*. In s. Me. the Common and Acadian Sharp-tails intergrade, producing individuals that are very difficult to place. (4) James Bay Sharp-tailed Sparrow, *A. c. altera*; breeds in marshes of s. James Bay, Can.; in migration from O. and

Mass. to Ga. Somewhat like Nelson's Sharp-tailed Sparrow (breast buffy with indistinct streakings) but back streakings duller and more washed out, like a rather brown Acadian. Most of the migrants that were once called *nelsoni* in N.Y. and N.E. are probably of this race. Sight records cannot be accepted. (5) Southern Sharp-tailed Sparrow, *A. c. diversa*; breeds from s. N.J. to Va.; winters to Ga. Probably not safe to try to distinguish in the field. Like a Common Sharp-tail (sharply defined breast-streakings) but with a slightly buffier wash across the breast.

SEASIDE SPARROW. *Ammospiza maritima:* (1) Northern Seaside Sparrow, *A. m. maritima*; Breeds from Mass. to Va. (2) Macgillivray's Seaside Sparrow, *A. m. macgillivraii*; salt marshes from N.C. to the S. Edisto River, S.C. (3) Smyrna Seaside Sparrow, *A. m. pelonota*; Atlantic Coast of ne. Fla. from Nassau Co. to New Smyrna. (4) Scott's Seaside Sparrow. *A. m. peninsulæ*; Gulf Coast of Fla. from Indian Pass to Pepperfish Keys. (5) Wakulla Seaside Sparrow, *A. m. juncicola*; Gulf Coast of w. Fla. from St. Andrew's Bay w. to range of next race (nw. Fla.). (6) Louisiana Seaside Sparrow, *A. m. fisheri*; Gulf Coast from ne. Tex. to Pensacola, Fla. (7) Texas Seaside Sparrow. *A. m. sennetti*; coast of Tex. from Galveston to Corpus Christi.

PINE-WOODS SPARROW. *Aimophila æstivalis:* (1) Florida Pine-woods Sparrow, *A. a. æstivalis*; Fla. and se. Ga. (2) Bachman's Pine-woods Sparrow, *A. a. bachmanii*; from s. O., sw. Pa. (sporadically), Va., and Md. (occasionally) s. along coastal plains and Appalachian plateau to Ga. and Ala. (3) Illinois Pine-woods Sparrow, *A. a. illinoiensis*; Lower Miss. Valley from sw. Ind. and s. Ill. s. to s. Miss., La., and e. Tex.

JUNCO. *Junco hyemalis:* (1) Boreal Slate-colored Junco, *J. h. hyemalis*; breeds from tree-limit in Can. s. to n. Minn., n. Mich., ne. O., Me., and mts. of Mass., N.Y., and Pa. (2) Carolina Slate-colored Junco, *J. h. carolinensis*; breeds in s. Appalachians from Md. and W. Va. to n. Ga. Said to be readily separated in mixed flocks in the field by large size, grayer color (devoid of brown cast) and pale gray or horn-colored bill (*J. h. hyemalis*, flesh-colored).

WHITE-CROWNED SPARROW. *Zonotrichia leucophrys:* (1) Eastern White-crowned Sparrow, *Z. l. leucophrys*; breeds near limit of trees in Can.; winters from O. Valley s. to Gulf. (2) Gambel's White-crowned Sparrow, *Z. l. gambelii*; migrates through Great Plains region, casual e. of Miss. River. Adult like White-crown but white eye-stripe *starts from bill* instead of near eye.

SWAMP SPARROW. *Melospiza georgiana:* (1) Eastern Swamp Sparrow, *M. g. georgiana*; breeds from s. Ont., s. Que., and N S. s. to n. Neb., n. Mo., W. Va. (mts.), and N.J. (2) Western Swamp Sparrow, *M. g. ericrypta*; breeds from Alb. and Man. to N.D., and w. across Can. (n. of range of *georgiana*) to n. shore of Gulf of St. Lawrence and N.F. Both races mingle in s. U.S. in winter.

SONG SPARROW. *Melospiza melodia:* (1) Eastern Song Sparrow, *M. m. melodia*; breeds in N.E. States and Maritime Provinces from Gulf of St. Lawrence and N.F. s. to Md. except where following races are found. (2) Atlantic Song Sparrow, *M. m. atlantica*; grayer; resident of the coastal strips and edge of mainland from L.I. to N.C. (3) Mississippi Song Sparrow, *M. m. euphonia* (Appalachian Song Sparrow would be more appropriate) breeds from s. Ont. Peninsula, s. Mich., and w. N.Y. e. through Appalachian Plateau to Va. and s. to Ga. (4) Dakota Song Sparrow, *M. m. juddi*; n. plains and n. Miss. Valley region.

Appendix III

HOME REFERENCE SUGGESTIONS

THIS HANDBOOK is primarily a field guide. *The Audubon Bird Guide* (2 volumes), *Land Birds* (1946) and *Water Birds* (to be published), by Pough and Eckelberry, is recommended for supplementary use at home. It contains a complete series of colored portraits of Eastern birds and sections on habits and nesting which were not practicable in a single book of *Field Guide* size. *The Book of Birds* (2 volumes) published by the National Geographic Society, Washington, D.C., is also recommended for home use. It contains a complete series of bird portraits of both Eastern and Western birds. Another useful work for general information, illustrated with one of the finest series of bird portraits ever made (the famous *Birds of Massachusetts* plates) is *A Natural History of the Birds*, by Forbush and May.

There are many local lists and state publications. I am not listing them here, but you will find a very full discussion of them in the *annotated list of bird books* in Joseph Hickey's stimulating book *A Guide to Bird Watching*. Most of these regional works outline the distribution, abundance, and seasonal movements of different species in limited regions. This is very useful knowledge if you live in one of those areas. Some of the larger state books have more than local interest and include life-histories and detailed descriptions of plumages and are lavishly illustrated in color. Among the most representative of these are *The Birds of Massachusetts and Other New England States* (3 volumes), by E. H. Forbush, State House, Boston; *The Birds of Minnesota* (2 volumes), by T. S. Roberts, University of Minnesota Press, Minneapolis; *Birds of Western Pennsylvania*, by W. E. Clyde Todd, Carnegie Museum, Pittsburgh; *Florida Bird Life*, by A. H. Howell, distributed by the National Audubon Society, New York City; and *Birds of Canada*, by P. A. Taverner, Musson Book Co. Inc., Toronto.

For general reference covering the entire East, I have long found Chapman's *Handbook of Birds of Eastern North America* (D. Appleton-Century Company) very useful, and for extended accounts of distribution, migration, and life-history, Bent's *Life Histories of North American Birds*, United States National Museum.

If you are interested in waterfowl do not miss Kortright's *The Ducks, Geese, and Swans of North America* with its abundance of color plates by T. M. Shortt. Even eclipse plumages, hybrids, and downy young are figured.

For complete data on the ranges of North American birds, *The*

A.O.U. Check-List of North American Birds is the standard. The fifth edition is now in preparation.

The most useful works on bird songs are (1) *A Guide to Bird Songs* by Aretas A. Saunders (D. Appleton-Century Company), a system of learning songs by symbols, and (2) *American Bird Songs*, 6 double-disc records with 72 songs recorded by the Albert R. Brand Bird Song Foundation (Laboratory of Ornithology, Cornell University), Comstock Publishing Company, Ithaca, N.Y.

This brief list of references is related almost entirely in some way to the identification of birds. For a much broader list covering the biology of birds and a score of other phases, see Hickey's *A Guide to Bird Watching*, Oxford.

Someone has aptly said that Joseph Hickey's book carries on where Peterson's *Field Guide* leaves off. After you have learned the names of the birds, if you are a thoughtful person, you become interested in their way of life, travels, ecology, populations, psychology, or whatever teases your curiosity. Mr. Hickey takes you by the hand and shows you that bird-study need not stop when you no longer can add new birds to your list, but can last a lifetime.

INDEX

In the field, the reader will find it most practical to go directly to the illustration. In most cases his problem will be settled there without the necessity of referring to the text.

Page numbers in bold-faced type refer to the illustrations. They are placed only after the common English names of species. They are not used after the scientific names. Nor are they used after the vernacular names of subspecies except in those few instances where a subspecies has been pictured in the book. Most subspecies cannot be safely identified in the field.